SUFISM IN THE SECRET HISTORY OF PERSIA

T0393215

Gnostica
Texts and Interpretations

Series Editors
Garry Trompf (Sydney), Jason BeDuhn (Northern Arizona) and Jay Johnston (Sydney)

Advisory Board
Antoine Faivre (Paris), Iain Gardner (Sydney), Wouter Hanegraaff (Amsterdam), Jean-Pierre Mahé (Paris), Raol Mortley (Newcastle) and Brikha Nasoraia (Mardin)

Gnostica publishes the latest scholarship on esoteric movements, including the Gnostic, Hermetic, Manichaean, Theosophical and related traditions. Contributions also include critical editions of texts, historical case studies, critical analyses, cross-cultural comparisons and state-of-the-art surveys.

Published by and available from Acumen

Sufism in the Secret History of Persia
Milad Milani

Histories of the Hidden God: Concealment and Revelation in Western Gnostic, Esoteric, and Mystical Traditions
Edited by April DeConick and Grant Adamson

Contemporary Esotericism
Edited by Egil Asprem and Kennet Granholm

Angels of Desire: Esoteric Bodies, Aesthetics and Ethics
Jay Johnston

Published by Peeters

Schamanismus und Esoterik: Kutlur- und wissenschaftsgeschichtliche Betrachtungen
Kocku von Stuckrad

Ésotérisme, Gnoses et imaginaire symbolique: Mélanges offerts à Antoine Faivre
Edited by Richard Caron, Joscelyn Godwin, Wouter Hanegraaff and Jean-Louis Vieillard-Baron

Western Esotericism and the Science of Religion
Edited by Antoine Faivre and Wouter Hanegraaff

Adamantius, *Dialogues on the True Faith in God*
Translation and commentary by Robert Pretty

SUFISM IN THE SECRET HISTORY OF PERSIA

MILAD MILANI

Routledge
Taylor & Francis Group

LONDON AND NEW YORK

First published 2013 by Acumen

2 Park Square, Milton Park, Abingdon, Oxon OX14 4RN
605 Third Avenue, New York, NY 10017

Routledge is an imprint of the Taylor & Francis Group, an informa business

First issued in paperback 2021

British Library Cataloguing-in-Publication Data
A catalogue record for this book is available from the British Library.

Designed and typeset in Warnock Pro by JS Typesetting Ltd, Porthcawl, Mid Glamorgan2

ISBN 13: 978-1-8446-5677-6 (hbk)
ISBN 13: 978-1-03-217979-7 (pbk)
DOI: 10.4324/9781315728995

For Homa

CONTENTS

PREFACE

There has never been an intention to confine this monograph series to texts and interpretations in the Western esoteric tradition. The first number, devoted to the only surviving dialogue from Late Antiquity, between five gnostics and an orthodox Christian, has its likely provenance in southern Asia Minor (Turkey) or Syria. More recently, the study of the religion of the Yezidis by Garrik Asatrian and Victoria Arekalova takes us to the Kurdish region straddling the Near and Middle East. In this present volume we find concentrated study on a host of materials almost completely separated from the Western tradition, and it is both a pleasure and honour to celebrate it as the first among an emergent cluster of textual and interpretative studies intensely focused on Near and Middle Eastern Gnosis, and on a living tradition at that.

In undertaking a work such as this, on Persian Sufism and its long-term historical roots, daunting problems can put off even the most enthusiastic authors, because there are swathes of Iran's complex and extraordinary past left quite undocumented. This is not only because there have been significant pockets of purely oral culture in the Middle Eastern and Central Asian regions, but because of destructive invasions, those by Alexander ("the Terrible", not the Great in Persian eyes!), by iconoclastic Moslem Arabs, by the Mongols and by the Turkish Tamerlaine, to name key agents. Considering these drawbacks, how estimable are Dr Milani's labours to fill in the gaps and uncover so many connecting pieces in the jigsaw of the Iranian peoples' mysterious spiritual heritage.

In the course of this exercise, Milad Milani has forced himself to walk along something of an intellectual tightrope. This comes from essaying a critical macrohistory or *Überschau* of Persia's religious variegations through time by responding to cues in Persianate Sufi contemplations and uses of the past, particularly those provided by the long-inured Nematollahi (or Ni'matullâhî) order. A fascinating conversation is created in this book between in-house Sufi outlooks (in all a mix of poetic motifs, suggestions, clues, surviving innuen-dos, anti-establishment proclivities, daring flights of spiritual insight and more recent theosophical reflection) and the sharp mind of a younger critical histo-rian of socio-religious ideas. Dr Milani has respected the voice of the believer, and let it provide footprints to follow for his investigations, yet not as a naïve tracker who could be easily deceived, but as one well trained historically, lin-guistically equipped and sensitive to literary creativity. The result is a credit to the standards of scholarship we seek to be maintained in this series and to the insights of the Sufi tradition of which Dr Milani strives to give a just and accurate account.

My personal association with Milad Milani goes back to his undergraduate student days. Soon after his honours year in Studies in Religion, he became my colleague and collaborator as an historian of ideas and spiritualities, and completed his doctorate by 2008 on the difficult data and issues that were eventually to constitute the subject of this volume. Our collegiality continued after Dr Milani continued his academic career in other universities, and he has become one of the five founding members of the new Institute for the Study of Religion, Politics and Society. Expanding our contacts in the world of ethno-religious variety in the Near and Middle East has widened our respec-tive agendas for research and helped make possible the prospective number of new and related studies in this series.

Scholars learn much from each other by comparing their own method-ologies. In meeting the challenge of writing this book, Dr Milani has had to face an array of apparently disordered materials and, like a detective, to "make some sense of a mess" left over from the stamping grounds of many differ-ent worldviews and collective human interferences. I myself would have been tempted to apply a neo-Vichian analysis, that is, one concerned to distinguish layers in the history of consciousness or "place" the different mental diction-aries of Persia's peoples from the stage when the divine was more immediate (as in Zarathushtra's hymns of dialogue with the ever-present Ahura Mazda), through the age of heroes (conveyed by the fabled figures in Hakîm Ferdowsi's poetic epic *Shahnameh*), on to our current state of prosaic reflectiveness on the long-term Iranian past as an exercise in historiography. This would fol-low but upgrade the guidelines of the founder figure of Social Science him-self, the profound Giambattista Vico. The chosen approach of Milad Milani, by comparison, is different. His is a voice – and perhaps this should have been acknowledged straightaway – that is an indigenous Persian one, and needs to be heard as such. He looks upon his country's former times as a seamless tap-estry (like a fabulous carpet from the region!), sensing there is necessarily a chronological order in its making (and recognizing this in the flow of Sufi wis-dom) but then applying taxing critical historical analysis from his academic education, especially informed by the generations of impressive scholars, both Western and Iranian, from over the last hundred years. I am not sure whether my approach would have worked as well; indeed, it might have faltered, and

I am thus all the more in admiration of my colleague's attempts. It has been alleged of Alexander Pushkin that he read history as a riddle needing decipherment: like him, Milad Milani shows us the skills to combine scholarly caution with the gifts of divining many forgotten atmospheres and re-invoking the powerful poesis of a Rumi and Hafez.

It is a very great pleasure to welcome this book.

Garry W. Trompf
University of Sydney

ACKNOWLEDGEMENTS

This book is dedicated to all Iranians (or Persians, as some may prefer) – I think about the truly enchanting land that is *Iran* and, above all, the tenacious spirit of her legacy. I wrote the book with my own children, Nala and Nhura, in mind; they are only half Persian, but may one day want to know more about their paternal heritage. I had imagined this book to be a point of entry into the religious history of Persia, making plain the spiritual consciousness that underpins its religiosity. Many thanks go to my wife, Nadia, having taught herself the subtleties of Persianate customs – including, to my good fortune, those culinary – for her feedback when thinking and writing this book.

Many thanks also go to my first mentor, Garry W. Trompf, who taught me history of religion, but especially for opening my eyes to the disciplines of "history of ideas" and "macrohistory" and for seeing this work through from its early stages to doctoral dissertation and then to its becoming a book. There are also aspects of this work that render special hermeneutic approaches to literature and thought, and I am thankful to Edward Crangle for help with methodology in this regard.

I would like to mention the Department of Studies in Religion of the University of Sydney, where I spent the first eight years of my academic life, and whose members of staff have offered their support throughout: these are, in no special order of significance, Garry Trompf, Jay Johnston, Iain Gardner, Carole Cusack, Christopher Hartney and Edward Crangle.

I wish to acknowledge my friends and colleagues at the University of Western Sydney; in particular the Religion and Society Research Centre, where I currently function as an Adjunct Fellow. I am especially grateful to Adam Possamai, the Centre Co-Director, for his continued support and encouragement.

Outside the department and beyond the borders of the university, I recall Vassilios Adrahtas and Vrasidas Karalis, with whom I became deeply immersed in philosophical discourse. Going back to the beginning, I thank Rahim Kheradi for introducing me to Sufi thought and Mehravar Marzbani for disclosing her knowledge of the Zoroastrian/Parsee culture. There are others who will remain anonymous for reasons explained in the work. But, in particular, I express my thanks to Terry Graham for his generous effort in shedding further light on the subject of Sufism; to Adnan Kasamanie for educating me about the mysterious wisdom of the Druzes; and to the Mandaean high priest Ganzibra Professor Brikha Nasoraia both for his sheer soulful presence and for his attention to my work as one of its readers for the series.

ABBREVIATIONS

Av.   *Avesta*, Irach J. S. Taraporewala (ed. and trans.). *The Divine Songs of Zarathushtra*. Bombay: Hukhta Foundation, 1993.

CHI   *The Cambridge History of Iran*, 7 vols, E. Yarshater *et al.* (eds). Cambridge: Cambridge University Press, 1968–91.

DGE   *Dictionary of Gnosis and Esotericism*, 2 vols. W. J. Hanegraaff *et al.* (eds). Leiden: Brill, 2005.

EIr   *Encyclopaedia Iranica*, E. Yarshater (ed.). London: Routledge, 1985–2004.

EIs   *The Encyclopaedia of Islam*, H. A. R Gibb *et al.* (eds). Leiden: Brill, 1960–2006.

EQ   *The Encyclopaedia of the Qoran*, Jane Dammen McAuliffe (ed). Leiden: Brill, 2005.

ER2   *The Encyclopedia of Religion*, 2nd edn, M. Eliade and C. J. Adams *et al.* (eds). New York: Macmillan, 1995.

M   *The Masnavi: Book One*, J. Mojaddedi (trans.). Oxford: Oxford University Press, 2004.

MJR   *The Mathnawi of Jalaluddin Rumi*, 6 vols, R. A. Nicholson (ed. and trans.). Cambridge: Trustees of the E. J. W. Gibb Memorial, 1925–40.

Sira Ibn Ishaq, *The Life of Muhammad: A Translation of Ishaq's Sirat Rasul Allah*, A. Guillaume (trans.). Oxford: Oxford University Press, 2004.

IRANIAN OR PERSIAN? THE RELIGIOUS LANDSCAPE OF IRANIAN IDENTITY

INTRODUCTION

This book has been a part of my continuing journey to excavate the socio-religious identity of Iran, and in the process to learn a thing or two about my ancestral past. Persia is an ancient land, possessing a long-standing cultural heritage that few others, apart perhaps from the Greeks, Egyptians and Chinese, could boast. Persia's mystique is probably owed to the early Orientalist scholars who set up the picture of the East, in particular Persia, as the exotic other – and especially as the source of all mystery, in the way that Egypt captures the imagination today. This attitude of nineteenth- and twentieth-century scholarship, that is, thinking of Persia as the origin of religious ideas, has since been revised, but it is one which regardless lingers in the discourse of contemporary Iranians. Interesting as it may be to entertain such notions, Persia would be better thought of as the land of extraordinary innovations. Possibly much to the dismay of my Iranian readers, Persia did not invent "everything", but Persians have certainly been among the finest innovators: from empire building, religion, culture and language to architecture, alcohol and astronomy. The centralized geographical location of the land itself lends to the nature of her people.

Iran differs from the Arab nations of the Middle East and should not be lumped together with them. Iran is, in fact, part of an Indo-European heritage, complete with its own distinct language, separate from its Semitic neighbours in the Near East. Sure enough, one of the most remarkable aspects about Iran is that it has retained its unique cultural, and to a degree its religious, identity through many episodes of invasion (Greek, Arab, Turk, Mongol), the most lasting of which has been the Arab (Islamic). And while noticing how Iran's theocratic regime has received a great deal of negative portrayal through tabloid media, we need reminding that the nation has always had a strained relationship with the UK and US as more recent invasive powers. There is growing interest in Iran among both academics and the general public, prompting desire to learn more about her special resilience. This book is written to respond to such interest, and aims to explain Iranian religious identity for those wanting to understand contemporary Iran more intimately.

A recurring motif in popular Iranian attitudes is the unremitting desire to be distinguished from an "Arab". Having become the subject of lighthearted jokes among Iranians themselves, this attitude nevertheless voices an underlying concern of a repressed aspect of Iranian identity. It typically crops up in the way that some Iranians idealize the past (either the Shah's regime or pre-Islamic Iran) and is especially acute in the way Iranians deal with the Arab-Moslem conquest of Iran. When observing contemporary Iran, one is not only presented with a dense cultural and religious content, but also by an unmistakable feeling that something has been repressed in the past. Iran's complex religious identity is owed to the unique synthesis of Iranian and Arab Islamic elements, Iran being unique in that it has preserved pertinent themes of its long-standing heritage, though these are now blanketed over with Islamic culture. Soon to be revealed is that this "blanket" of Islam was tucked in to fit the contours of the Iranian cultural landscape, and began to form its own expression through Twelver Shi'ism. While Iranian Shi'ism has accommodated many of Iran's cultural and spiritual needs, certain fundamentalist manifestations of it have in the long run subdued that liberal aptitude detectable in the poetry of an Omar Khayyam or an Hafiz-e Shirazi. In short, general observations would comfortably reveal that Iranians, whether they are conscious of it or not, consider themselves first and foremost "Persian" (culturally), and then Moslem, so far as their Islam is forged out of their "Iranianness". It may be difficult to get some Iranians, especially those steeped in their Shi'ism, to admit to this special datum, and it would perhaps make for an interesting sociological study at some future date, but Iran certainly has all the trappings of a repressed culture.

The case for "Persianate" Sufism can be contextualized in the peculiarities of Iran's rich and diverse cultural and religious past. As a result, Sufism in Iran can be nationalistic, and somewhat racist. As such, the study of Sufism in Iran must involve questions about the politics of identity. The Nematollahiya[1] are a case in point, since they carry all the right symptoms of a Sufi community affected by the after-effects of the 1979 revolution. That is, for the bulk of its Iranian contingent, Sufism is very much about pre-Islamic Iran and the heritage of Persianate culture which harbours the spirituality of its past. "Sufism", therefore, for the Nematollahiya, is introduced to Islam. More precisely, such Iranian virtues as *javanmardi* (chivalry) and *adab* (etiquette) have been

---

1. The Nematollahi Sufi Order is prominent in Iran and has a growing presence in the West through its popular branch the Nematollahi Khaneqahi Sufi Order (under the leadership of Javad Nurbakhsh and now his son Alireza Nurbakhsh). L. Ridgeon, "Nimatullahiyya", in *The Encyclopedia of Islamic Civilization and Religion* (ed. I. R. Netton) (London, 2007).

infused into Islam to make up the bulk of the "spiritual" content of "Persian Sufism". This is certainly the special case for the Khaneqahi Nematollahi Sufi order, which this study uses as the model for discussing a basic framework for exploring so-named "Persianate Sufism". To be clear, this study only observes a certain dynamic of Nematollahi Sufism as lived by a majority of its Iranian members (whether migrant or not), while the order itself is extremely diverse culturally, with quite a large non-Iranian following, most of whom go about their Sufi practice without paying much attention at all to the Iranian agenda. The order, having its roots in Iran, yet having transplanted itself, within the UK and the US primarily, caters for the needs of both its Iranian and non-Iranian adherents.

THE RELIGIOUS LANDSCAPE OF IRANIAN IDENTITY: THE MODEL OF "HIDDEN HISTORY"

Peeling back the layers, what this book explores is a part of Persia's intellectual and spiritual consciousness, without which one could certainly never understand her greatest mystics, let alone the many peculiarities of her complex "ethno-national" and institutional tradition, such as the Imamate. The question is how does one talk about this repression? Does it take the form of "hidden history", as suggested by Yuri Stoyanov, of Zoroastrianism lurking behind spiritual alternatives in southern European spiritual history?[2] Stoyanov's thesis is a good point of departure, although for the Persian case we prefer to write of a "hidden *macro*history", that is, history over a huge space of time, throughout which, if our attention is attuned to them, cultural and religious anomalies that persist in Persian historical consciousness can be detected. Stoyanov's thesis utilized the Bogomil heresy to explain the crucial character of the Balkan religious identity. This, of course, was by way of divulging a "hidden history" of Christianity. He argued that the Bogomils represented a secret current, which he carefully explained as cropping up in the past through a series of Gnostic Christian heresies ultimately underpinned by Zoroastrianism. In so doing, he explained how this "hidden history" accounts for the peculiar nature, character and place of "Bosnian Islam" in the Balkans. There is a similar "feel" about our own macrohistorical adventure, yet the difference in the Persian case is not *one* particular cultural and religious symbol or phenomenon that is in question, but rather several links of a number of associated phenomena in the intellectual life (and historical events) that make up the "past" or the background of Persian Sufism – our major focus – and to some extent the *personae* of "Persianate Islam" in general. The Twelver Shi'ite character of "Iranian

---

2. Yuri Stoyanov, *The Hidden Tradition in Europe: The Secret History of Medieval Christian Heresy* (London, 1994).

Islam", and speculative Imamology linked to it, also certainly reflects motifs and identity issues peculiar to Iranian Islam, yet in the context of the Gnostica series, our investigations in this book will be much more heavily fixed on certain Persian Sufi traditions and their powerful link to Persia's past.

In this big sweep of history, a number of distinct configurations or what may be called key "stepping-stones" in the form of movements and religious impetuses will be defined. When these are "lined up", they will result in a panorama of persistent themes, or a macro-vision with remarkable coherence. At the heart of this book, a number of fundamental issues will be raised which, given the concern with Iranian cultural and religious *resilience*, cannot but produce results that are both tantalizing and controversial in nature. The chapters of this book will be touching on (or re-touching!) sensitive issues of the past that may upset prevailing views about religious traditions. The established Moslem view, for instance, has it that Sufism is an essentially Islamic development; but here alternative expressions are explored. Distinctions will be made between what is called "Islamic mysticism" or "spirituality" (which was inherent to the practices of the Prophet, the literature of the Qur'an and the Islamic tradition) and what was born and developed in the "Sufi tradition (of mysticism)" in the years to follow. Regarding the history of Islam, again alternative views are discussed, as found in autochthonous, resilient currents of Iranian cultural, religious and spiritual movements, including Persian Sufism in particular. The case for the Persian origins of Islam is likewise revisited, in particular for its intrinsically Persianate nature, which draws on an indigenous tradition going back to Zarathushtra, even perhaps on a forgotten pristine Moslem theology that has Persian roots. This book does not attempt to make the case for "Persian Sufism" through Orientalist theories, but rather to explore Persianate features of Sufism in Iran by reading the revered past of its leading Sufi schools, the Nematollahiya. To understand the intricate landscape of the Iranian religious and spiritual identity from a historical point of view, many aspects of its past must be considered for a fuller view of how Iran's mystics are to be located within the framework of contemporary Islam. Each chapter in this book will consider a particular era of Persian history, taking the reader step by step through the ages of its past up until the Sufis, while also showing how Iranian mystical poetry reflects the multiple layers of Persia's cultural landscape.

CHAPTER 1

THE MACROHISTORICAL PURSUIT OF SECRET PERSIA AND THE SUFI MYTH-HISTORY

PRE-ISLAMIC SUFISM AND THE IRANIAN ROOTS OF SUFI MYSTICISM

Sufism does not predate Islam. Certain features of it that are characteristic of pre-Islamic traditions common among Iranians, however, can be detected in Sufism generally, but specifically pertaining to Sufis of Iran. These include the heroic tradition of champions (*ghahreman*), now known in Sufism as *javanmardi* or *futuwwat*; aspects of which include service (*khedmat*) and a selfless attitude of generosity (*sekhavat*) and sacrifice (*ithar*). Others require greater in-depth appreciation of ancient Persian ideas and heritage both religious and moral, which flow into Islamic Iran and are appropriated by early mediaeval Moslem-Iranian thinkers, such as Ferdowsi and Sohravardi. Earlier on, Salman-e Farsi (Chapter 8) is a paradigmatic example of this transition and flow of ideas from past to present.

Of those who contend for the pre-Islamic origins of Sufism, the previous head of the Khaneqahi Nimatollahi Sufi order, Javad Nurbakhsh (1926–2008), insisted that "Persian Sufism" is a distinctly Iranian phenomenon – independent of Islamic history – and one that assuredly predated Islam (Chapter 9). The nature of Nurbakhsh's claims are largely ahistorical, but they do warrant further review if only for their delineation of Persian cultural components, now part of Islamic mysticism. The case of the Nematollahiya, however, is also relevant to the present study because Nurbakhsh surmised the existence of a legitimate line of masters that are connected through a secret sapiential tradition referred to as *hekmat-e khosravani* (Chapter 2). Although the validity of such a "line of wisdom" is the subject of proper historical investigation in this book, there is little reason to believe it to be anything more than conjecture and properly identified as a composite attribute of Khaneqahi Nematollahi Sufi imagination or myth-history.

Indeed, what might be a better case to argue is that Sufism is an Iranian invention; but, to be exact, it has to be the product of an Iranian–Islamic marriage in which the offspring of these two great cultures harbours the genetic tendencies of both its parents. There is no way that Sufism could literally predate Islam, but there is no reason why it could not carry the germs of a distant ancestral religion within it. The fact of the matter is that Iranian and Arab cultures are intimately bound following the Arab-Islamic conquest of Sasanid Iran. This is verified by the fact that Salman the Persian, who was the first Persian convert, was also the first to translate the Qur'an and hadith into Persian. Moreover, the majority of Moslem scholars who laid the foundation of Arabic-Islamic sciences and arts were of Iranian and generally non-Arab origin. It remains the case that the Arabs and Iranians of this era immediately following the conquests had a close bond that was founded on the ideals of the early Islamic community, and which was headed under the guidance of the *caliph al-rashidun*. However, this bond is severed gradually during the Umayyad period, whereby the new Arab overlords ruled with a firm and elitist method that belittled and devalued the non-Arab. The rise of the Shi'a, proper, is a direct result of the non-Arab Moslem population taking control of the situation in a bid to avenge the unjust murder and usurpation of the members of the Prophet's House (*bait al-nabi*). The very special relationship of Iranian Moslems and the Islamic tradition is that Iranians saw themselves as the special guardians of the Prophet's House, and stewards of his true teachings (Islam), until the return of the rightful heir and leader of Islamic community, Imam Mahdi (*imam ghayeb*).

MACROHISTORY AND THE SUFI MYTH-HISTORY

Wherever the hints of a hidden *macro*history are provided, there are problems in detecting and following its "traces". A very difficult task faces anyone trying to make up for missing materials just by "tracking footprints" (sometimes seeming to "chase shadows") until reaching the Sufis – when the whole, strange exercise falls into place. Methodologically, there are genuine problems for the enterprise. From the very start, there are huge gaps or lacunae of evidence that can only be filled by inference. One danger in this method is that of subjective deduction, of being too keen to theorize in the endeavour to explain what has been repressed. However, upon collecting and sieving through all the available material on relevant-looking "religious" ideas and movements, what remain are crucial indicators in "periodic pockets", or "nuggets", that constitute the "stepping-stones" of a larger underground trajectory. It has been of some advantage to have access to the phenomenon and awe-inspiring, hard-to-fathom body of Sufi poesis. This book is not the first in its attempt to explain the peculiarity of the Iranian spiritual story; others have done so, but simply in terms of non-hidden ("exoteric") historical materials, albeit including the special and "public" nature of Shi'ite gnoseology and immamology. What is unique about the approach of this book is the appropriation of the rich ingredients of Sufi poetry to better explain the proposed macrohistory of religious currents, trajectories, threads and factors that have been "shelved" by the mainstream, this mainstream not just being the Islamic establishment, but also the Zoroastrian one earlier on. Indeed, Sufism has absorbed the impulses of ideas and movements that have been partly (or almost) hidden from view, and so it is adequately "placed" through the efforts of this book by tracking down the repressed elements that have gone into its making. Sufi poetry, therefore, serves as a useful point of entry into the highly nuanced character of Persianate Sufism.

This brings us to a related problem to do with the "esoteric", a term with at least three meanings in the following pages. The first is to do with the excavated subterranean currents being a "hidden history" (i.e. not open to easy view, as with the kind of exoteric history of the Islamic world written by Jarir al-Tabari). The second is that the materials (i.e. ideas/movements) making up the hidden history are of an esoteric nature anyway, and in this connection at least three specific elements need to be considered: the "inner life", the idea of "occultation" (as with the grand Imams) and secrecy (people often cannot afford to expose themselves). And third, coming to the final chapter on Sufi poets, one can find that they defy academic inquiry in many different ways – this being through a still deeper esotericism than the two former meanings can reveal. The endpoint of this work is thus very difficult to discuss and divulge under ordinary methods, but this volume is about the background for understanding what are undoubtedly very profound matters that can really only be hinted at through objective empirical research such as this. These matters certainly impinge on *gnostika*, that is, matters of an inner knowing that sit alongside yet should be explored in tandem with exoteric research. Yet of course not everything in Persian spirituality that is esoteric will be considered here. Except where the material is pertinent, this book is not about the "formerly esoteric side" to establishment traditions (such as Zoroastrianism or Islam in the case of Persian history),[1] but it more persistently pursues what comes out of a study of materials that have been "left behind", or in a "minority" position, or made "marginal", or had only "temporary prominence" before being forced "underground". Indeed this book is very often about what has been put "under threat" of extinction and "de-memorialization", but has somehow "survived", if only as covert and subtle impresses picked up by the trained and discerning eye.

The methods for this book derive mainly from the discipline of Studies in Religion (History of Religions/Comparative Religion), which is already

---

1. S. Shaked, "Esoteric Trends in Zoroastrianism", *Proceedings of the Israel Academy of Sciences and Humanities* 3(7) (1969), 175–321; J. R. Russell, "On Mysticism and Esotericism among the Zoroastrians", *Iranian Studies* 26(1–2) (1993), 73–94; M. A. Moezzi, *The Divine Guide in Early Shi'ism: The Sources of Esotericism in Islam*, (trans. D. Streight) (Albany, NY, 1994).

polymethodic and multidisciplinary. This discipline provides the flexibility to examine sensitive "religious materials" from various viewpoints. Above all, the sub-disciplines of the History of Religions and the History of Religious Ideas, including the manifold possibilities of the discipline of History itself, have assisted with the major procedures used in this study. The methods of these disciplines help develop a keen eye and special appreciation for the underlying "stream of consciousness" that alternatively bubbles up and apparently disappears in Iran's mysterious past. Indeed, the task here is a historical one: to uncover a hidden subterranean history over at least four and a half millennia, spotting the special lineaments of Persian thought and spirituality from Mithra to Rumi that best unravel the intriguing phenomena of Sufism. Therefore, this undertaking is indeed *macro*-historical.

"Macrohistory" we take to be "the representation of history as a whole", or the representation of a great passage of time. Macrohistory implies that all or a great sweep of history can somehow be held in the "mind's eye" of any putative observer and interpreter. Doing "macrohistory", moreover, is not exclusively the act of those critical minds probing "real" or "actual" history (or historical occurrences); it could be, in fact, highly fictional or imaginary, even a travesty of the past. As Garry Trompf explains:

> [Macrohistory] comprises all general(ized) visions of human destiny, whether as great stages or a procession of cycles through time, as an overall progress or regress, or as an encasement of the known order between determinative primordial events and some extraordinary eschaton. Macrohistory encompasses but is not limited to metahistory ... Macrohistory must also take in any broad prospectus of change that is decidedly imaginal, or highly speculative.[2]

Sufis themselves have propagated macrohistories, and somewhat suspicious as they may be, they are treated as "mythic" in some way, furthermore providing crucial assistance when discerning the "macro-historical prehistory" of their poetry, that is, the prior, hidden material into which they delve or to which they allude. The relevant materials of this great "prior history" are received in quite variable ways. Sometimes, in special contexts, one finds "full-blown" schemata or schemes of history that reflect the trajectory being traced, where they can be written into the current grander one as documents that fill out the whole story and make up for our "lack" in evidence of an overall hidden history. Most often one only gets a "scent" of what is going on, and every past attempt to derive an "alternative vision" of Persia's heritage will be grist to our research mill. Sufi suggestions of this "different overview" have been the most

---

2. Cf. G. Trompf, "Macrohistory", in *Dictionary of Gnosis and Esotericism* (eds W. J. Hanegraaff *et al.*) (Leiden, 2005), vol. 2, 701a–16a.

important macrohistorical materials of all for this project; the book alludes to them along the way and attempts to expound their purport.

Among Sufi (mythic-)macrohistories, one in particular, the Khaneqahi Nematollahi Sufi order, a major branch of the Nematolliya, attracts the interest of this book. In what is their alleged view, the past is quite remarkably explained in terms of the hidden wisdom tradition of Persia, *hekmat-e khosravani* or "the Khosravan Wisdom", also referred to as the "Khosravan Path". The Nematollahis do not imagine their macrohistory as an esoteric current or "movement", but rather see it as a doctrinal consistency passed on along a line of designated masters, unofficially beginning with Zarathushtra right down to noted Persian Sufis. This macrohistory and others like it offer crucial clues for unravelling the repressed past we seek to probe, claiming to preserve the pre-Islamic origin and subtle development of "Persian Sufism". This research is inspired by such available "Sufi" macrohistories, received first-hand from time spent with their purveyors (although their identities cannot be revealed for reasons of their safety). This book, however, provides a far more structured, critical investigation and a much fuller coverage than they have offered; so it is an independent historical exposition of a likely history. The macrohistory offered here really goes on to *interpret* Sufi visions of the past and what they are trying to convey esoterically. It should be noted that the intention of this book is not to impart esoteric truth, or a claim to construct a hypothetical "esoteric history" of human and cosmic affairs (like, for example, Abu Razi's).[3] This book is *about* esoteric issues, strictly concerned with the "esoteric macrohistory" of alternate or hidden lineaments in Persian culture or ones hitherto neglected. The approach is from an "esotericist" (rather than an "esoterist") point of view. The difference being that the "esoterist" is one who in fact subscribes to a single theosophical theory or model, while the "esotericist" is one who writes and thinks *about* esoteric thought.[4] This book is a history of ideas and hidden currents with special reference to esoteric forms of spirituality, and as such those holding them have had to be careful to protect themselves and their sensitive knowledge from "religious establishments", often choosing anonymity.

It should also be pointed out that a major premise of this undertaking takes its cue from Garry W. Trompf, in his attempt to set an agenda for Persian studies.[5] He maintains that certain conundrums in Persia's history demand

---

3. Abu Hatim-e Razi, *Kitab A'lam al-Obowwat*, cited in Trompf, "Macrohistory", 706a.
4. See A. Faivre & W. Hanegraaff (eds), *Western Esotericism and the Science of Religion*, Gnostica 2 (Leuven, 1998).
5. Cf. G. Trompf, "An Agenda for Persian Studies", in *Mehregan in Sydney: Proceedings of the Seminar in Persian Studies during the Mehregan Persian Cultural Festival, Sydney, Australia, 28 October–6 November 1994* (eds Trompf & M. Honari), Sydney Studies in Religion 1 (Sydney, 1998), 1–6; Trompf, "A New Agenda for Persian Studies?", *Iran and the Caucasus* 12(2) (2008), 385–95.

better explaining, among them the non-Islamic features of mediaeval Persian mystical poesis, and this book follows this quest, paying careful attention to ignored components in the previous histories of Iranian religious conscious-ness. As the book deals with such huge spaces of time, of course, it does not presume to expostulate on every known movement and idea within the pro-posed period, but rather to deal with what comes into focus as the landmarks – those stepping-stones – in the current macrohistorical reconstruction.

In presenting the scale of Iranian history – from approximately 3000BCE until now, or from pagan Iran to the Islamic Revolution – the present recon-struction finds real difficulties with standard approaches. These tend to read things by "establishments", be they Zoroastrian or Moslem, neglecting many other long-term and continuing impulses of Persian heritage, such as Mithraism and Mazdakism. The task here is to detect and take a fairer and proper note of "unnoticed" or "ignored" elements that often sit apart from a normative cultural and religious progress. Consider establishment and exo-teric Islam in Iran: there are peculiarities in Persian Islam, even Islam *eo ipso*, that have not yet been adequately accounted for in scholarship, and one of our tasks is to comprehend these properly, for the Moslem establishment tends to "paper over" many subterranean contours spread over a long period of time (with movements often kept at bay, or rejected and/or persecuted). There is a need to uncover these covert currents, because their continuing life through the history of Persian consciousness not only constitutes an alternate hidden history, but also explains the "public peculiarities" of Iranian Islam, and more especially Persian Sufism.

CHANGING HATS: ZOROASTRIANISM AND ISLAM

The Pahlavi dynasty of Reza Shah "The Great" – as dubbed by his successor and son Mohammad Reza Shah – was an attempt to radically modernize Iran. Muhammad Reza Shah, a more religious man than his father, took the ancient Achaemenian tributary titles of *Shahanshah* "King of Kings" and *Aryamehr* "Light of the Aryans", but his rather superficial attempt to fuse Persian heritage and its Islamic identity did not work to his favour. The founding of the Pahlavi dynasty was the last attempt at a restored "Kayyanid"-styled Persia – a native Persian dynasty – claiming the ancestry of the Achaemenians (Mohammed Reza Shah was the second ruler of the Pahlavi dynasty and the last Shah of the Persian monarchy). Although a closer analysis of the Pahlavi dynasty would be pertinent for a better understanding of Iranian identity, it is an exercise bet-ter suited to a modern historical endeavour. Here the more relevant example of the Sasanian dynasty (224–651CE) vitally demonstrates the point at hand. Its period marks the beginning of a major paradigm shift: the traditional line of the kings of Persia was broken with the coming of Islam and Arab domina-tion of the Umayyads (660–750). The subsequent Abbasid rule (750–1248), however, brought a Persian renaissance, moving the capital from Damascus to the more "Persianized" Iraq (building the capital on the Tigris in Baghdad), the seat of the ancient kings of Persia. The Abbasids' rule was still an Arab one, however, and as their grip on Iran weakened, several independent dynasties arose that were particularly important for the continual revival of Persian cultural and religious elements, re-establishing the line of kings that lasted until the 1979 Islamic Revolution of Iran. Among the first independent native Iranian dynasties were the Saffarids (861–1003), who annexed the regions of Greater Khorasan (from the first official dynasty independent of the Abbasids, the Tahirids [821–873]). The Saffarids' power lasted until the death of their founder, Yaqub ibn Laith al-Saffar (d. 879); they were defeated by the Samanids (819–999), a line of dynasts founded by the ex-Zoroastrian and theocratic convert to Sunni Islam, Saman Khoda (flor. 720s). Out of the military faction arose the Persianized Turkic Mamluk dynasty of the Ghaznavids (975–1187), and of course the famed Azarbaijanian–Kurdish Safavids (1501/2–1722) who formed the first Iranian Shi'a dynasty. The Safavids created the first united Iranian state since the Sasanids, using Shi'ism instead of Zoroastrianism as the official state religion. The 200-year legacy of the Safavids retained its effect on the Afsharid (1736–1750), Zand (1750–1794), Qajar (1781–1925) and Pahlavi (1925–1979) dynasties that followed, even on the fully fledged theocratic Shi'a regime of present-day Iran.

To return to the Sasanids, the cult of Zurvanism rose to become the generally accepted mode of the Zoroastrian establishment, in particular in the southwest of Iran, near the Sasanian capital. Zurvanism was a prominent philosophical trend of the "establishment" religion, which illustrates the continuity of Persian consciousness that flowed into the Islamic world. The Zurvanite creed of course presented a strict "monotheism" that idealized Zurvan (a minor god of the Avesta)[6] as the major divinity in the Sasanian era. Zurvan was conceived as "Father/Lord [of] Time", who oversaw the forces of light and darkness with Ormazd (Ahura Mazda) and Ahriman accordingly appropriated into the overarching monotheism. The Zurvanist cult was led by a strict and elite priestly class. This Persian formulation had its pragmatic uses for the Sasanian Zoroastrian state in the face of a growing Christian presence (both within and without the empire), hence the view held by some scholars that Zurvanism typically reveals Greek and Byzantine influences, and that it also developed out of a close contact with Babylonia (and was thus strongly influenced by Chaldaean astrology).[7] It is clear that Zurvanism was a Persian attempt at reconciling the notable dualistic and monotheistic inconsistencies

---

6. Cf. *Av.*, Yasna 72.10, where Zurvan is invoked in relation to "space" and "air" (*vata-vayu*) and in Yasht 13.56.
7. Cf. the position of F. Cumont and H. H. Shaeder, which was reiterated in the view of W. B. Henning. Cf. M. Boyce, "Some Reflections on Zurvanism", *Bulletin of the School of Oriental and African Studies* (*SOAS*), 19(2) (1957), 304.

in the Zoroastrian Holy Texts, the *Avesta*, and it succeeded under the Sasanids. However, Zurvanism came to a sudden end with the coming of Islam, whereas Mazdaeism, the more dualistic version of Zoroastrianism, continued. There are problems with the perceived notion of dualism which will be addressed throughout this volume, but the point is that the more "apparent" dualistic quality of Mazdaeism is a clear indication of its "Iranianness" or "Persianate" quality (compared with Zurvanism's syncretic "westernization"). Robert Charles Zaehner explains Zurvanism as a ghost of monotheism from Persia's past, an old monotheism that had withered away because it had had no real "mystical" foundation and only a distant hold on the Persian population.[8] Mary Boyce, however, has interestingly pointed out that Zurvanism and Mazdaeism occupied their own respective geographical locations in Iran. Zurvanism was native to southwestern Iran, and was thus closer to the Babylonian and Greek influence, while the latter belonged primarily to its native northeastern provinces of Iran, such as Bactria and Margiana (Merv in modern-day Turkmenistan) and was thus closer to the homeland of Zarathushtra.[9] As Persia was slow to convert to Islam, and proved to be most resilient to the Arab and Moslem culture, the Sasanian capital (in Iraq, and thus the southwest) was the first to fall to the Moslems. As a result, Zurvanism can hardly be said to have disappeared as a vulnerable "ghost" (as Zaehner suggested), but rather was totally assimilated into the Islamic domain. Hence the view of Jacques Duchesne-Guillemin is correct: it was Zurvanism not Mazdaeism that would leave its mark on the Twelver Shi'a formulation of "Iranian Islam".[10] At the same time it is true that geographical differences in the religious landscape already made Persia a complicated place, all the more so when other, neglected currents are taken into account.

Prima facie the crossover of Persian Zoroastrian elements into the Moslem world was as a "general movement" of cultural and religious change towards Islamization. But facets which this book is choosing to examine reveal special developments hitherto undisclosed by standard historiographical chronicling(s). Components from Zoroastrianism and other currents under its prior establishment (already indicative of resistance) survived the Islamic age and formed an alternative body of beliefs *vis-à-vis* the Islamic establishment. This can be first spotted in philosophical developments, with allegorical readings of the Qur'an in Avicenna (Ibn Sina, d. 1037) and Averroes (Ibn Rushd, d. 1198), for instance, and still more noticeably with the theosophical and mystical appropriations of Shihab al-Din Sohravardi (d. 1191) and Jalaladdin Rumi (d. 1273), who will be considered throughout. Military expressions of resistance, moreover, which began in the eighth and ninth centuries, were masked as internal disputes of succession. They were driven by discrete propagandist

---

8. R. C. Zaehner, *Dawn and Twilight of Zoroastrianism* (New York, 1961).
9. Boyce, "Some Reflections on Zurvanism", 308–9.
10. Cf. J. Duchesne-Guillemin, *Religion of Ancient Iran* (Bombay, 1973), 238.

agendas, typically of local Persian, and often of other anti-Arab/Moslem – Jewish, Christian and Gnostic – colour. As a result, these resilient movements were grouped together under the alias of the *ghulat* or extremist (often non-Twelver) Shi'a, the Iranian component of which was to have been fed by neo-Mazdakite revivalism. Another stream of strictly Persian sentimentality (as focused in the revival of Persian culture and mannerisms) arose with the *shuubiyya* ("national" reactionary) figures like Ferdowsi (d. 1020), for example, who occupied the more educated class of Iranian *mawali* (Arab clients). This group, typically those holding prominent governmental positions or wealthy landowners, were nevertheless not immune from allegations of heresy and conspiracy against the establishment, as in the case of Ibn al-Moqaffa (d. *c.*756). These two streams – the *ghulat* and the *shuubiyya* – along with the neo-Mazdakite phenomenon will be treated in detail.

THE NOTION OF A SECRET PERSIA

All this preliminary evidence, and much more as revealed in the following pages, point to "another history" of Persia that warrants both explanation and clarification. Tracing lines of thinking or "tendrils of thought", even "little threads that are seemingly cut off" (creating breaks in chronology), the strands often begin in one form but end up in another quite different one. For example, Mithraism, which began with the cult of a major divinity of ancient Iran, was later formulated as a syncretic occult movement among the Roman military. Therefore, an apparent tear in the thread does not finalize a discontinuity, nor does it determine an end to the flow of ideas. The detection of these various lineaments can be used to reconstruct an overall pattern, bringing back into clearer view collective signs of "living" and "continuing" traditions of orality.

What is detected along the way is a special sense of continuity in instances of "wisdom" and "self-knowledge", as recurring motifs within the Persian milieu, which have been identified in this study. However, this is not a view placed on the lips of figures, imposed upon groups or read into any specific outlook documented from the past. Rather, the alternative trajectory has emerged from poring over texts and from doing detective work, a cumulative body of evidence then calling for a macroscopic vision to reveal Persia's undisclosed story. Many recurring motifs hint at a deep-structural, and cultural and spiritual stability within the Persian history of consciousness, motifs that are always bubbling up "perennially", in this case as reinforcing the image of an "eternal Persia" or instilling the "indelibly Persian" – thus preserving the collective sense that something remains or "sticks" all the time in spite of external changes.

A consistently resilient force "within and/or alongside" the Moslem establishment, as already suggested, is the mystical tradition of Sufism. The study of a history of Sufism brings to the fore important initial questions regarding its contextualization as a movement *vis-à-vis* that establishment. Its origin and development are particularly intriguing for the historian of ideas, especially considering Sufisms kaleidoscopic nature. The very presence of Sufism has presented an existential crisis not only for Islamic theology, as detected from the works of al-Ghazali, but also for Islamic historiography and sacred history at large. At times, Sufism – especially its "Persianate" form – appears distinctly cut off from the Islamic norm; at other times, the thin crust of Islamic formalities is barely stretched over the body of mystical doctrine (as in the case of the great exponents of *fana* or mystical annihilation, Bayazid al-Bistami and Mansour al-Hallaj). Where a somewhat superficial, but nonetheless necessary, reconciliation was achieved with al-Ghazali, it was truly the intellectual and spiritual works of Sohravardi Maqtol, Ibn Arabi and Rumi that brought together a lasting and deep impression of Sufi insights on the Islamic body. And it was Rumi, in particular, who best managed to transmit and disperse the heart of Sufism across cultural and religious barriers – perhaps the earliest example of "transnational" Sufism – naturally through the means of poetry, to a truly universal audience. This may help establish that Persian Sufism serves as a crucial window into the hidden discourse that has concerned "the Secret Persia" over the ages.

The "special qualities" of Persian Sufism and those of the "inspirations" of those Persian poets such as Ferdowsi (d. 1020), Khayyam (d. 1131), Rumi, Sa'di (d. 1283/91?) and Hafez (d. *c.*1390) clearly accentuate a distinctive sense of the past.[11] Note that the great father of Persian wisdom himself, Zarathushtra, wrote the ancient *Gathas* in poetic verse. The immense value placed on poesy in Persia's culture becomes central to her Sufi tradition. In looking at Islam, a similar trend is detected with the qur'anic prose-poetry, granting an even greater clue to the collective sense of connection between poetry and the divine.[12] With regard to Islam in Persia, one could intuit the Qur'an to generate a linguistic and religious renewal, a fresh point of departure from which the great poets of Persia began their quest for the reclaiming of the divine in *poesis*. And the need for this freshness was very pressing in the Sufi case, because Sufism can be read as a broader reaction set off by the increasing trend of Islamic legalism. In any case, the Persian revitalization of poetry becomes a characteristic feature of the resilience of Persian culture in general. Such poetry is perhaps to accommodate "introduced" with "indigenous" spiritualities, but proves nevertheless an effective method to protect against establishment norms.

---

11. Trompf, "An Agenda for Persian Studies", 5.
12. G. B. Vico, *The New Science* (trans. T. G. Berger & M. N. Fisch) (Ithaca, NY, 1968).

CHAPTER 2

FROM MITHRA TO ZARATHUSHTRA

ZARATHUSHTRA IN HISTORY AND IMAGINATION

The earliest records for "Zoroastrian" religious life on the Iranian plateau point to the enigmatic *Gathas*, reputably authored by an equally inscrutable figure, Zarathushtra. The heritage of Persia being one of the most ancient in the world, the benefit is given to the older date for Zarathushtra – synonymous with the *Gathas* – placing him in the first millennium BCE.[1] Zarathushtra (Grk. "Zoroaster"), who gives his name to the Iranian religion eventually named after him, Zoroastrianism, becomes for many Western theologians a foundation figure of the monotheistic idea. Yet there is more to Zarathushtra in the way that he is understood and incorporated into the mystical stream of Iran. In contrast to the Zoroastrian establishment, the Sufi view rather depicts him as an early (or "proto") gnostic[2] who promoted arcane ideas of a mystical lore that were already well entrenched on the Iranian plateau and that flowed from the psyche and imagery of a pagan spirituality. The term "gnostic" is here used to reflect its corresponding notions in the terms *magi*, *kavi* or *zaotar*, which denote a level of required initiation into mysteries, to which a priest or poet like Zarathushtra would have access. As to the actual teachings

---

1. S. H. Taqizadeh, "The 'Era of Zoroaster'", *Journal of the Royal Asiatic Society* 1–2 (1947), 33–40; G. Gnoli, "Agathias and the Date of Zoroaster", *Eran ud Aneran* (Webfestschrift Marshak), www.transoxiana.org/Eran/Articles/gnoli; A. S. Shahbazi, "The 'Traditional Date of Zoroaster' Explained", *Bulletin of the School of Oriental and African Studies* 40(1) (1977), 25–35. J. M. Chatterji, *Atharvan Zarathustra – The Foremost Prophet: A Comparative Study of Hinduism, Zoroastrianism, and Islam* (Calcutta, 1971), maintains the language of the *Gathas* is older than many parts of the *Rig-veda*.
2. Cf. M. Boyce, *History of Zoroastrianism* (Leiden, 1975), vol. 1, 5–12; see also the index of L. J. S. Taraporawala, *The Divine Songs of Zarathushtra* (Bombay, 1993), on the meaning and function of the three terms in Ancient Iran and the *Gathas*.

of this figure, historians and scholars of religion remain uncertain, yet in spite of this no one can understand Persia without coming to terms with the effect of Zarathushtra's teachings.

The influence of the Zoroastrian ethos upon the current state of Iranian religion, Twelver Shi'ism and Sufism, serves as a useful window to the soul of Persia's past. An analogy can be drawn with the spoken English of foreign speakers, which can reveal the detail of the structure and logic of the native tongue from the errors made in grammar. Likewise the Shi'ite tone of current Iran speaks an accent of her cultural past, and indeed her religious and spiritual identity. The Arabian Wahabist may certainly detect the syntactical errors in the Shi'ite accent (finding it pure heresy), just as hardline Moslem orthodoxy has for centuries detected the alien tone of Sufi groups speaking the language of Islam. This only goes to show that something non-Islamic has been perceived; but what exactly is being detected? It is not difficult to peel back dominant layers of religion to find underneath a reality complicated by further national, cultural, religious, intellectual and spiritual intricacies. These phenomena usually lie dormant or remain pulsating under the skin of the establishment, looking for an opportunity to surface.

The search for the "Persianate" Sufi identity takes us invariably back to two points of reference: the *Gathas* and pre-Zoroastrian Mithra-worship. The *Gathas* constitute the earliest textual reference point to religiosity in Iran, yet before this time, in the ancient worship of Mithra, we might find the oldest Indo-Iranian source for a just, merciful and loving god. (We will return to this point later, when parallels are drawn in relation to the Moslem concept of a just and merciful god.) For this reason Roman Mithraism is important to this study, since it was the only living cult of the Roman era that bore witness to the almost forgotten mysteries of Mithra back in Iran.[3] (Alternations between "Mithra" and "Mithras" will designate the Persian and Roman periods respectively.) In fact, "Mithra*ism*", that is, Mithra-worship, was not completely lost to the Persians, surviving the apparent Zoroastrian Achaemenids and, later, the Hellenic Seleucids. Mithra-worship was well ingrained within the Iranian consciousness and kept its influence, however subtle, over Iranian religion. Mithra-worship was a feature of Parthian religion in Nisa (Turkmenistan), which was later modified by the Romans who came into contact with them during the Parthian wars. The connection between Roman and Iranian Mithra-worship is strengthened by the archaeological evidence and inscriptions (graffiti) of the Mithraeum at Dura-Eurupo, most likely involving the

---

3. Cf. Roger Beck, "Mithraism: The Cult of Mithra as it Developed in the West, Its Origins, Its Features, and Its Probable Connections with Mithra Worship in Iran", in *EIr*, 20 July 2002 (www.iranica.com/articles/mithraism). Also James R. Russell, "On the Armeno-Iranian Roots of Mithraism", in *Studies in Mithraism*, (ed. J. Hinnells) (Rome, 1994), 183–93.

Magi in the spread of Mithraism to the West.[4] The Romans, as was customary, adopted the Parthian religion and incorporated Mithra-worship into their religious lifestyle. Mithraism first sprang from the *sacred cult* of Mithra, elements of which began among Persian soldiers during the Achaemenian period,[5] although at a later stage it was an esoteric-looking movement that was "mystified" – in connection with the Hellenized Magi – and popularized mainly among the Roman Legions in the West from the first century until the fifth century CE.

A chronological sketch of events is provided by the following:

(pre-Zarathushtra)

↓

Zarathushtra
(pre-Zoroastrian)

↓

Indo-Iranian Pantheon
(Achamaenid Zoroastrianism)

↓

Mithra-worship – revival
(Parthian)

↓

Roman Mithraism – Mystery Religions

↓

Zoroastrianism
(Sasanian)

The *Gathas* and Mithraism play an important part in the history of Sufism with respect to the cultural themes that dominate its heritage. The *Gathas* stand as a wellspring of ideas that consistently recur in Iranian religions, while Mithraism, as it became a popular syncretic tradition combining East and West, serves as one of the last explicit ideological stepping-stones (and heir to mysteries of Persia's ancient world) in Asia Minor before the coming of Islam.

---

4. Cf. M. P. Speidel, "Parthia and the Mithraism of the Roman Army", *Acta Iranica: Études Mithraiques* (Actes du 2e Congrès International Téhéran, du 1er au 8 Septembre 1975) (Leiden, 1978), vol. 4, 479–83; Pliny, *Natural History*, 28, 4, cited in *ibid.*, 480n; H. D. Kayoji Mirza, *Ancient and Middle Iranian Studies* (Mumbai, 2000), 128.

5. Cf. R. A. Bowman, *Aramaic Ritual Texts from Persepolis* (Chicago, 1970), 15.

The *Gathas* are stanzas invoking and dwelling upon the notions of wisdom, justice and love as major components of divine transformation and earthly service. By examining this poetry, we can identify the fundamental roots of Iranian religiosity from which the basic make-up of "Iranian Mysticism" (*tasavvof-e irani*), and later Persian Sufism, is founded. Mithra-worship, as a mystery religion, also signifies an important pre-Islamic "spiritual" component that may have some measure of effect upon the nature of qur'anic discourse in Islamic Iran. Both the *Gathas* and the Mithraic impulses are crucial long-term sources of Sufi sensibilities. While not asserting any "mechanical-causal" connection between the *Gathas*, Mithraism and Sufism, or imagining the one "continuing entity", there are peculiar correlations or "recurring themes" in the *Gathas*, Mithraism and Sufism worth exploring in detail. Persians as a whole have always been keenly aware of their past, and this is still witnessed in the persistence of old festivities, of *chahar shambeh suri* (the Fire Festival), *nawruz* (Persian New Year), *shab-e yaldaa* or *shab-e chelleh* (celebration of the Winter Solstice)[6] and others. These derive from Old Iranian times, the last two being definitely connected to the worship of Mithra. A closer analysis of Persian Sufism reveals its deeper origins beyond the boundaries of the Islamic body as defined through the Qur'an and hadith. As will be seen, too, the mystical and spiritual quality of the *Gathas* is perpetuated through the resilience of Persia's ancient heritage and later revived in the "mysticism" of Persian Sufism. However, from a traditionalist point of view, "the perennial" is as unique to Islam as it is to Sufism *per se*, in that Islam traditionally sees itself as a continuation of the "Abrahamic religion" descended from the first man and prophet, Adam. Hence, similar to the *Gathas'* adaptation of certain prior-Mithraic insights, the Qur'an demonstrates the Moslem capacity for absorption and integration of ancient wisdom into its original revelation.

To define references to "religion" and "Sufism" in this work, I am inclined to refer to the "greater" and "smaller" religious body, the "expanded" and the "limited", or the "literal" and "imaginal" body of any so-called tradition, organization or community. To avoid the methodological problems of Clifford Geertz, I take the "greater form" of religion to be present beyond its face value. The "smaller" is identified in the light of its doctrine, legalism and socio-political identity. In this way, then, when speaking of "greater" Islam, the aim is to touch on the perceived "essential" part of its entity, or its "soul", however vague or (paradoxically) palpable it may be. Concordantly, where institutional experience is what defines the relation to the "smaller" identity, allowing us to spot its visible peculiarities, the "greater" defines the distinctly "religious" or "spiritual" experience. There may be therefore something not necessarily deeper and essential in, but rather behind and in the workings of, *both* "introduced Islam" and "indigenous Zoroastrianism" that could explain

---

6. P. Yagmaii, "Mehr and Mehregan", in Trompf & Honari (eds), *Mehregan in Sydney*, 7–16.

a special sense of continuity. This then brings us to the imaginal, where perhaps religious or spiritual traditions are, as presented in the methodology of Abdolkarim Soroush, only held to be separated in the spirit (or method) in which they attain to the divine; what then remains beyond the expressions cannot easily be discussed. Short of stating religion and spirituality as inherent to the human condition, it may suffice to say that a certain "mysticism" is inherent to the very depths of a culture. That is, "mysticism", imagined in a Confucian sense where the self is cultivated through cultural customs. This is definitely true of Iran, and also true is that the Persianate Sufism sought is precisely defined, empowered and motivated by the spirit of its cultural heritage. So much so that even the agnostic-cum-atheistic odes of Omar Khayyam and Hafez are laced with the most profound mystical insight – or they are at least interpreted as such by the Sufis. Like any good religious culture when observed closely, religion and spirituality weave themselves into the Persian daily routine and can be found in the most secular activity. In the case of the Iranians – and Persianate Sufism – this is a sign of a mysticism deeply entrenched in the psycho-spiritual existence of its people, and it is a sign that the "greater religion" of Iranian Islam reflects a unique composite of all the long-term historical forces that have gone into the making of Persia.

ZARATHUSHTRA, THE *KAVI* AND THE *MAGI*

So far, the idea has been to demonstrate the weight of ideas from its past that have retained their impress upon the Iranian religious consciousness until the present time. For now, the *Gathas* and the Mithraic cult demonstrate their importance to the developmental process of religious and spiritual thought in Iran. This does not constitute a theory for the origins of Sufism, but it does explain factors that contribute to the perceived notion of "Persian" Sufism. First let us consider the possibility of a Zoroastrian influence.

Zarathushtra

The "establishment" Zoroastrianism became the dominant religious air of a whole climate, but in the *Gathas* and the cult of Mithras, more specifically, we find recurring themes, ideas, and doctrinal and practical elements anticipating and corresponding with the ideals of Persian Sufism that do not derive from the formalities of any priestly power, doctrinal formulation, fire temple cult, or quest for religious structure and uniformity.

A distinction between Zarathushtra's teachings and Zoroastrianism is made explicit here, and this is for several important reasons. For one, Zarathushtra (according to the *Gathas*) showed little concern with either dualism or monotheism. Nowhere throughout the *Gathas* do we find an evil force placed on a

par with Mazda. Furthermore, Zarathushtra did not place particular importance upon the singularity of Ahura Mazda, as is the case with the strict monotheism of biblical religion (Judaism, Christianity and Islam); rather, stress is
instead laid upon the primacy of and reverence for Mazda. Second, it is unlikely
that Zarathushtra was the founder of a new religious order, "Zoroastrianism",
but more probable that he was involved in the reform of ancient Iranian values. Whatever the case, it seems he was an initiate of ancient Iranian wisdom
who spread his teachings to a small group of followers (probably consisting
of members of his own extended family) and spent most of his time in travel
and agriculture. The *Gathic* poems set Zarathushtra apart from a simple dual-
ist or monotheist.[7] Admittedly this view is culturally controversial, for it is the
antithesis of the established Zoroastrian depiction of Zarathushtra, steadily
built up in oral and literary traditions of Persian (and later Parsee) cultural
andreligious life to image him as a great "founder figure". This process is still
going on, and the prominence of Zarathushtra in Persia's heritage was especially accentuated in works over the past decades by the late Iranologist and
literary critic Abdol-Hossein Zarrinkub (1923–99) and by P. Nawruziyan, both
of whom are discussed in Chapter 9. Nawruziyan presents Zarathushtra as a
gnostic-type sage (promoting a theosophy rather than a theology), whereby
his work lends credence to a possible "Gathic" origin for Sufism.[8]

Zarathushtra is famed for the dictum "good thoughts, good words, good
deeds"; in Ridley Scott's *Kingdom of Heaven*, for example, when the protagonist Balian is at a loss and confesses that he is outside of God's grace, he is told
in return "piety is in right action … and goodness". Such are ideas which ring
true from the eternal imprint of "Zarathushtrian" sentiments on the West.
Even the character of Tolkien's Gandalf can be seen as a reflection of this influence from the classical and post-antique eras. For "Gandalf the Grey" is somewhat like Pliny the Elder's wandering Zoroaster, who also represents (in his
clash with "Saruman the White") the Voltairean and Nietzschean anti-establishment Zoroaster of the eighteenth and nineteenth centuries.[9] The ongoing
fame of this legendary figure in the West owes itself to those earlier Greek and
Latin appraisals of his philosophy and moral teachings by figures like Eudoxus
of Cnidus and Pliny himself. The oldest Greek reference to Zarathushtra is in

7. Cf. J. H. Moulton, *The Treasure of the Magi* (Oxford, 1917), 14–15. For background, e.g.
   Ahunavaiti 6.9, Yasna 33.9; cf. Taraporewala, *Divine Songs*, 333.
8. Cf. P. Nawruziyan, "Zartusht u hukamayi bastani-yi Iran", *Sufi* 49 (2000), 12–18. This
   view is also supported by the works of Chatterji, *Atharvan Zarathustra* and *The Gospel of
   Zarathustra in the Words of Moulana Jalal-ud-din Rumi* (Calcutta, 1973).
9. Cf. Pliny, *Natural History*, 30, 3; M. Stausberg, "Zoroaster: As Perceived in Western Europe
   after Antiquity", in *EIr* (online only): www.iranica.com/newsite/articles. See also Stausberg's
   "Faszination Zarathushtra. Zoroaster und die europäische Religionsgeschichte der Frühen
   Neuzeit", *Numen* 47(2) (2000), 205–7. Cf. Voltaire, "Zoroastre", in his *Dictionnaire
   philosophique* (London/Avignon, 1764); F. Nietzsche, *Also sprach Zarathustra (Thus Spoke
   Zarathustra): A Book for All and None* (ed. and trans. A. del Caro) (Cambridge, 2006).

the form of the mid-fifth-century BCE *Zôroástrês*,[10] whereby the Greeks record him as a "star watcher" or astronomist (with the epithet *ástra*, "stars", prefixed by *zôrós*, "undiluted", surely a no less respectable title than that of the Persian *Zarathushtra*). The Greek rendering, however, seems to reflect the way in which the western Magi presented their prophet to the Mesopotamians and Greeks. The Old Aryan term *Zaotar* (or Sanskrit *hotar*) used in the *Gathas* at Yasna 33.6, however, is distinctly Iranian, when depicting a "man of sacred responsibility", since the term means "invoker" or "singer of praises."[11] Both James Moulton and Jehangir Taraporewala press the point that this term (in its earlier use) did not necessarily define a member of a priestly class since, as Moulton proposed, even "the father of a family acted in this capacity".[12] In the Avestan form, *Zarathushtra* is rendered "He of the Golden Light"; K. R. Cama explained that the pseudonym sprang from the verb "to burn" or "shine", and was meant to resemble the colour of the Bactrian camel.[13] It was nevertheless a designation given to Spitama (the birth name of our hero) after achieving an illuminated state.[14] The Avestan rendition is supported by the Greek transcription, which indicates the older signification of "light" or "radiance".[15] Even the term *Spitama* is rendered "very white (or pure)".[16] Thus, to affirm an earlier statement, Zarathushtra is not necessarily connected to a priestly ideal, nor is he necessarily depicted as a Magus, unless we take a liberal reading of this term as a "sage-like" expression disconnected from the Median and Zoroastrian priesthood.

Such evocative semantics underline the oral traditions about Zarathushtra among Persian lore. The idea of Zarathushtra as a root of Sufism relates to the historical reflexivity in Persianate Sufi thought, which is seen in the invented myth-history detectable in the publications of Nematollahi Sufism (discussed in Chapter 9). In their view, the Sufi way amounts to a revival of "Zarathushtrian wisdom" – promoted as the "Khosravan tradition" or "Path". The notion of the "Khosravan Path" is derived in part from a combined reading

---

10. Xanthus, *Lydiaka*, fragment 32; cf. B. Schlerath, "Noch Einmal Zarathustra", *Die Sprache* 2(2) (1977), 127–35; A. de Jong, "Traditions of the Magi: Zoroastrianism in Greek and Latin literature" (doctoral dissertation, University of Utrecht) (Utrecht, 1966), esp. 219–23.
11. Cf. Taraporewala, *Divine Songs*, 323.
12. Cf. Moulton, *The Treasure of the Magi*, 15.
13. Taraporewala notes that there are only two names in the *Avesta* having the element *ushtra*: Zarathushtra and Farashaoshtra. In both cases, the *ushtra* means "light". Taraporewala, *Divine Songs*, 1049.
14. For a list of the variations of the terms *Zarathushtro, Zarathushtrai, Zarathushtrahe* and *Zarathushtra* appearing in the *Gathas*, cf. Taraporewala, *Divine Songs*, 1049.
15. Cf. *ibid.*
16. "Spitama himself was descended from the great Peshdadi family of the Royal-Sages of Iran", tracing his descent from Faridun (Fereydun; Avestan: *Oraetoaona*). Cf. *ibid.* Moulton, in *The Treasure of the Magi*, 14, agrees with Zarathushtra's noble lineage, whose "special divinity was 'the Wise Lord' Ahura Mazda".

of two major Persian texts – the *Shahnameh*, with its reference to the story of Kay Khosrow, and the philosophical works of Shihab al-din al-Sohravardi – and constitutes a special reading of the past on behalf of the Nematollahiya addressed in the final chapter of this book.[17]

Evidence suggests that Zarathushtra was born in northwestern Iran and migrated to the northeast.[18] This makes him a Mede, a man from the northwestern provinces of the Iranian plateau. Tradition (the Avestan *Zadspram* 16.1) explains that he ran away from home at the age of twenty, well into manhood, which by Old Iranian reckoning began at fifteen.[19] It seems he had abandoned his training to become a Magian priest, which began at the age of seven (*Yasna Heptanghaiti* 33.6, 13.94). Following this, he endured a period of solitary hardship leading up to his revelations (*Gath.* Y[as] 46.1) at the *Soma* festival, probably around the age of 30. The Magians were the ancient priestly class of the Medes, and it appears Zarathushtra rejected the religion of the Medes and their priesthood and then moved to eastern Iran, where he was successful in passing on his teaching, after an initial clash with the religious authority there, the *kavi*. In the *Gathas* the designation for the latter is *kavaya* and they are presented in a negative sense as denoting "Daeva-worshippers" who opposed Zarathushtra's teachings. Zoroastrian scripture explains that these were presumably the priests and teachers of pagan Iran who had erred from their own wisdom (Yas. 32.14) and were involved in leading society toward corruption (Yas. 46.11), thus being referred to in the Later *Avesta* as "the wilfully blind and deaf".[20] The term *kavaya* is originally related to the Vedic *kavi*, meaning "wise".[21] The Pahlavi form is *kay*, giving rise to the New Persian (NPers.) *kayani*: according to legend, the *Kavaya* were a "family of great and powerful rulers, who held sway amongst the ancient Iranian Aryans" in the time of Zarathushtra – all of these (except a certain *Kava* Vishtaspa) sided

---

17. On Kay Khosrow, see H. Ferdowsi, *The Shahnameh* (trans. J. Atkinson) (Tehran, 1369/1989), 160–243; and on Sohravardi, *Hekmat al-eshraq* in *Oeuvres philosophiques et mystiques: Opera metaphysica et mystica II* (ed. and intro. H. Corbin) (Tehran, 1954), 255; *al-Mashari' wa'l-motarahat* [ms. Leiden], or in *Opera metaphysica et mystica I* (which includes only Part 3: *On metaphysics*, of the texts *al-Mashari'*, *al-Talwihat*, and *al-Moqawamat* (ed. anon. and intro. Corbin) (Istanbul, 1945), 502–3; *Majmu'at-e asar-e farsi*, in *Opera metaphysica et mystica III* (which includes most of Sohravardi's Persian texts, plus the Arabic text of *Kissat al-ghorba al-gharbiyya*) (eds S. H. Nasr & H. Corbin) (Tehran, 1970), 76.

18. Moslem sources seem to favour his birthplace being in northwestern Iran (Azarbaijan). Greek and Latin sources are divided in their opinion: Cephalion, Eusebius and Justin believe it was in Bactria and the east, while Pliny and Origen suggest Media and the west; S. A. Negosian, *The Zoroastrian Faith* (Montreal, 1993), 17. Boyce's comments agree with Negosian in that she gives no conclusive remarks on the subject; cf. *History*, vol. 1, 190.

19. Cf. *ibid.*, 184.

20. Cf. Bartholomae, cited by Taraporewala, *Divine Songs*, 298–9.

21. Avestan and Sanskrit "sage", "intelligent" or even "eloquent". Cf. Boyce, *History*, vol. 1, 11. In later Persian legend it was applied to a line of kings, the *Kayanians*, discussed in the text below. Cf. Taraporewala, *Divine Songs*, 105.

with the pagan traditions (Daeva-worshippers), resulting in the disrepute of their family names among the later Zoroastrians.[22] Yet a subtlety long ago raised by Christian Bartholomae has it that the negative association of *kavaya* was carried over to *karapan* in the *Gathas*, and that the latter were the real perpetrators of obstruction. The *karapan* were the earlier ritualistic priests of the Old Iranian system who are specifically denounced throughout the whole of Yas. 32, presumably because of their attack on Zarathushtra, whose priestly legitimacy to teach a new path they deemed to be lacking.[23] Zarathushtra is no different here to his later *protégé*, Mazdak (d. 529CE), who claimed to have been preaching the original teachings of Zarathushtra in his social revolution, and who faced similar obstructions from the priesthood and the kings. Interestingly, Mazdak's patron, Kavad, also happened to be a Kayanid (one of the sage-kings from the line of *Kay* Khosrow), or so it seemed, since he took the title "Kay Kavad".

The Kavi

The Avestan tradition contains the legend of the ancient kings of Persia, the "Kavyan" (Kayanian) dynasty who are the forebears of Zarathushtra's patron, Kavi Vishtaspa.[24] They are eight in total, and are honoured together with the exception of one, "the great Haosravah [Kava Hooshravah]",[25] the *Shahnameh's* "Kay Khosrow", who is singled out and celebrated separately.[26] *In nuce*, he is pitched by Ferdowsi as the "great wise king" of ancient Persia, placed on a par with the idea of the perfect man. Kay Khosrow becomes a symbol of justice and all things good, as he was accompanied by divine favour (*Av. khvarenah* [Mid. Pers. *farr*]) – deemed "valorous, strong and wise".[27] This legend suggests that Zarathushtra's royal patronage should not be viewed as one-directional in favouring him alone: the more accurate picture deriving from these "Avestan legends" shows Vishtaspa and Zarathushtra in an equally profitable collaboration. Thus the teachings of Zarathushtra were well received by

22. Cf. Bartholomae, cited by Taraporewala, *Divine Songs*, 296.
23. Cf. *ibid.*, 687.
24. Cf. Boyce, *History*, vol. 1, 11. On the *Kavi*, see A. Christensen, *Les Kayanides* (Copenhagen, 1931), who accepted the interpretation of Gathic *kavi* simply as "prince, ruler", as did H. Lommel, *Die Yäsht's des Awesta* (German translation with notes) (Leipzig, 1927), 171–2. Against this see K. Barr, *Avesta* (Copenhagen, 1954), 206; I. Gershevitch, *The Avestan Hymn to Mithra* (Cambridge, 1959), 185–6. On the Indian *rsi vis-à-vis kavi*, see J. Gonda, *The Vision of the Vedic Poets* (The Hague, 1963).
25. *Ibid.*, vol 1, 105.
26. The Turfan form is *qavan*, as in *qavan'ud shahrdaran*, "kings and chieftains". In Armenian, too, we find the word *kav*, as in *Kav Xosrov*: Taraporewala, *Divine Songs*, 296.
27. Ferdowsi, *The Shahnameh*, 160–243. Cf. Boyce, *History*, vol. 1, 105, citing Yasht 19 (v. 71), and for *Haosravah* vv. 74–7.

Vishtaspa not because the ruler was "enlightened" but more likely because he was "enlivened" by the teachings of Zarathushtra and its fundamental affinity with the wisdom of the Kavyans in reviving ancient Iranian values, more specifically the wisdom of "Kay Khosrow" (*Haosravah*).

To be sure, there are signs of a distinct revival of this Old Iranian wisdom.[28] The making of the mythic Khosravan tradition (*ayin-e khosravani*) may just have been, for the Nematollahiya, a crucial component of Persia's most sacred past – which was to be picked up and cherished by them. Boyce has already established that Zarathushtra's teachings firmly indicate his membership of some kind of initiatory chain. Zarathushtra's gnosis arguably derived from the mantic or *manthraic* (*Av. mathra*), that is, "sacred teachings" and "utterances" that came from the traditions of both the *magai* and *kavi* – from twin lines of the religious forebears of western and eastern Iran.[29] These were both basically priestly traditions. Zarathushtra's revelation, though not syncretic, is possibly a natural unconscious synthesis of the two. The outcome, however, left him in a vulnerable position. The author of the *Gathas* openly confesses that he is an initiate, *vaedemna* "the wise one" or "one who knows".[30] Moulton notes that there is a distinction between *vaedemna* and *vîdvah*: the former is used for man and the latter for Mazda and for "men of illumination". Moulton admits that "it is risky to distinguish", yet he states that the nominative description "in this word implies 'realisation *within oneself*'".[31] Mary Boyce mentions that Henrik Nyberg sought to associate Zarathushtra with shamanism, but she believes that there was no need to leave the Indo-Iranian and Indo-European traditions of manticism to find his spiritual forebears.[32] In addition, Yas. 44, which is commended as "the great visionary hymn",[33] is composed in a literary style that "stretches back in unbroken continuity to Indo-European times",[34] and was a convention bound to mantic utterances.[35] Thus Boyce suggests a strong emphasis on Zarathushtra's contribution as having belonged to and derived from "a long line of lesser visionaries and priestly seers, whose literary and spiritual disciplines had been transmitted over countless generations".[36] But what is unique and extraordinary in the case of Zarathushtra is the fact that this *manthric* tradition was brought very early on into line with the "sage-kings". This given, the basis for the mythic notion of a Khosravan wisdom

---

28. Cf. Boyce, *History*, vol. 1, 11–13.
29. Skt. "manthra" denotes "sacred teachings" and "utterances"; cf. Boyce, *History*, vol. 1, 8.
30. See Yas. 28.5 and 48.3.
31. Taraporewala records (*Divine Songs*, 664),
32. H. S. Nyberg, *Die Religionen des Alten Iran* (trans. H. H. Schaeder) (Leipzig, 1938), cited and discussed in Boyce, *History*, vol. 1, 184.
33. *Ibid.*
34. Cf. Schaeder, "Ein indogermanischer Liedtypus in den Gathas", *Zeitschrift der Deutschen Morgenländischen Gesellschaft* 94 (1940): 404.
35. Boyce, *History*, vol. 1, 184.
36. *Ibid.*

or *hekmat-e khosravani* can actually be derived from the works of Ferdowsi and Sohravardi, albeit from a special (esoteric) reading.

Cyrus the Achaemenid

The rise of the Achaemenians under Cyrus II "the Great", *Kourosh-e Kabir*, in 550bce is paramount not only to the return of the initial character of Zarathushtra's teaching but also, once again, to the revitalization of the "Haosravanian" (Khosravan) tradition. Cyrus led the Persian people of Anshan to a conquest of their more powerful Indo-Aryan cousins, the Medes, uniting the two separate kingdoms (of the Persians and Medes). Soon after conquering Babylon and other neighbouring kingdoms, he created the largest Empire the world had yet seen. The Achaemenians appear to have belonged to the Vishtaspian lineage and quite possibly were the keepers of the "Khosravan tradition". Boyce suggests that the Achaemenians were originally an eastern Iranian clan who later joined the Persians in the southwest in the eighth century.[37] Cyrus's character is unique and important for the preservation of an inherently Persian Iranian ideal that seems to link back to the original (and iconic) treaty between Zarathushtra and Vishtaspa's marriage of theosophic wisdom with chivalric ideals. Nevertheless, there is no clear answer for the personal religious orientation of the Achaemenians or that of Cyrus, although the idea that he represents something more ancient and arcane is appealing and plausible given the common usage of the name "Vishtaspa"[38] in the Achaemenian family, and their alleged connection with eastern Iran. With the foundation of the Persian Empire, eastern and western Iran were brought closer, and this is reflected in the Achaemenian religious style. Here is a period when orthodox Zoroastrianism was not yet properly developed and puritanic elements were overshadowed by the newly promoted (Achaemenian) syncretistic model. Cyrus's newly innovative decree was to preserve the cultural and religious traditions of conquered lands and to incorporate each system into a collaborating network under Persian rule (maintaining increased efficiency and stability). He initially endorsed the influential Magian clergy of the Medes as a diplomatic manoeuvre to secure his rule. The Magi were soon incorporated into the expanding Zoroastrian picture, yet even with the eventual success of the Zoroastrian religion, Cyrus's own personal interests in "Magian Zoroastrianism", or conversion to it, carries little conviction (at least outwardly). This is because he promoted and supported religious freedom of expression and practice throughout his new world (with no evidence

---

37. The claimed link is made by Boyce (see notes below).
38. Cf. Boyce, *History*, vol. 2, 41–2. On the identification of Cyrus with Vishtaspa cf. *ibid.*, 68–9.

linking him to any one particular religion). This further strengthens our point with regard to a deeper religious sense attributed to Zarathushtra, comparable to the private (almost secular) spirituality of Cyrus the Great. Cyrus declares himself successful against the Babylonians due to the grace of Marduk; he frees the Jewish slaves of Babylon and orders the rebuilding of their temple in Jerusalem (an obvious honouring of their God).[39] He was also buried in the Old Iranian fashion and not in accordance with Zoroastrian custom.[40] The Greek sources that speak about Cyrus's religious practices likely reflect Magian propaganda in asserting that Cyrus was, indeed, a Zoroastrian convert. The decorations at Cyrus's capital, Pasargadae, are proof not of his Zoroastrian commitments but of his diplomatic treatment of the Magi, who, even prior to Zoroastrianism, were the instigators of fire worship.[41] To be sure, the stone inscriptions at Pasargadae reveal no declaration of religious belief.[42] Moreover, the "open air" design of Pasargadae was very much in line with Old Iranian tradition, to which the early Zoroastrian priests were also known to have adhered since they had "no need of sacred buildings or fixed altars", leaving no "traces for the archaeologist".[43] We suspect that the Magi at Cyrus's court were not of those early numbers who converted to Zoroastrianism. Even if they were, it seems the unorthodox hunch of the American historian and novelist Harold Lamb actually deserves a voice here, one of his last historical fiction works being a biographical portrayal of Cyrus the Great.[44] Lamb posited the view that Cyrus (though not Zoroastrian) held a "secret" admiration, or rather fascination, for the teachings of Zarathushtra through his contact with a particular Zoroastrian magus whom he encountered (and with whom he formed a mysterious bond) on his adventures as a young man. To be sure, Lamb cannot be taken to buttress evidence, yet we do find that the court Magi were ill-content with the Achaemenian approach to religion in general and thus made an attempt at a court coup during the rule of Cyrus's son, Cambyses II (d. 522BCE), only to be definitively crushed by Darius I "the Great" (c.549–485BCE).[45] The coup was led by a Gaumata the Magian, who posed as Bardiya

---

39. Cf. M. A. Dandamayev, "Cyrus; iii. Cyrus II the Great", in *EIr*, vol. 6, 516–21.

40. Cf. M. Boyce, *Zoroastrians: Their Religious Beliefs and Practices* (London, 1979), 52.

41. Cf. *ibid.*, 50. Note new evidence of pre-Zoroastrian fire temples, starting with V. Sarianidi, *I zdjesv govoril Zaratushtra* (Moscow, 1990), plate 25; V. I. Ionesov, *The Struggle Between Life and Death in Proto-Bactrian Culture* (New York, 2002), esp. 157–9, in advance of yet-to-be-published work by O. Basirov, School of African and Oriental Studies, University of London, and the University of Sydney's A. Betts unpublished lecture on "Pre-Zoroastrian Fire Temples" (UNESCO Conference on Zarathushtra, Morling College, Macquarie University, 2003).

42. Boyce, *Zoroastrians*, 50.

43. *Ibid.*, 46 and 50.

44. H. Lamb, *Cyrus the Great* (New York, 1960).

45. Herodotus, *Hist.* iii, 61–79); Darius's own inscriptions at Behistun. Cf. G. Gnoli, "Magi", in *ER2*, vol. 9, 79a.

(Grk. Smerdis), the murdered brother of Cambyses II; after failing to regain control, Cambyses II takes his own life.[46] It is Darius who re-establishes the Achaemenid rule (as alleged heir to Achaemenes) and restores the power of the Aryan aristocracy. This tension between dynasts and the Magians continues until the demise of the Achaemenid Empire under Alexander "the Great" of Macedon. The Magi subsequently regained their former ecclesiastical strength and royal patronage, and eventually came to power with the Sasanids; the Magi were known as the *mobeds*, the supreme religious orthodoxy of the empire.[47]

As it appears Zoroastrianism was firmly established in eastern Iran before it was gradually introduced to its western Iranian cousins,[48] this may explain how the first Magi were introduced to the Zoroastrian faith (see below). A further consideration, purely on an etymological basis, suggests that the Magi, or *Magai* as the word appears in the *Gathas* (Yas. 29.11), were named as such by Zarathushtra, yet it is doubtful if he introduced the term, but rather incorporated it into his teaching. Why this would appear in the *Gathas*, given the fact that Zarathushtra apparently abandoned the priestly (Magian) life, is answered by analogy. As we will see in later chapters, individual poets and rogue Sufis were later to be faced with the same problem of securing "identity". Attar, Sa'di, Hafez and others would use the term "Sufi", or rather "darvish", quite freely and without any connection to Sufi organizations or fraternities, thereby even calling into question those pretenders to its name.[49] We are then inclined to envision Zarathushtra as somewhat akin to these later enigmatics of Iran, in particular to Rumi, for example, where we can see a character of strict religious training and upbringing in the first part of his life yet to whom the wonders of a spiritual world beyond prevenient "narrow confines" are suddenly revealed.

The Magi

Mary Boyce notes the probable migration of Zoroastrianism from the east to west of Iran, a point overlooked by Gherardo Gnoli.[50] Having argued that all Mazda-worshippers were necessarily followers of Zoroaster, Gnoli was forced to assume that the Medes and Persians were "partly or wholly" adherents of

---

46. Cf. Moulton, *The Treasure of the Magi*, 62. Cf. Henning, "The Murder of the Magi", *Journal of the Royal Asiatic Society*, 3–4 (1944), 133; Gnoli, "Magi"; J. Duchesne-Guillemin, "Magi", in *New Catholic Encyclopedia* (Detroit, 2003), vol. 9, 33b–35b; A. de Jong, "Magi", *ER2*, vol. 8, 5559a–62a.

47. There are records of a clash between the clergy and the royal syncretism of Acaemenids as late as Artaxerxes III (358–338 BCE).

48. Cf. Boyce, *History*, vol. 2, 7 and 40.

49. For Rumi's verse on "false Sufi masters", see *The Masnavi: Book One* (trans. J. Mojaddedi) (Oxford, 2004), 140, lines 2275ff. (hereafter *M* [e.g. 1:2275]).

50. Cf. Boyce, *History*, vol. 1, 7; G. Gnoli, *Zoroaster's Time and Homeland* (Naples, 1980), 199.

the prophet "right from the beginnings of their history."[51] The Magi, Gnoli suggests, were members of a priestly tribe of Median origin, who offered their priestly services to the Medes and the Persians; but an interesting perspective was presented by Nigosian that three dominant religions competed for the patronage of Achaemenid Persia, namely the Zoroastrian, Magian and Persian, which were eventually synthesized by the time of the Sasanids.[52] It is believed that the Magi introduced consanguineous marriage, fire temples (or fire-worship), and the funeral rites of feeding the dead to animals and vultures, while the Persians did not engage in either of these previously nor is there any evidence of these in the *Gathas*.[53]

A closer investigation of the Magi reveals an unclear ethnic origin, however, possibly (*à la* Herodotus) being from a Median tribe and widely accepted as the hereditary priests of the western Iranians. Whoever these ancient Magi(cians)[54] were, they were the probable cause of Zarathushtra's migration to eastern Iran, since they rejected his unorthodox ideas. In Aristotle's reckoning, the order of the Magi was more ancient than the Egyptian priesthood, an important point of reflection on their mysterious heritage and lasting significance (e.g. as the wise men of Christmas).[55] We know something of their sacerdotal practices from before Zoroastrianism, in that some led a strict ascetically styled life and were clad in white; but even this varies with different "magi", since asceticism (as with the Sufis) was most likely an occasional (prescribed) practice rather than a trend. Of those who accepted Zoroastrianism, some adhered to the old pagan religion, while others even embraced a "secular" calling.[56] Bartholemae tells us that in Zarathushtra's own time, the alias "magi" was carried by the intimate Brotherhood of his disciples, who in later ages seem to have fallen in reputation and to have scattered.[57] Moulton re-interpreted this so-called dispersal as a division between western and eastern Iranian Magi.[58] This suspected dichotomizing points to the fact that two very different traditions (possibly originating from the same Median tribe) were operating under

---

51. Cf. Boyce, *History*, vol. 2, 5 note.
52. Gnoli, "Magi"; S. A. Nigosian, *Zoroastrian Faith* (Montreal, 1993), 30.
53. See Herodotus, *Hist.* (using A. D. Godley trans., London, 1920–1924, 4 vols), i, 101, 107, 132 and 140; also cited in Negosian, *The Zoroastrian Faith*, 8, and mentioned by Moulton, *The Treasure of the Magi*, and Gnoli, "Magi", 79bf.
54. The dialogue *Alcibiades*, ascribed to Plato, demonstrates Greek knowledge of the Magi. One finds there (122a) the distinction between two kinds of magic: popular magic, which was tantamount to sorcery, and the authentic or "Persian magic", which was a form of religion. See Duschesne-Guillemin, "Magi", 34a. Gnoli suggests this was why the term *magos* had a pejorative sense in Greek, like *goes*, "expert in the magic arts": Gnoli, "Magi", 80b.
55. D. Ross (ed.) *The Works of Aristotle, vol. 12: Selected Fragments* (Oxford, 1952), 79, fig. 6. Also cited by Boyce, *History*, vol. 2, 281.
56. Cf. *ibid.*, vol. 2, 67, 84–5 and 137.
57. Bartholomae, cited in Taraporawala, *Divine Songs*, 87.
58. Moulton, *The Treasure of the Magi*, 64; Boyce, *History*, vol. 1, 11 notes.

the alias of *magi*. It is possible that not all Magi were Zoroastrian, nor were they all considered priests, a datum stressed by both Moulton and Boyce.[59] It is true, though, that the Magi are generally seen as responsible for the priestly stamp over the whole system that extended Zoroastrianism into an arduous and complex ritual state, and as making themselves priests, "the one indispensable intermediary between God and his worshippers".[60] In fact, Boyce is correct in saying that "the search for an answer" to the "magi problem" "is not helped by the Greek practice of terming all Zoroastrian priests, whether from east or west of Iran, magi, and often calling Persians Medes". It is important then to make a distinction between the Zoroastrian Magi of the east and those of the west of Iran, who were later Hellenized.[61] The latter, those of the Iranian diaspora (in Asia Minor, Syria, Mesopotamia and Armenia), came into contact with diverse religious traditions and were to various degrees influenced by syncretic concepts.[62] Boyce detects a late antique division in the Zoroastrian tradition between the west and east of Persia, perhaps confirming Moulton's earlier suspicions of a separately developing Magi tradition. She, however, shows this to be the development of Zurvanism in the southwest (at the capital Ctesiphon) under the Sasanids, and Mazdaeism in the northeast.[63] The so-called "western" Zoroastrian Magi introduced the faith to pagan Mesopotamia, partaking in the cultural and religious exchange between Persian and Semitic notions. Therefore the history of the Magi can be divided into three distinct periodic and conceptual groups: first, the Median priestcraft before Zarathushtra, to which he himself may have at one point belonged; second, one nomenclature for the early disciples of Zarathushtra (with its reference in the *Gathas*); and finally, the Institutionalized Zoroastrian Magi of the Achaemenians, who survived into the Hellenized Magi of Parthians as an influential priesthood, and the Zoroastrian clergy of Sasanian Persia. It should be cautioned that the term "magi" is not always clearly defined and cited in texts, and the above precise categorizations are typically missed or glossed over too loosely.

The Magi help underline the distinction made between Zarathushtra and Zoroastrianism. It seems plausible to assert that it was the converted Magi who were responsible for the creation of the "Zoroastrian *religion*". Over centuries they were cultivating an adaptation of Zarathushtra's essential teachings to a syncretic formula of Semitic and western Iranian religious ideas;

---

59. *Ibid.*

60. Moulton, *The Treasure of the Magi*, 65; Gnoli, "Magi", 80b.

61. In the Hellenistic period, the Magi were often seen in Greek literature as a secular school of wisdom, and their writings on magic, astrology and alchemy, deriving authority from such prestigious names as Zarathushtra, Ostanes and Hystaspes, formed an abundant apocryphal literature. Cf. J. Bidez & F. Cumont, *Les Mages hélénisés: Zoroastre, Ostanes et Hystaspe d'après la tradition grecque* (New York, 1975). Cf. Gnoli, "Magi", 81.

62. *Ibid.*, 80b.

63. Cf. Boyce, "Some Reflections on Zurvanism", 308–9.

indeed, there was a strong propensity for eclecticism and syncretism among the Magi, which helped the diffusion of Zoroastrian ideas in the communities of the Iranian diaspora.[64] By the time of the Sasanid era, Zoroastrianism (now at its peak) had firmly developed the idea of heaven and hell, the doctrine of the Messiah, angelology, the concept of evil, and so on. It had become a fundamental monotheism, constructed by the elite ecclesiastical force of the *mobeds* or Zoroastrian clergy. This "Sasanian Zoroastrianism" enthusiastically preserved the writings of Zarathushra, but in practice became far more elitist than its attributed founder had intended. In short, the former Magian power (that had existed prior to Zarathushtra) was, in this Sasanian period, reasserting itself through the "Zoroastrian" institution. Although the *Gathas* carried the seed for all the above noted theological ideas, they are hardly developed (in the obvious Semitic fashion) and remain elusive, shrouded in the enigmatic poetry of the *Gathas'* author, and never made theologically explicit. Two important points need considering here: first and foremost that the Magi, posing as the alleged creators of "Zoroastrianism", represented the renewal of a former power. This also explains why the Achaemenids did not have a discernible (Zoroastrian) religion. And second, that the teachings of Zarathushtra were far more subtle than typically accredited. Now, the monotheism that is traditionally taken to hail from the Zoroastrian house of theology is best seen, in my opinion, as deriving from the direct meeting of the two distinct cultures of the Iranian and the Mesopotamian religious complexes. Again, this corroborates the view that Zarathushtra was not preoccupied with monotheistic or dualistic concerns, and that the content of his beloved *Gathas* was not produced out of such concerns – let alone intended to formulate a general religious reform or revival.

Even Ilya Gershevitch's distinction of the three time-frames of Zoroastrian history can be of help to our argument, since he, too, clearly highlights notable discrepancies. "Zarathushtrianism" (which defines the period of Zarathushtra) is taken here to be independent of "Zarathustriacism" (the faith during the rule of the Achaemenians kings) and (later) "Zoroastrianism" (the faith under the Sasanians).[65] His approach does not suggest that the three are inextricably separate, nor does it deny the unique character and life that each possesses in their relative periods. Zarathushtra never composed a textual form of the *Gathas*, for its teachings were preserved through the oral tradition that gave life to Persian esoterica in the very long run. Along with the *Avesta*, the *Gathas* were committed to writing from the third to the seventh centuries CE, with the texts' earliest records dating back to the Sasanid era.[66] The *Gathas* are crucial because they preserve the archaic wisdom and language of Zarathushtra's

---

64. Cf. Gnoli "Magi", 81a.
65. I. Gershevitch, "Zoroaster's own Contribution", *Journal of Near Eastern Studies* 23 (1964), 12–38.
66. Nigosian, *The Zoroastrian Faith*, 17.

time. The teachings that are found within the *Gathas* present a distinctive quality that can yield a personalized moral/spiritual content, which in the end affected the Magi and was absorbed by them.

The aim here is not to reconstruct a "mystical Magian movement", but to promote the obvious fact that the Magi's mystical tendencies were inherent in their priestcraft. Indeed from the very beginning it seems this group was etched in Persian memory as teachers of men and prophets and masters of oriental wisdom whose appeal was said to have spread to distinguished occidental figures. For Gnoli, the Magi were indeed rumoured to have been the custodians of Zarathushtra's revelation and the teachers of some of the greatest Greek thinkers such as Pythagoras, Democritus and Plato; they were the wise men who arrived at Bethlehem; they were the propagators of a cult of the sun in India; and they were also known as the Chaldaeans, or the priesthood of Babylon, renowned for its occultism.[67] The Magi are linked with the introduction of Mithra-worship to the Roman Legions and the inauguration of its cult in the Greco-Roman world,[68] one major source of its Iranian origins being that in Iran the entire fire temple is known as *dar-e Mehr*, "the gateway of Mithra".[69] The paucity of archaeological evidence for the existence of a cult of Mithra in Iran does not count against an Iranian connection or origin for Mithraism, but on the contrary it simply underscores the need to re-examine Mithraic graphic and statuesque iconography as an introduced style truly unique among the West's Graeco-Roman cultic life and to plot its evolution westward (Chapter 3).

The Magi, being at the heart of Zoroastrian history, are a vestige profusely honoured in the literary expression of Persian Sufi poetry. What is often referred to there as "magianism", however, is not to be confused with the praise of Zoroastrian clergy. When the poets mention the "Magian Master" (*pir-e moghan*), it is an epithet for the "Sufi Master". The immediate connection denotes the strong sense of Persia's past as revived by the Persian poets and retained in the tradition of Persia's mystics. It is a direct psychological link to Persia's spiritual heritage and deep wisdom tradition, while an indirect

---

67. Gnoli, "Magi", 81a. The Greeks did take an interest in Magian doctrine (Xanthus of Lydia, Hermodorus, Aristotle, Theopompus, Hermippus, Dinon). Classical historians and geographers, including Herodotus and Strabo, document their customs, while the philosophers dwell on their doctrines. See R. M. Afnan, *Zoroaster's Influence on Greek Thought* (New York, 1965); B. Centrone in "Pythagoras", in *ER2*, vol. 11, 7528b.

68. Speidel, "Parthia and the Mithraism of the Roman Army", 479–83; and contrarily, M. Volken, "The Development of the Cult of Mithras in the Western Roman Empire: A Social-archaeological Perspective" (Lausanne, 2003), online article, University of de Huelva, at http://www.hums.canterbury.ac.nz/clas/ejms/papers/Volume4Papers/volken_mithras_socio_archaeological_04.pdf.

69. J. R. Hinnells, "The Iranian Background of Mithraic Iconography", *Acta Iranica* (Première série: Commémoration), vol. 1 (1974), 248. He further notes, "To name the whole temple thus clearly demonstrates the paramount importance of the god in ritual matters."

establishment of their adherence to Zarathushtra. This is expressed in verse by the eighteenth-century poet Hatef-e Esfehani (d. 1783):

> The urge to meet You driving my heart crazy
> At last led me charging to the temple of the Magi.
>
> I found there sanctuary far from evil spell
> Bright with light of God, not with fire of hell.
>
> Everywhere I saw the fire which that night
> Moses, Imran's son, saw on Sinai's height.
>
> The Master with a torch moved in solemn rites
> Around the Magian priest, and his acolytes.[70]

THE STRUCTURE OF SUFI HISTORICAL IMAGINATION AND RECOGNITION OF THE PERSIAN PAST

Khorasan

Aside from Tabriz and Shiraz, Greater Khorasan holds a special place for the Nematollahiya, who see Sufism, which is really "Hekmat-e Khosravani", as the mystical tradition of the Aryan race before the rise of Islam. Khorasan is the birthplace of Mawlana Jalaleddin Balkhi, known in the West as "Rumi" (d. 1273), but it is also the birthplace of Ferdowsi (d. 1020) and Sohravardi Maqtol (d. 1191), who with their *Shahnameh* and the *hekmat-e eshraqi* (Illuminationist Wisdom) are two important figures to be incorporated by the Nematollahiya as invoking the Persianate *mythos*. There is some historical truth to this, since the *Shahnameh* is the first "Islamic-Iranian" link to this ancient vestige through the wisdom of Kay Khosrow, and Ferdowsi's grand epic can basically be summed up as a revitalization and popularization of the Avestan traditions and the ancient wisdom of Iranian culture and religion. A crucial element in the *Shahnameh*, and one which will be discussed in close connection with the wisdom tradition of Iran, is the notion of chivalry or *javânmardî*, as idealized in the epic via Ferdowsi's finest protagonist, Rostam. As for Sohravardi, it was he who fleshed out the idea of ancient wisdom (*hekmat-e atiq*) even more, and in his works put forward a strong case for the wisdom tradition of Iran as the main source of Persian Sufism.[71]

---

70. T. Graham, "Hatif-i Isfihani: Poet of Divine Unity", *Sufi* 61 (Spring 2004), 24–7; W. Dastgirdi, *Diwan-i Hatif-i Isfihani* (Tehran, 1966).
71. Cf. M. Milani, "Mystical Experience and its Critique of Pure Reason in the Spiritual Epistemology of Suhrawardi and Rumi", in *Through a Glass Darkly: Reflections on the Sacred* (selected papers from the Religion, Literature and the Arts Society's ninth Australian

Granted eastern Iran holds special historical significance (Chapter 7), especially with regard to the theme of "light", since "Khorasan", the eastern Iranian province, means "where the sun rises". The special relationship with "light imagery", which is a prominent theme in the Iranian Sufi *mythos*, is carried through into Persian Sufism and emphasized as a crucial link by the Nematollahiyya.[72] The connection of "wisdom" and "light" is also no coincidence in both Ferdowsi and Sohravardi, nor is Rumi, in the renowned *Mathnawi*, shy about invoking this, most obviously through his intimate (and constant) references to Shams, though he is of Tabriz! Again, the idea is thematic, and there is no need to make too much of Khorasan, as does Javad Nurbakhsh in his works (Chapter 9).

Hekmat-e khosravani

Admittedly, *hekmat-e khosravani* is a phrase that springs from the imagination of Islamic Iran's contemplative works, but from the outset it was quite clearly an echo from an ancient time. By way of hermeneutics, the *khosravan* tradition traces in itself the earliest recorded reference to a sapiential tradition that runs through the current of Iranian consciousness to its most current religious and spiritual expression. In a way, elements of this perceived wisdom tradition are rooted in Persia's most ancient past. These dispersed artefacts of historical and symbolic representation of Iran's religious heritage have on occasion been revived and retained as an esoteric history. Evidence of this can be found with Ferdowsi's popularization of Persian language and mythos and Sohravardi Maqtol's mystical opus. In the more recent history of Iran, a new revival of the Persian mythos emerged with the Nematollahiya, who have expounded on and permeated such views within the tradition of "Persian Sufism".

The "Hekmat" tradition was formally referred to and traced by Shihab al-Din al-Sohravardi (Soravardi Maqtol) in his theosophical history (*Hekmat-e atiq*). Sohravardi sourced this wisdom tradition based on the coming together of two principal strands originating with Hermes: first, the Greek, transmitted through Pythagoras and revived by the Sufis Dho'l Nun al-Mesri and Sahl Tostari; and second, the Persian, transmitted through Kay Khosrow and revived by the Sufis Bayazid Bestami, Hallaj and Abol-Hasan Kharaqani.[73] The

---

and International Conference, 30 September–2 October 2005) (ed. F. Di Lauro and intro. V. Barker) (Sydney, 2006), 230–48.

72. On the theme of "light" in Persian Sufism, cf. H. Corbin, *Man of Light in Iranian Sufism* (New York, 1978). For the Nematollahiyya (i.e. Nematollahi Order), cf. L. Lewisohn, "Persian Sufism in the Contemporary West: Reflections on the Ni'matullahi Diaspora", in *Sufism in the West* (eds J. Malik & J. Hinnells) (London, 2006), 49–70.

73. See Corbin (ed.), *Opera: Al-Mashari' wa'l-motarahat*, 502–3; *Hekmat al-eshraq*, 255; *Majmu'at-e asar-e farsi*, 76.

significance of the term "Khosravan" (*khosravani*) was originally sourced in the *Avesta* and adapted by Ferdowsi – if we recall the connection made with "Haosravah", as earlier mentioned.[74] The twin traditions of the "Khorasanian Path" (*tariq-e khorasan*) and "Khosravan tradition" (*ayin-e khosravani*), which are later taken up by the Nematollahiyya as the core of Sufism (see Chapter 9), permeate the collective "mystical" consciousness of the Iranians. The view of this book is that whatever the case of the Khosravan wisdom tradition within the imagination of the Nematollahiya, it is essentially a Persian sapiential current that underlines an informal lineage made up of various figures and relevant events throughout its long history – and it is the task of this book therefore to outline a periodic (macrohistorical) analysis of these.

The conflating Nematollahi view has the "Path" linked to the principal doctrines of "love" and "kindness", which have here been sourced independently in the tradition of Mithra and Anahita (Mehr-Aban=mehraban, "[loving-]kindness") – both taken to sit at the heart of Sufi spirituality and *gnosis* in Persia. This is further crystallized in the concept of *javânmardî* (Arabic *futuwwat*), or the tradition of "spiritual chivalry", typically attributed to the prophet Mohammed in the form of self-knowledge[75] and *jihad*.[76] Revered as the noblest of qualities, self-knowledge and chivalry remain a key Sufi prescription for the attainment of "perfection of being" and "annihilation in God"; both these notions were seen to be compatible with that which was imparted to Mohammed as *ihsan* (the third and most profound state of Islam).[77] In the

---

74. Cf. Boyce, *History*, vol. 1, 105, citing the "Later Avestan" Yasht (Yt.) 19 (v. 71), and for *Haosravah*, see vv. 74–7. On "the great Haosravah", esp. notes 24ff. Note "khosrow" in S. Haim, *The Shorter Persian–English Dictionary* (Tehran, 1984), 267. For *Av. Xshathra* ("good rule") and other themes, see P. D. Kolsawalla, *Avesta–English Dictionary* (Sydney, 1991), 446f, and Taraporewala, *Divine Songs*, 970f.

75. Cf. Hadith Qudsi, "He who knows himself, knows his Lord" (*man arafa nafsahu fa-qad arafa rabbahu*). Cf. Fariddaddin Attar, *Tadhkirat al-awliya'* (ed. R. A. Nicholson) (London, 1905–7), vol. 2, 291. It does not feature in major hadith collections, but has circulated widely and has been ascribed to Mohammed by the Sufis. Cf. W. A. Graham, *Divine Word and Prophetic Word in Early Islam* (The Hague, 1977), 72. Though not accepted by Sunni Islam, the saying finds support through Qur'an and other *Sunna*. The Sunni claim it reflects the established hadith, "Be mindful of Allah, and you will find Him before you", related by Tirmidhi (d. 892). Al-Tirmidhi, *Sunan* (Cairo, 1350–2/1931–4), 7 vols.

76. The "greater jihad", relating to inward struggle, develops in the first half of the ninth century from a growing passive Sufi attitude. Its aim was to re-interpret the aggressive tone of the Qur'an and hadith and shift the mood of warfare into a "spiritual" paradigm; hence "spiritual warfare". Cf. D. Cook, *Understanding Jihad* (Berkley, 2005), 35f. Cf. also the saying of the Prophet, "A number of fighters came to the Messenger of Allah, and he said: 'You have done well in coming from the "lesser jihad" to the "greater jihad".' They said: 'What is the "greater jihad?' He said: 'For the servant [of God] to fight his passions.'" Cf. Al-Bayhaqi, *Al-Zuhd al-Kabir* (The Major Book of Asceticism) (Beirut, n.d.), 165, note 373.

77. The Arabic term means "perfection" or "excellence" (of inner worship), but carries a strong sense of social responsibility as borne from religious convictions. Cf. Hadith of Gabriel,

Persian imagination, the concept of "spiritual chivalry" (*javânmardî/futuwwat*) is connected to an earlier notion of "[spiritual] poverty" (*faqr*), known among the Moslem Arabs. The pre-Islamic tribes of the Peninsula were certainly aware of the concept of "manliness" (*muruwwat*) as distinguished from *futuwwat*, which was introduced through the Qur'an (see Chapter 5). We have to ask, though, what is the source of this qur'anic virtue? As it happens, and this will be discussed at length, such a notion existed in pre-Islamic Iran. Evidence for this is found in the etymological roots of the distinct Iranian reference to Sufism as *darvishi* (Mid. Pers. *driyôshih*) (see Chapter 4).[78] In any case, spiritual chivalry was further augmented by a third and crucial insight purveyed to this day in Sufi consciousness as "service" (*khedmat*). Indeed, the so-called principles of the Khosravan Path, being unity, love, service and chivalry, can be recognized across all Sufi orders, but it is the Nematollahiya, in particular, who define their order based on its practice. For them, Sufism is to achieve the state of Unity of Being, the consciousness of which is attained through love, with the practice of the disciples being *khedmat* and *javânmardî* and its end being the annihilation of self (*nafs*).

The etymology of *hekmat-e khosravani* is brought to light through the tradition of *Kava Hos[h]ravah* (or, as spelt by Boyce, *Haosravah* = Kay Khosrow), who is the revered sage-king of ancient Iran even mentioned in the *Avesta*.[79] Here again the themes of regality, sagacity and chivalry are intertwined in a trinitarian concept defining the Perfect Man. Repetitive patterns of this are found in the legend of Zarathushtra and Vishtaspa, and those attributed to Cyrus and the Magi, building on the older models of Iranian folklore preserved in the *Avesta* and reverberating in Ferdowsi's *Shahnameh* in the story of the wise king, Kay Khosrow. However, the specific usage of *hekmat-e khosravani* in the works of Soharawardi is of a doctrinal and theosophical nature: it defines the ancient sapiential tradition of Persia and directs the reader's attention to an imagined "essential" and mystical purport. For this reason it is necessary to expound on the etymological significance of the term in order to gain insight into this theosophical reckoning.

The connection between *hekmat-e khosravani* and self-knowledge is found in an analysis of the etymology of "khosravan". I am grateful here to James Russell's valuable linguistic analysis, exploring the use of the terms "Khosro" and "Khosrov" to connote "good repute" and verifying this as cognate to

cf. Al-Bokhari, *Sahih al-Bukhari* (trans. M. Mohsen Khan) (New Delhi, c.1984), vol. 1, 41; Al-Tabrizi, *Mishkat al-Masabih* (trans. J. Robson) (Lahore, 1975), 5.

78. I.e., from Avestan to Pahlavi to Farsi. Cf. M. Shaki & H. Algar, "Darvish", in *EIr*, vol. 7, 72a–76b.

79. Discussion relating to "the great Haosravah", esp. notes 24ff. Note also references to regality in NPers. dictionary under "khosrow"; cf. Haim, *The Shorter Persian–English Dictionary*, 267. For connections with *Av. Xshathra* ("good rule") and other relevant themes, see P. D. Kolsawalla, *Avesta–English Dictionary* (Sydney, 1991), 446f, and Taraporewala, *Divine Songs*, 970f.

Sanskrit *sushravas* (*Av. hushravah*). There are numerous estimated derivatives for the term *khosravan* or (as it is found in its Avestan form) *hos[h]ravah*.[80] Our proposed etymology for the term, however, explores an unconventional avenue, if still firmly placed in a recognized linguistic framework. We attempt such an approach simply because there is a need for refreshed analysis of standard translations. As such, we take the term to be partitioned into two segments that together give greater meaning to the whole. By regular sound changes, the "kh" is taken to be the grammatical evolution from the "hu" sound and the "s" a derivative of "sh", as is commonly seen in the transition of terms in the Persian language. It is a common occurrence for the "hu" sound to become a "kh" sound in Mid. Pers. (Pahlavi) and NPers. (Farsi), as with the word for "God" in NPers. "Khoda" and the Avestan *Hoda*.[81] Therefore we have compartmentalized the word *khosravan* into what is believed to be the original statement *hoosh* (awareness) and *rawan* (fluidity). There are combinations of various terms that are relative to the first component "khos", which are words that either imply or directly communicate "wisdom", "illumination" and/or "light", and by extension "awareness", "cognition", "consciousness", "contemplation" and/or "recognition". The words that have a genetic or structural connection with the first component, which are to be noted in accordance with the rule of regular sound changes, are outlined as follows: *xvar* – to illumine; *xvan* – sun; *xvaratha* – light, illumined, insight; *xvathra* – light; *xvarathya* – directed to righteous ends.[82] In our view *hoosh* derives from the infinitive Av. *hu* meaning "good", "noble", "holy", that is, an epithet of the divine. In NPers. *hoosh* has been translated as "intelligence", "memory", "consciousness" and "sense",[83] with *hooshmand*, by extension, being "wise".[84] The term *hooshmand* has a direct Avestan connection with the Avestan term *huzantu* meaning "the wise one",[85] so the wider association between "wisdom", "consciousness", "awareness" and "light" or "illumination" is an obvious one. The second component of *khosravan*, being "ravan", simply means "fluid" or "effortless motion" and, by extension, "constant", "consistent", "perpetual" or "continual". *Ravan* is translated in modern Persian as "flowing", "running", "fluent", and also refers to "soul" or "spirit".[86] There is some debate about whether this word derives from

---

80. *Ibid.*, 1101; cf. page 296.
81. Cf. *ibid.*, 1055f.
82. Cf. *ibid.*, 1058f.
83. Cf. Haim, *The Shorter Persian–English Dictionary*, 803.
84. *Ibid.*, 804.
85. Taraporewala, *Divine Songs*, 1056. This translates in the modern Persian name of "Hooshang". Rather "Hushang" is the second king to rule the earth in Ferdowsi's *Shahnameh* (using trans. W. M. Pierce, *Germania Orientalia*, Washington DC, 1993, 62.). It is also a derivative of the root "hu".
86. Cf. Haim, *The Shorter Persian–English Dictionary*, 348. It is worth noting a possible Avestan origin for the term found in the infinitive *ri*, to pour, to flow. Its derivative is noted as *roithwa*, "stream". Cf. Taraporewala, *Divine Songs*, 1028.

fravas[h]i, which, through the Mid. Pers. *fravahr*, comes down to NPers. as *ravan*.[87] The compound *"khosravan"* therefore generally conveys the concept of an "aware mind", "illumined consciousness" or a "perfected soul" that is in "perpetual reflection", "contemplation", and moreover "flowing", which implies the prerogative of continuation on an endless path of learning. Our point is better placed in perspective when considering the Platonic maxim that "one does not learn anything new, rather one recollects" through the activity of the soul. Thus *hekmat-e khosravani* literally spells out "wisdom of the aware/ reflective flow of mind". The very concept of *hos[h]ravah* is infused with the idea of self-knowledge, and clearly entails in its etymological foundation the basis for theosophy built on the doctrine of self-realizsation, self-recognition and self-knowledge. By extension, we can see the early foundations for the Sufi practice of Ar. *dhikr*, NPers. *zekr* (remembrance [of God]) and *moraqebeh* (meditation), which is discussed below.

Sufism, the mystical tradition

Jalaluddin Rumi (d. 1271) will surely provide initial assistance in familiarizing readers with the subtleties of Sufi literature in the following chapters. It can be said that the overarching theme to Rumi's work is simply "death" and "love";[88] two parts or rather two faces of the doctrine of self-knowledge. It is honoured by the Sufi sentiment that love (far from just an attribute) is an entire mode of being; it is the whole personality of the lover. In fact, an idea fast developing among the early Sufis was the "doctrine of love", or "pure love" as first introduced in the eighth century by the female mystic Rabea al-Adawiya (d. 801). Initially, emphasis was placed on the Arabic term *muhabba*, which was later replaced with the Persian term *eshq*. The latter, often translated as "passionate love", is adequately characterized by its overbearing and consuming effect in annihilating the ego for the sake of the "beloved". Such a concept was not utterly alien to Islam; however, it was neither overtly practised among Moslems, nor was it clearly defined in the Qur'an. The notion of an "all consuming" love was adapted by the Sufis, who were inspired either by mystical experience or through their encounter with foreign – Persian or Hindu –

---

87. Boyce notes *"rovan"* as the common term used by today's Zoroastrians in referring to the departing spirit/soul at funerals. Cf. Boyce, "Fravasi", in *EIr*, vol. 10, 198a. The expression is *rawan shaad* (roughly "joyous spirit").

88. Rumi, *Masnavi-ye manavi* (ed. and trans. R. A. Nicholson as *The Mathnawi of Jalaluddin Rumi*), E. J. W Gibb Memorial Series N.S. (Cambridge, 1930), vol. 4, 215, line 3838. In the *Mathnawi*, Rumi alludes to the interplay between contradictions and union: "Life is the reconciliation of opposites." See Abdolkarim Soroush, "Rumi Lectures" at Harvard University in 2002, available online at www.drsoroushlectures.com/English/Lectures/2002.11.26-1.mp3; cf. Rumi, "How the lover, impelled by love, said, 'I don't care' to the person who counseled and scolded him", in *MJR*, 3830ff (vol. 4, 214–16).

elements. At this early stage, neither Judaism nor Christianity had developed a "tradition" of love, in the (ninth-century) Sufistic sense already described, the seeds for which would be nurtured by later Sufi mystics during the Middle Ages.[89] Indeed, the Qur'an, not to mention the Torah and the Bible, were full of potentially mystical passages and ideas, but these had to be recognized by the mystic thinker and brought to the fore by the mystical tradition(s) − of Kabbalah, Christian mysticism and Sufism − that were formally established during the Middle Ages.

It seems that Abol Hosayn al-Nuri (d. 907) was the first to incorporate the word *eshq* in a significant way, and, indeed, to retrace the steps of Annemarie Schimmel here, it was Hallaj who openly expressed the fullness of its effect until Fakhreddin Eraqi (d. 1289) "poetically changed the words of the profession of faith" into *la ilaha illa'l-'ishq* ("there is no deity save Love").[90] On the whole, the doctrine of love was met with objection by the orthodox. Strangely enough it was the great champion of orthodoxy, the theologian Abu Hamid al-Ghazali (d. 1111) who reflected on the story of Abraham's refusal to accept the call of the angel of death, where Abraham only submits after the angel remarks, "Have you ever seen a lover who refuses to go to his beloved?"[91] This is a fact that indicates to us that even in some "dry" and "dull" version, the doctrine of love could not be kept out of Sufism. We can understand, then, that when Rumi began to rekindle the "passionate" sense in Sufism − three hundred years after it was first formed − he would carefully superimpose the conventional Islamic idiom that it was by God's will and grace alone that Man would come to achieve any spiritual satisfaction. For he says: "Not a single lover would seek union if the beloved were not seeking it" (*M*, 3:4394).

For Rumi, however, death (in the way that al-Ghazali put it) marked the end of separation and the beginning of unity, which he describes as one of the characteristics of love.[92] Here we can see a distinct variance between al-Ghazali's "love of God"[93] and the Sufi's appeal to *eshq*, which placed the emphasis on the omnipresence of God, a feeling of God's all-embracing presence becoming so common among the Persian poets since Attar's shortened phrase *ham-e oost*, "Everything is He".[94] Such a view was often seen as denying the transcendence of God and further as straying from the absolute monotheism

---

89. Note, for example, the Kabbalist thinkers: Nachmanides "Ramban" (d. 1270), Isaac the Blind (d. 1235) and Moses de Leon (d. 1305); and Christian Mystics: Hildegard of Bingen (d. 1179), Francis of Assissi (d. 1226), Beatrice of Nazareth (d. 1268), Ramon Llull (d. 1315) and Theresa of Ávila (d. 1582).

90. Cf. A. Schimmel, *Mystical Dimensions of Islam* (Chapel Hill, 1975), 137.

91. Cf. Abu Hamid al-Ghazali, *Ihya' ulum al-din* (Bulaq, 1289/1872–2, vol. 4, 253).

92. Soroush, Rumi Lectures.

93. Whoever looks at the world ... and loves because it is God's work, does not look save to God ... and does not love save God ..."; cf. al-Ghazali, *Ihya'*, 276.

94. Farriduddin Attar, *Musibatname* (ed. N. Fisal) (Tehran, 1338/1959), 223, cited in Schimmel, *Mystical Dimensions of Islam*, 147.

that al-Ghazali would defend. Indeed, for the Sufi *eshq* would venture closer to the notion expressed in the Johannine maxim "God is love", since 1 John specifically says, "He who does not *love* does not know God", giving a distinct place to the act of love for its own sake, confident that (even in having no predilection for God) God is (yet) found in (and through) the experience of love. Rumi articulates the full potency of love in the verse "From love a *div* [demon] is made into a *huri* [angel]",[95] implying the unconditional quality of "divine (or true) love", *eshq-e haqqiqi*, and its unreserved promise of salvation. Naturally this becomes a central formulation in Rumi, the patron of "universal love", declaring that "when one gains an infinitesimal amount of love, he forgets about being a Gabir, a Magi, a Christian or an unbeliever".[96] Of course, the perfection of any love, as Rumi believed, was in Islam. Moslem mystics were certainly not in the habit of denouncing central tenets of their Moslem faith, although, on occasion, their words and poetry did reflect a carefree and highly "spiritualized" expression that could be easily mistaken for heterodoxy, if not outright heresy. Therefore, on some occasions particular Sufis would appear to be dangerously close to atheism, with the orthodox casting accusations of *itihad* ("[divine-human] union")[97] and *hulul* ("indwelling") not only towards Christians but also those Sufi representatives of love mysticism – allegedly the very same crime for which Hallaj was put to death.[98]

Now, our intention here is not to imply an affiliation between Christianity and Sufism, but rather that Sufism went *beyond* the "normative" religious boundaries, a point which is taken up at length throughout this book (but especially in Chapter 9, where we return to the case of the Sufis and the development of "Persianate Sufism" in full). It should be known that the Moslem mystic was very much in line with Islamic doctrine and practice, but that a distinctly dissident attitude emerged from the Persian component, which was part and parcel of the independent character of Iranian consciousness. This typically manifested itself as "love mysticism" or the "mystical tradition of love". Rumi was prudent to explain that love itself was not an attribute, and could never be thought of that way (nor can it ever be limited to words); to speak of it is to place a veil upon it.[99] As Rumi says, "While explanation sometimes makes things clear, True love through silence only one can hear."[100] Love itself is the only proof and explanation of love. "A donkey stuck in mud is

---

95. Cf. Rumi, *The Mathnawi of Rumi: The Spiritual Couplets of Maulana Jalalu-'D-Din Muhammad-i Rumi* (trans. E. H. Whinfield) (London, 2002), 84.
96. Cf. A. Reza Arasteh, *Rumi the Persian, the Sufi* (London, 1974), 73, citing *Diwan-e Shams* (no citation).
97. In that it presumes the existence of two independent beings.
98. Cf. Schimmel, *Mystical Dimensions of Islam*, 144.
99. *Ibid.*
100. Literally, "although the commentary of the tongue makes things clear, yet a tongueless love is clearer". For the rhyme verse Cf. Mojaddedi, in *M*, 1:113, 11.

logic's fate, Love's nature only love can demonstrate."[101] However, Abdolkarim Soroush, a current Iranian Reformist thinker and theologian, points out three specific characteristics that can be spoken of with regard to love. The first is unity, the other two are "humility" and "courage"; the meaning of the latter two are not to be taken in the conventional sense. They are not a mere indication of morals or etiquette. Far more than this, they, along with unity, represent (in the fullest sense) the state of selflessness – as an "alternate chivalry". This is known in Sufism, and emphatically pursued in the language of Rumi, as the complete and utter destruction of the egocentric construct and function of normative existence. This "selflessness", as expressed through *eshq*, is the profound allegorical implication of death in a Sufistic sense. Soroush informs us that it is Rumi who demonstrates the point of unity, humility and courage, summarized in the following words of Hallaj: "O come kill me, O come kill me; my life is in my being killed," *oqtoluni oqtoluni, an-nafi qatli hayaatan*.[102] In this understanding, death is a transition to becoming love; it is the gateway, the door(way) to the "real world", that is, to eternity, infinity, as opposed to its inverse shadow, the "unreal world" (as experienced through the limitations of the ego).[103] Of course, death and love are not opposites but relational subjects. However, Rumi's discourse on death and love works off the life/death paradox, paraphrased in the following: death is the only way to the "true" life or living; while the [egocentric] life is in fact death.[104] Hence, *hekmat-e khosravani* or the Khosravan Path is the specific example of such an idea, but in a wider scope, for the purpose of containing the valued content, i.e., the story of the journey of gnosis; or profoundly, the unfolding of God. Finally, another way in which all of this has been interpreted is found in the works of Javad Nurbakhsh as a psychology of Sufism. That is to say, "death" and "love" do not necessarily possess theological realities, and perhaps even not spiritual ones, but more importantly a psychological basis upon which personal transformation can be attained.[105] All this will help to explain what now comes next, in our treatment of Mithra and Zarathushtra.

---

101. *M*, 1:115.
102. *MJR*, 3849 (vol. 4, 215).
103. Soroush, Rumi Lectures.
104. *Ibid.*
105. Cf. J. Nurbakhsh, *The Psychology of Sufism* (London, 1992).

CHAPTER 3

THE *GATHAS* AND MITHRA

MORAL-SPIRITUALISM AND THEOLOGY IN THE *GATHAS*

Given that mystical elements can be read in to the *Gathas*, what the text itself actually conveys is a sense of moral-spiritualism. The *Gathas* or *gaat-haas* ("hymns" or "chants") are "divine songs" that celebrate Mazda and his cohort of angelic forces. The *Gathas* may be the oldest transcribed religious text based on an ancient oral tradition located dialectically in northeastern Iran. Its content is written in verse and metrical form – appearing in stanzas or *Yasnas* – and draws on a rich and diverse cultural and religious imagination that preceded its own. Like the poetry of Hafez or Rumi, the *Gathas* incorporate a rich symbolic language, but their content is not explicitly mystical in nature; instead they serve as an important source of cultural repository for later "Persian Mystics". One thing that remains consistent throughout the ages is the Persian inclination for synthesis and interpretation. Indeed, with the revival of Persian culture during the Abassid era 750–1258, learned Persians such as Ferdowsi, Khayyam, Avicenna and Sohravardi were acutely aware of their very ancient heritage, constantly referring to Persia's old "tradition of wisdom" (*hekmat-e atiq*). If we place Zarathushtra within this continuum, he too is perceived as uniting the religious symbolism of his ancestral past under the epithet Ahura Mazda or "Lord [of] Wisdom".[1]

We can deduce a basic summary of Zarathushtra's teachings from the content of the *Gathas*. The text speaks to the typical concerns of a religious community engaged in establishing its own boundaries and defining those of its adversaries. Zarathustra therefore makes a distinction between *ahuras* and *daevas* to denote the "angels" that support the faithful community and the "demons" that accompany those who denounce it. Another distinction

---

1. Cf. Taraporawala, *Divine Songs*, 952, 993 and 1015.

is made between Asha and Druj (the Truth and the Lie) through which all human beings were tested. Central to Zarathushtra's teaching was the "choice" with which every *intelligent* being was endowed; a limited freewill, since there were clearly "right" and "wrong" choices determined by one's allegiance to either the *ahuras* or *daevas*. The message of the *Gathas* is for the adherents of "Truth" (*asha*) and "the Lie" (*druj*), or to those who were correspondingly called *ashavan* or *dragvant* (Y. 30.2).[2] In other instances the *Gathas* mention "through As[h]a thou-hast-promised ... for those rich in discernment" (Yas. 31.3) as against those who "through-the-lures of the False-One, destroy the world of Truth" (Yas. 31.1).[3]

The correlation between the moral-spiritualism of the *Gathas* and the mysticism of Persian Sufism is found in the connective tissues that link the dominant features of the spiritual mode and practice found in both. First, in the *Gathas* there is a clear allusion to divine attraction (Yas. 48.3) and longing for the acquisition of divine knowledge (Yas. 50.9). The *Gathas* speak about the attainment of "wholeness" (*haurvatat*) and "immortality" (*amortat*), which lead to an "illumined mind" (Yas. 30.2), whereby God is realized (Yas. 34.11). Further, that the relation between Man and God is based on love (Yas. 46.2, 44.1).[4] The Gathic words "I am longing for your vision and communion (33.6) ... come to me in person and insight (33.7) ... rise within me (33.1)" echo and reverberate through Persianate literature. The Gathic material is therefore susceptive to a mystical rendering, but to read them as such would be to impose, ahead of time, what the Persian mind came to adapt its own. It may be that the seeds to a culture of mysticism were planted by Zarathushtra in the form of ideas such as "love", "wisdom", "kindness" and "friendship" – all of which later emerge in Persian Sufis discourse.

The second connecting tissue is the theme of "service" emphasized in several verses – Yas. 34.5, Yas. 51.1,[5] and Ys.34.14[6] – in the *Gathas*, as opposed to the practice of asceticism and hermitage. The third connecting tissue relates to meditation, which finds its correspondence in Sufism with *moraqebeh*. The word "meditation", deriving from its Latin (and Greek) origins *meditatio*,[7] relates an activity of the mind, the definition of which was not presumed in

---

2. *Ibid.*, 131.

3. Cf. *ibid.*, 172 and 178, and also Yas. 31.2, 175.

4. "Loving Mind", in Taraporawala, *Divine Songs*, 1040.

5. Adaptation of Taraporewala's free English rendering, *ibid.*, 765.

6. Adaptation of Taraporewala, *ibid.*, 394. F. A. Bode, *Songs of Zarathushtra: The Gathas* (London, 1952), reads: "The reward of happiness is given to those who serve the community with their deeds of good mind and promote the divine plan of wisdom through communal righteousness."

7. G. W. Trompf, "On the Origins of the Western Meditation Movement", *Proceedings of the Inaugural International Samadhi Forum* (ed. E. Crangle) (Bangkok, 2010), ch. 1 (referring also to the Greek *meletê*). Cf. C. T. Lewis & C. Short, *A Latin Dictionary* (Oxford, 1969), 445 and 1124; cf. esp. Marcus Aurelius, *Medit.*

the early periods between mind, soul, spirit and heart. Sufi *moraqebeh* denotes a threefold activity of "self reckoning", "the power of observation" and "communing." Javad Nurbakhsh argues that love is a definitive feature of meditation itself, perceiving love (divine attraction) as the cause of motivation for meditation.[8] Therefore, meditation is not an end in itself, but a means to illumination. The Sufis speak of it as the attraction to the divine that ensnares only the sincere lover. The *Gathas* specify that illumination can therefore be attained through profound concentration upon the divine. The text also defines the process as a "vision of the [inner] eye" or an "inner conception":

> Him shall I strive to turn to us with songs,
> For I have seen Him clear with eyes of the Soul;
>> Good thoughts, good words and good deeds taught me first,
>> And next through Asha did I realize,
>> That Mazda Ahura is Lord Supreme;
>> Songs of Devotion shall we offer Him.
>
> (Yas. 45.8)[9]

Sufi sages have made a curious comment about this third sense of *moraqebeh,* "communion" (or "looking after"): "Just as God takes care of and protects man, so Man in his heart must take care of and protect God."[10] This reiterates the qur'anic passages "For Allah Ever watches over you" (Q 4:1) and "And Allah does watch over all things" (Q 33:52). The practice of *moraqebeh* is akin to *ihsan* (whereby one achieves in Islam the highest station), which is marked by one's perpetual witnessing of the divine with every act, especially during prayer, since, "He sees you though you do not see Him."[11] Finally, the *Gathas* yield a distinct awareness of a corresponding concept incorporated into the textual litany:

> On You alone we ever meditate,[12]
>> And ponder over the words of Vohu Mana;
> We think about the acts of Holy Men,
>> Whose Souls accord most perfectly with Truth;
> So may we nearer come to You and Yours,
>> With adoration, Mazda, chanting hymns.
>
> (Yas. 34.2)[13]

---

8. For an explanation of *moraqebeh* in Sufi practice, J. Nurbakhsh, *The Path: Sufi Practices* (London, 2003).
9. Taraporewala's free English rendering, *Divine Songs*, 557.
10. J. Nurbakhsh, *In the Paradise of the Sufis* (New York, 1979), 71.
11. Cf. Al-Tabrizi, *Mishkat al-Masabih*, vol. 1, 5.
12. The word used here is *mananha*, translated as "with (full) heart". Cf. Taraporewala, *Divine Songs*, 356.
13. An adaptation of Taraporewala's free English rendering, *ibid.*, 355.

Through deeds I do, also through words I speak,
  Through meditation[14] deep within myself,
  I bring mankind Eternal Life and Truth,
  Strength through Perfection, Mazda, do I bring;
United may we be in Them and You,
  Ahura, ardent in our sacrifice.

(Yas. 34.1)[15]

You are Divine, I know, O Lord Supreme,
  Since Good found entrance to my heart through Love,
  This taught me that for steady inner growth
  Quiet and silent meditation[16] is best;
    No leader should with False Ones compromise,
    With those who think the Righteous are their foes.

(Yas. 43.15)[17]

The above three themes, namely "love", "service" and "meditation", form an important correlation of ideas between the *Gathas* and Sufism. In the Gathic context, "love", "light", "wisdom" and "truth" are implicit components for the realization of God. The notion of *Vohu Mana* is not only classically the "good mind" but more importantly the "illuminated" and "loving" mind.[18] This however does not constitute a predilection for an archaic mystical tradition that produced the *Gathas*. Therefore a careful reading maintains the above exercise as one which explores only the correlative relationship that particular themes in the *Gathas* have with later Sufi mystical ideas.

ANAHITA: THE DIVINE REFLECTION

One of the earliest reflections to Trinitarian thought and no doubt one of the most common hypotheses for the successful interface of Christian missionaries in Persian lands is the notion of the Ahuraic triad: Mazda, Mithra and

---

14. The word used here is *ya-yasna*. Taraporewala defines the term as "meditation" and the act of "thinking about the Deity rather than formal acts of worship or ceremonial", *ibid.*, 352.
15. An adaptation of Taraporewala's free English rendering, *ibid.*, 351.
16. The words used in this final verse referring to mediation particularly are *tushna+maitish*. Taraporewala accepts Christian Bartholomae's suggestion that the two should be read as a compound. E. K. E. Kanga reads it as "contended", whereas Bartholomae says it means "a quiet submissive mind". He also compares *tushnaa* with Skt. *tushni'm*, quietly, silently, which may ultimately be derived from *tush*, to be content. Taraporewala translates *maiti* as "meditation". Taraporewala takes the compound to mean "silent meditation". Cf. Taraporewala, *Divine Songs*, 454.
17. Adaptation of Taraporewala's free English rendering, *ibid.*, 453.
18. *Ibid.*, 1040.

Anahita – the Father, Son and the Mother of Creation. Zarathushtra's teaching is underpinned by the meaning found in two principal divinities, Anahita and Mithra, but in particular with regard to their conceptual interaction. In a free, almost New Age, rendering of historial events, Payam Nabarz singles out the presence of Mehr (Mithra) and Aban (Anahita) as forming the NPers. word *mehraban*.[19] His work is important as he points out an interesting, but hypothetical, connection between Anahita and Mithra, and in the way that Zarathushtra may have perceived these "forces". I am critical of Nabarz's interpretation, but inclined to navigate the hypothesis based on a probable interactive component that would have been innate to the ideological formulation of Anahita and Mithra within the religious paradigm of ancient Persia.

Anahita is a pre-Zoroastrian divinity associated with water (e.g. the rivers, the sea or the ocean), and Mithra is associated with fire, light, or typically the sun. Note, both are purificatory elements. Water is mirror-like or reflective, thus it can be taken to play the role of self-reflection and self-examination, while contributing to the purification of the soul. Reading into the triadic form, Mazda, Mithra and Anahita, they can also be taken to together present a formulaic principle of salvation as wisdom, insight and reflection respectively. This may divulge a contemplative methodology: wisdom comes from insight, and insight from (self) reflection (Table 3.1).

Table 3.1 A comparison of divinities and their corresponding interpretations

Anahidic		*Mithraic*		*Mazdaeic*
Water	⇒	Light	⇒	Illumination
Reflection	⇒	Insight	⇒	Wisdom
Anahita	⇒	Mithra	⇒	Mazda

It is in relation to "water" that Zarathushtra receives his epiphany. It is henceforth his epiphany of *Vohu Mana* ("good", "loving" mind), in the form of a radiant angelic figure that leads him to the highest realm of light, the throne of Ahura Mazda.[20] I want to point out the close correlation between Vohu Mana and Mithra (the Friend, the divinity of Light and Truth). This is important because they may be seen as the same expression of a fundamental feature or chief representative of Ahura Mazda. Looking at the "Zarathushtrian" divinities symbolically, the combination of Anahita (purity/reflection/examination)

19. Cf. P. Nabarz, "Anahita: Lady of Persia", *Sufi* 71 (2006), 35–8. The whole matter also relates to the Mother theme in Shiite Islam, as noted by Boyce in her article "Bibi Shahr Banu and the Lady of Pars", *Bulletin of the School of African and Oriental Studies* 30 (1967), 30–44.
20. This is alluded to in the *Gathas* (Yas. 43), and described in brief in the Pahlavi work *Wizidagiha i Zadspram* (ed. with English summary by B. T. Anklesaria) (Bombay, 1964), 20–21. Cf. Boyce, *Zoroastrians*, 18–19.

and Mithra (insight/love/friendship) appear to mediate Mazda (wisdom/illumination). This theme is present throughout Zoroastrian history, which must have its basis in Zarathushtra's own teachings, until its peak during the reign of the Sasanids (originally the guardians of a great temple to Anahid at Istakr in Pars) under whom Mithra and Anahita are worshipped along with Ahura Mazda.[21] In any case, the Sasanian "catholic" Zoroastrianism offers many instances of the simultaneous honouring of the divine trio: Ahura Mazda, Mithra and Anahita.

Historical evidence suggests the divinity Anahita originated in the northeast of Iran in association with the element of water (Av. *apas*, Mid. Pers. *aban*). She was then brought over into the plateau and introduced to western Iran as the "goddess of the planet Venus", there being associated with the Mesopotamian Ishtar and further west with Cybele. She is known as *Anahid* (Mid. Pers.), *Anahita* (Old Persian) and *Nahid* (New Pers.), while in Armenian *Anahit* and Greek *Anaïs*. She is also revered as *Ardwisur Anahid*, which is the Mid. Pers. name of a popular Zoroastrian *yazata* (angel) by the name of *Aradvi Sura Anahita*, who is celebrated in one of the longest and best preserved of the Avestan hymns, Yasht 5, known as the *Aban Yacht* ("Aban" = Anahita). Although Anahita is a word that does not directly appear in the *Gathas*, the veneration of its elemental nature, that is, "water" (along with earth and fire) features in the segment of *Yasna Heptanghyaiti* (Yasna of the seven chapters) located between the Gathic chapters 35–42. The *Heptanghaiti* are linguistically consistent with the *Gathas* and form the oldest part of the *Avesta*. There is no doubt that Anahita is the goddess of the waters or "lady of the waters" whose presence is paramount in the Iranian religious psyche.

Mary Boyce had pointed out that Anatita's initial connection with the dominant myth is that she is *Harahvati*, "the personification of a great mythical river and the source of all the waters of the world", making her in every way connected to almost every natural or man-made sanctuary situated with waterfalls or lakes.[22] She also notes the words *sura* and *anahita* are common adjectives, meaning respectively "strong, mighty" and "undefiled, immaculate". The term *aradvi* is special to this divinity on the etymological grounds that it is also interpreted as a feminine adjective meaning "moist, humid".[23] A further important connection that is made in relation to Anahita is the mantic link in many ancient cultures between water and wisdom, and priests and their pupils (no doubt in suit with Zarathushtra's own symbolic identification) who pray to Aradvi and Sura for knowledge (Yasht. 5.86).[24] Yet the impression of her as the "goddess" was also strongly at play. Indeed, Anahita comes into popular view

---

21. Cf. Boyce, *Zoroastrians*, 101. The relief at Taq-e Bastan at Kermanshah, Iran. For relevant plates cf. Boyce, "Anahid", in *EIr*.
22. Boyce, "Anahid", 1003b.
23. For the etymological renditions cf. Boyce, "Anahid", 1003b.
24. Boyce, "Anahid", 1003b.

with the reign of the Achaemenians (alongside Ahura Mazda and Mithra)[25] as the personified goddess, "Anahit"; and her cult, though formally extinguished today, has retained its essential significance into present-day Iran under the epithet *Bibi Shahr Banu*. A famous shrine on a mountain near the city of Ray seems to have been devoted to Anahid as "the Lady of the Land" (*Shahrbanu*). It was revered with such esteem that after the Arab conquest, it was rededicated to "Bibi Shahr banu", held to be a daughter of the last Sasanian king and the widow of Hussein, son of Ali Ibn Abi Talib.[26] (Moslem prayers and sacrifices are still offered there to this day, though now with reverence to Fatima.)

Anahita and the rise of Zoroastrianism

Anahita-worship predates both Zoroastrianism and the Achaemenids. During the course of its cultic worship, it appears to have been divided, but not at odds, since the eastern Iranians kept to their "water" divinity and the western Iranians adorned their goddess. When Anahita-worship came to prominence during Achaemenid times, she already represented a unique synthesis of the two impressions. The western Iranians knew her as the divinity "Anahiti", which correlated with the cult of Ishtar (venerated as the goddess of love and war) and the Mesopotamian astrology attached to it. Thus, from very early on the venerated Anahiti, "the Pure One", was identified by the Persians with the planet Venus — in fact, the modern Persian "Nahid" is used for Venus. Boyce had suggested that the ancient pagan Iranians who settled in the land of the Elamites learned to worship the goddess in connection with celestial appearances of Venus and to associate her with the powerful Ishtar, called "the Lady".[27] The rise of Zoroastrianism in the east, however, brought new challenges for the western Iranians. The new faith began to spread over into their lands, and the situation was intensified when western Iranians began to convert to the Zoroastrian faith. The tension was somewhat relieved when the new faith was adapted to a "western syncretic" style of Zoroastrianism that reflected the Mesopotamian attitude. Yet this did not resolve the competing ideologies of Zoroastrianism with Anahita-worship entirely. Artexerxes II (404–359BCE) eventually solved the problem by fusing the western Anahiti into the eastern *Harahvati Aradvi Sura Anahita*. Under her new epithet, "Anahit", the goddess was for the first time publicly acknowledged by an Achamaenian king who invoked her after Ahura Mazda and Mithra. It is then rightly suggested by Boyce that her warrior prowess, which is incongruent with an originally water divinity, is an additional quality picked up during the encounter with the Semitic cult of Ishtar. Boyce further points out that it is here that the verses

---

25. Cf. Boyce, "Anahid", 1004a.
26. Cf. Boyce, "Bibi Shahr Banu", 1004a.
27. Cf. Boyce, "Anahid: ii. Anaitis", 1006a.

relating to her warrior qualities and regal demeanour were incorporated in Yasht 5, apparently describing a temple statue built by Artexerxes II (one of many) in devotion to her.[28] Evidence seems to suggest that there was constant resistance from orthodox priests, who rejected the royally favoured syncretic cult; and in resentment towards its alien (Mesopotamian) elements of "enclosed"[29] temple and image worship, they introduced the rival characteristic Zoroastrian temple cult of fire worship.[30] Despite priestly resistance, the cult of Anahita was made popular and was successful especially during the Achaemenid and Parthian periods; even so, this continuity was not broken under the Sasanids, the original guardians of the temple of Anahita.[31]

The promotion of the triadic formula "Aramazd-Mihr-Anahid" in Achaemenian and Sasanian prayers and invocations could suggest a continuity with the royal *farr* (divine favour) towards her line of kings. The cult of Anahita, however, had a significant place for both the Achaemenians and Sasanians, who wanted to preserve Iranian nobility and cultural identity. For the Achaemenians the cult's syncretic character was handy in the balance of power against the rising power of the formidable Zoroastrian priesthood.[32] Something of this strategy was retained under the Sasanid catholic Zoroastrianism but with the cult of the fire quite overshadowing that of water.[33] In my view, it was not Zarathushtra who affects the apparent influences on Semitic theology, but more directly, the Zoroastrianism of the Magi, who had adapted their own peculiar pagan practices. Two dominant strands have always featured in Iranian religiosity: one that reflects the pietistic, puritanical and ascetic mode, as defined and guarded by its history of priesthood, while the other is hedonistic, love-based, and liberal in its gnosis and wisdom tradition. Regardless, the indelible quality of Anahita (and indeed Mithra) within the Persian religious psyche should be apparent, as her temple survives the conquest of Alexander and the Seleucid domination and is again restored to glory by the Parthians, this time under the epithet *Ab Nahid* ("Anahid of water"),[34] a linguistic conjoining of "Aban" ("the waters") and "Anahid".

---

28. *Ibid.*, 1004a. Certain passages of the *Greater Bundahishn* appear to treat the divinity as separate through the old descriptions "Ardwisur" (associated with the waters) and "Anahiti" (with fertility and the planet Venus). Though in other chapters these two are united again as "the father and mother of the waters", e.g. 3.17 (*Ardwisur i Anahid, pi dud mad i Aban*); see Boyce., "Anahid", 1004a.

29. Boyce, *Zoroastrians*, 50 and 62.

30. Boyce, "Anahid", 1004b.

31. Boyce, *Zoroastrians*, 101.

32. See *ibid.*, chapter 1, "The Magi".

33. Boyce, "On the Zoroastrian Temple Cult of Fire", *Journal of the American Oriental Society* 95(3) (1975), 454. Also cf. R. C. Zaehner, *Zurvan: A Zoroastrian Dilemma* (New York, 1972).

34. Cf. Fakr al-din Asad Gorgani, *Vis o Ramin* (ed. M. Minovi) (Tehran, 1935), section 9.5; Boyce, "Anahid", 1004b.

Anahita and Sufism

In Persian Sufism, Anahid is a prevalent and subliminal feature. Here she is not invoked in name, but being "associated with the ocean" is metaphoric for the act of becoming the disciple of a master and of traversing the Sufi path.[35] In the Sufi tradition, the ocean is temperament, the dangers contained within it, and the subtle rules that govern it govern the rules of engagement with the master of the path or, in effect, God.[36] Traditionally, Zarathushtra received his revelation at dawn, at the foot of a riverbank during the *Haoma* (*Soma*) ceremony, whereby young priests would offer penitents to the waters (*Aban*).[37] *Haoma* is associated with the Amesha Spenta *Vohu Manah* (good, loving mind). The ceremony is the ritual re-enactment of the divine state through the consumption of the plant. In fact, the linguistic affinity between the *haoma* and *vohu mana* is close enough to suggest they are one and the same. One myth relates that Zarathushtra was conceived after his parents had first prepared and consumed the sacred *haoma* drink. This myth suggests the importance of the "proper state of being" for the immaculate conception of the prophet. Furthermore, his parents were in fact adherents of the divinity Vohu Mana, the very mediation revealed in Zarathushtra's epiphany.[38] The details of Zarathushtra's revelation are of significant importance in relation to the psychological and spiritual processes of Sufism. His revelation occurs in spring (during the spring festival feast, *noruz*). There are three noteworthy factors: his contact with water, his appealing state, and the moment or time of his epiphany in relation to the sun and water divinities. The first two points convey the generic symbolic value of purification and submission. The time of his epiphany (by the riverbank) at dawn signifies the meeting-point between the sun and the waters, discerning for us the themes of "conception", "illumination" and "spiritual ascent". This seems to have given rise to the subtle distinction and competition between the Noruz and Mehregan festivals in Persian culture. We know that both the spring and autumn festivals were celebrated in exuberant manner in Persia from the time of the Achaemenians; but whereas spring marks the Iranian New Year (*No-Ruz*) today, it was autumn which fulfilled this role in ancient times and still continues to do so in certain parts of southern Iran.[39] With the spring festival dominating, the autumn festival

---

35. J. Nurbakhsh, "Associating with the Ocean: Becoming the Disciple of a Master", *Sufi* 50 (Summer 2001), 18; "The Drop and the Ocean", in J. Nurbakhsh, *Discourses on the Path* (London, 1996), 30–31. Nurbakhsh, of course, had adapted Rumi, in whose verse the analogy of water and reference to the "ocean" is a constant theme throughout; cf. *M*, 5:3853–9 ("Love is an [infinite] Ocean, on which the heavens are [but] a flake of foam").
36. *Ibid.*
37. See *Gathas* (Yas. 43) and Pahlavi work (Zadspram 20–21) for details of this event.
38. Cf. J. R. Hinnells, *Persian Mythology* (London, 1973), 94–9.
39. E. Imoto, "Mithra, the Mediator", *Acta Iranica* 7 (1981), 301. See also Abu Raihan al-Biruni, *The Chronology of Ancient Nations* (trans. C. E. Sachau) (London, 1879), 209.

retained its significance by virtue of Mehregan (celebrated today during the months of Mehr and Aban), holding implicit the quality of Mithra and Anahita in Persian tradition. Neither the spring nor autumn festival lacks the essential symbolic ingredients that encapsulate Mithra and Anahita (or even Mazda) – the governing "will" and "wisdom" behind the Mithraic justice, light and love, and the Anahitic "mirror-like" reflection and "water-like" fertility. Regardless, the symbolic significance of *dawn* relating to the "spring festival" would imply Zarathushtra's illumined state that followed the importance of the "autumn festival" (as a period of sowing before the winter months) incorporated by Zarathushtra as the months of prayers and preparation (since in autumn the demons were at their strongest).[40]

The linking of Anahita and Mithra is not only found in the celebration of Mehregan, but a covert representation of the two also comes into play with the modern Persian usage of *mehrabani* (literally, loving-kindness), as argued by Nabarz. There are basically two moments that define the meeting of the sun and waters: dawn and dusk. With the rising sun, the "re-birth" of wisdom; and with the setting sun, its temporary death. Anahita, the typification of "purity" and "perfection", is thus aligned with virginity and fertility in bearing ideas of "life", "birth" and "matriarchy" in a multitude of spiritual and religious symbols and symbolic nuances. Mithra, representing "truth" and "light", came to typify "friendship" and "union" and ultimately the component of love in Iranian thought. The relationship of Anahita and Mithra and the significance of their interaction have been sighted in the remains of the Sasanian Temple[41] of Anahita at Bishapur, which sees both replication of the ancient myth of Aban[42] and signs of the formation of the current Persian calendar.

The ancient and recurrent themes in the Modern Persian calendar in the months Mehr and Aban stand out in relation to the Iranian themes found in Sufism. The cultural and religious quality of the calendar months is deeply embedded in the imagination of the Iranians – they are seen as symbols of fire and water (or the sun and the ocean). These ancient and indigenous representations of masculine and feminine energies are given new impetus in the evolution of Iranian thought and in its re-imagination in Iranian expressions of Sufism. With the unification of the calendar months. *Mehr* and *Aban* (modern Persian names for Mithra and Anahita), the month of the sun god Mithra, which is followed by the month of the sea goddess, Anahita, are seemingly

---

40. Boyce, *Zoroastrians*, 32.

41. Cf. Nabarz, "Anahita: Lady of Persia", www.vohuman.org/slideshow/anahita20bishapur/anahitabishapur00.htm.

42. The *Bundahishn* tells of a great sea that was fed by a mighty river (*harahvati*, Avestan: *Aredvi Sura*, Middle Persian: *Ardvisur*). Two rivers, one to the east and one to the west, flowed out of it and encircled the Earth, where they were then cleansed by *Puitika* (Avestan, middle Persian: *Putik*), the tidal sea, before flowing back into the *Harahvati* (*Bundahishn* 11.100.2; 28.8).

brought together. Nabarz is keen on the joining of Mehr and Aban to mean the NPers. word *mehraban*, literally "kind" (or someone who is kind).[43] The implication is "loving-kindness", since the modern Iranian term *mehr* bears a special sense of "love" and "affection", which is consistent with the love imagery from ancient to modern Iranian spirituality.[44]

MITHRA(S) AND MITHRAISM

According to John Hinnells, in deciphering a history of Mithraism, it is essential, if paradoxical, to give preference of order to the analysis of the Roman material before engaging the Iranian material, since the cult of Mithras first appears to be a predominantly Western phenomenon.[45] A lack of archaeological evidence in Iran provides difficulties in establishing a continuity between Iranian Mithra-worship and Roman Mithraism, but the linguistic, ritual and ideological roots of the term "Mithra" invariably point back to his significance for Iranian heritage. John Hinnells argues that three primary connections of Mithraism to a Persian background cannot be ignored:[46] the *Yasna* ceremony, the *Mehragan*, and Zoroastrian ritual. Raymond Bowman had earlier made the claim to have evidence for the existence of a cult of Mithras at Persepolis, material which he interpreted as ancestral to later Mithraic mysteries.[47] This was an idea largely rejected for its neglect of the evolutionary process and development of the Mithraic cult, and further criticized for its assumption of a living proto-Mithraic cult operating within the Persian army.[48] But his detection of the older origins of the Mithraic mystery still holds some truth, for Hinnells has found that the invocation of the sun before entering battle was crucial for the Achaemenians, and has also pointed out that the Persian army rode behind banners depicting a shining sun when entering battle.[49] A study of the history of Mithraism requires "Mithraic phenomena" to be placed in three distinct chronological categories: the worship of Mithra as attested in the Old Persian and Avestan texts for the Achaemenid period; the cult of Mithra in the

---

43. Nabarz, "Anahita: Lady of Persia", 38.
44. Farsi–English dictionary. M. Aryanpur Kashani, *The Aryanpur Progressive Persian–English Dictionary* (Tehran, 1384/2006), 868.
45. Hinnells, "The Iranian Background of Mithraic Iconography", 247–50. Cf. R. Beck, *Religion of the Mithras Cult in the Roman Empire: Mysteries of the Unconquered Sun* (Oxford, 2006). Beck confirms Franz Cumont's hypothesis for the Iranian origins of Roman Mithraism. Cf. R. Beck, *Beck on Mithraism: Collected Works with New Essays* (Aldershot, 2004).
46. Hinnells, "Iranian Background".
47. R.A. Bowman, *Aramaic Ritual Texts from Persepolis* (Chicago, 1970).
48. For this cf. E. M. Yamauchi, "The Apocalypse of Adam, Mithraism and pre-Christian Gnosticism", *Acta Iranica* (also in *Études Mithraiques: Textes et Mémoires*, ed. J. Duchesne-Guillemin), vol. 4 (1978), 551.
49. Hinnells, *Persian Mythology*, 76, citing Quintus Curtius Rufus, *Hist. Alex.*, IV, 13, 2.

Figure 3.1 The lion of summer (bas-relief in Persepolis). Photo by Ipaat, Wikimedia Commons (CC BY-SA-3.0).

Parthian-cum-Hellenistic period; and the mysteries of Mithra in the Roman Empire.[50] Samuel Laeuchli discusses the correspondence between "Christ and Mithras", and has argued for the periodic and contextual difference between Mithraism of the second century BCE and that of the third century CE.[51] Taking into account the periodic spread of Mithraism, Michael Speidel has also proposed an archaeologically based theory to explain the introduction of Mithra to Rome during the Parthian wars, his view having found archaeological and theoretical support from Richard Frye.[52]

Evidence for Mithraic thought can surely be procured through the iconography in the archaeological remains of Persepolis or *Takht-e Jamshid*. Two images in particular can be compared to the Tauroctone scene – Mithras slaying the bull. One image found at the ancient capital is the classic icon of the lion attacking a bull. The piece is rendered as "The lion of summer devours the bull of winter."[53]

---

50. J. Hinnells (ed.), *Mithraic Studies: Proceedings of the First International Congress of Mithraic Studies* (Manchester, 1975).

51. S. Laeuchli, *Mithraism in Ostia. Mystery Religion and Christianity in the Ancient Port of Rome* (Chicago, 1967), 88, and his article "Urban Mithraism", *The Biblical Archaeologist* 31(3) (1968), 74.

52. Speidel, "Parthia and the Mithraism of the Roman Army", 479–83; R. N. Frye, "Mithra in Iranian Archaeology", *Acta Iranica* 17 (1978), 205–11.

53. Cf. D. Ulansey, *The Origins of the Mithraic Mysteries: Cosmology and Salvation in the Ancient World* (Oxford, 1989), 91–2.

Figure 3.2 The king's triumph (Persepolis in Shiraz). Photo by Mardetanha, Wikimedia Commons (GFDL, CC BY-SA-3.0 or CC BY-2.5).

Hinnells has already hinted at the Mithraic link here where one interpretation of the creatures he suggests is that of the astrological signs of Leo and Taurus and the sequence of the seasons. This motif of a lion attacking a bull occurs twenty-seven times at Persepolis, appearing in key locations – near the throne room. The motif recurs in much Persian art thereafter, suggesting an important symbolic significance.[54] Another motif at Persepolis that resembles Mithras slaying the bull is the portrayal of the king as a hero overcoming wild beasts. In one particular scene, "King's triumph over the Creature", the

---

54. For the image and a brief description, see Hinnells, *Persian Mythology*, 104.

emphasis is on the cosmic nature of the beast: a lion with wings, a scorpion's tail and clawed feet.[55]

The king is shown defeating the creature by stabbing it in two symbolic points, the head and the stomach, or lower abdomen. This may demonstrate nothing more than the king as a proficient hunter – within the context of Sufism the representation of the strike points can be a symbolic indication of victory over the "intellect" and the "self". Such a rendition makes sense in light of the Zoroastrian legends about the origins of the cosmos. The obvious rendering of this motif would suggest the destruction of cosmos by Ahura Mazda and along with it Ahriman (the polluter of the cosmos) in the Zoroastrian eschatology. In Zoroastrian theology God creates the cosmos (originally a good creation) as a trap set for Ahriman (who attacks the good creation and thereby corrupts it). This then becomes the centre-stage for the battle of good and evil and ultimately the final annihilation of the latter. Here, the rule is set whereby mankind must make the choice between good and evil without direct divine interference. The importance of the choice is in the idea that the cosmic world is not everlasting. However, the relief is not purely Zoroastrian, and what creates an even stronger ideological connection between the Mithraism of the Roman Empire and Persepolis is the Near Eastern influence in the art suggesting the complexity of the religious appreciation of the Persians. What is peculiar to both the motifs at Persepolis and the later cult of Mithras is the obvious thematic synthesis between Eastern and Western cosmology and astrology.[56]

In early Sufism, the dominant focus is on breaking the *nafs* (and its hold over the intellect and the self), often through prescribed rigorous ascetic practices – although Rumi suddenly seems to make it effortless in his lines "When love calls the heart to it, the heart flees from all creation."[57] In Sufism, this is generally portrayed as the battle between the *nafs*, which represents the domain of "multiplicity", and the spirit (*ruh*), taken as the domain of "unity".[58] The *spiritual* war is waged within, whereby both the *nafs* and the spirit compete for the heart ("the site of all knowledge and perfections of the spirit and … the appearance of the revelations of Divine Manifestations").[59] Traditionally, the *nafs* is the fallen state of "spirit" from God that was breathed into Man's body by Him (Q 38:72 and 73). Therefore, in Sufism the idea prevails that one's enemy is one's own self; hence the Prophetic tradition, "Your worst enemy

55. For the image, see *ibid.*, 104–5. For background, see G. Gropp, *Zarathustra und die Mithras-Mysterien* (Hamburg, 1993), 74–5.
56. Hinnells, *Persian Mythology*, 104–5.
57. Cited by J. Nurbakhsh, *The Psychology of Sufism* (London, 1992), 72.
58. Nurbakhsh explains that the "spirit is the source of all good, and the *nafs* of all evil" and that "love constitutes the army of the spirit, and the passions that of the *nafs*", *ibid.*, 71.
59. *Ibid.*, 72; cf., M. Milani, "Sufism and the Subtle Body", in *Between Mind and Body: Subtle Body Practices in Asia and the West* (eds Geoffrey Samuel & Jay Johnson) (Oxford, 2012).

is your own carnal soul inside you."[60] The basis of the tradition comes from the tri-figurative description of the stages of the *nafs* in the Qur'an, at the end of which the individual fulfils his return unto His Lord.[61] Rumi unveils the complexity of dealing with the *nafs* since it is in fact the task of dealing with oneself. His works, as do Sufi texts generally, assert that it is not the *nafs* that is the problem, but attachment to what it wants. This is why the symbolic strike-points (in the carving at Persepolis) are important to us here. To paraphrase Rumi's idea, the heart that is attached to worldly phenomena is strangled by the *nafs*' desire; whereas those whose hearts are free from material nature are in fact aided by the *nafs*. Rumi uses the metaphor of a boat (as the person) and water (as the *nafs*) to illustrate this in the *Mathnawi*: the attached are like the boat with water inside sinking it; the free are like the boat with water under it (keeping it afloat).[62]

In both the Persepolis reliefs, however ("Lion of Summer" and "the King's Triumph"), what is not explained is the obvious fact that the slain bull, which is to feed the lion, is a generous act of greater providence than the victorious striking itself. In this way, a very clear correspondence can be made with the role of the *nafs* in Sufism and the Qur'an. Just as outlined in the sacrificial festival of Mehregan,[63] the bull is recognized not only as the good creation of Ahura Mazda but also as a source of life, which is indicated by the corn spurring from the tail of the moribund victim in the Mithraic tauroctone. Similarly, the slaying of the creature by the king is a killing symbolic of a victory of the heart, and with it the hope and promise of renewal through love. The later Mithraic tauroctonous scenes that portray a range of conventionally evil symbols, such as the scorpion or snake, are similarly understood to represent an aspect of the life-giving force. In this way, a complex appreciation of theology can be discerned, and one with a continuous, quite hidden history, from Achaemenian to Roman times, and then beyond. The conventional mistake of Orientalist scholars has largely been in interpreting Zoroastrian thought in terms of a strict dichotomy of good and evil and in emphasizing their "conflict". As Hinnells points out, in re-thinking Franz Cumont's interpretation of the tauroctone, the problem is not in the Iranian sources but in the way they are used.[64] Boyce's paper on the Iranian festivals also shows a highly complex understanding of the interaction of good and evil contrary to

---

60. B. Foruzanfar, *Ahadith-e Mathnawi* (Tehran, 1968), 9, cited by M. Estalami, "The Gnosis of Self in Rumi's *Mathnawi*", *Sufi* 20 (Winter 1993/4), 5–9.

61. The stages: *nafs-e ammara* "inciteful soul" (Qur'an, henceforth Q, 12:53), *nafs-e lawwama* "reproachful soul" (Q 75:2), and *nafs-e motma'enna* "soul at rest" (Q 89:27). For the motif of all returning to God in Q, esp. Q 9:107; cf. also e.g. surah 7, 11, 21, 23, 24, 29, 31, 32, 35, 38, 40, 41, 45 and 64.

62. *MJR* 1, 2842–3, 155.

63. M. Boyce's paper on Iranian festival, cited in Hinnells, "Iranian Background", 248.

64. Hinnells, "Iranian Background".

the rigid dualism to which scholarship is accustomed.[65] Hinnells may be right that, despite various interpretations, the bull sacrifice is soteriological and that the ambiguous symbols explain transformation and renewal. Furthermore, the concept of salvation through sacrifice and the renewal of life and immortality are ultimately derived from Iran, but the Mithraic art that preserved these ancient ideas came to express them in terms meaningful to both a Graeco-Roman and an Iranian audience.[66] Mithraism was enriched by but not dominated by Zoroastrian theology,[67] and should be viewed rather as belonging to the historical frame of a "Greater Iran".[68] Still, it should be noted that Roman Mithraism and Zoroastrianism represent two distinct worldviews that cannot be literally converged. Far from it, indeed, Mithraism "represents a survival of archaic Iranian ritual practice, a survival which was adapted cultically as well as iconographically", through a large space of time.[69] Most importantly still for our macrohistory, the real point of the Persian aspect of Mithraism is to be detected not in the art so much as in the idea of salvation through the divine mediator[70] (this bearing important correlation with the hypostatized role of the Sufi Master or *Pir*).

Like Anahita ("the warrior maiden" and "goddess of fertility"), Mithra also represents the dual notion of peace and war. In addition, as is common with Indo-Iranian divinities, gender is obsolete. Mithra was originally both masculine and feminine; He represents both the sun and the moon, and is both "protector" and "punisher".[71] This is important for understanding the development of Mithra's character as both "friend" and "foe" in the Graeco-Roman mysteries and in the later Sufic idea that the Master's wrath and kindness are derived from love. Originally discovered in the *Rig Veda* (3.59) as "Lord of Heavenly Light" and "Protector of Truth", in Persia Mithra was the protector god of tribal society until his fusion with Ahura Mazda in Zarathushtra's vision (Yas. 1.11 and 2.11); in the *Avesta*, the "Twin of Mithra" is

---

65. Boyce, "Iranian Festivals", in *CHI*, vol. 3(2), 792–818.

66. Hinnells, "Iranian Background", 249–50; C. Colpe, "Development of Religious Thought" and "The Parthian Period", in *CHI*, vol. 3(2), 834–57.

67. Colpe, "Development of Religious Thought", 834.

68. R. N. Frye, *Greater Iran: A 20th Century Odyssey* (Costa Mesa, 2005).

69. Hinnells, "Iranian Background", 250.

70. Similarly, Cumont postulated that the Mithraic mysteries were brought to the West via Asia Minor by Parthian Magis (see Speidel, "Parthia and the Mithraism of the Roman Army", 479–80), though this was sidetracked by Cumont's grand assumptions of a purely Iranian origin of Mithraism. Cf. F. Cumont, *The Mysteries of Mithra* (ed. and trans. T. J. MacCormack) (Chicago, 1903). For the French, cf. Cumont, *Textes et monuments figurés relatifs aus mystères de Mithra* (Brussels, 1896–9), 2 vols.

71. "Mithra is the "protector" of the man who respects order and truth [and] Mithra is ferocious against those who are false to him, who follow Falsehood, who break the contract." Cf. G. Bonfante, "The Name of Mithra", *Acta Iranica* 4 (1978), 48.

Ahura.[72] The tripartite affinity of His name slowly pans out in a linguistic and ideological evolution of *mitram* ("the contract"), *Mitrah* ("the God"), and finally *mitrah* ("the friend"). In Iran the personification of this deity was prevalent and his association as the "friend" was taken from the Sanskrit *mitrah*, in contradistinction to *sakhi*, which denoted "friendship" between two parties on an equal plane. The former connotation was reserved for the relationship that took place between the gods and Man. Thus the character of the Iranian "Mithra" fuses all three notions (contract, god, friend) in its final form "as a beneficent 'friend' or ally to whom the ideas of equality and association are no more necessarily applicable than the expectation of [divine] reciprocity".[73]

Mithra's role as mediator and judge made him the "gatekeeper", "curator" or "preserver/keeper" (note the Islamic period, *al-hafiz*, one of the ninety-nine divine names of Allah) of the divine light, love and wisdom. He was then placed at the centre of the renowned Mithraic cult of the divine mysteries as the custodian of secrets and sacred knowledge, revealed to those initiated into the mystery. Mithra was not only a source of wisdom for the ancient Persians, but the sacred teachings associated with him, and held by its initiates, spread to every corner of the Roman Empire (as a movement lasting from the middle of the second century CE to the fourth). The decline of the Roman "Cult of Mithras" is linked with the rise of Christianity in the West and later Islam in the East. However, this did not mean the disappearance of "Mithraism" or the ideas associated with "Mithra", which was pushed further into the subconscious layers of Iranian religiosity. His cult's sacred teachings survived through numerous cultural myths that it connected with all across the old world. In the West, persecuted by the Christian establishment, the cult appears to have gone underground, its adherents placing increasing emphasis on initiation and secrecy. The only clues that remain are archaeological evidence of temple remains and reliefs, the writings of Porphyry, and Christian polemics. From these, important information regarding Mithraic Mysteries, its initiatic rites, and symbology has been garnished. In the East, and the Persian heartland, Mithra is already a part of the divine triad, as we have shown, and his influence is then brought over to the later Islamic and Sufic theological and theosophical developments in Iran, usually with intriguing subtlety.

In Hellenistic and Roman times the Western image of Persia was of a land of mystery, wisdom and learning, so it is not surprising that Mithraism was known to its contemporaries as "the Persian Mysteries", and Mithras himself was referred to as "the Persian god".[74] This portended a deeper idea of Persia's significance found with late mediaeval and early modern perennialists,

---

72. Cited in the *Gathas* and in Yt. 10 (Mihr), 113 and 145. Also in the Old Pers. inscription of Artxerxes I and III. Bartholomae says that the association is a continuation from the Aryan days. Cf. Taraporewala, *Divine Songs*, 598.
73. Bonfante, "The Name of Mithra", 47.
74. Hinnells, *Persian Mythology*, 76.

who hypothesized a prophetic trajectory (as transmitters and protectors of a sacred wisdom) with Zarathushtra at its fount and with the implication that he was a purveyor of still earlier wisdom.[75] To link the Mithraic teachings to Zarathushtra, of course, is not the same thing as connecting it with Zoroastrianism. Zarathushtra and his teachings are a distinct and unique aspect of the overall Persian wisdom tradition which he adapted in his unique context. There is a quotation from the third-century Neoplatonic philosopher Porphyry, who says:

> The Persians call the place a cave where they introduce the initiate to the mysteries, revealing to him the path by which souls descend and go back again. For Eubulus [an ancient writer on Mithrasim whose works have been lost] tells us that Zoroaster was the first to dedicate a natural cave in honour of Mithras, the creator and father of all; it was located in the mountains near Persia and had flowers and springs. This cave bore for him the image of the cosmos, which Mithras had created, and the things, which the cave contained, by their proportionate arrangement, provided him with symbols of the elements and climates of the cosmos.[76]

It appears that the Neoplatonic thinkers were somewhat attuned to an alternate history of Zarathushtra (and that of his "secret" teachings) in Persian religiosity, and Porphyry was not the only one affected by this arena of great intrigue. The father of Neoplatonism, the Egyptian born Plotinus (204–270CE) showed a keen interest to study the wisdom of Persia (and India),[77] but it is in Fritz Heinemann's chronological arrangement of Plotinus's life that he allows for a curious Persian influence, suggesting that Plotinus himself to some extent admits a Persian background to Greek philosophy toward the end of his life.[78] Of course the presence of (Platonic and) Neoplatonic thought in Islamic and later Sufistic thought cannot be denied, yet it is a salient point of this book to locate the heritage of Persian Sufism primarily in distinct Persian cultural and religious elements that have preveniently informed Neoplatonic speculation. There are certainly elements of hard-to-perceive currents of Persian wisdom in deeper Antiquity. Many of the motifs of these lines of thought and practice may seem to elude to ordinary historical narration, but they leave their traces (more broadly) on the imagination, ideas and mythologies of their times and through the undocumented interstices of time. With Mithras already melting

---

75. M. J. B. Allen, "Marsilio Ficino", in *DGE*, 361b–2a.

76. *De Antro Nympharum*, 6 (trans. John M. Duffy), in Porphyry, *The Cave of the Nymph in the Odyssey* (Greek and English texts) (Buffalo, 1969), cited in Hinnells, *Persian Mythology*, 80.

77. See A. H. Armstrong (ed.), *Plotinus I: Porphyry on Plotinus. Ennead 1* (London, 1966), 88.

78. F. Heinemann, *Plotin. Forschungen über die plotinische Frage, Plotins Entwicklung und sein System* (Leipzig, 1921).

into the Zoroastrian (Sasanid) orthodoxy and Mithraism overshadowed by the Church throughout the Roman Empire (and the eventual rise of Islam), the elements of Mithra(ism) ultimately dissolve into the gnostic and mystical trends within Christianity and Islam. These elements linger in the form of key ritual symbols – as in the (Islamic) sacrifice of the lamb and in the Eucharist – promoting central doctrines of unity, love, purification and sacrifice, but more distinctly and in the longer term engendering the special qualities of Persian Sufism (meaning Persianate Sufism as distinct from "Islamic Mysticism").

CHAPTER 4

MITHRAISM AND THE PARALLELS OF SUFISM

The following offers a comparative analysis between symbolic artefacts of Mythraic and Sufic traditions. These components are no doubt found in the historical archives of the traditions in question, but to be clear, I do not intend to make a case for a direct historical connection between Mithraism and Sufism.

THE IRANIAN MITHRA, ROMAN MITHRAISM AND THE TAUROCTONE

The most intriguing aspect of Mithra is that he is attributed the role of "mediator", or *mesiten*, as he is called by the Persians. In his eschatological role, Mithra is also the god of the "boundary" between heaven and earth; good and evil; Mazda and Ahriman. Imoto states that, "According to Plutarch, Oromazes is most comparable to the light, and Areimanios, on the contrary, to the obscurity and ignorance, and between them is Mithra ... Also, according to al-Biruni, Mithra is the mediator between the light and the darkness."[1] This is also an extension of his prior contractual role, in which in connection with the spirit of Mehregan festival, Mithra is seen as "the lord of the silent trade of the winter-solstice".[2] Classically, Noruz and Mehregan represent the feasts of summer and winter. However, the two festivals accurately coincide with the spring and autumn equinoxes. Regardless, Mehregan (day of Mehr, love and light)[3] is

---

1. E. Imoto, "Mithra, the Mediator", 299.
2. *Ibid.*, 304.
3. The ancient Persians had twelve months of thirty days each, in which the days where named. Within the thirty day cycle there were twelve days that were named after the months. When the name of the day coincided with the name of the month, that day was celebrated. Thus the sixteenth day (Mehr-Ruz, i.e. "day of Mehr") of the sixteenth month (Mehr) was celebrated as Mehrigan. Cf. P. Yaghmaii, "Mehr and Mehrigan", in Trompf & Honari (eds), *Mehregan in Sydney*, 7. For the names of the days see *ibid.*, notes; also M. Honari, *Now-Ruz Traditions* (Tehran, 1974).

Figure 4.1 Mithras slaying the bull (Kunsthistorisches Museum, Vienna). Photo by CristianChirita, Wikimedia Commons (CC BY-SA-3.0).

placed during the cold seasons and is a celebration of thanksgiving between friends, family and the poor. Here those wishing for renewal, strength, and purification (either for the first time or renewing their vows) would enter into a religious pact with the deity.

This is an important concept to consider in light of the notions of *fana* (the idea of spiritual "annihilation" of one's selfish attributes) and *baqa* (spiritual "subsistence" in God through his attributes).[4] These ideas form part of a special Sufic understanding to be discussed throughout this chapter, and particularly in relation to the Khorasanian Sufi, Abu Yazid al-Bistam (Pers. Bayazid-e Bistami), who elaborated upon it at great length as the key to the Sufi path.[5] This teaching has significant symbolic and conceptual parallels with the seasonal poles ("winter solstice" and "summer solstice" and the spring and autumn equinoxes).

---

4. F. Rahman, "Baka wa-Fana", in *EIs*, vol. 1.
5. R. A. Nicholson (ed. and trans.), *Studies in Islamic Mysticism* (Cambridge, 1994), 77, note 2, and for a summary on this cf. Farin al-Din Attar, *Muslim Saints and Mystics: Episodes from the Tadhkirat al-Auliya* (ed. A. J. Arberry) (London, 1966), 100.

Mithra is of course associated with the solar cycles, but he also presides over the changing seasons; in this role he is the master of both the "apocalypse" and the resurrection as represented by the beginning of the expansion of the sun (in winter solstice) to its full capacity (until summer solstice) and the zodiacal shift in the seasonal equinoxes. In other words, he rules over the moments of death (*fana*) of the old, followed by a [re-]birth (*baqa*) of the continuing spirit of life. Turning now to what we can reconstruct from Partho-Roman times, this mediating power of Mithra is represented in the striking Tauroctanous scene by the "torchbearers" who flank Mithra in the ritual within the cavernous Mithraeum.[6] The torchbearers represent the equinoxes, and the torches are an indicative presence of the solar cycles. Cautes (spring equinox) is shown with torch pointing upwards, depicting "dawn" and "summer solstice", and Cautopates (autumn equinox) with torch pointing downwards symbolizes "dusk" and "winter solstice". Implicit within the Sufi concept of *fana*, and as hinted at by the seasonal and solar cycles, the idea of death does not represent an absolute end. It illustrates a double function, similar to the proto-Indo-Iranian myth of the sacred bull of life, reflected in the *Bundahishn*, wherein the killing of the bull rejuvenates the cycle of life.[7] In the case of the *Bundahishn*, it is from the life essence of the sacred bull that all cosmic life continues to generate, although in this "saga" the bull is slain by Ahriman (Angra Mainyu = "angry mind"), intending to destroy life. In the account of creation in *Bundahishn* 4.12, the cosmic (or primal) bull is slain but the seeds of the dying bull are rescued by the moon from which come forth all of creation. The later Pahlavi text *Dadistan i-denig* explains Ormuz's (Ahura Mazda) omnipotence in knowing his enemy's intent, thus the prominent theme presented there is that an act of negativity or destruction is transformed positively into an act of creation.[8] In later Mithraism this motif is adapted to a more subtle formulation with Mithra as the apparent "slayer". Overall, what is made obvious in both mythologies is perhaps the insignificance of evil in the grander scheme and its limited effect on the ultimate course of life. Indeed, at the deepest level of the Sufi contemplative mode, there is no "evil".

If in the tauroctony of Partho-Roman ritual Mithras is said to "slay" the bull, we must understand that he actually does not *kill*. According to Hinnells, Mithraism had adapted the ancient myth of the sacred bull to a more complex and subtle interpretation, which in fact underlines a previously neglected Mithraic trait; the Mithraic myth, even in its earlier extant guise(s), portrays disfavour towards the act of killing. As already seen with the *Bundahishn*, the

---

6. For the image, see the painted Mithraic relief at Marino near Rome, Hinnells, *Persian Mythology*, 82–3. It is also visible in the Mithraic relief found in the 1970s near Dunaujváros in Hungary, and the finds from the first Mithraeum at Heddernheim, displayed in the Städtisches Museum, Wiesbaden: *ibid.*, 78–9.

7. B. T. Anklesaria, *Zand-akasih: Iranian or Greater Bundahishn* (Bombay, 1956), 53.

8. Cf. J. Duchesne-Guillemin, "Ahriman", in *EIr*, vol. 1, 670–73.

act of "killing" is quickly rectified by the omnipotent Ormazd as an act of crea-tion: the essential message being that life at its source is unaffected (by the darkness), and that its flow is therefore eternal. Whereas in the earlier Pahlavi works we have a "cosmogonic" presentation, the later Mithraic myth of Roman times is deemed microcosmic, that is, concerning an initiatic rite, where the renowned scene of the tauroctony is a telling depiction of its apex. This basic idea carries through into the Sufi notion of *fana* and *baqa*, carrying a central doctrinal significance. Where *fana* is classically taken as the death or destruc-tion of the *nafs*, the key message of the Sufi doctrine, however, is not a literal "annihilation". The doctrine of *baqa* and *fana* states the end of the egoic and base self, through which the transformation of the soul (i.e. its return to God) is then allowed and/or fulfilled (Chapter 2). The idea is better related through the popular Sufi analogy of the maturation of wine in a vat, connoting the act of perfecting oneself, and still reinforcing the parallel between Mithraism and Sufism. However, what is specific about both Rumi's perspective and indeed the Mithraic rite itself, especially as retrieved, for instance, from Porphyry and archaeological evidence at Ostia, is that the *nafs*, as idealized by the bull, is not the enemy, but rather the victim.

THE TAUROCTONE SCENE AND THE STORY OF "THE KING AND THE HANDMAIDEN" IN RUMI'S *MATHNAWI*

An interesting parallel is noted here between the stages of the Mithraic Taur-octone and the first story of the *Mathnawi* by Rumi.[9] The poet reproduces the Sufi doctrine of *knowing oneself* in a witty tale that reveals "the essence of our inner state".[10] Here he conveys his theosophical position in terms of a love story between the King, who symbolizes *ruh* = spirit, and the Handmaiden, *nafs* = soul or selfhood.[11] "Love" is the major theme in this story, and a close reading of the *Mathnawi* reveals a fundamental repetition of the moral tale throughout the entire text. A similar notion is discovered in a reading of the Mithraic Mystery (Tauroctone). For Rumi, *love* motivates the knowledge and transformation of self. The tauroctonous scene is likewise in its entirety symbolic of the power of love to move the entire universe. According to the

---

9. *MJR*, 36–221 and 6–15. These stages (and the sources for them in Porphyry, Origen, Jerome, etc.) are discussed in G. Trompf, "From the Esoteric to the Exoteric and Back Again", in *Esotericism and the Control of Knowledge* (ed. E. Crangle), Sydney Studies in Religion 5 (Sydney, 2004), 29–31.

10. S. G. Safavi, "Synoptic Approach to Story of the King and the Handmaiden of Book One of the *Mathnawi* of Rumi", *Transcendental Philosophy: An International Journal for Comparative Philosophy and Mysticism* 6(1a2) (December 2005), 45; Nurbakhsh, "Irfan va ravaan-shenaasi mawlana: dar daasstaneh paadeshah va kanizak", *Sufi* 8 (Autumn 1369/ 1991), 7–10 [Persian].

11. Safavi, "The King and the Handmaiden", 46.

seven well-known initiatic stages of Mithraism, the tauroctone does not actually show Mithras but the (fifth) station of Persis (or "the Persian"). Through an interlinked reading of the stages, at this final stage the initiate is ready to conquer his own self, as exemplified by the bull, in order to be in a state of "friendship" with the sun (Mithra). Like Rumi's story, the Mithraic initiate accomplishes this task only with the help of the Father, the highest stage in the Mithraic stations, or as imagined in Rumi's story, the "perfected guide" (*morshed-e kamel*) on par with the idea of the "Perfect Man" (*insan-e kamel*) in Sufism.[12] This perfected figure in Sufism is hailed as the *Pir*, literally: "father" – "Master of the Path".

Our two sources coincide in the following allegorical manner. Mithras, who is beckoned by the sun to conquer the bull, hunts the bull and, picking it up by its hind legs, drags it back to the cave of his birth. Subduing the bull, Mithras does not kill it as normally perceived. Hinnells points to the fact that, had the scene wanted to depict a killing, it would have put the knife at the throat of the bull.[13] The stab wound is to the shoulder, whereby the emphasis is again not on death, but (spiritual) transformation and the continuance of the life force as indicated by various elements in the reliefs (corn sprouting from the bull's tail, the blood pouring from the wound, and so on).[14] The King, in Rumi's story, is similarly out hunting and comes across a beautiful maiden whom he buys and with whom he falls in love. However, soon after she is taken back to the King's palace she falls ill and cannot be cured by all the courtly physicians, who are wittingly made to represent the rational intellect by Rumi. The king in the end falls before God, drowning in tears and begging for a cure for his beloved maiden. In a dream it is revealed that a sage – the perfect man – will be sent to his aid. As promised the sage arrives and promptly identifies the ailment. The girl, being the symbol of *nafs* in the story, had been secretly in love with a certain goldsmith, who then represents attachment to the material world or worldly pleasures.[15] On the advice of the sage, the king sends for the goldsmith and joins the two in marriage. The girl begins to recover her health, but the sage also instructed that the goldsmith is to be slowly poisoned. As his good looks fade, so does the maiden's superficial attachment to him. Upon his death, the maiden is then free to pursue true love with the king. Now, the sage represents the important symbol of "the mediator" in this story, and the fact that the king is helpless to do anything for the sick girl is another insightful analogy demonstrating the love of God for Man, but also Man's distraction with worldly prospects. In effect, the battle for the heart, in Sufism, and the success of the spirit, is dependent on the *mediation* of the master of the path – or the intervention of the sage – analogous to Mithra in his freeing of new life.

---

12. *Ibid.*
13. Hinnells, "Iranian Background", 249.
14. *Ibid.*, 247.
15. Safavi, "The King and the Handmaiden", 38.

Reaching the state of *fana*, for the Sufi, encompasses the first stage in the cycle of spiritual purification, perfection, growth and transformation. Its notion of death means the beginning of another cycle, *baqa*. With the background of Mithra as "the lord of silent trade" in mind,[16] the Sufi makes the pledge through initiation to offer his selfish attributes as sacrifice in utter submission so that God may provide His own (attributes) in exchange. For the Sufi, this "trade" is (in one sense) performed during *moraqebeh* (through reflection, observation, self-examination) and *zekr* (remembrance), but prominently through acts of service; yet essentially it is a silent exchange that takes place between Man and God. An important aspect of *moraqebeh*, as an exchange between two parties, however, is related to the central concepts of "love" and "friendship". In Sufism, the *Pir* (who is the earthly representative of God and in Mithraism being Mithra's earthly representative) acts as the intercessor for the salvation of Man.[17]

MITHRAIC STAGES OF INITIATION AND NEMATOLLAHI SUFI SYMBOLISM

Prior to the station of *fana*, the Sufi seeker or wayfarer (*salek*) undergoes certain ordeals to prepare him for the final conquest of the *nafs* (i.e. becoming *fana*). Two important junctures that mark the beginning and end of this journey are found in the symbolic significance of "the cave" in later Mithraism and "the ritual meal", both of which are common to Mithraism and Sufism. The metaphor of "the cave" is a significant representative of the "innermost part of the self" as idealized by the realm of the heart in Sufism. Its simplest function is that it is a "place of power", its outward manifestation being the *khaneqah* (Sufi house of worship) and its poetic alias the "goblet", "cup" or "grail" that holds the wine of divine unity (where it is said, "O Saqi, brighten our cup's depth with the light of the wine").[18] The terms goblet, cup and grail are used for the vessel of wine that represents the Sufi's heart. There are subtle differences, though, in their mystical meaning. The "goblet" (*saghar*) stands for "an object in which the Sufis witness the lights of the Unseen (*ghaib*) and perceive supersensory realities (*mana*)"; the "cup" or "grail" (*jaam*) portrays "the place where divine theophanies and illuminations of the Infinite Being

---

16. Imoto, "Mithra, the Mediator", 304.
17. P. Mohaghegh, "Mithra the Friend", *Sufi* 32 (Winter 1996/7), 8–9. For the following section, I am indebted to the research of Mohaghegh. Although a brief article and poorly sourced, Mohaghegh's insightful comparative illustrations were useful for elaborating further clues in connection between the practices and symbology of Mithraism and Sufism.
18. Hafez, cited in J. Nurbakhsh, *Sufi Symbolism* (The Nurbakhsh Encyclopedia of Sufi Terminology [*Farhang-e Nurbakhsh*]) (trans. L. Lewisohn & T. Graham) (London, 1984–92), vol. 1 (of 16), 130. On *Khaneqahs*, start with M. E. Bastini-Parizi, "Khaneqah: A Phenomenon in the Social History of Iran", in Trompf & Honari (eds), *Mehregan in Sydney*, ch. 12.

appear".[19] The realm of the heart is the sacred (internal) space to which the initiate retreats and draws on the power of the Spirit (that is, primarily through the act of meditation [*moraqebeh*] and *zekr* "remembrance"); this is symbolically illustrated in the use of either literal caves by Mithraists or temples made to look like a cave.[20] We will turn to the ritual meal in a moment, but before we do this, it is useful to expound on two other important factors in Sufism and Mithraism.

The allegorical correlation alluded to hitherto regarding the Sufi idea of the *nafs* and the Mithraic emblem of the bull is our own hypothesis for continuity of ritual significance. Therefore, the bull, here taken as corresponding with the Sufi notion of the "lower self", is forcefully brought to the Cave and there engaged on the terms and conditions of the higher self, and conquered. The Cave is both a synonymous allegory of the internal (heart) and external (temple) sacred space, both of which are necessary strategic components for the ultimate defeat of the *nafs* or bull being allegories of material nature. The bull and the *nafs* may be ideas totally unrelated, but this is because there has never been any prior examination of its possibility. In our view, it is more than likely for such an accidental (thematic or ideological) connection to exist, even if no direct continuity is (or can ever be) established. We are tapping the underlying (often covert) structures of Persian thought, even while the intricate (lost) history of linkages eludes us; and in our account we are responding to Sufi ways of picking up these structures.

The ritual meal

The ritual meal shared in its pristine sense is a symbolic demonstration of the victory. It is agreed that this meal was partaken as a regular ceremonial re-enactment of ritual significance for the Mithraic cult and community. The ritual meal scene on the Mithraic monuments is celebrated either over the body of the dead bull or over a table draped with the skin of the bull, as on an unpublished monument from Heidelberg.[21] This is similarly the case in Islam with the sacrifice (of lambs) at the *hajj* or on various celebratory occasions, but in Sufism the idea is taken beyond the Moslem norm. For the Sufi, the ritual meal of the lamb[22] is where the initiate declares inwardly "I have come

---

19. Nurbakhsh, *Sufi Symbolism*, vol. 1, 129–30.
20. Hinnells, *Persian Mythology*, 81.
21. Cf. Hinnells, "Iranian Background", 247.
22. The lamb substitutes the bull. See, Duchesne-Guillemin on the Middle Persian term *gospand* (also the modern Farsi for sheep) – derived from *gav* and *spenta* ("sacred cow/bull"). Cf. A. S. Melikian-Chirvani, "The Wine-Bull and the Magian Master", in *Recurrent Patterns in Iranian Religions: From Mazdaism to Sufism* (ed. P. Gignoux), Special Issue of *Studia Iranica* (vol. 11) (Paris, 1992), 124. The Zoroastrians of Iran were known to have the *Mehr Izad* (Yazata Mithra) ceremony, a great sacrifice of cows and other animals (cf. *Aban*

to sacrifice myself for the Friend."[23] The Mithraic ritual meal was celebrated over a table draped with the skin of the bull, which is rich in the symbolism already outlined regarding the slaying of the bull.[24] The Sufis similarly partake in ritual meal, known as *dig-jush* ("the sacrifice of the *nafs*"). In this ceremony, the bull's skin is symbolically replaced with a white cloth, but the meaning is maintained. The white cloth is the symbolic representation of the Sufi initiate's shroud, which becomes like a dead body in the hands of the *ghassal* (one who washes the dead).[25] This corresponds with the first stage of the seven Mithraic stations, the Corax ("raven"), representing the symbolic death of the "neophyte and his rebirth into the spiritual path".[26]

At this point, the Sufi and the Mithraic initiate share commonalities that are defined by the thematic and often symbolic and allegorical representation of their formal initiatic rites. Connecting itself with Khorasanian Sufism,[27] Nimatollahi Sufism sees itself as linked with one of the earliest Sufi schools: the school of "intoxication", marking itself as the Sufism of love. It goes even further in declaring itself as carrying the legacy of one the earliest fathers of Sufism, Bayazid-e Bistami – thus, adopting the lineage of "Bayazidian Sufism" (to be considered in the last chapter). This is of course not to say that Bayazid initiated such a movement. The phrase is very much a reflective identity on the "style" of Sufism for which Bayazid was famed. Hence, it is the "style" to which the Nematollahiyya generally adhere.[28] Corresponding to the second phase of the search for love in the Mithraic rite (the Nymphus, "male-bride") we find

---

Yasht, 41–3) up until the nineteenth century, reduced now to the slaughter of sheep and goats to Mithra due to a request to cease the slaying of cows from a Parsi from India. Cf. R. Hamzehee, "Structural and Organizational Analogies between Mazdaism and Sufism and the Kurdish Religions", in Gignoux (ed.), *Recurrent Patterns*, 34, notes 23 and 24. On the "living cow" and the "beneficent cow" in the Yasna ceremony, W. A. V. Jackson, *Persia Past and Present* (New York, 1975), 370–71; cf. also L. H. Mills, "The Pahlavi texts of Yasna xxii", *The Journal of the Royal Asiatic Society* 86 (1907), note 3, cited in Hamzehee, "Structural and Organizational Analogies" (who considers correlations between Persian and Kurdish religions).

23. See *dig-jush* ceremony in J. Nurbakhsh, *The Path: Sufi Practices* (London, 2002), 192.
24. A Mithraic ritual meal scene dated *c.*140CE discovered at Ladenburgh by Dr B. Heükemes in 1965 shows Mithras and Sol with drinking cups reclining on a couch draped with a bull skin behind a table with bulls' legs on which fruit is set. The stylized arch appears to represent a cave. Cf. Hinnells, *Persian Mythology*, 89. This appears to have correlations with a possibly earlier Sasanian bas-relief depicting a similar scene. See Melikian-Chirvani, "Wine-Bull", 130.
25. Nurbakhsh, *The Path*, 189.
26. Mohaghegh, "Mithra", 8.
27. T. Graham, "The Khorasanian Path: From Zoroaster to Plato and Beyond", *Sufi* 56 (Winter 2002/3), 42–6.
28. Cf. A. Nurbakhsh, "Bayazidian Sufism: Annihilation without Ritual", *Sufi*, 46 (Summer 2000), 8–13. (Note that Alireza Nurbakhsh is the son and successor to Javad Nurbakhsh of the Nematollahi Sufi Order; thus hereafter, the initials will be cited consistently).

the Sufi initiate vows to travel the path guided by devotional love.[29] The next two Mithraic stages (Miles, "soldier", and Leo, "lion") broadly correspond to the commitment of "service" in Sufism. Specifically, soldiers were those who were ready to engage in spiritual combat.[30] In a comparison with Sufi symbology, the lions represented a longstanding commitment to the Order, particularly those who were consumed in the fire of love.[31] Here showing no trace of the intellect, Leo's cup (which was once offered with water) is now filled with the wine of divine love; signifying the master's spiritual attention.[32] The following two stages represent the initiative of conquering the self, under Persis: "the Persian" subduing the bull, and reaching illumination, Heliodrumus: "Sun Runner", attaining friendship with Sol: "sun", which is done with the grace and favour of the *Pir* ("Father"), who represents the highest and final stage in the Mithraic rite.[33] The *Pir* or Father, who is often in Persian poetic imagination portrayed as the *saqi* or wine pourer, is a humble figure; the Master in the image of the generous "friend" (in connection with the Sanskrit *sakhi* = friend) pouring the sweet wine of love and light.[34] In short, the Father is the earthly manifestation of Mithras. It is his love and guidance that draws the initiate toward the realm of unity and truth. The various stages of the Mithraic ritual are apparent descriptions of his indispensable aid. To go back to the "key strike points" in both the relief at Persepolis and "the poisoning of the goldsmith" in Rumi's tale, the Father's mediation of divine love and wisdom become the sacred "tools of wisdom" with which initiates are empowered to overcome the obstacles of the intellect and the carnal self. Here is the ideal, reflected in the

---

29. The male-bride signifies "a lover of Mithras". This may indicate a period of celibacy or strict devotion to Mithras. A bowl of water is offered by the initiate, whereby the bowl/cup symbolized his heart and the water his love (substituting wine or "divine love" later received in the higher stages). See Mohaghegh, "Mithra", 9. As one of the ornaments of "spiritual poverty", the Sufi offers rock candy as a double gesture of his re-birth from the world of multiplicity to the world of love (*eshq*), loving-kindness (*mohebbat*) and unity (*tawhid*), also as a remembrance of travelling the path with "peace of mind" and "gladness" rather than depression and displeasure. See J. Nurbakhsh, *The Path*, 190.
30. In Sufism the battle is with what is termed "the *nafs*" and in Mithraism with what is depicted as "the bull". See images from the Mithraeum of Felicissimus at Ostia in Hinnells, *Persian Mythology*, 84–5. Here what appears to be the hind leg of a bull with its hoof set against the helmet (symbolizing soldier) is believed to depict this struggle.
31. Mohaghegh, "Mithra", 9. At Ostia represented by the furnace shovel, which also indicates their involvement with the preparation of the ritual meal and also acting as the protectors or defenders of the Order illustrated by the thunderbolts (the planet Jupiter). Cf. Hinnells, *Persian Mythology*, 85.
32. Mohaghegh, "Mithra", 9.
33. The images that represent this stage are the sun-crown, torch and whip. In the Mithraic tradition, Mithras here ascends to the sky (after the ritual meal) in Sol's chariot. Hinnells, *Persian Mythology*, 84–5. On the Father: Mohaghegh, "Mithra", 9.
34. For extensive discourse on the development of Persian thought on wine as love and light and its association with the Magian Master, Melikian-Chirvani, "Wine-Bull", 101–33 (also discussed below).

Mithraeum initiatory journey and what seems to correlate in Sufi teaching, that justice, truth, goodness, equality and liberty are muted at the slightest hint of anger, hatred, frustration, disappointment, lust and darkness. They can only be embraced through love, kindness, peace and light. This then brings us to the *pièce de resistance* of the tauroctone: the "bull slaying scene". Mithras is deliberately depicted as looking away from the bull while making the insertion.

This has the direct implication of an act of divine providence motivated by love rather than elements of an intellectual or carnal nature.[35] This emphasizes the crucial point of the tauroctony and the soteriological apex of the Mithraic mystery. Embedded within is also the heart of the chivalric ideal and the just hero.

COMPARATIVE ILLUSTRATIONS OF SUFI POETRY WITH MITHRAIC SYMBOLOGY

The development of this segment is greatly indebted to the research of Assadullah Melikian-Chirvani. He underlines the importance of Iranian poetry as a significant "archaeological field of notions and themes rooted in the most ancient past", fully acknowledging the power of this literature to unlock the key to Persia's past. His unique co-joined examination of both Persian poetry and art objects is of great assistance for a much-needed re-examination of recurrent patterns in Iranian thought (from Antiquity until the present). However, his two articles cited here differ from my own macrohistorical endeavour in that I am specifically plotting the hidden history of Persia with reference to the esoteric, while his work observes the thematic correspondence between long-term pre-Islamic and Islamic Persian symbolism. Certainly however, his is an essential contribution to the area of Iranian studies, especially his careful examination of the connection between Mazdaeism and Sufism.[36]

The blood that pours from the moribund victim in the tauroctone in one sense reconfirms the ancient rite of the bull sacrifice.[37] A particular passage from the *Bundahishn* further consolidates the connection of wine with that of bull's blood: "It is said in the scripture: when the sole-created Gav passed away ... out of the blood grew the gourd of the wine grape from which they prepare wine."[38] The blood is symbolic of the life essence and the soul-rejuvenating elixir.[39] In a collective sense, the whole scene represents a pre-Islamic notion

---

35. Mohaghegh, "Mithra", 9.
36. Cf. Melikian-Chirvani, "Wine-Bull"; cf. *idem*, "From the Royal Boat to the Beggar's Bowl", *Islamic Art* 4 (1990/1), 3–111.
37. Cf. Hinnells, "Iranian Background", 248.
38. Anklesaria, *Greater Bundahishn*, 53.
39. The first offering of which in the Zoroastrian Mehregan ritual is given to the dog. Cf. Hinnells, "Iranian Background", 248, citing Boyce. Of interest, both the dog and the snake are drinking from the blood of the bull.

of a "perfect man" as idealized in the accomplishment of Mithras. Later, in Sufi terms, this *ensan-e kamel* or "perfect man" becomes the fountain of love and light for those around him, since "from thousands one became *darvish*; the rest dwell in his grace".[40] This is the significance of the theme of *Pir-e Moghan* or "Magian Master" and his connection with sacrificial bull's blood, who is later understood to supervise the symbolic "wine drinking" for the Sufis, a double theme that is transmitted right throughout Persian Sufi poetry depicting the sacred passage of mystical initiation.[41] From this point in our account we can see various symbols coming together that recap on the entire journey from before Zarathushtra's epiphany right through to the rise of Persian Sufism. That is, celebrations during sunrise and sunset,[42] master and cupbearer, and bull's blood, wine and light all are the constant themes in Iranian religiosity and they continually regenerate its identity. These ancient rites now provide the iconic and conceptual force of Sufi symbolism, decorating Sufism's prolific literature. The outward aim of the poets has always been in part nostalgia in appealing to the sentimentality of ancient glory, while inwardly their writing encoded and preserved core teachings for those initiated into its *gnosis*. Appealing to ancient glories is not just sentimentality but a method of historiographical importance. Accordingly, Melikian-Chirvani underlines the significance of a thematic study, which typically receives "little attention from scholars concerned with the history of art, or religion".[43] Thus it is that Persian Sufi literature came to feature three primary elements that conveyed the ancient ingredients of its sacred alchemy: Master, Cup and Wine, with the addition of a fourth common and continuing feature, Light (often substituted for wine). Ibn al-Motazz invokes the sacred imagery of Iranian religiosity from its roots to the present in a swift poetic sweep:

> And people uttered praise saying they saw a surprising thing
> Light made of water in a fire made of grapes[44]

The "Master" appears under various aliases: cupbearer (*saqi*), boon companion, friend and so on. Melikian-Chirvani draws a parallel between the "cup" or "goblet" (*badeh*) and crescent shaped "wine-boats" that represent the Sufi's

---

40. Adaptation of Mawlana Rumi, cited in J. Nurbakhsh, "Veracity and Sincerity", *Sufi* 48 (Winter 2000/01), 42.

41. See Melikian-Chirvani, "Wine-Bull", 101–33.

42. The importance of dusk and dawn relate to wine libations, and point to periods of prayer, sacrifice, meditation. It is a practice attributed to Xenophon's Cyrus, whose prayers three times a day correspond to the pagan days (sunrise, noon and sunset); according to Boyce, later elaborated into five prayer times by Zoroaster. Cf. Boyce, *Zoroastrians*, 32–3. For Cyrus facing east at dawn, Boyce, *History*, vol. 2, 214.

43. Melikian-Chirvani, "Wine-Bull", 101.

44. *Diwan Ibn al-Mu'tazz* (ed. Dar Sadir) (Beirut, n.d.), 76, cited in Melikian-Chirvani, "Wine-Bull", 104.

begging bowl (*kashkul*). Wine would be poured out of a vessel known in literature as a "bull" into drinking cups reproducing the crescent shape boat. The *kashkul* is meant to have served as a wine vessel as is demonstrated by many verses inscribed on it.[45] Now, "Wine" is the classic symbol of illumination, initiation and sacred knowledge as argued by Melikian-Chirvani.[46] Javad Nurbakhsh, however, gives a detailed distinction between the uses of "wine" in Sufi symbology – that is, between "wine" as *mai* and "wine" as *sharab*, both of which are an obvious cognate with the theme of illumination, initiation and sacred knowledge, as also suggested by Melikian-Chirvani. According to Nurbakhsh, the former is "the intuitive savour of the recollection of God within a Sufi's heart, inducing a heady intoxication in him. It may also signify the exhilaration (*nasha'a*) brought on by the divine remembrance (*dhekr*) and the boiling-up of love." On the latter we learn that this term "denotes an excess of affection or the perfection of love". Furthermore, *sharab* signifies "the overwhelming force of love concomitant with a certain kind of conduct on the wayfarer's part which brings public reproach (*malamat*) down upon him. This love is possessed by those who are perfect, and is only realized at the end of the path." The etymology of the terms are of significant interest, where Nurbakhsh traces the origin of *mai* as deriving from the Sanskrit and Avestan *madhu*, meaning "an intoxicated beverage" or "wine". He also suggests that *madhu* is "cognate with the English word 'mead', while ancient Greek has a cognate in its poetic word for wine, *methu*". *Sharab* originally meant "any potable drink in Arabic, coming from the paradigm meaning 'to drink'; in Persian it has come to solely signify wine".[47]

A significant thematic correspondence is here drawn with Mithraism, where the Sufi "master" (like Mithra) has the (personal) power with which to retrieve (the bull's blood) and disseminate the "illuminating wine". There are many elaborate descriptions in the Sufi poetry of Nezami and Khaqani in the second half of the twelfth century of what appears to be the "ceremonial drinking of wine poured out of a wine-bull into a crescent-moon cup, i.e. a wine-boat".[48] These ceremonies in fact describe the theme of initiation of the Sufi lover (*asheq*) by the Magian Master. Further correlations are visible in a panegyric by Khaqani evoking the esoteric symbolism of an initiation rite involving "the drinking of wine poured out of a silver bull vessel into the golden boat filled with wine, symbolizing the conjunction of the moon and the sun".[49] We are already made aware of the ongoing ritual and allegorical

45. Melikian-Chirvani, "Wine-Bull", 101, and his "Royal Boat to the Beggar's Bowl". See also J. Nurbakhsh on the Sufi meaning of these terms in *Sufi Symbolism*, note 217.
46. Melikian-Chirvani, "Wine-Bull", 101.
47. J. Nurbakhsh, *Sufi Symbolism*, 143, 143n, 149 and 149n.
48. *Ibid.*, notes 243-4.
49. Khaqani, *Diwan-e Afzal al-Din Badil ibn Ali Najjar-e Khaqani-e Shirvani* (ed. Ziya al-Din Sajjadi) (Tehran, 1357/1978), 491–2, cited in Melikian-Chirvani, "Wine-Bull", 117.

importance of sacred acts and sacred times, as shown in discussion on Mithras and Mithraism. The exchange between the master and disciple is also symbolized by the conjunction of the sun and the moon, marking their inward bond through the "wine" of love and the "illumination" of *gnosis*. A verse by Qatran of Tabriz (d. 1072) captures this fine sentiment:

> From the reflection of your face, the crystal [cup] takes on the hue of carnelian
> > The rays of wine of like colour fall from the cup on your face.[50]

As Ibn al-Motazz sings:

> Night has become dark, oh my boon companion:
> > Pour out the fire with the wine
> > 'Tis as if we and all humans were asleep
> > Kissing the sun in darkness.[51]

The idea of "drinking" triggered the experience of drunkenness, which replicated the outward feeling of the powerful inward states as procured by way of *moraqebeh* and *zekr* in Sufism. With wine and light allegorically linked, the heart became the beacon for the Sufi as the Sufi Master became the beacon of light for the world. In the following two verses, the poets Zo'l-Feqar Shirvani, Khwaju Kermani, and Emad Kermani respectively describe such an experience:

> At peep of dawn drain the sun out of Jamshid's bowl from the hands of a moon-faced beauty
> For the [heavenly] king with its retinue of stars has raised its banner out of Capricorn[52]
> Give me, cupbearer, that bowl of Jamshid
> > That shining sun in the dark[est] night.[53]

And:

> In the dark[est] night I look inside the cup
> > And see the rays of the sun.[54]

---

50. *Divan-e Qatran-e Tabrizi* (eds Badi oz-Zaman Foruzanfar, Zabihollah Safa & S. H. Taqizadeh) (Tehran, 1362/1983), 36, cited in Melikian-Chirvani, "Wine-Bull", 104.

51. Ibn al-Motazz, *Diwan*, 408, cited in Melikian-Chirvani, "Wine-Bull", 104.

52. Zol-Faqar Shirvani, *Divan* (*Diwan-i Zu'l-Fakar*) (ed. E. Edwards) (London, 1934), 125, cited in Melikian-Chirvani, "Wine-Bull", 104.

53. Khwaju Kermani, *Homay o Homayun* (ed. Kamal Eyni) (Tehran, 1348/1969), 15, cited in Melikian-Chirvani, "Wine-Bull", 105.

54. *Divan-e 'Emad-e Faqih-e Kermani* (ed. Rokn ad-Din Homayunfarrokh) (Tehran, 1348/1969), 213, cited in Melikian-Chirvani, "Wine-Bull", 105.

In addition, Hafez confesses:

> I dare not sit in solitude without the luminary of the bowl:
> The corner of the people of the soul [Sufis] must be illuminated[55]

The *kashkul* ("begging bowl") had a dual function posing both as the metaphoric heart longing to be filled with divine wine or light,[56] and at the same time being the vessel (*kashti*) with which the *dervish* (i.e. Sufi) would travel towards the beloved.[57] The ritual and symbolism in short were only to "remind" the initiate of the experience, and to help "re-connect" with the source of that experience, for the actual alchemy was the reality that occurred within. Thus from the elaborate ancient ritual festivals of "bull sacrifice" to the ornamented Sufi poetry of the early to late Middle Ages, the intention to achieve such inward change remained basically the same:

> See the King of the World who in the fashion of Keykhosrow
>   In a single reflection of his wine bowl shows the two worlds[58]
> Request from the Magians liquid fire in a pottery vessel
>   That, of the fire, your pottery vessel may show the fragrance
> You want sunset light and daybreak, look at the wine and the vessel
>   [See] if in the sunset light daybreak is shown to be hidden
> From the silver-bodied gazelle, request a golden bull vessel
>   That at the celebration the blood of the sacrificial victim may be
>   shown in it.[59]

Here in the "ultimate synthesis" the relation between the Pahlavi and the Mithraic tauroctony is clearly spelled out. Moreover, Khaqani again invokes the memory of Kayanid Persia (the lineage of Kay Khosrow), Zarathushtra's legacy, and that of Sufism in the following panegyric:

---

55. *Diwan-e Khwaje Shams ad-Din Mohammad Hafez Shirazi* (eds. S. M. Reza Jalali Naini & N. Ahmad) (Tehran, 1976), 175, cited in Melikian-Chirvani, "Wine-Bull", 105.
56. On the connection between light and wine, Melikian-Chirvani, "Wine-Bull", 102–8.
57. Melikian-Chirvani, "From the Royal Boat to the Beggar's Bowl", 3–111.
58. The Cup of Jamshid in the *Shâhnâmeh* shows how the thread of Persian wisdom is connected through the invocation of Righteousness and Justice of the good kings of old. The great king belongs to the world of key symbols pursued, but drops out of later Mithraism because of its rite's "democratization" among Romans.
59. Khaqani, *Diwan*, 128, cited in Melikian-Chirvani, "Wine Bull", 113. Melikian-Chirvani mentions that the phrase "silver-bodied gazelle" (*ahu-ye simin*) echoes Abu Nuwas in the eighth century, who refers to the "cupbearer" as a gazelle. Abu Nuwas, born of an Iranian mother and an Arab father, has been long recognized by scholars to echo many Iranian themes and used many Iranian words. For further detail on the figure, Melikian-Chirvani, "Wine-Bull", 102, note 3.

Remember the precepts of the Magian master
    Remember the clamour of the bird that speaks the Zandavasta
Fill up the cup with Tigris rivers of wine
As high as the Baghdad parallel and remember the Ancient
Dynasty [*Keyan*]
The esoteric knowledge of the drunken ones has been divulged
    "The morning draught": that shout has been divulged
The Cupbearer was drawing blood from the cephalic vein of the jar
    The golden tray[60] fell out of Heaven
The ascetic in the mountain was flinging about his sleeve
    Out of it there fell the key to the tavern
The Sufi *Qoran* reader tore his blue robe
    His wine cup fell out from the top of its mast.[61]

A more contemporary image is perhaps fitting for a final example. An image from 1969 illustrating a scene from the *Diwan* of Hafez demonstrates just how pertinent the ancient Iranian and Mithraic symbology is to the Sufi, and more broadly the Iranian, imagination.

Figure 4.2 Hafiz and the Muse. Image from *Divan e Hafez* (Amir Kabir Publishers, 1969).

---

60. Melikian-Chirvani notes that it is a "standard metaphor of the sun disc", "Wine-Bull", 115.
61. Khaqani, *Diwan*, 473–4, cited in *ibid.*, 115.

Both the moon and torch are (simultaneously) present, representing day and night, hot and cold, good and evil, illumination and ignorance, wisdom and emotion, and so on. At the centre is the fair Maiden (feminine Mithras – remembering that a shift occurs in the representation of Mithras as Mitra [in the feminine] in modern Persian thought) or in mystical terms, "the silver-bodied gazelle", strumming the harp whose structure resembles the bull's horns, thereby signifying the subduing of the bull not with brute force but with love. The symbolic wine bowl to the maiden's right, while she is sitting on a larger bowl that signifies her as the fountain of life's elixir, indicates that she mediates the flow of "wine" or love, light and wisdom (which the lover seeks). The lover, who is Hafez, is depicted sitting in perplexity and contemplation. In fact, it can be rendered that "he is sitting in the ruin of his ego" (*dar kharabat*),[62] too drunken with humility and shame to appeal to his beloved or to engage in any senseless act of piety. Of interest is the notion that the lovers are situated "indoors" (internal, inward reality that is illuminated by the torch) and the moon hovers over the night sky (outward form) apparent through the arched window that is symbolic of the Mithraic Cave.[63] The whole scene can indeed be taken as depicting, therefore, a sacred rite of passage that is reimagined by the artist in a modern formulation, all being an iconic epitome of a hidden macrohistorical master-thread.

Before offering any conclusive remarks on the continuity of Mithraic doctrine and practice in Sufism, however, it is important to mention that this macrohistory only serves to define the immediate thematic correspondence of "Persian Sufism" and not Sufism as a huge, general topic or Islamic Mysticism as the inherent spiritual component of the religious tradition of Islam. Relevant issues to do with the more general history of Sufism remain to be discussed, but we cannot reach that point without first tracing the key stepping-stones of our macrohistory which allow us to explain the role of Sufism in Persia and its significance in preserving crucial aspects of the history of Persian consciousness. As we shall see, of special interest is a uniquely Persian trajectory of Sufi masters outlined by the Nematollahiyya, who interpret Sufism as the spirituality of the pre-Islamic Aryan culture of Iran, which is reformulated by Ferdowsi and intellectualized by Sohravardi and finally revived by Rumi, who defines the key features of Sufism as *love* and *gnosis* of self. With regard to our discussion of Mithraism and Persian Sufism, it is difficult to ignore the presence of continuing Persian themes in Roman Mithraism, since we have just shown how the development of "Persian Sufism" can hardly be accounted for without reference to the later Mithraic initiatory material. The growth of later Mithraism's popularity only goes to show how well the Iranian themes were

---

62. This is to refer to the title and content of J. Nurbakhsh's *In the Tavern of Ruin: Seven Essays on Sufism* (London, 1978).
63. Hinnells, *Persian Mythology*, 89ns.

adapted to alternate cultures even if we sadly lack good evidence of continuing Mithraism in Persia as the Zoroastrian establishment consolidated. In any case, the parallels between Sufi doctrine and practice to that of Mithraism are powerful enough to suggest a covert transmigration of secret teachings, via art, ritual and doctrine, out of the ancient Indo-Iranian and Graeco-Roman world into succeeding periods of Persian religious life. If we thought the cult of Mithras was eclipsed, its re-manifestations in Persianate Sufism will prove this wrong, for all the necessary features of Indo-Iranian and Graeco-Roman continuity are evident in the works of both Rumi and Sohravardi.

CHAPTER 5

THE RESURGENCE OF "PERSIANATE" IDENTITY IN THE TRANSMISSION AND FUSION OF ANCIENT IRANIAN IDEAS WITHIN ISLAM

The Sheikhs are the pourers of wine
And the dervish is the glass.
Love is the wine.[1]

DARVISH AND GNOSIS OF SELF IN PRE-ISLAMIC IRAN

In this chapter we will undertake a closer look at the translation of the "Persianate" themes even more specific to the Sufism of Iran. Important here are both the use of the term *darvish* as a distinctive Persian reference to "Sufi" – with its derivatives *darvishan* and *darvishi* defining "Sufis" and "Sufism" – and the place of gnosis (New Pers. *irfan*) as insight and awareness of self and the divine, linking to the pre-Islamic notion of *hekmat-e khosravani*. We will then observe the perpetual relevance of *javânmardî* (chivalry) and *âdâb* (moral etiquette), which sit at the centre of the doctrine and praxis of Persianate Sufism as prescribed by the Nematollahiya.

The New Persian term *darvish* derives from one of the earliest terms for pious individuals in pre-Islamic Iran. The word is implicitly endowed with a paradox between the spiritual and the mundane. Today's *darvish* is recognizable in Middle Persian as *driyôsh*, "the worthy poor, needy; one who lives in holy indigence", even as far back as Avestan *drigu, driyu*, "the needy one, dependent".[2] *Drigu* features only twice in the *Gathas* as *drigum*[3] and *drigaove*,[4]

---

1. M. Ozak, *Love is the Wine* (ed. R. Frager) (Putney, 1987), 8.
2. H. Lommel, "Awestisch Drigu. Vastra und Verwandtes," in *Pratidanam: Indian, Iranian and Indo-European Studies Presented to F. B. J. Kuiper* (eds J. C. Heesterman, G. H. Schokker & V. I. Subramoniam) (The Hague, 1968), 127–30.
3. Ahuna Vaiti, 7.5 – Yas. 34.5, in Taraporewala, *Divine Songs*, 365.
4. Vahishta Ishti, 9 – Yas. 53.9, in Taraporewala, *Divine Songs*, 854.

but is elaborated on extensively in Book VI of the Avestan *Denkard*, where it is given significant attention with respect to the *driyosh* and his way of life (*driyoshih*, NPers. *darvishi*). Both in terms of form and content, its concept is consistent with the use and understanding of *darvish* in modern Sufi parlance. In the *Gathas*, "meekness" is rendered as the chief characteristic of the *darvish*, which stood for "strong and rich in righteousness", a "deserving person" and "one who has restrained his lower self"; the reference to "poor" in a literal sense was a secondary meaning.[5] In the *Denkard*, both "humility" and "poverty" are brought together in reference to the *driyosh*:

> He to whom the worldly means of subsistence is merely toward keeping the body hale and healthy (*tuwân xwâstag î gêtîg rây tan padêxw ud bawandag*), whereupon he is with peace of mind (*axw ais[h] âsânîg*), of contented disposition (*menis[h] padis[h] hunsand*), and free from distress (*widang*).[6]

More importantly, "he does not hold the reputable (*c[h]as[h]mag*) and the opulent (*tuwânîg*) in disrespect (*tarmenis[h]n*)", this behaviour revealing an attitude that says "He with his reputation and wealth, [compared] with my [pious] indigence (*driyoshih*), he is [just a creature] the same as I am."[7] This is later developed in the language of Sufism as the idea of "spiritual poverty", denoting one who is empty of egoic self and free from worldly desire and yearning to be "filled" by God. There is a play on the words *darvish* and *faqir* (Arabic "poor") here to emphasize the state of the practising Sufi adherent. The terms "Sufi" and "*faqir*" were synonymous in the early Islamic period, while later the use of *darvish* became popular among the Persians. As such, *darvish* was to acquire a certain ascetic overtone that created the iconic image of the "wandering dervish", while *faqir* was reserved in Persian as generally referring to the literally poor. However, the usage of *faqr* (poverty) and *faqir* (poor) in early Persian Sufi literature unmistakably denotes the virtues of "spiritual poverty" in referring to the *darvish* and his qualities, whereby Sufis began to assimilate the distinct use of *darvish* to stress the inward state of being over and above outward poverty and the external ascetic behaviour.[8] To be clear, *faqir* and *darvish* denote the Arabic and Persian designations for a similar concept, and so too by comparison do they represent divergent attitudes within Sufism. The Persian *darvish* is not a mendicant ascetic or beggar, as denoted by *faqir*; but rather, he is a jubilant *majnoon* ("lover") who recites lyrical poems and plays the lute (*tanbour*)

---

5. *Drigu* is derived from the opposite to Rig Vedan term, *adhrigu* "excessiveness". Cf. Taraporewala, *Divine Songs*, 366–7.
6. D. M. Madan (ed.), *The Complete Text of the Pahlavi Denkard* (Bombay, 1911), 504; cited by M. Shaki, "Darvish i. In the Pre-Islamic Period", in *EIr*, vol. 7, 72a–b.
7. Madan, *The Complete Text of the Pahlavi Denkard*, 504; cited by Shaki, "Darvish i", 72a.
8. H. Algar, "Darvish ii. In the Islamic Period", in *EIr*, 73b–4a.

on his travels. Praised as the ideal way of life in the established Zoroastrian *Denkard*, those who took to poverty for its sublime indigence were deemed as ridding Ahriman from their lives and the demons from the world; yet an important distinction must be made between the Zoroastrian *driyosh* and the Sufi *darvish*. The *darvish*, although engaging in ascetic exercises at times, was by no means purely a "beggar", nor did he necessarily live a life of poverty or strict asceticism. The idea in Sufism is based on the combined influence of both Zoroastrian piety (*driyosh*) and the renowned Persian love of life (wine, food, music and poetry), integrated with the desired pursuits for good manners (*adab*) and being just (*javânmardî*). This is key in understanding not only Persian heritage, but also the driving attitude of Persianate Sufism.

The pre-Islamic pious individuals were men and women equally revered, beside the priestly class, because they were seen as excelling in mystical insight. It is admittedly possible that they were originally a group from within the learned clergy, but by no means limited to that caste; yet the concept and quality of the *darvish* looks to have been independent of the priesthood from early on, holding a status which was adapted and held in esteem by them as a constituent and legitimization of their own practice.[9] In fact, the renowned doctor of Zoroastrianism Adurbad-i Mahrspandan claimed the status of *driyosh* to be the best human quality, as did the high priest Adurbad-i Zardushtan, who prided himself upon his diligence and moderation in life as a *driyosh*.[10] What was required on the path for the *driyosh* were "diligence" and "moderation", but indispensable were the quintessential qualities of "contentment" and "right-mindedness", with emphasis on the former. Contentment was to play a similarly central role in the literature and doctrine of the mystical dervishes – the Sufis. As rendered in a verse by Hafez: "If there is any merit to be gained in this world, it is that attained by the contented *darvish*. O Lord, grant me the blessings of holy indigence and contentment",[11] though a lesser, even pejorative connotation had come into play in later Zoroastrian Sasanian society, whereby the *driyoshi* – as associated with the priestly class – were used as a way of ensuring mutual respect and benefit between the ranks of the priestly elite and privileged nobility. Note the parallel of later Safavid relations with state-sponsored Sufism – sometimes cited as "false Sufism".[12] This was found in a favourable exchange of duties between the two classes, whereupon the priestly *driyosh* would be promised paradise and deliverance from

---

9. The *darvish* is notably distinguished from the priestly class in the following prayer: "I celebrate the righteous men and women; I celebrate the *driyosh* men and women." Madan, *The Complete Text of the Pahlavi Denkard*, 621.

10. *The Pahlavi Texts Contained in the Codex Mk* (ed. Jamasp-Asana) (Bombay, 1897–1913), vol. 1, 67 and 81; Shaki, "Darvish i", 72b.

11. *Dar in bazaar agar soodi'st ba darvish-e khorsand ast/Khodaya mon'am am gardaan be darvishi o khorsandi.* Cf. Hafez, *Divan* (eds. M. Ghazvini and Q. Ghani) (Tehran, n.d.), 307, cited by Shaki, "Darvish i", 72b.

12. Roger M. Savory, *Iran under the Safavids* (Cambridge, 2007), 236–7.

evil were the priests to refrain from treating the nobility with disdain; and this was reciprocated by a guarantee of paradise for those who favoured the *driyosh*, and severe retribution for those who would turn a deaf ear to their complaints.[13] In its purer form, the term is empty of any suggestion of social prestige in that it is grounded in seeking an indigent life simply for its own sake,[14] an idea that becomes the *raison d'être* of the notion of "Persian Sufism" as embodied in the *darvish*.

In the Islamic period, *darvish* (or dervish) was directly applied to practitioners of Sufism – especially those subscribing to an undisciplined and antinomian type. The new impression broke with both the conventional image of its usage by the Sasanian priestly class and its association with asceticism in early Islam. With this move, the spiritual core of Persia's heritage was being invoked and disassociated from the two orthodoxies of the Zoroastrian and the Islamic establishments. Noted Sufi figures made it very clear that Sufism had nothing to do with "mendicancy" and its pretensions to sanctity, any more than it was to hold in reverence or to have recognition for the act of poverty.[15] But this was more a power-play on the Sufi part than anything else, while not doubting the sincerity of their devotion, but rather contextualizing their awkward socio-political positioning. The more influential of the Sufis were nevertheless adept at winning patronage, and they did this in the style and manner that befitted their pre-Islamic antecedents. At the level of practice, however, Sufism would not tolerate self-pride (nor recognition of such an act) or chosen lifestyle, which were taken as sure signs of a false *darvish*. The Sufis of Iran, in particular those aligned with imaginings about the heyday of Khorasan, were re-establishing a direct contact with Persia's ancient heritage and preserving the alleged wisdom of its suppressed culture and spirituality. It would seem that the Persianate expression began to surface gradually out of the dust of Antiquity, through various temperaments, often or typically shown by the mastery of the Persian Sufis over the Arabic language and its expressions of Islamic piety for "indigenous" purposes. In the eleventh century, Abol Hassan-e Kharaqani (d. 1034), in particular, described dervishhood "as an ocean fed from three sources: abstention (*parhiz*), generosity (*sakhawat*), and freedom from need (*bi niaz budan*)".[16] Then again the indelibly Persian character of its past would present itself much more abruptly, as in the case of the earlier Sufi Bayazid-e Bistami (d. 874), who, perhaps unconsciously,

---

13. S. Shaked, *The Wisdom of the Sasanian Sages (Denkard VI)* (Boulder, 1979), 58–9; P. Gignaux (trans.) *Le livre d'Arda Viraz* (Paris, 1984), chs 67 and 68.
14. Esp. Madan, *The Complete Text of the Pahlavi Denkard*, 503; Shaki, "Darvish i", 72b; and "a mere pious desire for 'intense holy indigence', with bare necessities of life, may render one righteous, provided [that] he does not look down on those who are not like him": Madan, *The Complete Text of the Pahlavi Denkard*, 542; Shaki, "Darvish i", 72b.
15. Cf. Algar, "Darvish ii", 73b.
16. *Ibid.*, 74a; *Ahwal wa aqwal-e Shaykh Abu'l Hasan Karaqani* (ed. M. Minovi) (Tehran, 1354/1975).

echoed themes from pagan Iran with regard to Mithra and Anahita. He proclaimed the *darvish* as one "upon whom God had bestowed three signs: kindness like that of the sun, generosity like that of the sea, and humility like that of the earth".[17] And whenever the idea of *darvishi* would wane, and Sufism would in odd moments accrue ascetic overtones from its preliminary association with *faqir* (one who "literally" has no worldly goods), the definition would soon enough be corrected, even tweaked to a new level. Take for example Kharaqani, who observed the dervish as:

> He whose heart is empty of cares; who speaks without awareness of speech; who hears without awareness of hearing; who eats without awareness of tasting; for whom motion and stillness are as one; and for whom grief and joy do not exist.[18]

In short, the idea of spiritual poverty was devoid of ascetic disdain for the world, but was perhaps best epitomized by the words of Jesus: "Father forgive them, for they know not what they do" (Luke 23:34). Hardly a refutation of the world, it was rather a rejection of "worldly existence" as defined by egocentric perception. Instead, the idea of spiritual poverty as defined by the Sufis was a profound love for the innermost reality of the world, which was, always for the Persians, a part of God's *good* creation. The early dervishes were careful to avoid the notion of asceticism, which could be misconstrued regarding their ways; and so laboured diligently in their writings to imply the prolific nature of the *darvish* as devoid of spiritual pomp and ascetic contempt. Note how Kwaja Abd Allah Ansari (d. 1089) continued to employ the doctrine of *fana* in his exegesis on the nature of the *darvish* for another example, but with a new twist. In deliberate exaggeration, he placed the *darvish* as one "who does not possess the slightest particle of being" and "who abandons both this world and the hereafter and does not even have any religion" (in the sense that the *darvish* has no selfhood, whereas religion presupposes the selfhood of its practitioner).[19] Al-Hojviri (d. 1073/7?) described the *darvish* in the same vein while averring that the actions of such a figure was "no more attributed to himself", since he *is* "the Way [and] not a wayfarer" he was to *be* a place over which "something is passing, not a wayfarer following his own will".[20] Similarly, another noted figure, Abu Sa'id Ibn Abol Khayr (d. 1049), proclaimed, "the dervishes are not they, for if they existed, they would not be dervishes", and, in

---

17. Cited by A. Nurbakhsh, "Bayazidian Sufism: Annihilation without Ritual", *Sufi* 46 (Summer 2000), 8.
18. *Ahwal wa aqwal*, 110, cited in Algar, "Darvish ii", 74a.
19. *Ibid.*, 74a; cf. *Rasa'el-e Khwaja 'Abd-Allah Ansari* (ed. H. Wahid Dastgerdi) (Tehran, 1368/1989), 137.
20. Ali ibn Othman Al-Jullabi al-Hojviri, *The "Kashf al-Mahjub": The Oldest Persian Treatise on Sufism* (trans. R. A. Nicholson), Gibb Memorial Series 17 (London, 1959), 28–9.

a vivid reflection of John 14:6, asserted: "in their name is their attribute; whosoever seeks a path to God must pass by the dervishes, for they are the gate to Him".[21]

In the post-Mongol trauma, the literature of the thirteenth and fourteenth centuries laboured to promote the ideal of *darvishi* and its qualities in order to restore some degree of social coherence. To this effect, Sa'di would describe the face of the *darvish* as "a mirror in which the light of truth is to be seen",[22] declaring "Seek the question of truth from the circle of *darvishes*, that from this circle you may fill your ear!"[23] In this later period, Hafez, in particular, draws a paradoxical yet clear distinction between dervishes and "the Sufis", admiring the former but rejecting the latter as hypocrites and formalists. By his time many of the Sufis had become followers of an established and commercialized form of spirituality.[24] The sentiment of Sa'di resonates in a *ghazal* by Hafez, further, where the latter described the intimate company of the dervishes as "the loftiest garden of immortality … the alchemy that turns blackened hearts to gold" and the dust at the doors of their cells as the source of the water of life.[25] But this went further during the Mongol and Turko-Timurid times "when political vicissitudes revealed the hollowness of worldly power", and the increasing contrast between dervishhood and kingship, which was constantly drawn in Sufi literature, began to suggest that a "darvish might enjoy a higher status than a king". Both Sa'di and Hafez proclaim: "Were they to desire kingship, they could plunder the realm of kings" and "The good fortune (*dawlat*) that is immune to harm and eclipse – hear it plainly from me! – is that of the dervishes."[26] It is likely the theme of a Sufi-king connection began with the "semi-legendary" figure of Ibrahim ibn Adham (d. 776 or 790), an alleged royal from Balkh who in a Buddha-like fashion abandoned his status to become a *darvish*. Regardless, close connections were to develop on occasion when certain Sufi orders were able to have some degree of influence over

---

21. *Darvish* also rendered: "one who goes from door to door" or "one who opens doors". Cf. *Dictionary of Islam*, http://answering-islam.org/Books/Hughes/d.htm. Note, John (NIV) 14:6, "I am the way and the truth and the life. No one comes to the Father except through me." For Abu Sa'id, cf. Algar, "Darvish ii", 74a; Mohammad ibn Monawwar, *Asrar al-tawhid fi maqamati'l – Shaykh Abi Sa'id* (ed. M. R. Shafii Kadkani) (Tehran, 1366/1987), vol. 1, 295.

22. Sa'di, ghazal No. 668. Hasan Anvari, *Kolliat Sa'di* (Tehran, 2004). Original Persian: *sokhaneh marifat az halgheyeh darvishaan pors/Sadiyaa shaayad az in halgheh to dar goosh koni*. There is a pun on the word *halqa*, meaning both "circle" of people and "ring" to put in the ear as a sign of slavery in the past or devotion in the context of Sufism. *Marifat* means both "gnosis" or "cognition of God" and "good conduct."

23. Sa'di, text unknown. Original Persian: *sokhaneh marifat az halgheyeh darvishaan pors/ Sadiyaa shaayad az in halgheh to dar goosh koni*. A saying cited on collectable postcards with miniature paintings of classical Persian art.

24. By then Sufism may be referred to as *Sufi-gari*; Algar, "Darvish ii", 74b; cf. B. Khorramshahi, *Hafez-nama* (Tehran, 1366/1987), vol. 1, 138–9.

25. Algar, "Darvish ii", 74b–75a; Hafez, *Divan* (eds. Ghazvini & Ghani), 35–6.

26. See Algar, "Darvish ii", 75a, citing Sa'di, *Qasa'ed*, 112–13, and Hafez, *Divan*, 35.

their royal patrons, such as those of the Naqshbandiyya with the descendants of Timur. On a broader scale, we can witness the incorporation of Sufism into the empire building of the Safavid (1501–1722), Moghal (1526–1857) and Ottoman (1299–1922) dynasties, who needed the Sufis for expansion and cultural integration, though all this hardly forms a neat picture.[27] The Safavids themselves went through several transformations, most notably from humble Sufi beginnings to extremist fundamentalist Shi'a monarchic rule, and in the meanwhile nearly wiped out all (non-compliant) Sufi orders of Persia – making no distinction between those of the Sunni or Shi'a affiliation – in their advancement. Both the Naqshbandi and Nematollahi orders of Iran found refuge outside of their homeland, but it was the Nematollahi revival in Iran that reintroduced organized Sufism at the end the eighteenth century. It was also the Nematollahis who purportedly lived true to the fullness of the term *darvish*, owing to their ecstatic and antinomian style in contrast to the Sunni and "sober" mood of the Naqshbandiyya who retained the epithet "Sufi". Indeed, from the time of its founder, Shah Nematollah Wali (d. 1431), the Nematollahiyya vividly upheld the "kingly nature of the dervish calling" and were the first to deal "imperiously with monarchs" and to incorporate "shah" into their Sufi names, usually coupled with the epithet Ali (the fourth of the rightly guided caliphs, issuing into Iranian popular tradition as *shah-e mardan*, "the king of true men").[28]

We will return to the Nematollahiyya and the particular calling of Persian Sufism later, but for now let us turn to a short anecdote told by Sheikh Muzaffer Ozak (d. 1985) of the Helveti-Jerrahi order, nicely capturing the essence of *dervish*, in the modern understanding of the term and its usage among contemporary Sufis. In the story Ibn Arabi once met a fisherman from Tunisia who would distribute his daily catch to the poor and keep only one fish head for his own supper. This fisherman would become a disciple to Arabi and eventually a sheikh in his own right. A day came that one of his own disciples was leaving for Spain and the fisherman thought this a chance to send word to Arabi and ask for some spiritual guidance (since he felt he had not made progress for years now). The disciple to his surprise found Ibn Arabi living in overwhelming luxury and worldly comfort. To his further surprise, Ibn Arabi's advice for the disciple's master was rather disturbing and seemingly contradictory, saying, "Tell your master his problem is that he is too attached to the world." Upon the disciple's return the fisherman eagerly enquired after the "great master" (i.e. Ibn Arabi) and his advice, but the disciple was reluctant to pass on the message as it seemed wrong in light of Arabi's own lavishness and his own sheikh's asceticism. When pressed, he told his master what Arabi

27. J. Malik & J. Hinnells (eds), *Sufism in the West* (London, 2006), 8.
28. Cf. Algar, "Darvish ii", 75a. On the relationship of Shah Nematollah and his dervishes with rulers of their age, H. Farzam, *Rawabet-e ma'nawi-e Shah Ne'mat-Allah Wali ba salatin-e Iran wa Hend* (Isfahan, 1351/1972).

had said, and the fisherman broke into tears. Baffled, the disciple asked how this could be, but the fisherman replied, "He is right. He really cares nothing for all that he has, but every night, when I [myself] have my fish-head, I wish it were a whole fish."[29]

A similar legend is told of Shah Nematollah, who was once visited by a wandering dervish seeking the master's council and company. The visiting dervish was surprised by the kingly estate of Shah Nematollah and thought to himself, "Is this the manner of a true dervish?" When it came time for him to leave, Shah decided to accompany him on his journey, and the dervish gladly accepted. Not long after their departure the dervish stopped (remembering he had left his *kashkul* or "begging-bowl" behind) and asked Shah to wait for him to run back for his *kashkul*. However Shah replied, "I have left all of my wealth and station to become your companion, and you cannot let go of one bowl?"[30]

PRACTICAL SUFISM: CHIVALRY (*JAVÂNMARDÎ*) AND MORAL ETIQUETTE (*ÂDÂB*) IN IRANIAN SUFISM

Chivalry is a deeply entrenched component within Persian society and religion, and has, in fact, been a significant contributor to her distinctiveness. The Iranian ideal of chivalry is defined by a necessary paradox, which explains the very heart of Iranian identity. Therefore, chivalry (and indeed moral etiquette) is set up in the nation's distant past, while the "old" and "new" (the pre-Islamic and Islamic) era of Iranian history is connected in an intimate way. Chivalrous ideals are as much a part of the ancient Iranian ethos, as they are a real part of the Iranian religious consciousness today, thus making it difficult to speak of the one without the other.

Lloyd Ridgeon's *Morals and Mysticism in Persian Sufism* deserves particular mention, since it is the single most comprehensive examination of *javân-mardî*.[31] Ridgeon brings to light the social realities of Persian Sufism and attempts to set forth a preliminary chronology. He critiques the typical patriotic, nationalist Iranian attitude that presents an ethic of chivalry "in an unbroken chain" that predates the Islamic conquest of Iran.[32] The history of chivalry, for Ridgeon, involves equal contributions from both periods, a fact that is easily noticed during the unique period of mediaeval Iran with the merging of the pre-Islamic and Islamic cultures.[33] Ridgeon highlights an important notion of the "Persian" as an amalgamation of two significant cultures: the Iranian and

---

29. Ozak, *Love is the Wine*, 16–17.
30. Adapted from a Nematollahi tale. Cf. J. Nurbakhsh, *The Path*, 56.
31. L. Ridgeon, *Morals and Mysticism in Persian Sufism: A History of Sufi-Futuwwat in Iran* (New York, 2010).
32. *Ibid.*, 5.
33. *Ibid.*, 10.

the Arab. In this way, "Persian", he argues, cannot be limited to any kind of chauvinistic idealism, be it Iranian, Persian, Sasanian, Islamic or Arab.[34] While I join Ridgeon in his criticism of those who tactlessly hold Iranian chivalry to predate Islam, I am wary of another factor that is implicit to the Iranian ethos. This is that the Iranian is so concerned with the past, due to the repressed trauma of repeated conquest, in particular the Islamic, and the lost opportunity to regain its footing in the ever-changing conditions of Middle Eastern politics. Indeed, the Islamic conquest has been the single most significant blow to the ancient Iranian cultural identity, simply because the impact of Islam was so great, having left a heavy mark in the areas of religion, nationality, culture and language. Yet, for all this, Iran was almost completely resurrected (in terms of its culture, nationality, religion and language), but not without conceding dramatic changes to its identity.[35] Again, I am inclined to agree with Ridgeon's critique of Karim Zayyani, in particular, though notwithstanding the fact that the latter's writings on the history of chivalry and Sufism are, first, not academic, and, second, they are highly nuanced and must be understood in their proper context. A good example is Karim Zayyani's claim to a 3000-year history of Sufi-chivalry, which predates Islam. Zayyani's claim actually rests on the fact that both *futuwwat* (chivalry) and *tasawwuf* (Sufism) originate in the Khorasan province.[36] In fact, this is a view that is based on the proposition of Javad Nurbakhsh, who believed that the chevaliers founded the creed of Sufism "on the basis of both Islam and chivalry".[37] Now Ridgeon never denies the importance of Khorasan and the role of the chevaliers in the early history of Sufism and chivalry in Iran, but pushes for the correct assessment of this fact. Even so, it will not do to reduce the Iranian claim for a pre-Islamic tradition of mysticism and chivalry to nationalistic or patriotic dogma. There is still much to be said for the direct influence of Persian culture on the Islamic Middle East.

The Iranians have a distinct word for chivalry, *javânmardî* (its Arabic equivalent *futuwat*). This term embodies two distinct facets of chivalry: the idea of the "strong man" and also the notion of gentility and ethics. The word *futuwwat*, meaning "chivalry", is taken from the Arabic root f.t.a, and in turn yields the noun *fata* (young man). Yet this term has no pre-Islamic origin among the Arabs of the Peninsula. There is another term used by the Arabs, *muruwwat* ("manliness"), which is sourced in Arab pre-Islamic poetry. It harbours similar connotations of "virtue" and "loyalty", but is different in essence to *futuwwat* because it is largely bound to tribal customs of reciprocation. The point of

34. *Ibid.*, 5.
35. M. Axeworthy, *Iran: Empire of the Mind* (London, 2008), 72f.
36. L. Lewisohn, "Persian Sufism in the Contemporary West: Reflections on the Ni'matullahi Diaspora", in Malik & Hinnells (eds), *Sufism in the West*, 59; Ridgeon, *Morals and Mysticism*, 5, 22 and note 1.
37. J. Nurbakhsh, *Discourses*, 13.

contention is that *futuwwat* signifies a unique ideal that is alien to Arabia, and quite likely that *javânmardî* (literally "young-manliness") is unique to Iran and stands in contrast to the Arab notion of *muruwwat*.[38] In other words, *futuwwat* was likely a new abstract concept that featured in the Qur'an and was introduced to the Arabs by Mohammed. Indeed, this is a factor additionally supported by the research of Laury Silvers,[39] who argues that the truest quality of *futuwwat* "chivalry" is to be "feminine and receptive towards God's command" yet also "properly masculine and active in the world".[40] Her research highlights the all-important innovative contribution of Sufism, but in this case, and as pertinent to us, the radically envisaged qualities of chivalry as kindness and selfless service. It is such that the *futuwwat* movement during the Middle Ages incorporated both men and women into its fold;[41] this was an idea quite different from *muruwwat*, a purely masculine notion of the pre-Islamic Arabs. Most significantly, Silvers points out that the Arab understanding of chivalry was challenged by the qur'anic notion of *futuwwat* during the lifetime of the Prophet.[42] What remains is that an institution of chivalry, as a counterpart to Persio-Mesopotamian models, did not as yet exist in Arabia, and moreover, the qur'anic ideals of chivalry were clearly foreign to the Arabs of the Hijaz. What will dominate our discussion henceforth is the primary role of the Sufis in adapting the concept of *futuwwat* in the broadest context of the Persian *javânmardî*; that is, in the way that the Sufis increasingly spiritualized the concept and practice of chivalry to such an extent that it even goes beyond the Qur'an and the traditions of the Prophet.

The Iranian origins of Sufi chivalry and etiquette

The late master of the Persian Nematollahi Khaneqahi Sufi Order, Javad Nurbakhsh, asserted the unmistakable impression that all of Sufism can be summed up in *javânmardî* (chivalry) and *âdâb* (moral etiquette) – a *practical* Sufism.[43] Such emphasis speaks boldly of the connections with pre-Islamic Iran and the Pahlawan religion (or custom of the "champions" [strongmen]) practised before the coming of Islam, and which was properly appropriated into the monotheistic faith of the Moslems of Iran. In fact, Javad Nurbakhsh clearly expressed this view in saying that "With the appearance of Islam, these

---

38. Ridgeon, *Morals and Mysticism*, 6ff.
39. L. Silvers, "Representations: Sufi Literature", in *Encyclopaedia of Women and Islamic Cultures* (ed. Saud Joseph), vol. 5.
40. *Ibid.*
41. *Ibid.*
42. *Ibid.*
43. Cf. J. Nurbakhsh, *The Truths of Love* (ed. W. C. Chittick and trans. L. Lewisohn) (London, 1982), 21. For an extensive elaboration on this, *idem, Javanmardi* (Tehran, 1385/2007).

chevaliers embraced the religion of Islam while retaining the conventions of chivalry."[44] Consequently, it has not been unusual that, for the Sufis of Iran, every single doctrine and theosophical excerpt is grounded in points of chivalry and etiquette, marking the *acts* of the Sufis. It is around these two points (of *âdâb* and *javânmardî*) that the quintessence of Sufism is shaped, to which the Sufi is ultimately bound, and the juncture at which *hekmat-e khosrawani*, *darvishi*, and gnosis of self actually meet. This comes out of the very stuff of old Persia.

In the Iranian tradition, both the ideas of chivalry and etiquette are well entrenched in pre-Islamic times and are often treated synonymously or concurrently in literature. Originally a reference in singular and later in plural with gradual categorization and formulation, both concerned the conduct and behaviour of a person and dealt with the proper measure of restraint with regard to it. Etiquette, in particular, is difficult to trace on its own, as it permeates almost every aspect of human interaction from the personal to the divine. Chivalry, in the classical sense, strongly associated with the virtue of warfare, was nevertheless predominantly an *ideal* that characterized the proper behaviour and conduct of a "warrior". What is unique about the two values is that neither were, nor are they still, the property or the exclusive trait of any particular class or privilege; and although eventual fraternities and organizations came to form individual communities with membership and specific codes, no discrepancy was adhered to in terms of social rank or racial (or even religious) origin.[45] In a strictly Persian milieu, the oldest reference can probably be traced to Achamaenian Persia and the legends that surround the acts of Cyrus the Great. The Persian cavalrymen and knights were a prominent feature of warfare in the ancient world. Since formally manhood in Persian culture has been associated with horses and the wearing of pants (*shalwar*) and belt, these components have become iconic symbols of the later *futuwwa* organizations and the *javanmardan*. Although not fully investigated, the life of Cyrus (*kurosh-e kabir*) is still very much a pillar for chivalry and moral etiquette in Persian culture – on top of which we believe the legendary figure of Ferdowsi's Rostam was modelled.[46] Since the Persians apparently did not commit much to writing till later in their history, the bulk of Persia's chivalric and moral tradition was to be reconstructed by the labour of post-Sasanid authors

---

44. He goes on to say, "thereby founding the creed of Sufism on the basis of both Islam and chivalry. Thus, the etiquette of the chevaliers became part of the practice of *khaniqah* and of the Sufis", *idem, Discourses on the Sufi Path* (London, 1996).

45. Cf. R. S. Simon, "Futuwwa", in *Encyclopedia of Islam and the Muslim World* (ed. R. C. Martin) (New York, 2004), vol. 1, 263.

46. M. A. Dandamayev, "Cyrus; iii. Cyrus II the Great", in *EIr*, vol. 6, 516–21. Note also the unfinished documentary by Cyrus Kar "In Search of Cyrus the Great", www.spentaproductions.com/Cyrus-the-Great-English/cyruspreview_english.htm.

such as Ferdowsi.[47] Despite the presence of Arabian components in the literature of the Islamic period, the Iranian origin of these chivalric motifs is undisputed.[48] Ibn al-Nadim, for example, takes for granted that the first storytellers were the early inhabitants of Fars: "After the stories of the early Persians had passed to the Arsacids and the Sasanians, the Arabs translated them into their own language and then began to compose similar stories themselves."[49] The Persian/Arab interaction is an old relation, mind you, with "Iranian Islam" being its most recent outcome. This is a matter which will be treated at length below, but suffice it to say that a great deal of religious and cultural interaction had taken place between Arabia and Persia, beginning with the Achaemenians, and especially under the Sasanians (in opening a serious flow of cultural exchange – with both positive and negative results – between the two). The Islamic period then added a new dimension to the Iranian heritage of chivalry and etiquette bringing about a specifically "Islamic" synthesis, which will be discussed later.

Adab

The virtue of *adab* (pl. *âdâb*) denoted by the Arabic is defined in Sufism as the "learning of the exercises of the carnal soul (*nafs*), the betterment of morals",[50] yet when taken independently of religion it defines "habit, hereditary norm of conduct, [and] custom". It is the equivalent of the Mid. Pers. term *frahang*, NPers. *farhang*,[51] which also corresponds with another Pahlavi word, *êwên*,

---

47. Cf. Rudaki (d. *c.*941), the founder of Persian literature and first to compose poetry in the New Persian language, combined Persian and Arabic script. Nezami (d. 1209) wrote the romance narrative of "Khosrow and Shirin" and "Leyli and Majnun" in *Panj Ganj* ("Five Jewels"). Ferdowsi's *Shâhnâmeh*, better known in the West, sought to revive Persian culture and language.

48. Abu Ishaq Hosri (d. 1061), the compiler of the Arabic anthology *Ketaab zahr al-aadaab* (ed. Z. Mobarak) (Cairo, 1925), vol. 1, 140, refers to the ten categories of *âdâb* as stated by the vizier Hasan b. Sahl (d. 850), six portions of which are Persian, three Arabian and one that is superior to the others. For these cf. D. J. Khaleghi-Motlagh's article "Adab", in *EIr*, vol. 1, 433b–4a. The tenth portion is noteworthy here for being "the recitation of pieces of story and fable at social gatherings", the Iranian origins of which are easily traced in Ibn al-Nadim, *Ketab al-Fehrest* (ed. G. Flügel) (Leipzig, 1871–72); *idem, Ketab al-Fehrist* (ed. M. R. Tajaddod) (Tehran, 1350/1971); and *idem, Ketab al-Fehrist* (trans. B. Dodge) as *The Fihrist of al-Nadim* (New York, 1970). The Iranian origin of the Arabian portion (poetry, genealogy and historiography) is demonstrated by Khaleghi-Motlagh, "Adab", 434a–b.

49. Ibn al-Nadim, *Fehrest*, 304, cited in Khaleghi-Motlagh, "Adab", 434a.

50. Mohammed ibn Mohammed al-Zabidi, *Taj al-'aruz* (Kuwait, 1974), vol. 2, 12.

51. Th. Nöldeke, "Geschichte des Artaschir-i Papakan aus dem Pahlevi übersetzt mit Erläuterungen und einer Einleitung versehen", *Bazzenberger's Beiträge zur Kunde der indogermanischen Sprache* 4 (1879), 38, note 3; H. S. Nyberg, *Hilfsbuch des Pehlevi* (Uppsala, 1931), vol. 2, 70.

Persian *âyîn*, meaning more or less the same things (i.e. education, culture, good behaviour, politeness and proper demeanour), being closely linked with the concept of ethics.[52] In Persia, the origin of this ideal can be found in its earliest reference to the Old Iranian Mithra as the major component of traditional ethics and moral conduct incumbent upon the individual.[53] The very heart of *âdâb* in Iran is purveyed extensively in the *Shahnameh* (and other works rooted in the Iranian cultural tradition) as the refinement of thought, word and deed, and as proportion (*andaza*) and moderation (*mianaravi*) in conduct.[54] These were expanded upon in detail with respect to the manner of one's speech and generosity, and colourfully portrayed in the *Shahnameh* through the conduct of its heroes. For example, "soft-spokenness" (*narm-guyi*) is consistently affirmed by Ferdowsi, stating that one should never "tear anyone's skin with words".[55] In the face of insult "silence" is prescribed; should it persist, a reply should be made with "smooth" and "fresh", in other words vigorous, but moderate, language.[56] Similarly the refinement of generosity is marked by the giver's indebtedness to the receiver, for it is in the act of (the receiver's) acceptance that peace and serenity of soul are bought with the gift.[57] The refinement of this cultural tradition is worth underlining by another example to really stress the significance of its role and continuity at the heart of Iranian social and religious doctrine. Several stories in the *Shahnameh* are relevant, but one in particular will suffice: this concerns the reception that the Iranian commander Godarz gives to Royin, sent by his father Piran with an offer of peace. Godarz, who has already suffered considerable losses (seventy sons and grandsons) in the war with Turan, walks with a cheerful countenance to greet his guest and embraces him, asking after the health of his family, himself and the other Turanians, and entertains him for one week before explaining that there can be no other solution except through battle.[58] Ferdowsi is little interested in simply enunciating "good manners" or "ethical maxims"

---

52. In certain Arabic works of early Islamic centuries, *êwên* is rendered either by *adab* and its pl. *âdâb*, or by *rasm* and its pl. *rosûm*; and sometimes the original word, in its Persian form *âyîn*, is retained. Cf. Khaleghi-Motlagh, "Adab", 432.

53. Imoto, "Mithra, the Mediator", 299. Cf. also Boyce, "Iranian Festivals", 801–3; J. Moulton, *Early Zoroastrianism* (London, 1913), 63–4. On A. Meillet's hypothesis cf. Taraporewala, *Divine Songs*, 588–9.

54. Khaleghi-Motlagh, "Adab", 432a.

55. Ferdowsi, *Shahnameh* (ed. and trans. J. Mohl) (Paris, 1838–78), vol. 6, 270, line 1339; similarly in a Pahlavi text it is emphasized that we should not "hurt people with words": cited in Khaleghi-Motlagh, "Adab", 432a–b.

56. Thus *Shahnameh* (Mohl), vol. 6, 506, lines 4185–9; cf. Khaleghi-Motlagh, "Adab", 432a–b.

57. *Shahnameh*, vol. 6, 260, lines 1204–8; cf. Khaleghi-Motlagh, "Adab", 432b. Sheik Ozak gives a notable illustration in the humorous story of the "host that beat up his guests" in *Love is the Wine*, 81–3.

58. *Shahnameh*, vol. 3, 512, lines 119–25. Other examples are given to show its counter effect: the story of Rostam and Esfandiar, *Shahnameh*, vol. 4, 520. Cf Khaleghi-Motlagh, "Adab", 432a–b.

here, but rather he is concerned to exemplify the proper conduct and behaviour of a refined soul. It is at this point that *âdâb* most clearly passes over into *javânmardî*, as outlined in the definitive sentence:

> That with your heart and soul you serve and seek the well-being of others, while in practice you are fair to others, not expecting fairness in return; and not disrupting the comfort of others with your own sufferings.[59]

Futuwwat

The term *futuwwat* was technically coined in the eighth century to illustrate the characteristic qualities of the ideal *fatâ*, pl. *fityân*, literally the "young man", which was already inferred in the Qur'an in the seventh century. By the twelfth century *futuwwa* organizations were flourishing throughout Iran, Asia Minor and the Fertile Crescent as well as in Europe. The late date is suggestive of its borrowing from earlier versions of "men's groups" already existing in the Middle East with both Byzantine and Sasanid fraternities.[60] In the Islamic period, *futuwwat* was translated by *javânmardî* among the Persians, meaning literally the same thing ("young-man") but emphasizing the Iranian character on its own, and continuing Persian tradition through its adherents' meeting in the "House of Strength" (*zourkhaneh*). The connotations of this term also connect to Mithra, a deity that functioned as both an emissary between heaven and earth, as well as between parties, possessing a dual function in epitomizing both the ethical staple of society and its heroic cornerstone. A pre-Zarathushtrian phenomenon, Mithras is documented as the god of justice and truth, keeping the balance and punishing wrongdoers (with vigorous vengeance). For a discussion of this, see Imoto's "Mithra".[61] Boyce makes a case for Mithra (or *Mehr*), who is honoured in the feast and festival of *Mehregan*. *Mehr* is one of the "great fighting divinities of Zoroastrianism, a champion for the kingdom of righteousness."[62] Hinnells points out, further, that "when a [Zoroastrian] priest is initiated he is given a *gurz* – the mace of Mithra which has at the end of it the head of a bull". And, "these maces are carried at major ceremonies and decorate the walls of Zoroastrian temples".[63] The idea of the "mace of justice" is a theme of ancient times that has concurrently carried through into Persian Sufism in the form of an axe: generally as an accompaniment to the travelling dervish (or *qalandar*) for chopping firewood or fending

---

59. Cf. J. Nurbakhsh, *Javanmardi*, 54.
60. Simon, "Futuwwa", 263.
61. Imoto, "Mithra, the Mediator", 299–307.
62. Boyce, "Iranian Festivals", 802.
63. Hinnells, "Iranian Background", 248.

Figure 5.1 Coat of arms of a Persian Sufi order. Courtesy House of Sufism.

off wild animals and highway robbers.[64] Figure 5.1 depicts the axe as part of the symbolic coat of arms for a Persian Sufi order.

In anticipatory parallel to the rise of Persian Sufism, *javânmardî* was increasingly associated with Mithraic morality and heroism in a distinctively social sense, giving rise to the practice of "service to society" (or social exertion, *kasb* and *amal*), which was adapted by Sufis of Transoxania and Khorasan (and the *akhis* of Turkic regions) into the mystical stream. There are already clear indications of this in the history of Sufism as in the case of the life of Mawlana Rumi and his renowned assistant, Hosamoddin Chalabi, who was head of an order of chivalry that integrated with Sufism when he joined Rumi's circle.[65] In Sufism chivalry took on an esoteric meaning in that it served to explain a significant purification method where the soul was brought closer towards perfection and union with the divine. For instance, where a young man initiated into knighthood would gain his "manhood" and "honour" through the trials of

---

64. Cf. Algar, "Darvish ii", 74b.
65. Cf. Mojaddedi, introducing *M*, xviii.

bravery and battle, the *javânmard* reflected this in a spiritual journey through the trials of the *tariqah* (Sufi path).

On a deeper plane still, this term helped open another dimension of esoteric dialogue: that the *javân* (young) *mard* (man) was a code for the "renewed man", "refreshed man",[66] a person "born again" (for want of a better word) but "re-born" into the world of spirituality and gnosis. This not only fully involved and encompassed a literal experience through the physical body, but the difference from the previous state of being amounted to "the opening" and "awakening" of the spiritual body. This has been described in many passages and captured in endless verses by the mystics as "gaining a heart through the grace of God", but a verse of Rumi that comes to mind encapsulates it even better: "I am not looking for the elixir or gold. Where is a receptive piece of copper? How can even a lukewarm disciple attain passionate love? What then if he's cold?"[67] Similarly, Hasan al-Basri, a patron of chivalry and one of the earliest Sufi saints, when asked "O Shaikh, our hearts are asleep ... What should we do?" would reply "Would that you were asleep, for a sleeping person can be shaken and woken up ... your hearts are dead!"[68] Hasan, when refusing to speak to the congregation in the absence of Rabea, would justify himself by saying, "that wine which we've made for the capacity of elephants can't be poured into the chest of ants".[69] The highest secret is here touched upon by Abu Sa'id when revealing that it (*javânmardi*) is in essence "a substance of God's grace (*latifa*) ... produced by the bounty and mercy of God, not by the acquisition and action of man",[70] and so this Persian Sufi continued to honour the Hallajian view from very early on, that "intention" held precedence over "action"[71] (as we will shortly explain below). In the Sufi path, the notion of *seyr wa soluk* ("travelling [the path] and social conduct") captured the finer relationship that was inherent in the acts of the Sufis.[72] With regard to Hasan al-Basri's remarks to his disciples, the words of Abu Sa'id are especially pertinent here in reminding the eager souls that this phenomenon "belongs to the Creator: the creatures have no part therein, and in the body it is a loan.

---

66. Again, *javanmard* in the context of "refreshed", "renewed", etc., has significant conceptual correspondence with the Av. *fravashi*, Mid. Pers. *faravahar*, NPers. *farvardin*. Cf. Boyce, "Fravashi", in *EIr* vol, 10, 198a.

67. Rumi, *Koliyateh Shams-e Tabrizi* (ed. Badi al-Zaman Forouzanfar) (Tehran, 1382/2003), 790, line 2206 (here trans. W. C. Chittick, *The Sufi Path of Love: The Spiritual Teachings of Rumi* [New York, 1983], 160).

68. J. Nurbakhsh, *Masters of the Path* (London, 1980), 9.

69. *Ibid.*, 7.

70. Mohammed ibn Monawwar, *Asraru'l-tawhid fi maqamati'l Shaykh Abi Sa'id* (ed. V. A. Zhukovski) (Petrograd, 1899), 385, cited in Nicholson, *Studies in Islamic Mysticism*, 51. Also, *Asraru'l-tawhid*, 385, 15, in Nicholson, *Studies*.

71. L. Massignon, "The Juridical Consequences of the Doctrines of al-Hallaj", in *Studies on Islam* (ed. M. Swartz) (Oxford, 1981), 140–63.

72. See an exposition on "travelling" and "social conduct" ("Seir-o Soluk") on the Sufi path by J. Nurbakhsh in his *Discourses*, 19–20.

Whoever possesses it is 'living' (*hayy*), and whoever lacks it is 'animal' (*haya-wan*). There is a great difference between the 'living' and the 'animal'".[73]

Mystical chivalry and the unification of the futuwwat guilds

Chevaliers were drawn to the Sufi path since Sufis would make prolific use of their terminology and customs. Prior to the rise of Persian Sufism, and parallel with it, chevaliers prominently featured among paramilitary fighters and had significant connections with artisan guilds. They were often broadly placed in society (given their vague social status) and at times fought with the dominant political regime, at other times defending local autonomies against the military invader, as well as indulging in extortion and looting the wealthy.[74] This last trait – acting as rabble forces and outlaws – earned them the pseudonym *ayyâr[rûn]*, meaning "vagrant, outlaw", among other possibilities.[75] Their function as urban militia in particular contributed to the social unrest common in the state during the ninth through to the twelfth centuries, supporting and helping to define the *ghulat* and *shuubiyya* activities, important cultural resistance movements we will soon have to consider. However, by the late mediaeval period, chivalry's various functions and associations, with strong-men fraternities, guilds and Sufi orders, had become interwoven. The instigator of this fusion was the Abbasid caliph al-Nasir al-din Allah (1181–1223) and its architect Omar al-Sohravardi (d. 1234). The caliph, upon fearing military threat and competition for leadership, moved quickly to gain control of the *futuwwa* movements through institutionalization, organized membership, and adaptation of genealogy, rites and ritual, and he made himself the immediate head of all orders.[76] This was a cunning move, since chivalric rituals and codes of honour represented small pockets of historical continuity in ideas and doctrine, usually setting the adherents apart from the rest of Moslem society. In this way, al-Nasir secured complete hegemony, at least in name. This move tightened the grip on centuries of subterranean cultural and religious resilience that had taken refuge among chivalric orders sometimes defined by their special clothing (consisting of *futuwwa* trousers and belt of honour) and who partook in their rituals of independent allegiance, such as the event of the *futuwwa* drink – a cup of salty water – taken during the initiation ceremony.[77]

---

73. *Asraru'l-tawhid*, 385, 3, cited in Nicholson, *Studies*, 51.
74. On the history of *futuwwa* as a military organization, see the Introduction to J. R. Crook (trans.), *The Royal Book of Spiritual Chivalry (Futuwat nama-yi Sultani)* (Chicago, 2000); C. Cahen, "Futuwwa", in *EIs*, vol. 2.
75. Also *awbâsh* "riff-raff", *shatir*, pl. *shuttar* "artful [ones]" and occasionally (from the time of the Saljuks) *rind* pl. *runûd* "scamp"; Cahen, "Futuwwa".
76. Simon, "Futuwwa", 264–5; Cahen "Futuwwa", 964–6.
77. A. Loewen, "The Initiation Rite", in his article "Proper Conduct (*Adab*) is Everything: The *Futuwwat-namah-i Sultani* of Husayn Va'izi-i Kashifi", *Iranian Studies* 36(4) (2003), 557–62.

All in all, the chivalric orders adhered to a general code of honour that upheld the virtues of generosity, solidarity, courage and hospitality,[78] principles that were adopted by Sufis into their doctrinal system in an alternative way. As such, chivalry and moral etiquette as an improvized and intuitive component of Sufi practice was gradually systematized and made available textually from the early eleventh century. In this period the manuals of Abd al-Rahman al-Solami al-Neyshaburi[79] (d. 1021), a celebrated Sufi and a noted instructor to Abu Sa'id,[80] mark the initial period in which *âdâb* and *javânmardî* became further ritualized. Yet it was the twelfth century that saw the "standardization" of the schools of chivalry and moral etiquette, as well as Sufism itself – everything being brought into a manageable sphere and increasingly married to the Islamic norm – because the establishment feared instability and resistance.

This had subsequent effects upon the practice of Sufism. Sufism *per se*, was meant to be the internal or spiritual component of Islamic faith. However, becoming increasingly institutionalized, Sufism too took on both internal and external aspects. These were distinguished by outward acts (*âdâb al-zahir*) and inward intention (*âdâb al-batin*). The *inner intention* of the Sufis was kept increasingly private, since observance of *outward* acts represented closer affinity with mainstream ideas about Sufism. Paramount in the memory of saints such as Abu Sa'id is the radical Hallajian tradition where *khedmat* (service) is greater than *ebadat* (servitude), *niyyat* (intention) is greater than *amal* (action), *ebaha* (permitting) is greater than *tahrim* (forbidding), and *muhabba* (love) is greater than *iman* (faith).[81] Where increasing appeal was made to the outward façade, Abu Sa'id would even reproach his own disciple for composing anecdotes in his honour saying, "O Abdo'l-Karim! Do not be a writer of anecdotes: be such a man that anecdotes are told of thee."[82] Building on al-Ghazali's earlier appropriation of the mystic creed to the Islamic institution, Omar al-Sohravardi, as the spiritual advisor to caliph al-Nasir, was among the first to legitimize the new regulations that were bound by tradition under the caliph's reign.[83] The work of Ibn al-Memar (d. 1248), moreover, with his most factual *Kitab al-Futuwwa*, remains as a testament to a strictly Islamic agenda incorporating *futuwwa* into the *sharia*, so that only a true believer could be a

---

78. *Futuwwat-namah-i Sultani*, attributed to Hosayn Vaizi-i Kashifi (d. 1504/5) (ed. M. J. Mahjub) (Tehran, 1971). Also Crook, *Royal Book of Spiritual Chivalry*.
79. E. Kohlberg (ed.), *Jawami adab al-sufiyya* (Jerusalem, 1976); F. Taeschner, "As-Sulami's *Kitab al-Futuwwa*", in *Studia Orientalia Ioanni Pedersen Septuagenario* (ed. F. Hvidberg) (Hauniae, 1953), 340–51.
80. Nicholson, *Studies*, 14.
81. Massignon, "The Juridical Consequences".
82. Nicholson, *Studies*, 67.
83. He was the first of a series of writers in Persian who inaugurated a literary category which in Irano-Turkish territories (and also in Egypt during the Ottoman period) was to continue until the beginning of modern times; Cahen, "Futuwwa", 964a–b.

fata.[84] Al-Nasir and his confidant (al-Sohravardi) effected a system that bound *futuwwa* and Sufi fraternities to the caliph. Indeed, Al-Nasir ensured the loyalty of all *futuwwa* organizations by becoming a member and declaring himself as their head throughout the Islamic world; in conjunction, al-Sohravardi founded his own order of Sufis, the Sohravardia (no relation to Shahab Al-Din Sohravardi), adapting popular *futuwwa* and promoting the caliph's significance as the head of both.[85] The introduction of *isnad*s or "spiritual chains" to Sufism in their claim to ancestry and legitimacy proved as ambivalent as the notions of "Sufi" and *fata*, and made directing allegiance from these movements to the state rather vague.[86] In Iran, for example, these chains most often returned to Ali as the *fata* exemplar and then to Salman the Persian, the patron of Irano-Mesopotamian artisan guilds,[87] but they were to become subtle ideological means of keeping indigenous Persian traditions alive, and what they actually represented will have to be explored later, especially with regard to Salman. In any case, by the twelfth century Sufism came to be fully infused with the dual tradition of *âdâb* and *javânmardî* under the principle of "spiritual warriorhood", based on the alleged tradition of the Prophet that the "inner [greater] *jihad*" had higher value than any other "struggle". The Sufi's inward struggle, though, developed in parallel to the increasingly feudalistic development of martial *futuwwa*, warriors of great honour who were employed as the private army to the Abbassid caliphate.[88]

The fusion of *âdâb* and *javânmardî* under Islam was an achievement largely owed to two prominent figures: Ibn al-Moqaffa (720–756), of noble heritage, and Ferdowsi (935–1020), a wealthy land owner.[89] Both were of the *shuubiyya*, a term borrowed from the Qur'an (49:13) by an early anti-Arab Persian Moslem movement – a non-extremist, "revivalist" group among the distinguished members of Moslem society, which was characterized by a

---

84. Ibn Memar Hanbali Baghdadi, *Kitab al-futuwwa* (intro. Mostafa Jawad), 12, cited in Simon, "Futuwwa", 264b.
85. Simon, "Futuwwa", 264b; Cahen, "Futuwwa", 964a–b. Cf. also M. J. Mahjub, "Chivalry and Early Persian Sufism", in *The Heritage of Persian Sufism* (trans. L. Lewisohn) (Oxford, 1999), vol. 1, 579–80. For a fuller discussion on Nasirian chivalry cf. Mahjub's article in *Sufi* 12 (Autumn 1370/1991), 6–18 [Persian].
86. Cahen, "Futuwwa", 964b; a useful resource on biographies and hierarchies in the history of Sufism is J. Mojaddedi, *The Biographical Tradition in Sufism: The Tabaqat Genre from al-Sulami to Jami* (Richmond, 2001).
87. Ali is attributed the phrase *la sayf illa dhu'l fiqar/la fata illa Ali* "There is no sword but Dhol-Fiqar [Ali's sword] and no *fata* but Ali". After the conquest of Ctesiphon, the Sasanian capital, Salman was made the governor, while maintaining a modest living as an artisan. Cf. A. H. Zarrinkub, "The Arab Conquest of Iran and its Aftermath", in *CHI*, vol. 4, 13.
88. This private guard was established by the Abbasid caliph al-Muqtafi al-Mustazhir (1136–60). Mahjub, "Chivalry and Early Persian Sufism", 580f.
89. F. Gabrieli, "Ibn Al-Mukaffa", in *EIs*, available at Brill Online, www.encquran.brill.nl/entries/encyclopaedia-of-islam-2/ibn-al-mukaffa-SIM_3304; C. Huart, H. Massé & V. L. Ménagge, "Firdawsi", in *EIs*, vol. 2.

strong attachment to Iranian culture and a somewhat superficial Islamic faith, a typical position in the early Islamic period among the majority of Persian *mawali*.[90] We may very briefly note here that Al-Moqaffa, Arabic author and translator of Persian origin, introduced many notable works of Indian (*Kalila we-Dimma*) and Iranian origin to the Arab world. Like Sohravardi Maqtol, he lived a short but prolific life, meeting his end through political and personal causes. Al-Moqaffa was suspected of being a Manichaean, or at least associated with this Gnostic heresy, and also significantly attributed to him was the transmission of *Kitab-i Mazdak*, the heretical Book of the Mazdakites, (these heresies will be discussed later). Charges were brought against him that he attempted to make an "imitation" of the sacred Book of Islam, which appeared to be an attack on Mohammed, the Qur'an and Islam in the name of another faith, suggested by Francesco Gabrieli to be Manichaeism. As for Ferdowsi, his monumental work served as a separate but equally important medium to channel material from ancient Pahlavi directly through versions of neo-Persian into his great "nationalist" epic that secretly told the history of Persia through mythical figures and colourful allegories. It seems that Ferdowsi had in his possession an "ancient book" passed down to him from his predecessor, the poet Daqiqi (d. *c*.980), ostensibly a series of attempted *Shahnamehs*.

A third element in the transmission and fusion of ancient Iranian ideas within Islam is the inevitable effect that the development of Persianate Sufism had on the Moslem world at large. The Sufis of Iran fused *âdâb* and *javânmardî* into the one tradition of mystical thought, and adapted these and other Persian elements to the Islamic sphere in a way that it became fixed components of the Islamic ideal and spirituality of Iran. The point of *âdâb* and *javânmardî* are no longer significant in and of themselves, but as cultural ornaments and ideals that cling to a decadent past. They become integral to Sufism and interwoven with its notion of *fanâ* and *baqâ* as the apex of refinement and practical sophistication. This single most significant aim of Sufi praxis, coupled with what *âdâb* and *javânmardî* now meant under its banner, consisted of such fervent "selflessness", so that naught could be accounted to the acts of the Sufi – whether to be "accredited" or "discredited" as good or bad manners – by observers. For example, Javad Nurbakhsh has said, "O Sufi, abandon the observance of manners; the people of the heart are beyond mere manners", yet it is prescribed, "While you are travelling the Path you must have manners; but when you reach God it is unbelief to observe manners."[91]

A good example of this kind of interpretation of *âdâb* and *javânmardî* within Sufism is found in anecdotes about the antinomian Sufi Abu Sa'id Abol Khayr, Retaining the consistent Sufi theme of *fanâ*, Abu Sa'id was asked, "What is evil and what is the worst evil?" He replied, "Evil is 'thou', and the

---

90. R. Hamzehee, *Land of Revolutions* (Göttingen, 1991), 51. Cf. D. J. Khaleghi-Motlagh, "The Fusion of Adab and Islam", "Adab", 438a–9a.

91. J. Nurbakhsh, "Silence and Etiquette of the Sufis" (poem), *Sufi* 9 (Spring 1991), 24–5.

worst evil is 'thou', when thou knowest it not."[92] This is clarified when Abu Sa'id recounts an early episode from his youth saying, "I opened the Qur'an, and my eye fell on the verse, *We will prove you with evil and with good, to try you; and unto Us shall ye return*."[93] He explains this by way of God indicating to him, "All this which I put in thy way is a trial. If it is good, it is a trial, and if it is evil, it is a trial. Do not stoop to good or to evil, but dwell with Me!" Then he concluded, "Once more my 'self' vanished, and His grace was all in all."[94] And so he was tested; where at one stage the dung from his horse was an object of veneration, at a later stage the very same folk saw his value to be no more than that object! Whence in realizing the transitoriness of both, he attained to the proper state of unity (as devoid of either the aspiration and anxiety for "good" or for "evil"),[95] whereupon Abu Sa'id would remark that "Whoever saw me in my first state became a *siddiq* (sincere [devotee]), and whoever saw me in my last state became a *zindiq* (heretic)."[96]

In Sufi practice, going beyond the self (and self-interest) allowed for a kind of "disinterested love" as the spiritual staple of the Sufis. Abu Sa'id learned from a very young age that all acts of piety are "to serve God" and "to love God", which was summarized for him by his teacher in the following lines:

> Perfect love proceeds from the lover who hopes naught for himself; what is there to desire in that which has a price? Certainly the Giver is better for you than the gift: How should you want the gift, when you possess the very Philosopher's stone?[97]

The notion of the perfect saint for Abu Sa'id being about such a one "who lives in friendly intercourse with his fellow-creatures, yet is never forgetful of God".[98] He is perhaps indicating that "there is no better and easier means of attaining to God than by bringing joy to the heart of a Moslem [i.e. brother]".[99] According to Hasan al-Basri, "the entire meaning of chivalry (*futuwwa*) is summed up in the following verse of the Qur'an: "Surely God bids to justice and good-doing and giving to kinsmen; and He forbids indecency, dishonour,

92. *Asrar*, 403, 3, in Nicholson, *Studies*, 53

93. Q 21:36; Nicholson, *Studies*, 17.

94. Mohammed ibn al-Monawwar, *Halat u Sukhunan-i Shaykh Abu Sa'id ibn Abi'l-Khayr*, 19, 6; *Asrar*, 37, 8, in Nicholson, *Studies*, 17.

95. *Halat*, 19, 6; *Asrar*, 37, 8, in *ibid.*, 16–17.

96. *Asrar*, 41, 19, in *ibid.*, 62.

97. *Asrar*, 16, 9, in *ibid.*, 5. An echo of this is heard in a verse by Hafez: "For years my heart sought the grail of Jamshid from me; a needless quest for a jewel it already possessed (*saal-ha del talab jaameh jam az maa meekard/va-aan ke khod daasht ze beegaaneh tamanna meekard*); Hafez, *Diwan* (ed. Kh. Khatib-Rawhbar), 193, *ghazal* 143, line 1.

98. *Asrar*, 258, 17, in Nicholson, *Studies*, 67.

99. *Asrar*, 380, 11, in *ibid.*, 55.

and insolence, admonishing you, so that happily you will remember [16:90]."[100] Of course, *javânmardî* was not limited to the Qur'an or to the Islamic tradition, and allegedly the Sufis would frequently quote from it to demonstrate its universality and all-embracing spiritual quality.

For the Nematollahiya, in Iran, Sufism increasingly came to be seen as nothing more than *javânmardi* and *âdâb* in the garb of Sufism and encompassed in the doctrine and practice of service and love. Therefore "service to" and "love for" all of creation was prescribed as the method for removing the obstacle of "the self" (*nafs*) and "self-interest" (*tama'*) for the purpose of unity (with God, i.e. *residan be haqqiqat*). Echoing the words of Abu Sa'id, Javad Nurbakhsh has said:

> If you travel on water, you are no more than a water bug;
> If you travel in the air, you are no more than a fly,
> Gain a heart, that you may become a human being.[101]

Gathering the threads of the foregoing analysis, to this point, let it be clear that we seek to explain *hekmat-e khosrawani* or Khosravan wisdom as the tradition that forms the collective reflection of a nation on its own history and development, consciously and sometimes in almost imperceptible and apparently unconscious ways. We are on the track of a uniquely Persian method of "imaginative historiography" that utilizes a mythic-macrohistorical system in re-collecting, re-constituting and re-telling Persia's envisioned past. More importantly, what it does is preserve the mysteries of its repressed, almost forgotten and hidden history. It is also a method prevalent among Sufis of the "Khorasanian tradition", the Nematollahiya, who adhere to the "Khosravanian path". Outside the Nematollahi instigation, it seems that its original architects were Shihab al-Din al-Sohravardi (Sohravardi Maqtol, d. 1191) and Ferdowsi, who appeared to be uncovering Persia's hidden history. Whatever the validity of assumptions, these two figures were keenly aware of the repressed character of Persia's past and diligently sought to recapture its essence in the new "Islamic age" of Iran. Directly and to the point, this "eastern Iranian" tradition of wisdom sets itself apart from "western Iran", which has now come to be predominantly Turkic/Kurdish and is promoted as the authentic "Persian" cultural and religious foundation. It was transmitted as the continuing tradition of a native Persian wisdom into which many noted early Sufis have been assimilated. To place the term *haosravah* or *khosravani* within context, it infers a "flowing mind" or "free-flowing consciousness", not only of the historical consciousness of the Iranians, but also as a mystical motif for the *darvish*. The pattern carries through to be summed up in the modes of *javânmardî* and

---

100. Using *The Koran Interpreted* (trans. A. J. Arberry) (Oxford, 1982); Ibn Memar, *Kitab al-futuwwa*, (intro. Mostafa Jawad), in Simon, "Futuwwa", 12.
101. J. Nurbakhsh, "Divine Reality", *Sufi* 47 (Autumn 2000), 44.

âdâb collaborating to impart the same discourse: the removal of the self and its desire(s) through refinement of conduct and behaviour; indeed serving as the ultimate demonstration that this has been achieved. Surprisingly, all this incorporates the sense of a way and a tradition that is felt as the heartbeat of Persian identity.

We will now begin to show how the vague myth-history of the Sufis took shape the way it did. In our own macrohistorical re-visioning we will elaborate on the cumulation of Persian resilient trends and esoteric currents of spirituality out from Later Antiquity and into the Islamic period. All this will better explain, as we shall see in the very last chapter, the special undercurrents to be found in Persianate Sufism, which contains within itself the footprints of a repressed series of indigenous Iranian impetuses.

CHAPTER 6

FROM LATE ANTIQUITY TO NEO-MAZDAKISM

dar azal partoveh hossnat ze tajalla dam zad
'eshq peydah shod o aatash be hameh 'aalam zad

In the beginning a ray of your beauty appeared with a breath
Love was found and set aflame the entire world![1]

MAZDAK: A MISSING LINK?

Between the eclipse of Mithraism, in the fourth century, until the coming of Islam to Persia, in the seventh, there appears the almost forgotten figure of Mazdak (d. 524/8), a socio-religious revolutionary active in Zoroastrian Sasanian Iran, whose radical re-thinking of religion and state held a short but influential patronage across Iran and into Arabia. The Zoroastrian clergy moved swiftly to end the widespread influence of his teachings, securing his death – as they had Mani's about three centuries before him, but on the whole they failed to eradicate the immortal impress of its ideals. Mazdak taught an unorthodox doctrine which was incredibly misconstrued by the *mobeds*, a deliberate misunderstanding carried over into the Islamic establishment that adopted a comparable view of Mazdak[ism] as heresy. Since these first accusations Mazdak and his followers have been negatively portrayed as excessively libertine – as sharing women along with their worldly possessions – sadly inflating what should perhaps be considered as probably the first "communistic" society in history.

One important question concerns the degree of Mazdak's connection, if any, to the "Khosravan Wisdom" or *hekmat-e khosravani* tradition as perceived by the Nematollahiya. Mazdak is certainly an important, but

---

1. Hafez, *Diwan*, 206.

overlooked, socio-political figure in the history of Iran, whose egalitarian constitution, resonating in Persia and as far as Mecca, may have had significant impact on the development of early Islam. Support for this view comes from dispersed sources, yet there is scant evidence that suggests the Arabs of the Hijaz were ever so briefly converted to the new movement, Mazdakism, by Mazdak's royal patron, Kavad. "Convert" is probably a strong word, if not an inaccurate way to describe the events that may have transpired, because Mazdak's movement was likely not seen as a new religion so much as a social movement or philosophy that worked within Zoroastrianism and Persian politics. Such a political shift may have been significant to building the basis of Mohammed's own Islamic social reform, at least initially, in Mecca. There are striking similarities. The effects of Mazdak's basic constitutional and humanitarian projects, characterized by the equal status of women, property and wealth, is on a par with that which motivated the early Islamic community, and gave hope to Iranian exiles in the Arab world through its long-term goal of overthrowing the incumbent Sasanian regime. A related but trickier figure to place in the history of Islam is Salman the Persian (Salman-e Farsi). This quietly grand personality may be part of a secret discourse pertaining to the perceived trajectory of Khosravan wisdom. Or so will run our argument to confirm the ongoing impetus of Persia's resilient wisdom tradition.

The link between Mazdak, Salman and Mohammed requires a step back from an orthodox historical approach, demanding a rethinking of available material in an "outside-the-box" fashion. The connections can be built nonetheless on substantial historical evidence, albeit not always conforming to strict chronology and of a somewhat controversial nature. To delve briefly into Salman in a preliminary way, traditionally Salman is placed as first meeting the Prophet in the Medinan period (622–630); but unorthodox traditions claim Salman was present even during Mohammed's first revelation, acting indeed as the emissary to God. The boldest reference to this link in our time comes from Salman Rushdie's best-selling novel *The Satanic Verses*,[2] an anti-Islamic *tour de force* that makes the angel Gabriel and Salman the Persian look to be the same person – a not wholly unanticipated view, for the limited material available on the subject has already encouraged this highly provocative and unorthodox idea. Any critical analysis of Rushdie is not necessary here, but it is well within our purpose to investigate the alleged identification via traditional and primary Islamic sources, namely the Hadith of Gabriel and certain other allusions to Salman's role which are made from the Qur'an (16:102–3), all of which will concern us later. In addition there are non-traditional sources, for instance among the Ahl-e Haqq (Yaresan)[3] and Alawites (or Nusayris) that

---

2. S. Rushdie, *Satanic Verses* (New York, 1997).

3. "Ahl-e Haqq" and "Yaresan" both represent the names of an important southern Kurdish community; R. Hamzehee, *The Yaresan: A Sociological, Historical and Religio-Historical Study of a Kurdish Community* (Berlin, 1990), 1.

will be looked at in this chapter, giving background to our detailed assessment of the Salman/Mohammed relationship. Mazdak's connection with Islam is initially based on the general and alleged influence that his principles had on the Arabian Peninsula, in particular in Najd and the Hijaz, but more importantly there is the tantalizing consideration of the mediation of Salman the Persian as a disciple of Mazdakite principles.

Independent of materials concerning Mazdak and Salman, yet requiring our scrutiny, are indications of the Mazdakites' later absorption into reactionary Shi'ite groups. Splinter movements of Shi'ism, such as Khoramiyya, can be interpreted as expressions of *neo*-Mazdakite endeavours in post-Sasanid times, for, in the "venture of Islam" Iranian and Arabian components came together in reaction to Moslem rule; they were what we will argue social and ideological reactions of negative reciprocity or of "payback",[4] grounded in experiences of social-economical and religious oppression.[5] The success of the Islamic [egalitarian] ideal was to be a short-lived victory, as the Arab/ Persian aristocratic element quickly re-established itself through and within the new religion: first by the Umayyads and later by the Abbassid cohort with Iran's privileged class. Thus a tit-for-tat conflict against "new establishments" issued initially from the egalitarian Kharijite resistance and was carried on when this gradually evolved into the reactive neo-Mazdakite movement, which directed its militant and reactionary ideologies through broader *ghulat* and *batini* Shi'a channels. With the eventual standardization of the orthodox Imami and Ismaiili Shi'ite branches, such reactionaries were forced further out of the conventional boundaries of Islam, and are recognized today as the Druzes, Nusayris (associated with the Syrian Alawis), Ahl-e Haqq, the Alevis of Turkish Kurdistan, and intriguingly the Yazidis mainly of northern Iranian/Iraqi Kurdistan. These groups, going under the mere outward garb of Islam, have successfully adapted arcane and indigenous religious doctrines to Islam while retaining their anti-Arab, and in certain cases anti-Moslem, agenda.[6] Our focus now shifts slightly to the northwest of Iran, and specifically to the areas of Azerbaijan and Kurdistan. As Greater Khorasan resisted Arabization in the northeast, the Arabs met further resilience in the northwest, with its eclectic and syncretic heritage more typical of "northwestern Greater Iran" going back to the Medes. Since Reza Hamzehee and Farhad Daftary have previously contributed significantly to the social and typological

---

4. See G. W. Trompf, *Payback: The Logic of Retribution in Melanesian Religions* (Cambridge, 1994), Prelim., for methodological orientation; cf. M. G. S. Hodgson, *Venture of Islam: Conscience and History In a World Civilization* (Chicago, 1974), for previous quotation.

5. For methodological clues as to how all these movements might be related sociologically, start with E. J. Hobsbawm, *Primitive Rebels: Studies in Archaic Forms of Social Movement in the 19th and 20th Centuries* (Manchester, 1959).

6. Y. Stoyanov, "Islamic and Christian Heterodox Water Cosmogonies from the Ottoman Period – Parallels and Contrasts", *Bulletin of the School of Oriental and African Studies* 64(1) (2001), 19–33.

study of reactionary movements in Iran, our work mainly concerns the role of these movements in the recurrence of key concepts and structures of thought detected right through Persia's obscured macrohistory.

There has been a long-term affair between the Persian and Arab worlds. These two worlds become increasingly entangled from the sixth century onwards, producing both positive and negative effects upon each other's socio-political climate and religious facets. For example, the success of the Islamic conquest of Iran was as much owing to the Iranian problematic components involved as it was to the Arabs' repulsion of the prevailing Iranian imperial dogmatism. Many Persians welcomed the Arabo-Islamic influence as a promise of salvation from oppressive political forces – and there is a strange *déjà vu* of these hopes with the 1979 Islamic Revolution that put an end to Iranian monarchy. In fact, the Iranians have always been staunch defenders of the "just" and "true" as inherited values from their beloved figurehead, Zarathushtra, and carried on by the virtue of the monarchs' subservience to the divine *farr* ("grace") – even if this archetype was to be transformed, in the years to come, with the call of a prophet from the far-flung land of the Arabs. Thus, the Iranians would go to extreme lengths to preserve the value of justice and liberty not only in the face of the Arab aristocracy – whose Moslem piety looked like a pretence – as they have always done against their own Persian overlords and religious elite of the Zoroastrian creed. Let us also note that, ultimately, a singlehanded attempt at the expulsion of Arab dominance in Iran failed, and the Persians were indebted to the Shi'ite (and other Moslem sectarian) innovations as compensation. In short, Iranian Islam, and especially Sufism, is a testament to this special ongoing legacy. Thus, here we wish to document the subtlety within materials concerning the Persian and Arab intrigue from the Mazdakites until after the Islamic conquest. In doing this, however, we will make what may seem a strange move: we will take large strides over Persian religious history and then come back to look at the cases of Mazdak and Salman in serious detail.

THE DOCTRINE OF THE AHL-E HAQQ, ALEVIS AND YAZIDIS

Though little is known of the origins of Kurdish religion, a common observance of their beliefs and practices reflects a unique syncretism, with a prevalent "Iranian" theme and a detectable presence of Mazdaeism and Mithraic elements.[7] The Kurds resisted the Islamic occupation of the sixth century with force, and subsequently played a central part in the formation of rebel movements

---

7. Cf. R. Hamzehee, "Mazdaism and Sufism and the Kurdish Religions", in Philippe Gignoux (ed.), "Recurrent Patterns in Iranian Religion: From Mazdaism to Sufism", in the special 1991 edition of *Studia Iranica* (number 11), Proceedings of the Round Table held in Bamberg, 30 September–4 October 1991, Paris, 1992.

and the activities of reactionary, protestative trends. With the eventual acceptance of Islam, prominent ideological currents were forced deeper into the
subconscious of Kurdish religion. Mehrdad R. Izady's (Kurdish) macrohistory
explains the course of this repressed religiosity as primarily taking form in the
Yazdani tradition ("the Cult of Angels"), based on a belief in and reverence for
"seven" cosmogonic components (angels) and accompanying theophanies.[8] It
also meant that within these traditions a distinctly Kurdish "cosmo-history"
or a "Gnostic myth-history"[9] was preserved, undermining the normative
stream of Islamic theology and historiography. In the case of the Ahl-e Haqq,
this involved a special reverence for the figure of Salman the Persian, who is
included among the list of prominent avatars associated with *Jibraiil* (Gabriel
and his manifestations).[10] This approach was more openly espoused and elaborated by the Nusayris, or Alawis (the name change made formally in 1924 to
"rid the Nusayris of their reputation for being heretics or even pagans" and
demonstrate that they were indeed true Twelver Shi'ites).[11] They hold a tripartite configuration of the divinity in that "the supreme God" who is "the
Essence" (*ma'na*), is always in every age accompanied by "two subordinate
hypostases", known as "the Name" (*ism*) and also "the Veil" (*hijab*) and "the
Gate" (*bab*).[12] In the Islamic period this conformed to a trio consisting of Ali
ibn Abi Talib (*ma'na*), Mohammed (*ism*) and Salman (*bab*). By the ninth century the *ghulat* produced *batini* systems of symbolic interpretation of the
Qur'an, which differed in asserting the supremacy of one or another principle,
as embodied in religious offices and persons. Thus, the Mimiyya exalted the
mim (*Mohammed*), as the truth and outer reality; the Ayniyya exalted the *ayn*
(Ali), the principle of inward meaning; and a third principle was also adhered
to by *sin* (Salman the Persian), as the Gate through whom men came to the
truth.[13] To place the Ahl-e Haqq, Nusayris and Yazidis into perspective, the
alleged reverence for Ali by the first two groups seems to be the checkpoint
with regard to their correlation with Islam. Paradoxically, though, their special
worship of him betrays an implicit act of defiance, wherein "Ali" becomes a
representative of a "hidden" and or "repressed" spiritual theme. A closer look

8. M. R. Izady, *Kurds: A Concise Handbook* (Cambridge, MA, 1992), ch. 5; V. Minorsky, "Ahl-i
Haqq", in *EIs*, vol. 3; and Hamzehee, "Mazdaism and Sufism and the Kurdish Religions";
P. H. Kreyenbroek, "Yazidi, Yazidiyya" in *EIs*; H. Halm, "Nusayriyya", in *EIs*, vol. 8.

9. G. W. Trompf, "Macrohistory and Acculturation: Between Myth and History in Modern
Melanesian and Ancient Gnosticism", *Comparative Studies in Society and History* 31(4)
(1989), 638–48; *idem*, "Macrohistory", 701–17.

10. Minorsky, "Ahl-i Haqq", table; see also table in C. J. Edmonds, "The Beliefs and Practices of
the Ahl-i Haqq of Iraq", *IRAN: Journal of the British Institute of Persian Studies* 7 (1969), 94.

11. H. Halm, "Nusayriyya; 4: History", in *EIs*.

12. Cf. *ibid.* and see also F. M. Pareja, "Les sectes de l'Islam", in Pareja *et al.*, *Islamologie* (Beirut,
1964), 844–5.

13. Cf. M. G. S. Hodgson, "Ghulat (singular, Ghali)", in *EIs*, vol. 2; cf. also Pereja, "Les sects de
l'Islam", 814–58.

at the doctrines of these traditions further yields that Ali is either totally over-shadowed by other figures, as for example, in the Ahl-e Haqq tradition (by other avatars),[14] while in the Nusayri tradition he is raised to such extreme heights that any recognition of him (as an historical figure) is outwardly inconsequential. Among the Yazidis, in contrast, Ali is by and large non-exist-ent, but this only confirms our point that, of the three movements, the Yazidis are the least assimilated into the Arab-Islamic garb and the most explicit living tradition among pre-Islamic religion(s) of the Old Persian domains.

A fundamental dogma common to all three, however, if more specific to the Ahl-e Haqq, is the belief in the successive manifestations of the Divinity, in accordance with the number seven.[15] This has significant correspondence with the seven Mithraic Stages of Initiation and the seven Amesha Spentas of the Mazdean theology, as already covered in detail in the previous chapter. More importantly, all this relates to our Sufi myth-history regarding the inner wis-dom and gnosis of self as connected to *hikmat-i khosrawani*. The Ahl-e Haqq compare the manifestations of God to "garments put on by the Divinity", a process that is summed up by the maxim "to become incarnate", which means "to come (to dwell) in a garment" (*libas, djama* or [Turk.] *dun*).[16] This is an idea that immediately reflects back to the *fall* of Adam, held by Kabbalists as the "clothing of flesh" of Adam and Eve, while Mandaeans discuss the *Lbuša* ("Sacred Garment"); such examples find important parallel in Christian the-ology (i.e. God made incarnate, Christ made flesh, etc.).[17] But in the deeper consciousness of Kurdish religion is the way that Ahura Mazda made him-self known to Zarathushtra, that is, through the manifestation of the "Loving Mind" (Vohu Mana), and how the "seven bodies" (or "garments", i.e. the *hep-tads*) of the Divine came to accompany Zarathushtra. For in the Yaresan "Stories of Creation", the pre-eternal form of God, "Ya", creates the first angel, Gabriel, out of Himself, after which He proceeds to create the other six in a similar fashion, hence forming the *haftan*, literally "seven-bodies".[18] Holding the Original Principle of the "Essence", the Yaresan give the designation *Haqq* (a commonly shared Sufi reference) to their "Supreme God", which is seen as a

---

14. Minorsky, "Ahl-i Haqq", 260a.
15. This may be taken as calling on an Ismaili element, which cannot be pursued in this work. Cf. F. Daftary, *The Ismailis: Their History and Doctrines* (Cambridge, 2007).
16. *Ibid.*, with Hamzehee, *The Yaresan*, 90.
17. For background, B. Layton (ed.), *The Gnostic Scriptures* (New York, 1995), 18 (ancient Gnostic ideas of flesh as "garment"); G. D. Ginsburg, *Kabbalah: Its Doctrines, Development and Literature* (Whitefish, MT, 2003), 112; B. Nasoraia & G. Trompf, "Mandaean Macrohistory", *ARAM* 22 (2010–11), 398–412; J. N. D. Kelly, *Early Christian Doctrines* (London, 1960), esp. 327–30.
18. Michael (from His breath), Esrafil (taken out of His mouth), Ezrail (created from His anger), Ruchiyar and Aywat (created from the light of His eyes [right and left, respectively]), and Marmuz (of feminine gender was created out of His sweat). Cf. Hamzehee, *The Yaresan*, 70–71.

deeper Truth vouchsafed to their keeping alone. The term *haqq*, far more than the Arabic, refers to an ultimate sense of "Truth", "Life", "Light" "Radiance", by implication the "Source" of creative intelligence.[19] This is especially important in light of the prominence of Mazda (as the Supreme Being) over the Persian pantheon. A further etymological connection should be noted (though it is by no means conclusive) with the derivation of the term *Yazid* as being from *ez da* ("I [i.e. God] created") and thus from *Maz[-]da*. There is evidence to suggest the connection, since there is an essential conceptual link between *yaz*[20] ("to worship", "to adore") and *maz*[21] ("great", "high", "lofty"). Again, the notion of "Yuzen" (the Holy Angels) and "Mazda" (the Supreme Being) forming one essential theo-cosmic compound is reflected in the cosmogony of the Yazidis. By extension, we may infer that the etymological correlation of *Yuzem*[22], *Mazda*[23], *mazoi*[24] and *Magai*, especially when the phrase *mazoi Magai* (Yas. 46. 14) is taken to infer the "brotherhood" or "secret society" of Zardusht,[25] corresponds to the nature of the communal rites of worship practised by all the socio-cultural derivatives of the Kurdish traditions. The continuous theme stressed is that of community rather than the individual,[26] put in a way that reflects the long-prevenient Zarathushtrian idea of community, unity and divine grace. The emphasis is transmitted in Cyrus's political parity,[27] in Mazdakite social egalitarianism and of course with the Islamic *umma*.[28] Hamzehee also tells us of the important "egalitarian tendencies" of the Yaresan (i.e. Ahl-e Haqq) tradition.[29]

The Ahle-e Haqq hold that, upon each appearance, the Divinity is accompanied with a number of Angels (*yaran*), usually also seven.[30] The formal initiator of the Ahl-e Haqq is held by all branches of the sect to be Sultan Ishaq (Sohak),[31] who is also the fourth Divine manifestation, the first three theophanies

---

19. The Avestan root *haithya* openly corresponds with *al-Hayy* (Arabic), *ad-Haii* (Mandaic). Cf. G. W. Trompf & B. Nasoraia, "Reflecting on the Rivers Scroll", *ARAM* (2010–11), 61–86.
20. Cf. Taraporewala, *Divine Songs*, 1023.
21. Cf. *ibid.*, 1015.
22. The plural applies to the Supreme Being and the Amesha Spenta; *ibid.*, 87.
23. As already noted, Highest Wisdom, Collective Mind.
24. Translated as "great", taking it as an adjective to *Magai*. Cf. *ibid.*, 87.
25. *Ibid.*
26. For a detailed record of the Yaresan community see Hamzehee, *The Yaresan*, ch. 7.
27. See "The Cyrus Cylinder" in *Ancient Near Eastern Texts relating to the Old Testament* (ed. J. E. Pritchard) (Princeton, 1958), 315b–16b.
28. Note the reference "Kakai" (brother[hood]) as the Ahl-i Haqq are generally called in Iraq. Cf. Edmonds, "The Beliefs and Practices of the Ahl-i Haqq of Iraq", 89.
29. Hamzehee, *The Yaresan*, 233.
30. For variations cf. Minorsky, "Ahl-i Haqq", 260b, and Edmonds, "The Beliefs and Practices of the Ahl-i Haqq in Iraq", 89; and for possible background the Biblical Lk. 10:1 and 17; cf. Num. 11:25.
31. The dates are not accurate; perhaps lived sometime from the second half of the fourteenth century to the first half of the fifteenth century; cf. Hamzehee, *The Yaresan*, 57–8.

being *khawandagar* (the creator), Ali and Salman.[32] The belief in this reincarnation of the theophanies is further elaborated by the parallel idea of human metempsychosis.[33] Minorsky quotes the phrase "Men! Do not fear the punishment of death! The death of a man is like the dive which the duck makes," in which case death becomes a necessary component for perfection and purification and by no means an indication of a finite end. The spirit is clothed in the garments of this world from birth, but the precise aim is to shed and become free of these upon its ultimate celestial return to the source. In fact, the world is seen as a place of striving and testing of the spirit, this being also the purpose behind the self-manifestations of the essence of God. Both the essence of God and the spirit of individuals are said to appear "one thousand and one times", the latter in order to become perfected, through the trials of the created world, the former for the assurance and guidance of the spirits.[34] While the line drawn between a literal "reincarnation" and a figurative one becomes blurred at times, the idea remains transparent enough that human beings must endure the trials of this world – through which they receive the reward of their actions. Thus every embodied spirit, regardless of social or religious affiliation, is accountable for its actions in this world. It is strongly held, however, that the prospect of purification is limited to the preconceived *nature* of beings: humanity is divided into two classes, each predisposed to the nature of its psycho-spiritual and physiological construct.[35]

This sense of determinism is a recurrent and concrete theme relayed from the *Gathas* to the Qur'an, and is reinforced by Gnosticism. Although resonating strongly in the Ahl-e Haqq, where a Gnostic "spiritual caste system" manifests itself, this spiritual dichotomy is muted in more major traditions and can always be overpowered by the determination of intent received from the initial act of repentance renewing the agent and placing him/her on the path toward divine purification.[36] It can be seen in the traditional account of Zararthushtra's revelation, for instance, where his purification in the water led to his vision of Vohu Mana. This follows in Mohammed's instruction in purification (*wuzu* or ritual ablution) before the Moslem ritual of prayer (*namaz*), five times daily. In Sufism, of course, this purifying takes a far more abstract and spiritual form, as illustrated in the following remark by a Sufi poet: "At each step a thousand bonds appear, thus a swift traveller is required, able to brake bonds."[37] Certainly, in a Jobian fashion, the bonds of "suffering" can be taken as a sign of God's favour, but the Sufi concept is conveyed by the para-Kabbalist

---

32. Minorsky, "Ahl-i Haqq"; Hamzehee, *The Yaresan*, 90.
33. Minorsky, "Ahl-i Haqq"; discussed at length by Hamzehee, *The Yaresan*, 128–33.
34. Edmonds, "The Beliefs and Practices of the Ahl-i Haqq of Iraq", 90.
35. A distinction is made between those originally created out of "yellow clay" (*zarda-gil*), the good, and those out of "black earth" (*siyah khak*), the evil. Cf. Minorsky, "Ahl-i Haqq", 261a.
36. Yas. 30.3; surah 24:35; see also the New Testament parable of the seed, Matt. 13:24–30.
37. J. Nurbakhsh, *The Path: Sufi Practices* (London, 2003), 110.

teaching of *resistance* whereby one becomes further illuminated through the act of "resisting" the impulses.[38] Rumi also plays on this theme throughout his poetry – it is (a prevalent Sufi theme) – and writes:

> O Brother stand the pain; Escape the poison of your impulses. The sky will bow to your beauty, if you do. Learn to light the candle. Rise with the sun. Turn away from the cave of your sleeping. That way a thorn expands to a rose. A particular glows with the universal.[39]

With the Ahl-e Haqq, correspondingly, the more "the good" go through the "world of garments and the more they suffer, the more they approach God and the more their luminous state increases [while the 'dark ones' shall never see the Sun]".[40]
In both the cases of the Ahl-e Haqq and the Yazidis, there is little mention of individual prayer; in fact, a peculiar passing over of such an important matter has something in common with Mazdakite practice (as will be shown below) in that prayer is usually regarded as a personal matter and to be done in private.[41] Now, the absence of a ritualistic component is also very distinctive of the "Khorasanian" and "Bayazidian" Sufism of Iran (also discussed later), and this apparently keeps up the Old Persian style of a spiritual chivalry setting right by action rather than ritual. Service through suffering is mentioned as part of the sacred rites of Kurdish religion, fittingly explained in the Sufi verse, "Unless you burnst, thou canst not give off the smell of incense."[42] In practice, the Ahli Haqq, Yazidis and Alevis mainly correspond with Sufi traditions of "gatherings" (*jam"*), "remembrance" (*zekr*) and "service" (*khedmat*), overseen by the *Pir* or "spiritual [and communal] leader".[43] The third of these rites for the Ahl-e Haqq is given a special place to the extent that garments are shed by those who *serve*, and those who are in service are in harmony with God, and for them worldly suffering and the cycle of dying and coming to life (1001 times) is made short and easy.[44] In this regard, the early father of Persian Sufism, Bayazid-e Bistami, once remarked, "I sought to polish the

---

38. On "resistance", see Y. Berg, *The Power of Kabbalah* (Kent, 2003), 57. Here the Kabbalist cosmology is explained as an act of defiance in resisting compliance with the innate desire to "receive" what the Jewish tradition describes as the "bread of shame".
39. Adaptation of Rumi's charming story of "the man from Qazvin". Cf. *MJR* 1, 3002–8, vol. 2, 163.
40. Minorsky, "Ahl-i Haqq", 261a.
41. Cf. Kreyenbroek, "Yazidi, Yazidiyya". Note also the admonition of Jesus in Matt. 5:5-8 on prayer, and good deeds.
42. M. Valiuddin, *Contemplative Disciplines in Sufism* (London, 1980), 1.
43. On the Yaresan rituals cf. Minorsky, "Ahl-i Haqq", and Hamzehee, *The Yaresan*, ch. 6.
44. Minorsky "Ahl-i Haqq"; Edmonds, "The Beliefs and Practices of the Ahl-i Haqq of Iraq", 90–91.

mirror [of my soul] with all acts of obedience and servitude."[45] The apparent doctrinal opposition – between a worldly renewal and an eternal one and thus between the Nematollahi view and that of the Ahl-e Haqq – may be resolved by recalling Kharaqani's restatement of the contradiction as superficial: "There are twenty four hours in a day. I die a thousand times an hour, and I cannot explain the other twenty three hours."[46] In any case, "service" holds a profound centrality in the esoteric realm of Persian and Kurdish spirituality, for instance where the Yaresan saint, Baba Taher of Hamedan (d. 1019?) is quoted as saying: "He who is controlled by the *nafs* must serve it; he who controls the *nafs* serves others."[47] As "love" and "friendship" are key components of mystical intimacy with the divine, the Ahl-e Haqq make particular mention of the Day of Reckoning when "The Lord of Time" shall come "to accomplish the Desires of the Friends". Essentially and fundamentally, the sect of the "Haqqiqat" is a religion of universal brotherhood and love, whereby to harm even the lowliest creature is a sin.[48]

Indispensable features of the so-called Yazdani tradition, as manifest in the Ahl-e Haqq, Yazidis and Alevis, are the communal assemblies and the offerings and sacrifices that take place ceremonially. These keep up an important relationship with older Iranian ideas behind such festivals as *Mehregan* and are expressed within Zarathushtrian and Mithraist doctrines, indeed Sufi ones to come. The entire continuity is above all maintained through the metaphor of sacrifice. The metaphoric correlation drawn by Rumi in the *Mathnawi* springs to mind: with regard to the buffalo or (male) oxen, "He [God] is the Feast of the Sacrifice, and the lover is the buffalo (for slaughter)."[49] In the Ahl-e Haqq ceremony of *nadhr wa-niyaz* two forms of offerings are made: "raw offerings" (usually including animals of the male sex) and "cooked or prepared victuals" that distinguish between "bloody" and "bloodless" sacrifice.[50] Picking up on the residual power of this kind of understanding, Rumi says that "death is a gate to perfection" – to freedom (from the bonds of material nature) and a pilgrimage – towards the ultimate destination, the Divine source (of pure Spirit).[51] In parallel and thus subtly invoked by the Sufi poet, the Old Iranian festival of *Mehregan* was seen as a sign of resurrection and an end, as "that which grows reaches its perfection".[52] In foregoing the council of reason, furthermore, Rumi

---

45. A. J. Arberry, "Anecdotes of Bayazid", in his *Muslim Saints*, 113.
46. Attar, *Tadhkirat al-Awliya* (ed. J. Salmasi-zadeh) (Tehran, 1381/2003), 690.
47. Baba Taher Oriyan Hamadani, *Sharh-e ahwal wa athar wa do-baitiha-ye Baba Taher*, including *Shahr wa tarjoma-ye kalamat-e qesar*, ascribed to Aino'l-Qodhat Hamadani (ed. J. Maqsud) (Tehran, 1975), cited in Nurbakhsh, *The Psychology of Sufism*, 39.
48. Edmonds, "The Beliefs and Practices of the Ahl-i Haqq of Iraq", 91.
49. *MJR*, 3895, vol. 4, 218.
50. Minorsky, "Ahl-i Haqq", 261b.
51. Soroush, Rumi Lectures.
52. Abu Raihan al-Biruni, *al-Athar al-baqiya* (ed. E. Sachau) (Leipzig, 1876), trans. by Sachau as *The Chronology of Ancient Nations* (London, 1879), 223; Boyce, "Iranian Festivals", 802.

explains through the words of the lover that "My bonds are more grievous than thy advice: thy doctor (who taught thee) was not acquainted with love,"[53] so getting underneath the ritual feast of sacrifice from a profound standpoint.

"Death" is then seen as a symbolic sacrifice of the "lovers" for the "beloved" to produce Sufi imagery. The pilgrimage (*hajj*) and the sacrifice (*ghorbani*) are idealized in a symbolic journey to the House of God (the internal Kaba), in other words the heart, whereupon the soul (*nafs*) is offered for the aim of perfection (through death) for the purpose of becoming more (spirit).[54] The precise designation of making this sacrifice is of course "to make sacred" or "to make [yourself] holy" through careful preparation.[55] A powerful intention behind this symbolic interpretation is that which corresponds with the general rule of normative sacrifice, that is, "the greater the sacrifice the greater the reward". In corroboration with the Mithraic tauroctony, the initiate must first capture the (great) bull to bring it to the Cave for the (great) sacrifice. And so Rumi makes it clear that the sacrifice is in fact the lover offered to the beloved. Thus, the entire purpose of Mithraic and Sufi soteriology is brought to bear in the metaphoric statement that, in order to be more valuable to the Beloved, so too the lover must have "excellences and perfections", in the sense of spiritual maturity and knowledge by experience. "It is not good for the lover [moreover] to be bare."[56] The act of sacrifice is the realization of the desire for union, with its fulfilment indicating the final unification of the particular soul (intellect) with that of the Universal Soul (Intellect),[57] as is remarked on from one of the odes of the Chishtiyya Sufis:

> None but the elegant are slaughtered on the altar of love,
> The ill-tempered and weak natured are just let off.
> Do not escape being slain, if thou art a true lover,
> He who is not slaughtered is just dead meat.[58]

The central doctrines of reincarnation and metempsychosis in the Yazdani, in particular, the Ahl-e Haqq traditions, are best embodied in an insight of Sufism preserving and transforming them. This is eloquently summed up by Mir Hossein ibn Moiin Maibudhi: "In the Path of the Sufis one finds Divine Light, perpetual self-manifestation of God and the gnosis of the ultimate reality of all things phenomenal."[59]

---

53. Cf. *MJR* 3, 3831, vol. 4, 214.
54. Soroush, Rumi Lectures.
55. *Ibid.*
56. *Ibid.*
57. For the terms "Particular Intellect" and "Universal Intellect", see the article by J. Nurbakhsh, "Psycho-analysis and Sufism, Part 2", *Sufi* 6 (Summer 1990), 5–6.
58. Valiuddin, *Contemplative Disciplines in Sufism*, xxiv–xxv.
59. *Ibid.*, xix.

The intention behind observing the doctrines of the Yazdani tradition(s) has been to demonstrate the presence of Persian themes in Kurdish esoterica and myth-history. These in turn help throw light on the doctrinal subtleties in Persian Sufism and its connections with the ongoing build-up of northwestern Iran's rich spiritual heritage. After all, the Ahl-e Haqq is usually (though mistakenly) taken as a Sufi tradition, and one might be tempted to refer to it as "Kurdish Sufism" in its own right. Even so, the complexity of Kurdistani religions cannot allow us to make such a passing statement. More work is certainly required to unravel the deeper material of Kurdish spirituality and the vexing issues of its historicity, which must be pursued elsewhere. Importantly, Kurdish heritage had continued to show formidable resistance to Arab-Moslem domination and acculturation, by keeping to their ancient beliefs and practices in the improvised and highly secretive manner we find in the Yazdani currents of belief and ritual life.

This macrohistorical investigation of persisting Iranian cultural components has hitherto demonstrated those repressed under the Zoroastrian and Islamic establishments – movements from Mazdak through to the proto-Shi'a insurrections and *ghulat* to the neo-Mazdakite Khorramiyya. With the Arab conquest, the Persians reacted both intellectually and militarily on two significant (yet disparate) levels and with almost entirely opposite goals. The former included the *shuubiyya* and the latter primarily the *ghulat* (extremist Shi'a). The *shuubiyya* were primarily of the well-to-do class of Persians, while the *ghulat* generally consisted of the middle and lower classes. While Persia was conquered from without, the *shuubiyya* and *ghulat* battled for the soul of Iran from within. It is out of this highly volatile and interactive socio-religious setting that various shades of Sufism resulted, quite often expressing themselves through either or both of these group impetuses.

THE *SHUUBIYYA* AND "ANTI-ARAB" IDEOLOGY

The Persian *shuubiyya* were among the various trajectories of "Persian-ism" to be detected. They were directly rooted in an old-established tradition and they saw their primary task to be its preservation. The *shuubiyya* were the educated, the poets and secretaries in high office to the caliph. Although some parallels with the *ghulat* may be drawn, the two cannot be confused, as the *shuubiyya* were a strictly non-military "national" resistance. The latter's quest for a "rediscovered national consciousness" was not necessarily a threat to the Moslem empire;[60] rather, their concern was more a matter of the influence in order to secure, and to ensure, the empire's future direction. In any case, the

---

60. I. Goldziher, *Muhammedanische Studien* (Halle, 1888), vol. 1, 147–55 (English version: *Muslim Studies (Muhammedanische Studien)* (ed. S. M. Stern) (London, 1967), 98–118).

aim of the *shuubiyya* "was not to destroy the Islamic empire … but to remould its political and social institutions and values, which represented in their eyes the highest political wisdom."[61] There may not have been signficant contact between the *shuubiyya* and *ghulat*, but both groups held in common strong resilient motifs.[62] The *shuubiyya* were counted among professional civil servants of the "continuing Sasanid" administration, put in place by the Abbasids as promising clients. At first indifferent, they later became more aggressive towards their Arab overlords when the social-demographic developments in the former garrisons of Kufa and Basra began to undermine their privileged social status (*c*.850s).[63] In an era of demilitarization, expansion of trade relations and flourishing of cities, social status and differences between Arabs and non-Arabs were gradually beginning to decrease, and the *shuubiyya* were fiercely concerned with maintaining reputation, privileges and status by remaining faithful to Sasanid tradition.[64] They actually circulated a crude form of anti-Arabism among the educated by way of sardonic remarks about "the Arabs".[65] For example, it is said: the Arabs were a disgrace in terms of their warfare in comparison to the Sasanids and Byzantines, while the Arabian habit of gesticulating with a stick in hand while speaking, and other linguistic and non-linguistic habits of speech, merely exposed the emptiness of the Arabian claim to eloquence. The text goes on to say that their language revealed the Arabs for what they really were, a people of camel-drivers, while the Persians alone were capable of possessing proper *âdâb* (in eloquence, delicacy and good conduct). Moreover, the arts and sciences were products of Greek and Indian cultures, not the Arabian, and, lastly, the Arabs could only claim just four prophets as their own, namely, Hud, Salih, Ismail and Mohammed, confirming the pedigree of their line as descending from Ismail, the son of a slave concubine.[66] Needless to say the presence of such ethnic crudism can still be detected in Persian society. On the whole, the *shuubiyya* were responsible for the preservation of significant Persian texts, not to mention the administration of the Arab Moslem empire. Their influence among the educated affected a major flow of ideas throughout the history of Iran with such cynical sentiments being picked up casually by other groups, and also creeping into the *ghulat* and Sufi streams.

---

61. S. D. Goitein, *Studies in the Islamic History and Institutions* (Leiden, 1966), 66.

62. Cf. S. Enderwitz, "al-Shu'ubiyya", in *EIs*, vol. 9.

63. On the formal inception of the *shuubiyya*, H. A. R Gibb, *Studies on the Civilization of Islam* (New York, 1962), 62–6; cf. Enderwitz, "al-Shu'ubiyya".

64. *Ibid.*

65. Jahiz, *Kitab al-Bayan wa'l-tabyin* (ed. A. M. Harun) (Cairo, 1960); Ibn Qutayba, *Kitab al-Arab*, in *Rasa'il al-bulagha'* (ed. Kurd Ali) (Cairo, 1946), 344–77; Ibn Abd al-Rabbih, *'Iqd al-Farid* (ed. A. Amin) (Cairo, 1949–53), vol. 3, 408–20; Enderwitz, "al-Shu'ubiyya".

66. I.e. through a prejudiced reading of the Hebrew Genesis (16:3; 21:10), not of the *Qur'an* (2:133).

THE *GHULAT* AND THE NEO-MAZDAKITE MOVEMENTS

The *ghulat* cannot be explained without referring to the movement initiated by Mazdak. Mazdak's movement, perhaps the first communist one in history, was a reaction against the social stranglehold of Persia by the Sasanian-Zoroastrian establishment. Mazdakism is in fact a Zoroastrian heresy. It is highly egalitarian in its influence and advocating the commonality of land, property and women, even democratizing religion itself so that the effects of the Old Indo-European caste arrangements – court, priests – no longer had force. It advocated "great simplicity of dress" and sometimes abstention of virtually all animal food,[67] and it became a movement of the needy and the common people in the ancient Persian history of "the lowly".[68] And in this way, subtle parallels can be drawn between Mazdakism and the Shi'ite cause, since Shi'ism traditionally represents the downtrodden. If anything, Mazdak's ideology may very well have been an early answer to social injustice felt by the people, and likely laid the principal grounds for the emergence of Shi'ism in Iran. This correlation will also explain the distinct affinity that the Iranian psyche has with Shi'ism. Indeed, Mazdakism, as an "in-house" dilemma, was important for the weakening of Zoroastrian Persia before the coming of Islam. From what is known about Mazdakite books, most having been destroyed, the transition to neo-Mazdakism is detectable, which then makes obvious the Shi'ite connection.[69]

Early Shi'a and the rise of the ghulat

To understand the importance and eventual impact of Mazdak's doctrine it is imperative to appreciate the complex background of the early Shi'a movements in Kufa in the eighth and ninth centuries. The focus will be the *ghulat*, the extremist Shi'a and the *batini* movements. The aim is to draw out the connection between Mazdakism and Shi'ism in order to demonstrate the transition. As such, the neo-Mazdakite intrigue during the Abbasid era will be discussed.[70] There is certainly one very important aspect of early Shi'ite history that should not be confused with events associated with the *ghulat*. That is, the advent of the fourth Caliph, Ali Ibn Abi Talib, and his progeny, who never took part in *ghulat* activities. Likely, it is their memory that was invoked

---

67. For introduction, see S. G. W. Benjamin, *Persia* (London, 1888), 219 (quotation).
68. Left unmentioned in the communist writer C. O. Ward's *The Ancient Lowly: A History of the Ancient Working People from the Earliest Known Period to the Adoption of Christianity by Constantine* (New York, [1900] 1970), vol. 2, although this would have come at the very end of his history.
69. See Hamzehee, *Land of Revolutions*.
70. Cf. Daftary, *The Ismailis: Their History and Doctrines*, esp. 57.

by radicals to motivate revolutionary activism under the banner of the Imams. Furthermore, the ensuing Shi'ite tradtions, the Twelver, Sevener and Fourer branches of Imami, Ismaili and Zaydi Shi'ism, were formed in honour of the Imams, who held a special significance for the people. What is interesting is that the *ghulat* were primarily composed of originally non-Moslim religious elements that sought political and religious reformation using the Shi'ite cause. Traditionally the first *ghulat* is deemed Abd Allah ibn Saba, alleged founder of the Shi"a, also known as Ibn al-Sawda, Ibn Harb, Ibn Wahb, a Yammanite Jew, according to the Sunni, who converted to Islam. He was responsible for exalting Ali's religious position or the glorification of Ali's person. However, Ali rejected the claims of Ibn Saba and, if various traditions are right, even prosecuted and executed the figure.[71] It is clear that the idea of the divinity of Ali is a foreign fabrication, appearing for the first time with Ibn Saba in the form of a pseudo-Islamic Christology, in the way that the material on Mansour-e Hallaj may have been rehabilitated in Sufi consciousness,[72] whereby the death of Ali is even denied in some extremist Shi'a traditions. It is possible that *ghulat* thinkers frequented the circle of Mohammed ibn al-Hanafiyya, Mohammed Baqir, and Jafar al-Sadiq (even as late as the eleventh Imam Hasan al-Askari), but any formal relation is dubious.[73] There is no indication of *ghulat* involvement on behalf of any of these figures, who, like Ali, were only later appropriated into an ideology that originally conflicted with them. The *ghulat* are noted as including a wide range of peoples from pre-Islamic tribal Arab origins to the variety of *movali* of Christian, Jewish, Gnostic and Zoroastrian background,[74] with the greater portion of them comprised of dissident Iranians unhappy with Umayyad, and later Abbasid, rule.

In its first stages, Islam presented a fresh ideal to the foreign imagination, in particular in the form of a new social order uniting all believers (regardless of race or class) with equality. Such egalitarian attitudes were promoted initially, and technically remained in theory.[75] In practice another reality manifested itself: the Islamic empire revealed itself as an "Arab kingdom", administered under the Arab aristocratic rule of the Umayyads. This inevitably resulted in social and religious disparity with the new subjects of the empire, in other

---

71. Ali is said to have had him "or" his followers burned for declaring him (Ali) God, cf. *ibid.*
72. The parallel between Hallaj's martyrdom and that of Jesus is of note; cf. Arberry's trans. of "The Passion of Hallaj" in his *Muslim Saints*, 266–71. Also M. Milani, "Representations of Jesus in Islamic Mysticism: Defining the 'Sufi Jesus'", *Literature & Aesthetics* 21(2), 2012, 45–64.
73. The sources are generally clear on this point. Cf. F. Buhl, "Aliderners stilling til de shi'itiske bevaegelser under umajjaderne", in *Kongelige Danske Videnskarbernes Selskab*, Forhandiling, 5 (1910); cited in Hodgson, "Ghulat".
74. Hodson, "Ghulat".
75. F. Daftary, "Sectarian and National Movements in Iran, Khurasan and Transoxania during Umayyad and Early Abbasid Times", in *History of Civilizations of Central Asia* (eds. M. S. Asimov & C. E. Bosworth) (Paris), vol. 4, Part 1, 41–60.

words the Iranians, Central Asians and other non-Arab peoples, becoming *movali* (clients of an Arab lord or clan) by virtue of converting to Islam. The clash of ethnicity immediately surfaced as these *movali* now acquired an inferior status compared to the Arab Moslems. Even below these clients in social rank were the "People of the Book" (*ahl al-dhimma*), that is, non-converting Jews, Christians and Zoroastrians, all of whom paid special taxes exempt for Arab Moslems. Tensions between Arab rulers and their clients, in the newly conquered Islamic lands, was inevitable. But no place was more troublesome for the empire than the remote provinces of Khorasan and Transoxania, where the majority of Iranians were superficially Islamized.[76] Situated far from the caliphal centres of power in Syria and Iraq, the northeastern frontiers of Greater Iran proved the strongest nodes of resistance against the Arabs, avoiding conversion to Islam for even longer. As a result, different religious-political currents of thought and sectarian movements often stirred popular insurrections, these activities persisting in one form or another until the early Abbasid period and later in various pockets of important Iranian regions. The common trend among these groups was the express opposition to the established caliphate, many of whom promoted anti-Arab, sometimes anti-Islamic, sentiments originating in Zoroastrianism, Mazdakism and other Iranian traditions.[77]

For these reasons, Iranians lent strong support to the Alid cause and to Shi'ism. The Shia or the *shiatu Ali* ("followers of Ali" or "Ali's Party") were originally a unified and exclusively Arab faction opposed to the established caliphate.[78] As earlier mentioned, Ali himself never opposed the caliphal authority of his predecessors: Abu Bakr, Omar and Othman, yet the people rallied in his name and spread propaganda that Ali was the rightful, but politically sidelined, caliph. The major branches of the Shi'ites – Kaysaniyya, Imamiyya, Zaydiyya and Ismailiyya – had by the ninth century acquired communities of followers throughout Iran, while other sectarian groups engaged in armed revolts remained specific to Khorasan and Transoxania, as well as Azarbaijan. Effectively, the northeast and northwest of Iranian highlands proved difficult for the Arabization process of Iran. These latter sectarian groups were generally referred to as the Khoramiyya, who largely held syncretic doctrines that aimed to merge indigenous Iranian religious traditions with aspects of Islamic teachings. These were distinct from the Shia. The Khoramiyya amounted to a staunchly anti-Arab/Moslem "para-establishment", whose revolts were always supported by the peasantry due to consistent social-economic grievances. From the second half of the ninth century the weakening grip of the Abbasid caliphate on remote outposts allowed for new opportunities of a nationalistic bent. This phase saw the revitalization of Iranian culture and identity,

---

76. Daftary, "Sectarian and National Movements", 41.
77. *Ibid.*
78. *Ibid.*, 42.

beginning with the Saffarid dynasty (861–1003) but especially flourishing under the ids (900–999) and, much later, the Safavids (1501–1722).

The extremist Shia and Khorramiyya (neo-Mazdakite)

Granted, a study of the Khorramiyya in Khorasan and Transoxania during the Umayyad and Abbasid periods presents certain limitations when rendering their doctrine.[79] There is scant information on the sectarian and revolutionary activities, as little contemporary sources have survived. Information is mainly derived from Sunni and Shi'ite heresiographers, who were either more interested in defending the legitimacy of their own orthodox history while writing on some aspects of these sects, or else freely attributing extremist ideas to them as refutation.[80] Although there are common features found across extremist Shia movements and the Khorramiyya, the two are not to be confused, since the latter either rejected Islam or claimed it as part of their syncretism

The Kharijites

Of the non-Khorramiyya movements, Kharijism is considered the first schismatic movement in Islam that originated in Iraq in connection with the conflict between Ali (d. 661) and Mu'awiya (d. 680). The Kharijites established a separate Islamic community that emphatically upheld Islamic egalitarianism as central to its doctrinal position.[81] Recurrent motifs are found in the Qarmatian movement, likely "the revolutionary movement inspired by Shi'ite chiliasm and Mazdakite egalitarianism, which succeeded to establish a sovereign state", which appeared for the first time during Abbasid rule in 892, spread throughout Syria and Iran, and even established a republic in Bahrain that lasted for almost 150 years.[82] The first set of connections between Mazdakism and the Shia is pointed out by Reza Hamzehee: Mazdak was to introduce and formulate an "egalitarian ideology", and that in fact, "Egalitarianism, which is referred to as Mazdakism by the historians, was a goal value for [most of] the Iranian oppositional movements of this period."[83] The strong and clear presence of egalitarian sentiments among the Kharijites proved appealing to

---

79. Note, e.g., E. Yarshater on the problem of sources in his article "Mazdakism", in *CHI*, vol. 3(2), 993–5, and also W. Madelung's article "Khurramiyya or Khurramdiniyya", in *EIs*, vol. 5.

80. For early Sunni orthodox heresiographers, cf. al-Ash'ari (d. 935), al-Baghdadi (d. 1037) and Ibn Hazm (d. 1064). On early Shiite heresiographers, cf. al-Nawbakhti and al-Qummi.

81. Daftary, "Sectarian and National Movements", 43.

82. Hamzehee, *Land of Revolutions*, 76. The republic was founded by only one part of the Qarmatians led by Abu Sa'id of Janabeh and his son Abu Taher (d. 944). Cf. Hamzehee, *Land of Revolutions*, 75.

83. *Ibid.*, 71.

the Persian and other *movali*. The revolutionary movement of the Kharijites opposed both to the caliphates of the Umayyads and the Abbasids in succession, soon became a channel of expression for Iranian anti-Arab sentiment. The Iraqi Kharijites, seeking refuge from military pressure, gradually made Iran their stronghold, and firmly established themselves there for prolonged programmes of anti-caliphal activities. With the decline of the Kharijites, in the ninth century, they were scattered (securing their long-term following in eastern Arabia and among the Berbers of North Africa), and it was Shi'ism that produced the most lasting effect on Iran despite the official Sunni supremacy until the beginning of the sixteenth-century Safavid period.[84]

The Kaysaniyya

The particular brand of Shi'ism that was to be diluted with the indigenous ideology of Iranian and other *movali* first emerged under the revolt of al-Mokhtar in 685, on behalf of Ali's son Mohammed ibn al-Hanafiyya. Al Mokhtar was a revolutionary who allegedly sought to avenge the death of Hussein Ibn Ali at the battle of Karbala (680CE), and who named al-Hanafiyya as the rightful leader of Moslems. The millennial aspirations of the revolt naming al-Hanafiyya as Mahdi drew considerable support for the Shi'ite cause from the *movali*. In return, many ideas, especially those coming from early *ghulat* trends rooted in Irano-Zoroastrian and other non-Islamic traditions, were introduced into Shi'ite ideology with long-term effect on its doctrinal development. The etymology of al-Mokhtar's title "Kaysan" is unclear, but his followers were known as the Kaysaniyya.[85] With the death of al-Mokhtar and al-Hanafiyya, the sect divided into several groups, each proclaiming their own Imam and doctrine.[86]

The bulk of the Kaysaniyya acknowledged the eldest son of al-Hanafiyya, Abu Hashim Abd Allah, and were called the Hashimiyya. The Hashimiyya were the earliest Shi'ite group whose revolutionary teachings and stance was to spread throughout Iran, finding adherents among both *movali* and Arab settlers, especially in Khorasan. Next in line and significance among the Hanafiyya sects were the Harbiyya – they rose to prominence following the death of Abu Hashim in the mid-eighth century. The Harbiyya organized themselves under the Imamate of Abd Allah ibn Mu'awiya, not to be confused with Mu'awiya ibn Sufyan, and found their main support in western and southern parts of Iran.[87] Ibn Mu'awiya was an Alid rebel and Imam, and a descendent of Imam Jafar ibn Abi Talib, the elder brother of Ali ibn Abi Talib. The Harbiyya were later also recognized as *Janahiyya* who expounded

---

84. Daftary, "Sectarian and National Movements", 44.
85. Yarshater, "Mazdakism", 1002; W. Madelung, "Kaysaniyya", in *EIs*, vol. 4.
86. Daftary, "Sectarian and National Movements", 45.
87. *Ibid.*

many extremist gnostic ideas, attributed by heresiographers to the enigmatic figure of Abd Allah ibn al-Harb. Al-Harb is reckoned to have initiated key foreign doctrines into Kaysaniyya thought, such as the pre-existence of souls as shadows (*azilla*), the transmigration of souls (*tanasukh al-arwah*), and the macro-cyclical history of eras (*adwar*) and aeons (*akwar*).[88] Close connections between the Harbiyya-Janahiyya and the neo-Mazdakites of western Iran have been noted in scholarship, with the possibility of partial recruitments from the latter serving as the backbone of the Khorramiyya movement (discussed below) who are arguably "the continuation of the Mazdakite movement in the Islamic period".[89] The main faction of the Hashimiyya, however, gave allegiance to the Abbasid Mohammed ibn Ali ibn Abdullah ibn Abd al-Muttalib (the great-grandson of the Prophet's uncle al-Abbas), as Abu Hashim's successor to the Imamate. Thus it was through a long underground propagandist campaign (using *ghulat*-cum-Hashimiyya as support) that the Abbasids were able to overthrow the Umayyads. Yet the Hashimiyya-Abbasid merger came to an abrupt end with the Abbasids disclaiming their Shi'ite and extremist Kaysani (Hashimiyya-Abbasiyya) connections by the 750s. In all, the Kaysaniyya did not survive as a sect; their supporters dispersed and eventually disappeared altogether.

The Khorramiyya as a neo-Mazdakite insurrection

The remaining Shi'ite sectarian movements operating in Iran continued a close connection with the Khorramiyya in the ensuing years of the Abbasid caliphate, at which time the main forces of the rebellions were focused and united under highly influential leaders who were specifically associated with Mazdakite/Khoramiyya, that is, with neo-Mazdakite motivations. Thus notification is given below as to the significant links between the resurfacing Mazdakites and prominent Persian *ghulat* figures such as Bihafarid the Magian, Abu Moslem, Sindbad, Ostadhis, al-Moqanna and Babak-e Khorrami, who formed some of the most influential movements that were to threaten caliphal power. Indeed the insurrections under these noted figures were opposed by the once powerful priestly class of the Majus (i.e. Zoroastrians), who sought to regain control in the Islamic era, after having been subject to persecution. The complexity of the religio-political nature of the situation (*c*.760) is twofold in its trajectory. First were the sectarian movements fighting for a "pristine" Islam, an idea already introduced through Kharijite and Alid sentiment that dealt with the corruption of faith or rather the diversion from, and loss of, the original egalitarian and universal ideal that moved the early Islamic community of the Prophet. Second, the genesis of this struggle

---

88. *Ibid.*; for Persian theories cycling aeons more generally, see H. Corbin, "Le temps cyclique dans le Mazdéisne et dans l'Ismaélisme", *Eranos–Jahrbuch* 20 (1951), 149–217.

89. Hamzehee, *Land of Revolutions*, 71; Daftary, "Sectarian and National Movements", 5.

began in pre-Islamic Iran with Mazdak's egalitarian "social revolution" against the religio-political monopoly of the Sasanian Zoroastrian Majus. Mazdak's eventual execution did not, however, see the end of his movement, which always remained a potential threat. With the rise of neo-Mazdakite trends, the two trajectories quickly merged into one general pseudo-Moslem force empowered by anti-establishment motives. In the Khorramiyya, we can spot the continuation of the movement of Mazdak that during the late Umayyad period began to coalesce with various extremist factions of the Kaysaniyya.[90] The largest proportion of reactionary activity, in consequence, belonged to Khorramiyya/Mazdakiyya trends, consuming or influencing sectarian movements all through Islamic Iran. These groups either incorporated what seemed to be Zoroastrian aid or were antagonized by Zoroastrian clergy who, seeking to destroy Zoroastrian heresies, occasionally sided with state officials. The Khorramiyya/Mazdakiyya movement certainly took "formal shape" as a separatist movement during the Umayyad and Abbasid caliphates, and it had gained credence and pace from the earlier reform of Mazdakism (which, to remind readers, pitched itself against the Sasanid state and Zoroastrian religious establishment). The leap is a logical one, and is connected with the historical continuity we have been plotting all along.

Following the Majus-provoked Sasanian persecution of Mazdak and his followers, the movement remained underground until the rise of Islam. Mazdakite presence in virtually all parts of Iran during the early periods of Islam are well attested. Sources also provide detailed lists of their regional strongholds, particularly located in the north-western and north-eastern provinces. Specifically important are those at Jibal, Azarbaijan, Isfihan and Ahvaz, in Gurgan and Tabaristan, and in Khorasan and Sogdiana.[91] The defeated Sasanian state and the weakened power of the Zoroastrian "church" gave the Mazdakites new opportunity to act. Thus the history of Mazdakism has been formally divided into two segments: the pre-Islamic Mazdakites and the post-Islamic Khorramiyya, a neo-Mazdakite resurrection. The (neo-)Mazdakites, now professing Islam, laid the foundations for the *ghulat* factions and inspired their ideas.[92] The formal connection between Mazdakism and the *ghulat* is certainly more than conjecture.[93] An-Nadim records, "the Khurramis are two

---

90. Madelung, "Khurramiyya".
91. See Yarshater, "Mazdakism", 1001–02; Madelung, "Khurramiyya".
92. Yarshater, "Mazdakism", 1002; Madelung, "Khurramiyya".
93. Cf. Yarshater, "Mazdakism", 1004; G. H. Sadighi, *Les Mouvements Religieux Iraniens au II et au VI Siècle de L'hégire* (Paris, 1938), 187–97. Cf. also Baghdadi, *al-Farq bain al-Firaq* (Cairo, 1948), 160, and Ibn Hazm, *Kitab al-milal wa'l-nihal* (Cairo, 1899–1903), vol. 1, 34 (confirming this); Abol-Maali Mohammed, *Bayan al-addyan* (ed. H. Razi) (Tehran, 1964), 22 (tracing the origins of the Khorramis to pre-Islamic Iran); M. T. Bahar (ed.), *Mujmal al-tawarikh wa'l-qisas* (Tehran, 1939), 353 (explicitly tracing the Khorramis to Mazdak). On the Khorrami affinity with the Mazdakites and other sects, Mohammed Ibn Jafar Tabari, *Ta'rikh al-rusul wa'l-muluk* (ed. M. J. de Goeje) (Leiden, 1879–1901), vol. 2, 1588;

categories; the early Khurramis [that] had been originally Zoroastrian, then their doctrine was reformed ... The founder of their doctrine was Mazdak."[94] Primary sources attest to positive doctrinal association and identification, leaving little disparity between the *ghulat* and neo-Mazdakites of the Islamic period. In fact, the reference to the Khorramiyya or Khorramdiniyya in the Islamic sources describes them synonymously with the religious movement of Mazdak in the fifth century and the various Iranian (anti-Arab) sects, which developed out of it under the impact of certain extremist Shi'a (i.e. *ghulat*) doctrines. Although the Khorramiyya are sometimes mentioned separately besides the Mazdakiyya, Ibn an-Nadim, following Abol-Qasim al-Balkhi, is correct in recording that the name Khorramiyya (also "Muhammira") originally meant the movement of Mazdak in general, and not merely a branch of it.[95] Shahrestani summed up the chief doctrinal points of the extremist Shi'ite by stating that these extremists were called by different names in different places: in Esfehan, *Khorramiyya* and *Kodakiyya*; in Rayy, *Mazdakiyya* and *Sonbadiyya*; in Azarbaijan, *Dhaquliyya*; in some places *Muhammira*; and in Transoxiana, *Mubayidha*.[96] The fact that sources make mention of other origins for the *ghulat*, such as the Sabians, Harranians or Judaeo-Christian sects, does not dramatically affect the *ghulat*/Mazdakite connection. Rather, granting the possibility that other social influences on the sects may have contributed to the *ghulat*, the clearest example of *ghulat* activity is still to be seen in the case of continuing Mazdakism. Our main point, in any case, is that Mazdakite activity and belief, marking the persistence of distinctly Iranian ideas from "the archaic" to "the new" under the Islamic Iran, clearly manifested in the *ghulat* activities in Iranian lands.[97] Various sources make the frequent link of characteristic doctrines of the *ghulat*, which are identified as the belief in incarnation (*hulul*), of the divinity of the prophets or imams, reincarnation (*tanasukh*), the occultation (*ghaiba*) and return (*raj'a*) of an imam, and recourse to the inner meanings (*batin*) of the scriptures, with those of the Mazdakites.[98] The Zoroastrian and Manichaean basis of these beliefs is also manifest; indeed, such beliefs should be attributed to a generic band of "gnoseological" affiliation. Closer observation will be made below concerning

---

Hasan Ibn Musa Naubakhti, *Firaq al-Shi'a* (ed. H. Ritter) (Istanbul, 1931), 32–3; Abol-Hasan al-Masudi, *Kitab al-tanbih wa'l-ishraf* (ed. de Goeje), Bibliotheca Geographrum Arabicorum 8 (Leiden, 1894), 353; J. W. Fück, "Sechs Ergänzungen zu Sachaus Ausgabe von al-Birunis 'Chronologie orientalishcher Volker'", Documenta Islamica Inedita (Berlin, 1952), 79.

94. Ibn al-Nadim, *Fehrest*, 342, and *The Fihrist of al-Nadim* (trans. B. Dodge) (New York, 1970), vol. 2, 817.

95. Madelung, "Khurramiyya".

96. Shahrestani, *al-Milal wa'l-nihal* (ed. W. Cureton) (Leiden, 1846), 132. Cf. Yarshater, "Mazdakism", 1001.

97. Yarshater, "Mazdakism", 1002.

98. Hodgson, "Ghulat".

the direct doctrinal relationship of Mazdakism and *ghulat* within a strictly Iranian framework, and, apart from their role behind Shi'ite Imamology, they amount to a general drift away from Islamic orthodoxy. It is possible that early heresiographers compiled such elaborate lists of sectarian positions to condone this drift, fabricating their association with well-known serious heresies and thereby obviously dissociating them from Islam, but this is unlikely, for it would completely undermine their historiographical credibility. A certain degree of truth has been countenanced therefore in their statements concerning the nature and activity of heretical sects, and its Mazdakite-*ghulat* linkage is underscored by their evidence.

The formative period of the extremist Shi'a is certainly defined by both foreign and indigenous doctrinal influence. Interestingly enough, much of *ghulat* thought can be traced to the impulse of early Islam itself and the experience of the Qur'an, either because of its innate universality or the particular nature of some of its key concepts, even though the *ghulat* approval represented an alternative interpretation of Islam to that of the leadership at Mecca and Medina.[99] But let us be open, we also have to reckon with the claims and possibility that Mazdakite doctrine was a source for the initial inspiration of Islam itself.[100] Before Islam, Mazdakism had already penetrated into Hira as well as the Arab Hijaz under Kavad, and had gained followers there; it also entered Kufa, a centre of religious heterodoxy and schisms, being a likely focus of Mazdakite activity.[101] On closer inspection, mind you, there are observed differences between the doctrine of Mazdak and that of the *ghulat*, and this is accounted for through noting contributions of other *movali* (of Middle Eastern origins) to the development of *ghulat* doctrine, making the *ghulat* clearly distinguishable from the Islamic establishment as further elucidated below.

The ghulat *as the face of neo-Mazdakism*

It is now important to offer a brief outline of key Khorramiyya revolutionaries that verify a strong neo-Mazdakite presence. It is through these *ghali* (i.e. plural of *ghulat*) in general that the Mazdakites were once again able to

---

99. Cf. *ibid.*

100. P. Crone & M. Cook, *Hagarism: The Making of the Islamic World* (Cambridge, 1977).

101. Cf. Yarshater, "Mazdakism", 1003, citing Ibn Wadih Yaqubi, *Ta'rikh* (ed. M. T. Houtsma) (Leiden, 1883), vol. 1, 298; Ibn Qutaiba, *Ma'arif* (ed. Th. Ukasha) (Cairo, 1960), 299; Motahhar Ibn Tahir Maqdesi, *Kitab al-bad' wa'l-ta'rikh* (ed. and trans. C. Huart) (Paris, 1899–1919), vol. 3, 167 and vol. 4, 31; T. Nöldeke, "Das iranische Nationalepos", in *Grundriss der iranischen Philologie II* (eds. W. Geiger, E. W. A. Kuhn & C. Bartholomae) (Strasbourg, 1896–1904), 170, note 1; A. Christensen, *Le Regne du Roi Kawadh I et le communisme Mazdakite* (Copenhagen, 1925), 77; C. E. Bosworth, "Iran and the Arabs before Islam", in *CHI*, vol. 3(1), 600–601.

instrumentalize their revolutionary ideas and esoteric beliefs. An exception to this rule was Bihafarid ibn Mahfurudin, who was of Zoroastrian descent, yet he may still be considered as a candidate for neo-Mazdakite insurrection considering the syncretic nature of his Zoroastrianism. Peasant uprisings in the eighth century, provoked by fiscal oppression in eastern Iran, gave occasion for the emergence of new antinomian, anti-establishment Zoroastrian sects.[102]

Bihafarid the Magian

The most successful of *ghulat* protests is accorded to Bihafarid the Magian (as he is also known),[103] who claimed to be a new prophet with a book in Persian.[104] He appeared in the last days of the Umayyad caliphate (747), at Khawf south of Nishabur, with the intention of a Zoroastrian reform. His attempt, however, seemed to have produced a syncretic concoction of Zoroastrianism and Islam, which succeeded for a short time until his death (*c*.750). He admonished against *zamzama*,[105] the use of wine and improperly prepared meat, consanguinous marriage, and fire worship, and he limited dowries to 400 dirhams, while endorsing charitable acts and service to society.[106] Further recurrence in ideas are noted with Bihafarid's predilection for the number "seven", for example seven years of stay in China (reportedly as a merchant, from where he reportedly brought back his famed green silk attire), the division of tax to the portion of one seventh, and the number of daily prayers very significantly made seven. The *qibla*, moreover, was made towards the sun, as practised by the Yazidis today, the ritual performed while kneeling on one knee.[107] His bid for what is an apparent synthesis between Magian and Islamic doctrine is a strong indication of neo-Mazdakite tendency. In effect, he sought to transcend specificities of religious identity and social class, with his support of the poor and debasing of Zoroastrian clergy making the connection with Mazdak full-circle (as this is what Mazdak had briefly achieved in his time).[108] In light of the increase in sectarian activities, the Zoroastrians themselves actually strove harder than the Moslems against these heresies. Although it was a group of certain *mobads* (religious priests) and *herbads* (religious masters) who provoked Abu Moslem to destroy the renegade ex-Zoroastrian Bihafarid, however, it was Abu Moslem himself, as the renowned arbitrator of the Abbasid takeover, who would become the motivation for the next series

---

102. Morony, "Madjus", in *EIs*, vol. 5.
103. "Behzadeh Magus"; Cf. G. H. Yusofi, "Behafarid", in *EIr*, vol. 4, 88a.
104. *Ibid.*, 89a–b.
105. Or the act of ritual droning during meals, M. Moiin, *Mazdayasna wa ta'tir-e an dar adabiyat-e farsi* (Tehran, 1326/1947), 254–7; cf. also Morony, "Madjus".
106. For a list of admonitions and endorsements, Yusofi, "Behafarid", 89a–b; for the elitist view of the Majus contrary to this, Morony, "Madjus".
107. Yusofi, "Behafardi", 89a–b.
108. B. S. Amoretti, "Sects and Heresies", in *CHI*, vol. 4, 489–90 and 513–17.

of insurrections.[109] These reactionary movements were specifically religious movements (unlike the "revivalist–nationalistic" *Shuubiyya*) and were held by a characteristic thread of messianic militancy.[110] These movements are technically classified as "active millenarian movements",[111] and were driven by an overarching egalitarian motivation that was, as we shall see, never absent of the "nationalistic impulse" typical of the Iranian revolts during the Arab domination of the Umayyad–Abbasid period (*ca.*786–861).

Abu Moslem Khorasani

Abu Moslem (*c.*700–755) was an Abbasid general of Persian descent. He was the first to lead a major organized liberal movement against the Umayyad dynasty. The history of Abu Moslem, having somewhat legendary proportions, apparently originated wth the rise of a Persian slave destined to become a revered political, military and religious figure.[112] He was recruited from among the *ghulat* in Kufa by Imam Ibrahim ibn Mohammed, under whose tutelage he was instructed and placed as the revolutionary leader of the Abbasid movement in Khorasan (*c.*750s). His special commission was to launch the long-term underground Abbasid propaganda against Umayyad forces.[113] His success inaugurates the Abbasid dynasty, but shortly afterwards he was betrayed and murdered under the second Abbasid Caliph Mansur (who also had his mentor Ibn Mohammed executed, the date being *c.*753–754, marking the beginning of formidable reactionary movements under and later inspired by the legend of Abu Moslem). Abu Moslem's original intentions had been to join the Abbasids, though what he hoped to gain through their association is a topic of debate, even if he was initially a faithful and loyal Abbasid subject, that is, loyal to the ideals of Abbasid propaganda.[114] It is more than likely that the deterioration of these ideals under the Abbasids, who soon declared Sunni orthodoxy and abandoned all extremist hopes, produced a strain in Abu Moslem's relationship with the new dynasty. It is not clear whether he was planning a revolt or whether he still continued to harbour extremist religious propaganda, but his growing prestige and power in Khorasan alone was

---

109. Despite Bihafarid's capture and death, his followers, the *Bihafaridiyya*, continued until the tenth century CE, expecting his return; cf. Abd al-Husain Zarrinkub, "The Arab Conquest of Iran and its Aftermath", 33. For sources on Bihafarid cf. Ibn al-Nadim, *Fihrist* (ed. Tajaddud), 407; Gardizi, *Zayn al-Akhbar* (ed. Abd al-Hayy Habibi) (Tehran, 1968), 119–20; and also Yusofi, "Behafarid", 88–90.
110. Hamzehee, *Land of Revolutions*, 64–72.
111. *Ibid.*
112. Sources are not unanimous, though inclined towards a Persian origin. Cf. Ibn al-Athir, *al-Kamil fi'l-ta'rikh* (Cairo, 1957), vol. 4, cited by Zarrinkub, "The Arab Conquest", 53; S. Moscati, "Abu Muslim", in *EIs*, vol. 1; G. H. Yusofi, "Abu Moslem", in *EIr*, vol. 1, 341–4.
113. *Ibid.*
114. *Ibid.*, 343.

enough to alarm the Abbasids. Some claim he wished to establish a national Iranian government and that he fought the Umayyads under the guise of a religious uprising in order to gain control of the caliphate, while other views attribute to him a purely religious motivation, yet devoid of ethnic overtones so that he would have eventually moved against the Abbasids.[115] Abu Moslem's success as an Abbasid visionary was due to his effective missionizing, careful planning and strategic military operations. The fact that he stopped Bihafarid had little to do with a soft spot he may have had for the Zoroastrian clergy (or Zoroastrianism), as has been proposed.[116] Rather, it had more to do with a political strategy to have all disparate forces on line for the Abbasid cause (or even his own alternate agenda). In fact, it is even mentioned that Behafarid was given a chance to be an ally, but was put to death solely on account of his auguring.[117] Abu Moslem ruled with absolute power from his base in Khorasan, to such an extent that his death made him into a legend. His memory was kept alive in the eastern provinces, and he was regarded by some as the Mahdi.[118] From this point on, Abu Moslem plays a central role in subsequent insurrections, his legacy inspirational for later leaders of these groups – as we shall see.

Sunbadh

In the next series of insurrections provoked by Abu Moslem's murder, the first occurs just two months after his death. It was led in 755 by a certain Sunbadh (or Sindbad), Abu Moslem's friend and associate (or general),[119] and his rebellion took place with the aid of Abu Moslem's supporters as an apparent act of vendetta. Sources describe him as a wealthy Zoroastrian supporter of Abu Moslem, but again, the nature of his "Zoroastrianism" is in doubt. The force with which Sunbadh moved against the caliphate, rising within two months and suppressed in seventy days, is a point of interest, in that it shows his rebellion was in haste. There is mention in the sources, however, that Abu Moslem suspected a plot to assassinate him, though nevertheless chose to obey the caliph's summons. Abu Moslem is then mentioned arriving with eight thousand men and entering the capital with one thousand. Given the reputation and legend surrounding Abu Moslem, it is likely, and to the credit of Sunbadh, that he had already organized Sunbadh's rebellion, and that in fact Sunbadh's rebellion was neither out of impulse nor ultimately in vain, but a carefully planned

---

115. For the variety of positions, *ibid.*; cf. also Hamzehee, *Land of Revolutions*, 67–8.
116. For the contrary view, see Yusofi, "Abu Moslem", 343b.
117. Al-Nadim, cited in Yusofi, "Abu Moslem", 90a, contains another tradition preserved by Biruni and Shahrestani about Bihafarid's servants and followers claiming that he mounted a golden horse and flew to heaven, and would return quickly to get even with his enemies.
118. Copious legends surround Abu Moslem; *ibid.*, 343b–4a.
119. Yarshater, "Mazdakism", 1002.

act under Abu Moslem's instructions. The fact of its failure should not really discredit the attempt. Sunbadh, denying Abu Moslem's death and exulting him, preached an arresting syncretic eschatology, expecting the return of Abu Moslem along with the Mahdi and Mazdak and securing support from Shi'ites and the Khorramiyya. According to Nizam al-Molk, all three would soon reappear and Abu Moslem would rule with Mazdak as his vizier, while the Rafizi Shi'ites, hearing the mention of Mahdi and Mazdak, joined in great numbers.[120] In any case, Sunbadh was generally regarded as a Mazdakite and accused of promoting libertinism.[121] Surviving him were the *Sunbadhiyya* for a short period. Little is known of them, and since they were falsely attributed by Nezam al-Molk with containing Mazdakite elements, there is no need to pursue their trajectory.[122] By this time, and largely due to Sunbadh's postulations, Abu Moslem had become a well-known legend, in some circles revered as the Mahdi.

Al-Moqanna

The second rebellion in Abu Moslem's name was led by the fabled al-Moqanna. Before it a revolt occurred in 767 in Badghis, northwestern Afghanistan, in connection with the legacy of Bihafarid. The town, already converted by Bihafarid before his death, gave their allegiance to the leadership of the local chief, Ustadhsis,[123] who revolted, together with numerous Kharijites and Lughayris (an obscure Zoroastrian sect, who like the Bihafaridiyya incorporated some Islamic practices and belief), and succeeded for a short time against caliph Mansur. This event was later overshadowed by a second insurrection launched under the renowned al-Moqanna (*c*.777), "the Veiled Prophet of Khorasan", because he hid his face behind a silk veil or golden mask that he created for himself.[124] A native of Marv, in the province of Khorasan, and his real name is not known (possibly Hakim ibn Hashim?). He was initially involved in Abu Moslem's campaign. His fellowship consisted of recruits from

---

120. Nezam al-Molk, *Siyar al-muluk (Siyasat nama)* (ed. H. Darke) (Tehran, 1968), trans. by Darke as *The Book of Government or Rules for Kings* (London, 1978), 279–81, and cf. W. Madelung, "Sunbadh", in *EIs*, vol. 9.

121. Yarshater, "Mazdakism", 1003. On Sunbadh, Tabari, *Ta'rikh al-rusul*, vol. 3, 119–25; Masudi, *Muruj al-dhahab* (ed. and trans. Barbier de Meynard & Pavet de Curteille) (Paris, 1861–77), vol. 6, 188–92; Nezam al-Molk, *Siyar al-muluk*, 279–83; and Sadighi, *Les Mouvements*, 132–6.

122. Daftary, "Sectarian and National Movements", 48–9.

123. See esp. Tabari, *Ta'rikh al-rusul*, vol. 3, 354–8 and 773; A. H. Zarrinkub, *Do qarn-e sokut* [Two Centuries of Silence] (Tehran, 1336/1957), 159–62; E. L. Daniel, *The Political and Social History of Khorasan under Abbasid Rule 747–820* (Chicago, 1979), 133–7.

124. Amoretti, "Sects and Heresies", 495–503; Daniel, *The Political and Social History of Khorasan*, 137–47.

among Turks and Mazdakites of the region (Soghdian peasants);[125] from the Soghdian dress in particular was derived the name Mubayyida[126] (the Arabic equivalent to Persian *sapid jamagan*), "wearers of white." The rebellion spread from Khorasan to Transoxania and lasted (approximately) six to eight years, before al-Moqanna's besiegement and subsequent suicide.[127] Al-Moqanna seems to have subscribed to a hybrid doctrine with Mazdakite and *ghulat* (and *batini*) components. Bosworth and Yarshater suggest his self-acclaimed divinity, or in the belief attached to him that God, having created Adam in His image, was then made incarnate in Seth, Noah, Abraham, Moses, Jesus, Mohammed, Ali, Mohammed ibn al-Hanafiyya, Abu Moslem and finally in its perfected form, al-Moqanna himself. His doctrine promoted the belief in anthropomorphism, incarnationism, and the transmigration of souls.

Babak-e Khorrami

The last and most celebrated Mazdakite/Khorramiyya resistance came from the leadership of Babak-e Khorrami (798–838), the great-grandson of Abu Moslem. Babak was native to Azarbaijan, and is remembered today as a nationalistic icon in that region. He is generally known as a great Persian hero who fought against Arab-Islamic rule of Iran.[128] Arising from the peasant class, and succeeding Javidan ibn Sahl, the Khorramiyya leader of northwestern Iran, he claimed that Javidan's spirit "had settled upon him"[129] and began to incite the locals. Many Khorrami groups in other areas of Iran, which had previously failed in their uprisings, joined Babak in comprising a final and formidable force. It is known, furthermore, that Babak's army was primarily made up of peasants and farmers and that his revolt was strictly anti-Arab, and to an extent anti-Moslem, with a desire for re-establishing the religion of Mazdak and a return to past Persian lifestyles. Sources indicate wine drinking and merrymaking, even at a time of war, which resonate with the chief Mazdakite doctrinal principle – Joy, from which the Mazdakites under Islam derive their name, Khorramiyya (*Khorram*, "happy", "joyous", etc.). Another point of consideration is the special position of women who were deemed

---

125. Bosworth, "al-Mukanna", in *EIs*, vol. 7; cf. also, Al-Biruni, *Athar*, 211, connects al-Moqanna and the Mazdakites, stating "He made obligatory for them [his followers] all the laws of Mazdak", cited in "Yarshater, "Mazdakism", 1003.
126. Shahristani counts the Mubayyida as one of the neo-Mazdakite sects and as a variety of the Khorramiyya; cf. Madelung, "Khurramiyya".
127. The event is dated to 783. Cf. Bosworth, "al-Mukanna"; Yarshater, "Mazdakism", 1003.
128. *Akhbar Baba* by Waqed Ibn Amr Tamimi, quoted in the *Fehrest* of al-Nadim (ed. Flügel), 406–7, and Ibn al-Nadim, *The Fihrist of al-Nadim* (trans. Dodge), 818–22. The "lost" text was likely used by Maqdesi, *Kitab al-Bad*, vol. 6, 114–18; cf. Sadighi, *Les mouvements*, 234.
129. Madelung, "Khurramiyya".

equal or as elevated as men – a key Mazdakite motif.[130] It was in fact Javidan's wife who appointed Babak as successor and then married him as a seal of the former's testament or last wishes.[131] A description of their marriage offers further insight into Khorrami doctrines, with special emphasis on their "un-Islamic" (i.e. "unorthodox [Moslem]") Iranian nature. The description is given in brief by al-Nadim:

> She called for a cow and ordered that it be slaughtered and flayed, and its skin spread out; then she placed on the skin a bowl filled with wine and into it she broke bread, which she placed around about the bowl. And she called them [the soldiers] one by one, and told each one to tread on the skin with his foot, and take a piece of bread, plunge it into the wine, and eat it, saying "I believe in you, O spirit of Babak, as I believed in the spirit of Javidan;" each was then to take the hand of Babak, do obeisance and kiss it. This they did until such time as food was made ready for her. Then she brought food and wine to them, seated Babak on her bed, and sat beside him publicly before them. When they had drunk three draughts each, she took a sprig of basil and offered it to Babak, and this was their marriage. Then they [the soldiers] came forth and did obeisance to the two, acknowledging their marriage.[132]

Reflected here are some peculiarities of esoteric practices and doctrine of a Mithraic nature that had effected Azarbaijan and Kurdistan. The Mithraic elements of the sacrifice of the cow, the use of its skin, wine and bread are indeed obvious, and that their presence signals a continuing hidden history of indigenous Persian sensibilities needs no defence.[133] Nor is there a need here to elaborate on Sufi and Yazidi expressions, the seeds of which are already inherent in this kind of suggestive ritual.

Secured in the mountainous regions of northwestern Iran, Babak's rebellion started in 816–817 and lasted approximately twenty years. It spread from Azarbaijan to the western and central parts of Iran, and ended in 838 with his gruelling defeat and dramatic execution.[134] With the fall of Babak, the neo-

---

130. Amoretti, "Sects and Heresies", 508 and 517–18.
131. Al-Nadim, *Fehrest* (trans. Dodge), 821; cf. also G. H. Yusofi, "Babak Khorrami", in *EIr*, vol. 3, 300b; Yarshater, "Mazdakism", 1010–11.
132. Al-Nadim, *Fehrest* (trans. Dodge), 821–2.
133. Cf. G. Widengren, "Babakiyya and Mithraic Mysteries", in *Mysteria Mithrae* (ed. U. Bianchi) (Leiden, 1979), 667–95.
134. In 835, after repeated futile attempts to defeat Babak, the Caliph al-Motasem sent Haydar ibn Kavos Afshin, who was lavishly provided for the campaign, against Babak. Afshin proved to be a success and defeated and captured Babak. Cf. Yusofi, "Babak Khurrami", *EIr*, vol. 3, 303a.

Mazdakite aspirations suffered a very serious blow, but were not entirely killed off. Under relentless persecution, however, the Mazdakite/Khorramiyya sects were gradually forced underground – into assimilation with Islamic sects.[135]

The important point to be considered thus far is not only the impact of Mazdakite doctrine on disparate heterodoxies in the Umayyad Abbasid times, but also the substantial influence of Mazdakite egalitarianism on both the Persian and Arabian mind-frame in general. It is because of this that the companionship of Salman the Persian and Mohammed (for the purposes of a study of Persian Sufism) is a central concern in this thesis. The presence of Mazdakite thought in post-Islamic Iran, especially in the early *ghulat* period (and the concern expressed by heresiographers at large regarding the Mazdakite heresy) is a clear indication of an existing heterodox trend persisting in that time (which found itself agreeable to or was able to incorporate *ghulat* and *movali* elements at large). Moreover, its general threat to orthodoxy has bearing on a much greater event – the essential core of the Sunni/Shi'a split – the former supported by the aristocracy and nobility, the latter upholding the faith of the lower and struggling economic class. The original economic struggle of the Mazdakites, admittedly, is echoed in the preliminary mission statement of the Islamic conquests during the initial "patriarchal reign", and later this "democratic-looking" impetus becomes an ethno-religious concern with the (*movali*-supported) Alid cause during the Umayyad Arab Empire. Under the Abbasid caliphate, after that, the Arab *vs. movali* scenario returns to a basic socio-economic struggle not necessarily motivated by, but continuing to reflect, ethnic and religious concerns, as by now Iranian elements of nobility and priestcraft were already integrated and assimilated into the orthodox regime.

The need for social liberties

The *khorram-dini* insurrections commencing after the murder of Abu Moslem are often misconstrued as being purely anti-Arab and anti-Moslem, when they are in fact pro-Mazdakite, meaning they were no longer struggling against an intruding ethnicity or rejection of what had previously been taken as an alien religion. Rather, these sectarian insurgents were primarily driven by the ideals of social, political, economic and religious egalitarianism. And along with this came a natural rejection of established orthodoxy, which in this case, and broadly speaking, was Islam. In reality, the general Mazdakite resistance movement was simply anti-establishment, based on an agreed level

---

135. Their traces as Mazdakites and Khorramites can be seen up to the Mongol period and beyond. Connections with Qarmatis and Batinis are considered but remain in question when overlapping with Ismaili origins. See Yarshater "Mazdakism", 1005–6, citing B. Spüler, *Iran in früh-islamischer Zeit* (Wiesbaden, 1952), 206; cf. also Spüler, *Die Mongolen in Iran* (Berlin, 1968), 241, note 10.

of injustice no longer tolerated by the middle and lower class. The Mazdakites, it needs to be pointed out, were not originally a religious reform movement; in their time they were already in a Zoroastrian world. Instead, they were fighting an economic war that was turned into a religious issue (by the opposing Zoroastrian priests) for easy disposal as a branded heresy. The concern is not with economics, of course, but with the continuity of religious thought, and so the examples of insurrections covered serve to demonstrate the continuity and impact of Mazdakite doctrine and practice throughout post-Zoroastrian Islamic thought. In a religious frame, their own apparent sectarian claim and religious reform was purely based on a struggle to redeem the fundamentals of Zarathushtra's teachings buried in the stockpile of priestly ritual, formalism and superstition. As for the re-enactment of Mazdakism, it occurs during the advent of Islam when early Moslems, suffering the same religio-economic fate, also formed anti-establishment regimes (as with the Kharijite reaction) to defend the basic religio-economic rights they saw laid down by the fundamental "Islamic" teachings of Mohammed. The argument here is more than just a pattern, a recurrent theme or "history repeating itself". Rather, it is about maintaining "Mazdakism" and "Islam" as essentially or deep-structurally synonymous on a social and doctrinal level. So we can see how, in the earlier Islamic period of Persia, pockets of heterodox Islam and neo-Mazdakite activities are seen hand-in-hand, or well nigh inexorably and in successive insurrections, typically instantiating the continuity of Persian values in Iran's "repressed past".

THE DOCTRINE OF MAZDAK AND ITS CURRENCY IN NEO-MAZDAKITE ASPIRATIONS IN THE ISLAMIC PERIOD

Up until now we have covered a major portion of historical events that signify the continuing presence of Mazdakite ideals in post-Sasanid Iran. In this last segment by touching on the doctrine of Mazdak the aim is to explore the validity of neo-Mazdakite activities as a sign of the continuing impetus of the imagined "sapiential tradition" of Iran, revered by the Nematollahiya as the Khosravan Path (*hikmat-e khosravi*). In highlighting some of the necessary points in the doctrine of Mazdak, it is important to begin with the etymological significance of the term from which the neo-Mazdakites derive their name, *khorram*. Two explanations for this, often regarded with caution, the first that the epithet came from "Khorrama", the wife of Mazdak, and the second that it derives from a district called Khorram, near Ardibil (Azarbaijan), hold significant intrigue, though they are probably equally inadequate.[136] The

136. Cf. Madelung, "Khurramiyya"; Yarshater, "Mazdakism", 1005–6; Amoretti, "Sects and Heresies", 508.

obvious etymological explanation concerns what is "happy" or "cheerful", and also "fresh" or "green", in this case pertaining to a new social order.[137] The choice of this word is quite telling in itself, for to the doctrinal nature and pre-dilection of the Mazdakite religion was not a base hedonism as portrayed by the heresiographers.[138] Founding itself on the core teachings of Zarathushtra, the principles of Mazdakism taught peace and happiness through a prescribed relationship with material possessions, which included the equal distribution of commodities, thereby eradicating competition and dispute, giving freely of oneself, and taking pleasure in life through moderation.[139] This twofold religious and economic doctrine, embodied within the neo-Mazdakite phrase *khorram-din*, is then rightly compared with the Zoroastrian *veh-din* ("good religion") and Mazdakite *dorist-din* ("right religion").[140]

The ancient Persians were well known for their hedonism, which was to be an indelible and consistent quality for appreciating life, apparent even among the most religious of them. In the Persian religious consciousness a most obvious continuity is that of two themes that consistently present themselves in Persian literature: "light" and "love", which on into Islamic times was accompanied by the negative and opposing themes of "resistance" and "death". We are not labouring any point about dualism here, but reiterating an earlier argument in Chapter 2 that the "dualism" of Iranian religion depicted a simple yet profound understanding of human purpose and destiny in the second cosmogonic age known to Zoroastrians as the age of creation or admixture. It was the philosophy that created more theological problems for later academics than its intention to solve the problem of evil for its adherents. For the Iranian, it was strictly understood that human destiny was based on the "ethical choice" that every individual would have to face; that is, between the Truth or the Lie. Later summarized in Sufi doctrine, the one who "chooses" God, is a person "dead to his own self and alive in God".[141] This is the theosophical expression of the principle of "gnosis of self" (*to know oneself is to know one's Lord*) generally adhered to in Islam.[142] The following is an account of the Mazdakite/Khorramiyya doctrine, accompanied by a basic hermeneutical analysis. Also, the teachings of Mazdak, as given by Abdul-Fath Shahrestani, are drawn upon and compared with those of the neo-Mazdakite impressions in the Khorramiyya sect, given by al-Maqdisi.

137. Also, "lush", "luxuriant", "verdant", "pleasant", "glad". Cf. M. Aryanpour Kashani, *Persian–English Dictionary* (Tehran, 1384/2006), 320.
138. Cf. Madelung, "Khurramiyya".
139. Al-Nadim, *Fehrest* (ed. Tajaddud), 342; Yarshater, "Mazdakism", 1005.
140. Sadighi, *Les Mouvements*, 195; and see previous note.
141. Jonayd, cited in Valiuddin, *Contemplative Disciplines in Sufism*, xxii.
142. Hadith Qudsi, *man arefeh nafsahu, faqat arefeh rabbahu*.

The doctrine of the Mazdakites

The teachings of the Mazdakites are primarily gathered from an all too brief mention by the Islamic heresiographer, Shahrestani (1076–1153).[143] His exposition begins with their belief in two primordial principles, Light and Darkness; but this is not to be taken at face value as that of the rigid dualism of the Zoroastrian priests. In Mazdak's religion, as with Zarathushtra, the Light is always more dominant than the Darkness,[144] even though his position may be all too subtle in presentation. It is explained: "Light is endowed with knowledge and feeling, and acts by design and free will, whereas Darkness is ignorant and blind, and acts at random and without direction."[145] In comparison, Abu al-Maqdisi[146] (writing in 966), another key Moslem source on the Khorramiyya doctrine, places them in one of the "categories" of *al-majus* (Mazdaeans) who mask themselves as Moslems.[147] He says that among the Khorramiyya, the principal force of the world was the light, with the exception of a portion of which was corrupted and turned into darkness.[148] This crucial understanding reflects the Mazdakite Khorramiyya "Model of the World", dictating its long-term outlook and overarching dogma. The doctrine can be viewed as denoting "consciousness" *vs.* "unconsciousness" or in a Gnostic sense: "knowledge" opposed to ignorance. This is an intimate description of human motivation, in that individuals are moved or motivated by intention or will. The idea conveyed is that light is a "state" that does not "react", but rather makes individuals subservient through the possibility of choice via awareness, which is especially true of Zarathushtra's insights. "Light", as noted there, refers to an "innate intelligence" (i.e. "knowledge and feeling"), which is

---

143. *Kitabo'l-milal wa'l-nihal*, from the British Library Ms, Add. 23, 349, dated 549 AH (After Hegra). A full translation of the BL copy is given by M. Shaki in "The Cosmogonical and Cosmological Teachings of Mazdak", Special Issue of *Acta Iranica: Papers in Honour of Prof. Mary Boyce* (Leiden, 1985), vol. 11, 527–43. Shahrestani's source is Abu Isa Harun al-Warraq (d. 247 AH), a (Zoroastrian or Manichaean?) scholar, converted to Islam, who appears to have had access to genuine Mazdakite sources. Other sources are noted for their usefulness in giving coherence to the Mazdakite belief system, such as Ibn al-Nadim's *Fehrist* and Ferdowsi's *Shahnameh*. Cf. Yarshater, "Mazdakism", 994 and 1006–8; and for the full excerpt of the reference in *Shahnameh*, cf. A. Bausani, *Religion in Iran: from Zoroaster to Baha'ullah* (trans. J. M. Marchesi) (New York, 2000), 97–100.
144. W. Müller, "Mazdak and the Alphabet Mysticism of the East", *History of Religions* 3(1) (1963), 74; yet cf. H. Jonas, *The Gnostic Religion: The Message of the Alien God and the Beginnings of Christianity* (Boston, 1963), ch. 9.
145. Cf. Shaki's Ms and Cureton's edition interchangeably for the purpose of invoking certain concepts and notions as transparent in the doctrine. Cf. also Yarshater, "Mazdakism", 1006.
146. *Kitab al-Bad*, Naubakhti, *Firaq al-Shi'a*. Maqdesi's account is based on his personal acquaintance with members of the sect and his reading of some of their books. Cf. also Yarshater, "Mazdakism", 1008, and Madelung, "Khurramiyya".
147. Maqdesi, *Kitab al-Bad*, vol. 1, 143.
148. *Ibid.*, vol. 1, 143. Cf. Madelung, "Khurramiyya"; Yarshater, "Mazdakism", 1009.

governed or "given direction" through choice ("free will"). The opposite principle of "Darkness", however, is on the contrary a "reactive" mode that has no direction because it is ignorant to choice. Note: there is no specific reference to "good" and "evil" at this point; and this is significant with respect to Sufi doctrine explored through the notions of *javânmardî* and *âdâb*.

For Mazdak, the notion of good and evil comes into play with the Mixture (as with Mazdean and Manichaean cosmogony/cosmology), initiating creation. According to Mazdak, this period of "admixture" has occurred by chance and at random, and so Separation or "the deliverance (of Light from Darkness)" also occurs at random (possibly constituting an unexplored and pre-eminent notion of "grace" in Mazdak's thinking). Mazdak also prescribed the subduing of passions (literally a "killing of the soul")[149] to deliver the soul from admixture (i.e. from evil and Darkness). Note here the theme of "death" and "resistance" (and its correspondence with the Sufi doctrine of *nafs* and the Ahl-e haqq and *ghuli* doctrine of transmigration) in order to promote Light. The combination specifically pinpoints a necessary "process" of purification and transformation that has to occur on an individualistic level (placing particular stress on awareness and choice). Mazdak's approach to "randomness" reveals an esoteric principle holding no fault with creation (humankind). This presumably did away with self-pity and regret; two major hindrances that lead to the opposite of joy: "sorrow" and "depression". Each person must strive to emulate the quality of Light within him or herself, in order to bring about change on a collective level. The point that the separation (of Light and Darkness) is also random further elucidates detachment from (mainstream) eschatological expectations. In this regard, Sufis openly claim: "do away with this world and the next",[150] eradicating both fear and anxiety as proponents of Darkness. The Mazdakite view has very little disparity with Khorramiyya doctrines with their beliefs in "incarnation" and "transmigration of souls" denoting the distinctness of spirit from body and its transitions of purification (from Darkness) and transformation (in Light). It is difficult to deny that such ideas have settled in the Sufi contemplative disciplines generally, for we find the four main stages of Sufi practice are: *tadhkiya-i nafs* ("purification of the self"), *tasfiya-i qalb* ("cleansing of the heart"), *takhliya-i sirr* ("emptying of the secret") and *tajliya-i ruh* ("illumination of the spirit").[151] The Sufi's struggle with his or her own *nafs* is likewise given life through one's bodily senses, which is outlined, in the eleventh century, by Hojwiri:

> The lust of the eye is sight; that of the ear, hearing; that of the nose, smell; that of the tongue, speech; that of the palate, taste; that of

149. Shaki, "The Cosmogonical and Cosmological Teachings of Mazdak", 528.

150. For example, Attar's account of Rabea setting out to burn paradise and to put out the fires of hell: Attar, *Muslim Saints* (ed. Arberry), 51.

151. Cf. Valiuddin, *Contemplative Disciplines in Sufism*, xxii–xxiii.

the limbs, touch; and that of the mind, thought. Hence the seeker must be his own keeper and governor, and spend day and night throughout his life keeping watch.[152]

The Mazdakites speak of three essential elements – Water, Fire and Earth – in what seems to be the recipe for Man, Man being made of clay in Islamic tradition. Interestingly, the Ahl-e Haqq refer to "yellow clay" and "black earth" in denoting the predisposed nature of individuals.[153] For Mazdak, two forms or types result from the "mingling": from their pure[154] constituents proceeds the Director of Good, and from their impure[155] constituents proceeds the Director of Evil.[156] In the Khorramiyya tradition, as in Zoroastrian, Mazdakite and Sufi ones, "cheerfulness" and "joy" are a sign of allegiance (or harmony) with "the Good". The Khorramiyya were particularly concerned with cleanliness and purity, a key Mazdean mandate associated with the Good, as they were apt to perform acts of kindness and strictly avoid bloodshed (with few exceptions).[157] This, coupled with their view of women (as being respected [either equally, if not elevated]) carries on a continuing Persian tone from the *Gathas* to the Qur'an.

Mazkak's original worldview is presented in the form of an analogy between the divine and worldly order. The Supreme Being or the "object of [Mazdak's] worship" (*mabuduhu*) is the Lord seated upon a "throne (*kursi*) in the world above, as the king of kings ([*k*]*husrau*) is seated in the world below"; four powers (*quwa*) stand before the Supreme Being: "Discernment (*tamyiz*), Understanding (*fahm*), Preservation (*hifz*) and Joy (*surur*)", as there are in the worldly realm four persons before the king: "the *Mobadan Mobad* [Chief Judge], the Chief *Herbad* [chief religious doctor], the Commander of the Army (*sepahbad*), and the Entertainment Master (*ramishgar*)".[158] The Four (primary) Powers also have their opposites in the force(s) of Darkness: blindness, ignorance, neglect and

---

152. Hujwiri, *Kashf al-Mahjub*, (ed. R. A. Nicholson), 263, cited by J. Nurbakhsh, *The Psychology of Sufism*, 37.

153. The missing element of Air may be in defiance to orthodox Zoroastrianism ("the Wind God (*Wat*)"). Cf. Shaki, "The Cosmogonical and Cosmological Teachings of Mazdak", 530f; cf. Boyce, *History*, vol. 1, esp. 72, 75 and 79f.

154. That is, "light" (elements); cf. Shaki, "The Cosmogonical and Cosmological Teachings of Mazdak", 528.

155. Or "dark" (elements); cf. *ibid.*

156. Cf. Shaki's translation of Shahrestani in "The Cosmogonical and Cosmological Teachings of Mazdak", 528.

157. This would change, for instance, given a decided rebellion. See, Yusofi, "Babak", 299f.; Maqdesi, *Kitab al-Bad*, vol. 4, 30–31. Cf. Madelung, "Khurramiyya"; Yarshater, "Mazdakism", 1008.

158. Al-Biruni, *Athar*, 209; Khwarazmi, *Mafatih al-'ulum* (ed. G. van Vloten) (Leiden, 1895), 37; E. G. Browne (trans.), "Some Account of the Arabic Work entitled 'Nihayatu'l-irab fi akhbari'l Furs wa'l-'Arab'", *Journal of Royal Asiatic Society* 32 (London), 227; also cf. Yarshater, "Mazdakism", 1006.

sorrow.[159] Once again, the principal forces of Light and Darkness continue to have their effect on the world through the creation as specific to an individual's natural disposition. Accordingly, the world can be directed by any of these four powers depending on individual level of awareness and choice. According to Mazdak, the good are ruled by the "four powers" of the Supreme Being (or in Sufi terms, "the divine attributes of God") who are assisted by Seven viziers[160] revolving within Twelve spiritual forces.[161] The bad or evil suffer their fate in becoming subject to the opposite "four" (based on a lack of awareness and neglect of choice). A particularly *hurufi* interpretation could take the doctrine to be an allegory of a profound spiritual principle: when the powers of the Four, the Seven and the Twelve are united in a person, that human being then "becomes godly (*rabbani*)" or "(part of) God",[162] and is then relieved from religious duties and obligations (*irtafa'a anhut-taklif*). This Mazdakite belief follows through in practice and doctrine in *ghulat* and neo-Mazdakite beliefs, and especially in Sufi schools of thought. Much of the *ghulat* doctrine flows into the Sufi stream (via the *Hurufis*) and examples abound.[163] In the first instance one is immediately reminded of the numerological representation of the major Shi'a branches: the Fourers (*Zaidiyya*), Seveners (*Isma'iliyya*) and the Twelvers (*Imamiyya*). In a second more profound sense, this remarkable claim is also associated with the formula given for the prominent Sufi idea of the Perfect Man (*al-insan al-kamil*), which feeds on the twin doctrines of *fana* and *baqa*. Moreover, the unification of the powers (four, seven and twelve) means that the individual is made complete, a true "human being" (*ensaan*),[164] resulting in the ultimate harmony with the Divine. The terms employed by Shahrestani for both the ruler of the world above and the king in this world are the appellatives *husrau al-'alami'l-a'la* and *husrau*, which are definitive in highlighting the *khosrawan*.

---

159. Shaki offers five: unawareness (as blindness), ignorance, oblivion, stupidity and sorrow. These are interactive notions depicting principle elements. Cf. Yarshater, "Mazdakism", 1007; Shaki, "The Cosmogonical and Cosmological Teachings of Mazdak", 529.

160. Cf. Yarshater, "Mazdakism", 1007; Christensen, *Le Regne du Roi Kawadh*, 81; O. Klima, *Mazdak, Geschichte einer sozialen Bewegung im sassanidischen Persien* (Prague, 1957), 188–98.

161. Ms. cited in Shaki, "The Cosmogonical and Cosmological Teachings of Mazdak", 528f; Yarshater, "Mazdakism", 1007

162. Ms. cited in Shaki, "The Cosmogonical and Cosmological Teachings of Mazdak", 529; Yarshater, "Mazdakism", 1007.

163. Ms. cited in Shaki, "The Cosmogonical and Cosmological Teachings of Mazdak", 529. For the *ghulat* side, Hodgson, "Ghulat", specifically: "tolerance and agreement, these are our customs". Cf. J. Nurbakhsh, *The Truths of Love: Sufi Poetry*, 40: "One who is annihilated in God, transcends manners, and closes the book on them". Cf. *idem*, "Silence and Etiquette of the Sufis", 24b; "The Sufi Path", *Sufi* 7 (Autumn 1990), 4.

164. The idea is connected to the Avestan root of the word "human", i.e. Hooman (*Vohu-Man[a]*) Good/Loving Mind (*Vohu Mana*), a complete and fulfilled person who by extension is fundamentally divine.

Mazdakite belief that the Supreme Being rules by the power of the letters whose totality forms the Supreme Name (*al-ismu'l-a'zam*), corresponds in the first instance to Zarathushtra introducing "Mazda" (or "Mazda Ahura", i.e. Ahura Mazda) as the Supreme Name, and as the culmination or unification of the old pantheon therein. Moreover, this is observed in the Sufi and Kabbalist theosophies, where the principal names of God and their essences amalgamate, culminate, and are contained within the "the Supreme Name" (e.g. the ninety-nine names of Allah; seventy-two names of God). In addition, the specific instruction is given in Mazdakism that a comprehension of these letters is the key to the Great Secret (*al-sirro'l-akbar*), significantly corresponding to the practice of *zekr* (remembrance of the name/s of God) in Sufism.[165] The fact that "becoming (part of) God" is principally followed by "being relieved" from religious duties points to the zenith of Mazdakite (and neo-Mazdakite) esotericism, whereby religion itself becomes redundant for such an individual. A fascinating point, and one that reminds us of countless examples of Sufi anecdotes and phrases concerning this. Note those of Bayazid, Hallaj and Abu Sa'id (to be discussed in Chapter 9), all of which are wittily rendered in a summary verse by Hafez: "Colour the prayer rug with the stain of wine if the Magian Master [*pir-e moghan*] proclaims it; that the seeker not remain ignorant of the way and custom of the House."[166]

As we have seen, the fervour of *neo*-Mazdakism, the resurgence of the Mazdakite impetus in its post-Islamic appearance and engulfed with *ghulat* and *movali* aspirations, melded with Iranian forms of Islam that wanted a return to what appears to be an idealistic "Islam" (as first reflected in brief in the early Kharijite movement). Neo-Mazdakism only goes to demonstrate the continuing course of an informal trajectory with discernible impetuses of social resistance and doctrinal correspondence of a distinctly Persianate character. Therefore, despite the serious intervention of Islam, our macro-vision has followed the cultural and religious resilience of Persian religious consciousness from beyond Mithra and Zarathushtra, and has moved on to cover the ongoing story behind Sufism. Significant spaces in this history, however, will have to be filled out in the next chapters regarding Persian influences at the very origins of Islam itself and the mysterious role of Salman the Persian.

---

165. Valiuddin, *Contemplative Disciplines*, xxii–xxiii (overview); the reference to Shahrestani in Yarshater's, "Mazdakism", 1007.

166. *Be mey sajjadeh rangeen kon garat pir-e moghan gooyad/ke saalek bikhabar nab-wad ze raah-o rassm-e manzel-ha*; Hafez, *Diwan*, 1.

CHAPTER 7

LATER ANTIQUITY: MAZDAK AND THE SASANIAN CRISIS

Moving deeper, we look at Later Antiquity and begin an examination of Mazdak and Mazdakism as the key building-block in our macroscopic vision of Persian cultural and religious continuities from pre- to Islamic Iran. Specifically, we must consider the transmigration of ideas from Mazdak to Mohammed. It is important to appreciate that the place of Mazdakism in the history of Persia has remained a subject almost totally ignored, or else glossed over as a Persian mistake best forgotten.[1] The advent of Mazdak brings to attention one of the most successful Persian reactive movements, apart from the earlier implant of Manichaeism. Yet Mazdak is the face of a hidden tradition (allegedly going back to Zarathushtra) that for a time won the favour of the Sasanid court and was rapidly spread throughout the empire and, we should stress, as far as Arabia. If Mazdak and Mazdakism indeed form one of two crucial pieces in the jigsaw puzzle for filling out our alternative Persian macrohistory, the other piece, Salman the Persian, looks like the very joining of Iran and Islam.

MAZDAK'S SOCIO-RELIGIOUS REFORM

The history of the world is filled with some of the most atrocious events that taint the spirit of humanity. The Zoroastrian persecution of Mazdak and his followers is a dark chapter in Iran's history. And it would seem that the Moslem conquest of Persia, as previously implied, was a premeditated act of retribution. However, the finger does not necessarily have to point to the Mazdakite, or rather neo-Mazdakite, resurgents alone, since Salman the Persian is very much a suspect in the fall of Sasanian Iran. The fact that these events may be

---

1. Yarshater, "Mazdaksim", 990–1024; P. Crone, "Zoroastrian Communism", *Comparative Studies in Society and History* 36(3) (1994), 447–62.

in any way linked adds further to the intrigue of Persia's secret past, but nevertheless, this is precisely what encompasses the "Sasanian crisis" upon which we are about to embark.

Al-Masudi states that Mazdak was the first to interpret the *Avesta* according to its hidden meanings (*batin*): "Mazdak was the interpreter (*al-muta'awwil*) of the Book of Zoroaster, the Avesta ... and he is first among those who believed in interpretation (*ta'wil*) and in inner meanings (*batin*)."[2] It would seem the popular and egalitarian reform of Mazdak was only the tip of an ingrained esoteric and anti-establishment current originating in an alternate interpretation of Zarathushtra's teachings.[3] Its doctrine appears to have been founded by one Zaradosht-e Pasa (Fasa/Farsi, i.e. from Fars), son of Khorragan, a *mobad* (chief) whose followers were called Zaradoshtagan.[4] Given the fact that he is only mentioned by Moslem sources and no dates are specified for him leaves possible room for postulating this figure as actually a reference to the original Zarathushtra.[5] Regardless, the epithet "Zaradosht" is taken here as a title rather than a name like Zaratosht-e Pasa (which could represent a continuation gone unrecorded, perhaps initiated by Zarathushtra or his immediate followers), as was "Mazdak", which meant a kind of "little Mazda" (as a derogative phrase) or "like Mazda" (in praise).[6] The sources indicate that Zaradosht of Pars was the leader of a long-standing Zoroastrian occultism (or hidden tradition known only by initiation) whose leadership was passed to Mazdak, under whom it was made public (for the first time).[7] The change in epithet probably owes itself to the fact that Mazdak renewed the Zaradushtagan doctrine, giving it new impetus, to the extent of adapting it as his own. The link from Zarathushtra (through a series of "Zaradoshts") to Mazdak is not imagined as directly connected, but more an informal trajectory, much like the later chain

---

2. Cf. al-Masudi, *Kitab al-tanbih*, 101; Yarshater, "Mazdakism", 997; cf. M. Guidi, "Mazdak", in *EIs*, vol. 6.

3. The earliest account of Mazdakism is found in the Syriac *Chronicle* of Pseudo-Joshua the Stylite (ed. and trans. W. Wright) (Cambridge, 1882), paras ix, xx and xxi–xxiv. For the Greek, Persian and Arab sources and discussion on them, see Guidi, "Mazdak"; Yarshater, "Mazdakism", 993–5.

4. Cf. Tabari, *Ta'rikh*, vol. 1, 893; Yaqubi, *Ta'rikh*, vol. 1, 185, cited in Yarshater's "Mazdakism", 995. The date for Zardosht is 431CE, contemporary with the emergence of Monophysitism in Byzantium. Crone places him as early as Mani: "Zoroastrian Communism", 448.

5. Tabari, *Geschichte der Perser and Araber zur Zeit der Sasaniden* (ed. and trans. T. Nöldeke) (Leiden, 1973), 461, note 2; Christensen, *Le Regne du Roi Kawadh*, 59 and 66; O. Klima, *Beiträge zur Geschichte des Mazdakismus* (Prague, 1977), 55–65. Cf. Yarshater, "Mazdakism", 995.

6. Klima regarded the name of Mazdak as a conflation of an Iranian name, Mazdak, or Mizdak, or Muzhdak ("the justifier"), with a Semitic name, Mazdeq, from the root *zdq* ("righteous"). He supports the thesis that *mazdak* may have been a title for the leaders of the movement, as opposed to a proper name; possibly even what its members were called. Cf. Klima, *Mazdak*, 155–9.

7. Cf. Yarshater, "Mazdaksim".

of events connecting the Mazdakite and the later Khorramiyya (who form a major branch of the neo-Mazdakite resurrection).[8]

Socially, Mazdakism preached what appears to have been a communist agenda favouring the equitable distribution of property and women, essentially an anti-caste system that sought to break traditional barriers that benefited only the privileged classes. The idea was to allow equal opportunity for all men to take a wife, the abolition of harems, and that wealth be distributed among the poor. The acclaimed counts of promiscuity and the sharing of women were standard accusations against heretical sects, most probably untrue; in any case such allegations reflected a bruised ego among the social and religious elite because of Mazdakism's challenges. Patricia Crone discredits both the conventional viewpoints, which have either claimed the libertine and hedonist approach of Mazdak (and the later neo-Mazdakites) or characterized it as a form of asceticism and devotional piety. She restricts the Mazdakite phenomenon to a pre-modern communist trend and probably overplays "the heretical" claims of (implicitly promiscuous) "women-sharing" among the Mazdakites, implying that they treated land and women as communal commodities (with unrestricted access by all of its members), a fact, Crone argues, most scholars are only too keen to explain away or ignore.[9] However, we have to be careful how we conceive Mazdak's social and communal outlook towards women and property, because his principles (like those of Marx!) are easily made to conform to a given "communistic" stereotype or agenda. The Mazdakites were sharply aware that "women" and "property" were two major reasons for war, hatred and discord,[10] and it is therefore likely they sought to minimize their impact. Clearly the Mazdakite doctrine is not simply a hollow principle ("communistic" or otherwise). Instead, Mazdakism has an underlying austerity which is misinterpreted in light of prominent religious themes. Crone's work does not pretend to interpret the subtleties of Mazdakite religious life. There is no mistaking, as Patricia Crone and Mansour Shaki point out,[11] that the concern with women and property is a pivotal one.[12] Ehsan Yarshater probes more deeply, however, in showing how Mazdak's prohibition sought to prevent a social imbalance based on reformist religious principles that identified the general cause of suffering and injustice. Perhaps adding to Crone's slant on Mazdak's treatment of women, Yarshater suggests the Mazdakites specifically targeted the accumulation of women – or the possession of more than one wife by the privileged class – and sought to reduce the financial requirement

---

8. Cf. the thesis of G. H. Sadighi, *Les Mouvements*.
9. Crone, "Zoroastrian Communism", 451–63.
10. Cf. e.g. al-Nadim, *Fehrest* (ed. Tajaddud), 342; Yarshater, "Mazdakism", 1005.
11. Shaki, "The Cosmogonical and Cosmological Teachings of Mazdak", 527–43.
12. P. Crone, "Kavad's Heresy and Mazdak's Revolt", *Iran* 29 (1991), 21–42; and M. Shaki, "The Social Doctrine of Mazdak in Light of Middle Persian Evidence", *Archiv Orientali* 46 (1978), 289–306.

of marriage, such as the dowry (and marriage portion for the wife [*kabin*]) so that the less well-off members of society could have fair opportunities in the prospect of marriage. The Mazdakite worldview also extended to the breaking up of the harems and it allowed intermarriage among social estates, a fact to which Crone also admits.[13] Indeed, Mazdak never attacked the family nucleus of Persian society, and marriage continued among the later Khorramiyya.[14]

A gnostic or sapiential heritage?

Mazdakism outwardly functioned as a reformed Zoroastrianism that was later, under Khosrow I (Anushirvan) (ruled 531–579),[15] branded a heretical interpretation of Zoroastrian Holy Scriptures. It went underground as a result of its brutal suppression but reappeared in various sectarian forms after the advent of Islam and the fall of the Sasanian Empire in the mid seventh century.[16] The contention is that Mazdakism may quite possibly have been a continuation of the Iranian gnostic or sapiential tradition that began with or was inspired by Zarathushtra. Mazdakism's apparent innovation, however, lies in its adaptation of the sacredness of numbers and letters, as seen from the report of Shahrestani (d. 1153).[17] Although Mani had earlier made a similar appeal to the authenticity of Zarathushtra's revelation, through his own syncretic and macro-prophetic vision, the central appeal of his particular faith was primarily to a Christian audience.[18] Connections between Manichaeism and Mazdakism are worth exploring within a broader comparative spectrum of Gnostic activity in the Iranian heartland; yet Mazdakism did not originate in Manichaeism, as earlier presumed,[19] even if a similar stress on a monistic theological frame, carefully disguised as dualism, suggests some overlap.[20] An intriguing hypothesis has it that Mazdakism stems from noting an irregularity from within the official Manichaean body. A rogue Manichaean by the name of Bundos appeared in Diocletian Rome professing that "the good god had already accomplished victory over the evil one and that the victory

---

13. Yarshater, "Mazdakism" (2), in *ER2* (ed. L. Jones), 5800a; Yarshater "Mazdakism", 991–1024; Crone, "Zoroastrian Communism", 454.
14. Cf. *ibid.*
15. Khosrow's era falls in conjunction with the reign of the eastern Roman Emperors, Justinian I (527–565) and Justin II (565–578).
16. Yarshater, "Mazdakism" (2), 5800a.
17. Shahrestani, *al-Milal wa'l-nihal*; also, Shaki, "Mazdakism", and Yarshater, "Mazdakism".
18. L. J. R. Ort, *Mani: A Religio-Historical Description of his Personality* (Leiden, 1967), esp. 195–202.
19. Concerning Mazdakism as a reform of Manichaeism, Christensen, *Le Regne*, 108–19.
20. Müller, "Mazdak and the Alphabet Mysticism of the East", 74. Cf. also F. Altheim & R. Stiehl, *Ein asiatischer Staat* (Wiesbaden, 1954), 189, and *Finanzgeschichte der Spätantike* (Frankfurt, 1947), 24–36.

should be honoured".[21] He was allegedly banished by the Manichaean community there and travelled to Persia to propagate his doctrine, which the Persians
came to call *dorost dinan*.[22] But that is probably only a sideshow in a mainly
Zoroastrian story.

The appeal to *dorost dinan* as a way of running the Manichaean and
Mazdakian traditions together does not help in our analysis. In Sufi macrohistories, or projected images of their ancestry, there seems to be no special
interest paid to Mani, nor does he retain a role in their tradition. Mani appears
to sit on a parallel trajectory that is not Iranian in origin – as the Persian Sufis
have sensed.[23] Still, it is important to explore this overlap in brief for clarification at this point. Arthur Christensen puts it that Bundos set the foundation
for Mazdakism, and in fact identified Bundos with Zaradosht,[24] implicating
Mazdakism as reforming a Manichaean sect.[25] However, this cannot be the
case, because Bundos is clearly a peculiarity even within the Manichaean
framework. Instead it could be argued that Christensen's demonstration of the
role of Bundos in Mazdakism usefully brings to the fore the probable presence
of a resistant trend operating within the Manichaean framework. Very much
like the versatile Sufi stream within Islam, there is a non-denominational factor
represented by Bundos and Mazdak, who at least share broadly the same unorthodox (religious) attitude and resilient culture. In this way, both Bundos and
Mazdak are perceived as parallel aberrations reflecting the same subterranean
tendency. In support of Christensen's hypothesis, Bundos (as a Manichaean
outcast) could have a place in the formation of early Mazdakism, especially
if he is to be associated with Zaradosht. However, this does not show that
Mazdakism was derived from Manichaeism, especially in the light of our hidden "indigenous" Iranian macrohistory.[26] Instead, Christensen's work becomes
important in taking Bundos as a clue for investigating resilient Persian trends
within Manichaeism itself. In the end, it seems this Bundos, like Mazdak,
cared less for religious formality, pointing to deeper spiritual foundations.

---

21. Müller, "Mazdak and the Alphabet Mysticism of the East", 75. The case of Bundos is argued
    by Christensen, *Le Regne du Roi Kawadh*, 96.
22. Müller, "Mazdak and the Alphabet Mysticism of the East", 74f; Yarshater "Mazdakism", 995.
23. G. Quispel, "Mani", in Trompf & Honari (eds), *Mehregan in Sydney*, 53–7.
24. Christensen, *Le Regne du Roi Kawadh*. Taking the name Bundos to be an honorific title of
    Zaradosht, from Mid. Pers. *bwynkh* ("the venerable"), cf. Guidi, "Mazdak".
25. But Klima held Zaradosht and Bundos as separate persons, in his *Mazdak* and *Beiträge
    zur Geschichte des Mazdakismus*; Yarshater gives the later date for Zaradosht in the fifth
    century CE. On E. Arrigoni's reckoning, Bundos is a fictitious "re-personalization" of the
    Buddha in a misreading of Budos; see Arrigoni's *Manicheismo, Mazdakismo e sconfessione
    dell'eresiarca romano–persiano Bundos* (Milan, 1982).
26. At the same time, Christensen's own intentions, however, remain unscrutinized and
    welcomed as one possible alternative version of the macrohistory we are delineating. I
    have pointed out problems that exist in assuming a general link between Mazdakism and
    Manichaeism.

Ultimately, Mazdak's endeavour would by-pass Manichaeism (and even a formal recognition of Mani), to place his movement in a Zoroastrian context and ground it in direct appeal to Zarathushtra. In the broader view, at any rate, a precise relationship between Mani and Mazdak is not the point; what is significant, rather, is the comparable nature of their attempts at disseminating the sacred teachings of the Iranian world (and of earnestly maintaining them so that they would eventually filter across into Islamic consciousness).

Mazdak and the court politics

The course of Mazdakism, however, was largely affected by the political intrigue procured by the social elite (*bozorgan*)[27] *vis-à-vis* the activities of Kavad I (488–531) and his son Khosrow I Anushirvan (531–79). Kavad, who is the movement's supporter, ascended the throne following the Hephthalite defeat of the Sasanians in 484. The defeat saw the death of the emperor Peroz I (459–484, Kavad's father), and initiating a seven-year period of chaos and famine in Iran. For a short period Peroz's brother Balash (484–548) was ruler, briefly enthroned by the nobility, but he was soon toppled at the behest of Magian priests who feared disruption to their laws.[28] In 488 Kavad was crowned by both the nobility and priesthood. It is in this upheaval that the egalitarian reform of Mazdak began to flourish, and the movement's ascension was also aided by increasing sectarian fragmentation and conflicts between Magians and Christians typical of the period. The Hephthalites had also decimated the military nobility and undermined their privileged status and power. Kavad, wanting autonomy from the nobility and the influence of the priests, sponsored the present leader of the Zartoshtagan movement, that is, Mazdak, and identified himself as paragon of *dorost-din* ("of the right faith") in stark contrast to the Zoroastrian indicator *veh-din* ("the good religion").[29] This was a double ploy to gain both religious and military support against the nobles and priests, as well as to use the movement for restoring and transforming his kingdom.[30] His employment of Mazdak's social doctrine was certainly a useful

---

27. Or "*Wuzurgan*"; Cf. M. Morony, "Sasanids", in *EIs*, vol. 9.
28. Cf. R. N. Frye, "The Political History of Iran under the Sassanians", in *CHI*, vol. 3(1), 149; Morony, "Sasanids".
29. The phrase *dorost din* = "right faith" or "religion", by implication: the "correct religion"; see Christensen, *Le Regne du Roi Kawadh*, 96–8. For the usage *Derosthenos*, associated with *dorost din*, Malalas of Antioch, *Chronographia*, in *Patrologiae Cursus Completus: Series Graeca* 97 (ed. J. P. Migne) (Paris, 1860); and for further association with the "Zaradushtagan", Joshua the Stylite, *Chronicle* (ed. and trans. W. Wright) (Cambridge, 1882), para. 20. Yarshater, "Mazdakism", 995–6.
30. Cf. Nöldeke's trans. of Tabari, *Geschichte der Perser*, 455–67, and Christensen's *Le Règne du Roi Kawadh*. Also, N. Pigulevskaya, "Mazdakitskoye dvizeniye", *Izvestiya Akademii nauk SSSR* 1 (Seriya Istorii i Filosofii) (1944), 171–81, and *Goroda Irana v rannem srednevekov'e*

pragmatic means to undermine the nobility: by depriving the exclusivity of nobility over women and property, Kavad intended to break down existing social barriers, and through allowing marriage between nobles and commoners, in particular, he sought to repopulate the state and restore agriculture.[31] However, due to the excesses of this Mazdakite "libertinism", major disruptive reactions occurred (in 494–495), forcing Kavad's dethronement in 496 at the hands of the nobility. They had him incarcerated and replaced by his brother, Jamasp (496–499). Yet Kavad escaped, fleeing to the Hephthalites, with whom he formed a familial bond (through marriage).

In 499, with Hephthalite support, Kavad returned to the throne. The affairs of state were stabilized, with the Mazdakites becoming the official state religion for approximately thirty years. Kavad's Mazdakite influence reached Arabia, prompting the conversion of the Lakhmids of al-Hira to Mazdakism (c.500s) even though Kavad's decree was refused by the Lakhmid king al-Munthir III (514–523?).[32] The latter was replaced with al-Harith ibn Amr al-Kinda (523–527),[33] who seems to have brought Mazdakism to the Arabs of Najd and the Hijaz.[34] Later, Khosrow I's subsequent anti-Mazdakite regime (from 531) nearly eradicated both the Kindis and Mazdakite leadership in Persia itself.[35] Nevertheless, the religion of Mazdak had apparently spread to two of the most prominent and sophisticated regions of Arabia.

Kavad gave his sons Kayanid names and was called by the prefix "Kay" (*Kay Kobad*) on his coins, a likely indication of the kingly tradition of Iran. The shift in Kavad's approach away from Mazdakism, however, was more than likely initiated at the behest of his son and successor, Khosrow, who doubtless had a personal vendetta against Mazdak.[36] It is understood that

---

(Moscow, 1956) (trans. *Les villes de l'État iranien aux époques parthe et sassanide* [Paris, 1963], 195–230).

31. Cf. Morony, "Sassanids".
32. Bosworth, "Iran and the Arabs before Islam", 600.
33. I. Shahid and A. F. L. Beeston, "Kinda; 1. The pre-Islamic period", in *EIs*, vol. 5.
34. Cf. M. J. Kister, *Studies in Jahiliyya and Early Islam* (London, 1980), 144–5. The account is recorded in Ibn Sa'id's *Naswat al-tarab*, Ms. Tübingen, fol. 96v; cf. F. Trummeter, *Ibn Sa'id's Geschichte der vorislamischen Araber* (Stuttgart, 1928), and G. Potiron, "Un polygraphe andalou du XIII Siècle", *Arabica* 13(2) (1966), 164.
35. Khosrow I restored al-Munthir to his throne in Hira (c. 527 or 528), where Munthir massacred the leading Kindis, with Harith fleeing to Byzantine territory; Bosworth, "Iran and the Arabs", 602.
36. Some scholars explain that Kavad (449–531) changed his political position over time and distanced himself from the Mazdakites gradually, withdrawing his support fully towards the end of his life. This is unlikely, as the decision to withdraw support occurs suddenly, at an old age (about 82), and as directed by Khosrow. There is a Middle Persian source, *Mazdak-namag*, that cites the story of Mazdak's asking Kavad for Khosrow's mother to be surrendered to him and for Khosrow's intervention. Cf. R. Kruke, "Sharaf Az-Zaman Tahir Marwazi (fl. c.1100AD): On Zoroaster, Mani, Mazdak, and other pseudo-Prophets", *Persica* 17 (2001), 51–68.

the Mazdakites favoured the eldest son, Kawus, to succeed, in which case his younger brother Khosrow moved quickly to bring the Mazdaean priests on side, and challenged Mazdak's influence over his father. Next, Khosrow cunningly engineered to draw the Mazdakites to Ctesiphon (for either a religious disputation or to proclaim Kawus as successor in 528 or 529). In this assembly he managed to convince Kavad that Mazdak's doctrines were false and had the latter and his followers, numbering in the thousands (approx. 80,000), massacred.[37] Khosrow I carries the epithet, "Khosrow the Just", but this soubriquet owes as much to his father's political idealism as it does to his own cunning. Kavad's move to implement fiscal, administrative and legal reforms, in conjunction with the Mazdakite social doctrine, was already, by the time of Khosrow I, in motion. In effect, Khosrow gained his so-called "Just" reputation because he was forced to administer some of Kavad's social policies, even though his counter-Mazdakite measures were also helpful to his cause in restoring the traditional social ethos.[38] In a very striking sense, this bit of historical account is directly replayed much later with the Abbasid betrayal of the Shi'a movement that placed it in power. According to Tabari, Kavad especially won favour among those affected by the radical Mazdakite social doctrine.[39] Aware of the influence of the nobility, Khosrow purged his rivals from among the royal family and the nobility, giving him complete autonomy to rule. His newly implemented economic program both prevented further rebellion and kept the nobility in check. New alliances with the Turks were made to destroy the Hephthalite threat to the east, marking the formal end of their empire in 557. Khosrow's achievements saw the restoration of the Sasanian Empire to its height as a recognized international power.

Regardless, deep-seated problems persisted at the core of the Sasanian social fabric that led to its own demise – with the arrival of Islam. Mazdak, the so-called "unsuccessful prophet"[40] of Iran, was in fact far more successful than currently given credit. The impetus of his ideas would provoke the rise of the neo-Mazdakites and the residue of his doctrine was already present in certain elements of the early Islamic theology and praxis. After forty years, the movement was driven underground only to re-emerge in the Islamic period under the Khorramiyya, and in association with other *ghulat* groups, the foundation for which was established by Kavad, who apparently introduced the religion of Mazdak to Arab thought. However, a prevalent factor connecting the Mazdakite and Islamic doctrine is the figure Salman the Persian, otherwise described in Islamic fringe gnostic imagination as *Jibraiil* (i.e. Gabriel – see Ahl-e Haqq, Nusayri, etc.).

---

37. The full account of this event is given in Ferdowsi's *Shahnameh*. For a translation of this, A. Bausani, *Religion in Iran: from Zoroaster to Baha'ullah*, 97–100.
38. And see Yarshater, "Mazdakism", 999–1000.
39. Tabari, *Ta'rikh*, vol. 1, 879; cf. Yarshater, "Mazdakism", 999–1000.
40. Bausani, *Religion in Iran: from Zoroaster to Baha'ullah*.

IRANIANS AND ARABS BEFORE ISLAM: THE PERSIAN AND MAZDAKI FACTOR IN THE EVENTS LEADING UP TO THE RISE AND DEVELOPMENT OF THE ISLAMIC SOCIO-RELIGIOUS DOCTRINE

There is little doubt about the influence the Persian way of life has had on Arabia. For instance, the influence of Persian culture is readily witnessed in the development of Arabic literature and poetry, though influence in the religious sphere is a topic of a somewhat more controversial nature, especially if one were to contend that the religious heritage of Iran affected the birth and development of the so-called "Arabian faith" of Islam. The idea of the Iranian origin of Islam, a topic hotly pursued in the early 1900s but since abandoned, has not received the attention it requires in recent years. Edgar Blochet, Ignaz Goldziher and Alessandro Bausani were among the earliest to facilitate a discourse on the importance of Iran and her pre-Islamic heritage.[41] The idea of "Iranian influence", moreover, which until now has remained in the shadow of Zoroastrianism, needs to be considered independently as extending to Mithraism and Mazdakism, and, indeed, even Manichaeism, as other major building blocks of the Iranian complex. There is no need to expand on the influence of Irano-Zoroastrian themes on Islamic literature, previously analysed by others.[42] Instead we bring to the fore those materials connected with a Mazdakite/Moslem "correspondence", as part of the hidden history of Iran. In this regard, it is important to give close scrutiny to the pre-Islamic Arab civilizations within the Persian, and also Byzantine, ambience, also noting their particular socio-religious context *vis-à-vis* the pretensions of the great empires. From a literary standpoint, the splendours and luxury of Persian court life were proverbial in early Arabia, and many pre-Islamic poets would record the features and manners of the Persian lifestyle with which they were obviously in contact.[43] The Qur'an, too, yields signs of such influence, more

---

41. Cf. Edgar Blochet, "Études sur l'histoire religieuse del 'Iran, I", *Revue de l'histoire des religions* 38 (1898), 26–63, and "II", vol. 40 (1899), 1–25 and 203–36; "Études sur l'ésoterisme musulman", *Journal Asiatique* 19 (1902), 489–531, and 20 (1903), 49–111; and *Études sur le gnosticisme musulman* (Extrait de la *Rivista degli studi orientali*, 2, 3, 4, 6) (Rome, 1913). Cf. Goldziher, *Muhammedanische Studien*, 101–20, and "Islamisme et parsisme", in *Actes du Ier Congrès International d'Histoire des Religions* (Paris, 1901), vol. 1, 119–47 (repr. in *idem*, *Gesammelte Schriften* [Hildesheim, 1967–73], vol. 4, 232–60). Also A. Bausani, *Religion in Iran*; *La Persia religiosa, da Zarathustra a Baha'ullah* (Milan, 1959), 138–50.

42. Cf. S. Shaked, "Some Iranian Themes in Islamic Literature", in *Studia Iranica 11: Recurrent Patterns in Iranian Religions: From Mazdaism to Sufism* (ed. P. Gignoux), 143–58, and other related articles therein; see also Bosworth and his sources in "Iran and the Arabs", 609–18.

43. E.g., in the al-Namara inscription of Mar al-Qais and in several pre-Islamic and Mokhadram poets: thus M. Lidzbarski, *Ephemeris für semitische Epigraphik* (Giessen, 1903–7), vol. 2, 34–6; cf. Bosworth, "Iran and the Arabs", 610.

particularly in significant theological and moral threads.[44] And Mohammed would indeed impress his audience with occasional recourse to Persian terms when describing "the joys in store for the righteous".[45]

It is quite clear that Mohammed was acquainted with literary and cultural customs abroad and was aware of foreign economic and political relations. In a nutshell, the success of Mohammed's military campaign depended on the control of Mecca, Yathrib and Hira, because they were monopolized by Persian and Byzantine forces, in conjunction with pagan Arab and Jewish mediations. Therefore, it was a potent economic stratagem of his to disarm Pagan Arab, Jewish, Persian and Byzantine control of Arabia, a success ultimately achieved through key alliances with components of these groups. The Qur'an, on the other hand, which is argued to have been completed and available as a text prior to Mohammed's death, is still the best example of foreign influence.[46] There is no need to pursue an elaborate examination of the Qur'an here, because reference to any of the critical works on the subject suffice to establish the case.[47] What needs to be explained instead is the importance of the key regions and cities in relation to Mohammed's mission and revelation, cities which have particular relation to our theme of Iranian cultural resistance.

Long before Ardashir I (*c.*226–241) sacked Charax and made Mesene into a dependent province of his empire,[48] Cyrus the Great would create a short-lived satrapy of *Arabaya* (the Arabs) in northern Arabia, and Darius(h) I The Great, encouraging trade through the Persian Gulf, sent expeditions around

---

44. Such as: *'ifrit* "demon" (early Mid. Pers. *afritan*, later Mid. Pers. *afridan* "to create", "creature"); *junah* "crime" (early MP *winah* "crime, sin", MP and NPers. *gunah*); and of course terms defining Paradise and its delights. The Arabic *firdaus* "Paradise" (Avestan *pairidaeza*) has been suggested to have passed into Greek and most Middle Eastern languages, and probably via the Christians of Iraq into Arabic. The delights of Paradise such as *istabraq* "silk brocade" (Mid. Pers. *stabraq stabr* "thick, strong") worn by the dwellers in Paradise; *namariq* "cushions" (Parthian *namr*, MPers. and NPers. *narm* "soft") and more. See Bosworth, "Iran and the Arabs", 610; cf. also, e.g., Imam Rohollah Al-Mosawi al-Khomayni, *Forty Hadith: An Exposition of Ethical and Mystical Traditions* (trans. M. M. Qaraii) (Tehran, 1989), Part, 1, 137.

45. And perhaps to counter the influence of his rival in Mecca, al-Nadr ibn al-Harith, who told stories of the Persian heroes Rostam and Esfandiyar and distracted the Prophet's audience. Cf. Ibn Ishaq *The Life of Muhammad: A Translation of Ishaq's Sirat Rasul Allah* [*Sira*] (trans. A. Guillaume) (Oxford, 2004), 162–3; cf. Bosworth, "Iran and the Arabs", 611.

46. Cf. A. T. Welch, R. Paret & J. D. Pearson, "al-Kur'an; 2. Muhammad and the Kur'an", in *EIs*, vol. 5.

47. *Ibid.*, and esp. cf. Ibn Warraq (ed.), *Origins of the Koran: Classic Essays on Islam's Holy Book* (New York, 1998); see also P. Crone and M. Cook on the subject, esp.: M. Cook, *The Koran, A Very Short Introduction* (Oxford, 2000); P. Crone, *Meccan Trade and the Rise of Islam* (Princeton, NJ, 1987); Crone & Cook, *Hagarism*.

48. With the decay of the Seleucid Empire, an Arab principality was established there in the later second century BCE (post 129) on the banks of the lower Tigris, by Hyspaosines son of Sagodonacus (known as "Charax of Hyspaosines"); Bosworth, "Iran and the Arabs", 594.

the coasts of the Arabian peninsula.[49] Naturally, the Parthians and then the Sasanians made Ctesiphon their capital. Being on the eastern bank of the Tigris in central Mesopotamia, it became the centre from which Iranian power was extended over Aramaic, and then increasingly Arab-affected Iraq. By the middle of the first century BCE the Arab infiltration into Iraq was mainly focused on Hatra (Ar. Al-Hazr), a settlement in northern Iraq (southwest of Mosul) well into present-day Kurdistani regions.[50] The point of mentioning Kurdistan is to remind us of our previous discussion about the deeper layer of cultural and religious consciousness in this Persian region, and the preservation there of the older indigenous religious (esoteric) themes of ancient Iran and Mesopotamia. At the time of the first-century intrusions, in fact, Arab principalities were found along the desert fringes of the Fertile Crescent stretching through northern Mesopotamia and Commagene to Edessa, serving as vassals to the western or eastern powers of Byzantium and Persia.[51] As ally to the Parthians, Hatra repelled Roman attacks even after Trajan (116–117) and Septimus Severus's (198–199) capture of the Parthian capital, Ctesiphon. We can certainly infer from this that Iranian cultural influences affected the Arab interlopers.

Hatra flourished as both a caravan city and as the site of a religious shrine dedicated to the cult of the Sun God.[52] There is strong interplay between ancient Mesopotamian and Persian ideas here, with the "sun god" having links with both the Mesopotamian *Shamash* and the Iranian *Mithras*. During the first and second centuries CE, Hatra (as a semiautonomous Arab state) was subject to Parthia's influence, with its revival of Iranian religion and culture entailing the special veneration of Mithra (widely spread throughout the Parthian empire). The Parthian revival was a reaction against Hellenism in the first century (*c.*300BCE–100CE), indicating that even though Persia was for a time Hellenized under the Seleucids, Iranian cultural and religious consciousness remained resilient and alive. The decree to reclaim the teachings of Zarathushtra (i.e. the *Avesta* and *Zand*) also began under the Parthians[53] and was completed by the Sasanians in its final form under the Khosrow I (Anushirvan).[54] The Parthians brought with them the impetus for the Oriental Mystery religions that swept into northwestern Iran, Mesopotamia and then throughout the Roman Empire as far as Britain.

With the overthrow of the Parthian Empire by the Sasanians in 224–226, Hatra was garrisoned for a while by the Romans against the Sasanians, until it

---

49. The voyage was delegated to the Greek Scylax of Caryanda. Cf. *ibid.*, 593.
50. *Ibid.*, 595.
51. Certain early rulers of Edessa bore Iranian names. J. B. Segal, *Edessa, "the Blessed City"* (Oxford, 1970), 16; cf. Bosworth, "Iran and the Arabs", 596.
52. *Ibid.*
53. Madan, *The Complete Text of the Pahlavi Denkard*, 412. Cf. J. Duchesne-Guillamin, *Religion of Ancient Iran*, 153.
54. Duchesne-Guillamin, "Religion of Ancient Iran", 8.

was ransacked and abolished by Shapur I in 241, under the decree of an official "monotheistic" Zoroastrian orthodoxy, and was to disappear into the romance genre of Arab consciousness. In its stead rose Hira, which became the capital of the Lakhmid dynasty, the Lakhmids being vassals of Sasanian power who guarded the desert fringes against nomadic pressure from the interior of Arabia and against the Byzantines and their Ghassanid ("Monophysite") allies of Syria.[55] Hira was the commercial centre on the east–west caravan route between Syria, Iraq and Persia, and it provided a unique encounter between the three cultures of Sasanid Zoroastrian Iran, Christian (including Nestorian) Byzantine and indigenous pagan Arabia.[56] Hira was also home to the 'Ibad ("devotees"), who were Nestorian Christians using Syriac as their liturgical and cultural language, but Arabic for common daily use.[57] Famed for their literacy, traditions tell of their influence on Meccan traders visiting Hira (who would return with a newly evolved Arabic alphabet).[58]

The Lakhmids, in securing caravan routes (through eastern Arabia) to the Hijaz and Yemen, also helped extend Sasanian influence westward across the peninsula. The Persians had always recognized the importance of the Hira–Mecca commercial and cultural highway, and well before the sixth century attempted to exert their influence even in Mecca and Yathrib to counter the Byzantium Ghassanid influence in the Hijaz.[59] Kavad may have, to some extent, imposed Mazdakism on the Arabs of Najd and Hijaz, through the success of Harith al-Kindi (which lasted no longer than his reign, 523–527), and was nevertheless a part of the attempt by Persia to control Mecca.[60] Ibn Sa'id records that some Arabs did embrace the tenets of Mazdak at the time (*faminhum man tazandaqa*), and that, later on, former Mazdakites (*zanadiqa*)[61] were recognizable during the early Islamic period.[62] In Yathrib, Persian control of the oasis was mediated by the prominent Jewish settlements of al-Nadir and Quraiza, which dominated the Arabs of Banu Qaila (Aus and Khazraj).[63] With the Arabs gaining the upper hand during the latter part of the sixth century,

55. Bosworth, "Iran and the Arabs", 596.
56. *Ibid.*, 597.
57. *Ibid.*, 598.
58. *Ibid.*
59. *Ibid.*, 596.
60. Cf. Kister, *Studies*, 144–7.
61. J. Ali (ed.), *Ta'rih al-Arab qabla'l-Islam* (Baghdad, 1957), vol. 6, 287–8. There is a list of "zanadiqa" of Quraysh in Ibn Habib's *al-Muhabbar* (ed. I. Lichtenstäder) (Hyderabad, 1942), 161.
62. Cf. M. J. Kister, "al-Hira. Some Notes on its Relations with Arabia", *Arabica* 15 (1968), 144–5; G. Olinder, "The Kings of Kinda of the Family of Akil al-Murar", *Lunds Universitets Arsskrift*, N.F. Avd. 1, Bd 26, No. 6 (1927), 63–4.
63. F. Altheim and R. Stiehl, *Finanzgeschichte der Spätantike* (Frankfurt, 1957), 149–50.

the Lakhmids continued to maintain control,[64] and the Jewish tribes constituted a significant element right up to the time of the *hijra*. In opposition to
the Lakhmids, the Banu Tamim, one of the mightiest tribes of Nejd, offered
prominent resistance to foreign rule. They were also important in playing
an especially poignant role in the defeat of the Persians as early converts to
Islam. Yet, their acceptance of Islam was questionable, for they were as quick
to renounce their ties upon Mohammed's death as they were in establishing
them with his rise to power.[65] Their interests, far from the new faith, were ide-
ally political, or so it is imagined. Indeed, the Banu Tamim, as part of the general resistance of the Arabs of Nejd (or the pre-Islamic Banu Hanifa) remained
a plausible threat to the existence of Islam, leaving a bloody battle on the hands
of Abu Bakr.[66] The strategic locations of Nejd and the Hijaz, in particular the
cities of Yathrib (=Medina), Hira and also Mecca, played a key role in the control of Arabia for both Persia and Byzantium as it did for Mohammed (and
the Islamic conquests over these two superpowers). With the rule of the two
great empires being held in the balance of volatile and eruptive Arab/Bedouin
tribal relations, the success of Islam was primarily gained in the unification
of these dispersed tribes through the charisma and strategic allegiances of
Mohammed.[67]

Earlier on, Shapur II (309/310–379) was especially famed for his harsh suppression of the Arab invasions into Persian lands, and achieved the control of
eastern Arabia in stationing Persian soldiers and officials there, subsequently
implanting Zoroastrianism.[68] Another point of interest concerns the Persian
military aid sent to support the Yemeni nationalist reaction against Ethiopian
control in eastern Arabia. After failing to negotiate with the Byzantines, the
leader of the insurrection, Saif ibn Dhi Yazan, directly contacted the Sasanian
Anushirvan, who reluctantly sent a force of 800 men (originally destined for
execution but allowed to redeem themselves in battle) under the leadership of a
certain Vahriz.[69] Successful in defeating the Ethiopians, Dhi Yazan was planted
as the king of Himyar and vassal to the Sasanians. A second uprising took
place in the absence of the Persian garrison, but Vahriz ultimately returned to
banish the Ethiopians from Yemen (and thus Christian Monophysite influence

---

64. Al-Numan III Ibn al-Munthir placed Amr ibn Itnaba al-Khazraji (referred to as "king of the
Arabs" by Sa'id) as his representative in the oasis. Cited in Kister, *Studies in Jahiliyya and
Early Islam*, 146–8; cf. Bosworth, "Iran and the Arabs", 601.
65. Bokhari, *Sahih*, vol. 5, 459, 652, and Sahih Moslem, Book 5, 2323. Cf. www.usc.edu/dept/
MSA/fundamentals/hadithsunnah/muslim/005. smt.html#005.2323.
66. A. Guillaume, *Islam* (Harmondsworth, 1956), 79.
67. Indeed the Lakhmids, knowing this, were adept at taking advantage of tribal feuds and
vendettas within Arabia, playing off one group against its rivals. Cf. Bosworth, "Iran and
the Arabs", 601.
68. *Ibid.*, 603.
69. *Ibid.*, 607.

with it). A Persian occupation force remained in Yemen until post-*hijra*, where Mohammed entered into agreements with the Persian governor and then his son.[70] This again illustrates Mohammed's active political engagement with foreign components for control of Arabia. Heraclius's victories in Iraq isolated the Persian colony of officials and soldiers and the fate of the Persian forces in northwest Arabia was to join the new faith (Islam) in supporting Moslem commanders to suppress revolts of the local prophet al-Aswad.[71] Yet some retained their Zoroastrian faith and were subjected to religious tax.[72] As the large tide turned, the current of events worked in favour of the Moslems. Within Medina, the Jews were losing their prominence, followed by the subsequent decline of Lakhmid influence in the Hijaz. By the 630s, in a short period of time, the increasing vulnerability of the Persians encouraged the Arabs to advance, and Iraq and Hira were taken by the famed Moslem general, Khalid Ibn al-Walid. In eastern Arabia, too, the Persians lost control and the Persian marzban of Hajar (who was called Sebukht) and his retinue joined Islam; there were those, however, who remained faithful to Zoroastrianism and who were taxed accordingly as People of the Book.[73]

Kavad's move to bring Mazdakism to the Arabs is an especially important factor to consider here. Persian and Zoroastrian influence in Iran and Arabia amounted to the norm for the elitist Sasanian regime, and so the rule of Kavad and his advisor Mazdak was an exception to it. If Mazdakism was known in sophisticated regions of Arabia (the Hijaz and Najd), and had converts from among them after Kavad's push for religious change in Persian lands, some social aspects of this may very well have particular pertinence to the social application of Mohammed's views. Another point is the possible role of Mazdakite elements for the support of the Islamic conquest of Persia, grounded in a "payback" mentality, considering Khosrow I's persecution of Mazdakism. This is the implication of Tabari's account of Mohammed's confidence when Khosrow rebuffs his envoy.[74] In an exercise of charting the history of ideas, the likely presence of Mazdakism in Arabia becomes an important and uncharted event underlining the conventional beginnings of Islam. Given that Mazdakism is supposed to have entered Arabia officially, it is more than likely that it survived Khosrow's persecution in the isolated regions of western Arabia. Considering Khosrow drove the remaining Persian Mazdakis underground, we perhaps have no reason to expect a great deal of evidence to tell us

---

70. *Ibid.*, 607–8.
71. Tabari, *Geschichte der Perser*, 264 and 349–51; A. Christensen, *L'Iran sous les Sassanides* (Copenhagen, 1936), 368–9; W. M. Watt, *Muhammad at Medina* (Oxford, 1956), 121–30; K. V. Zetterstéen, "Abna", in *EIs*, vol. 1; Bosworth, "Iran and the Arabs", 607.
72. Bosworth, "Iran and the Arabs", 607.
73. *Ibid.*, 608–9.
74. Cf. Tabari, *Ta'rikh al-rusul*, discussed in L. Caetani, *Annali dell'Islam: Compilati de Leone Caetani* (Milan, 1907) (Hildesheim repr. 1972), vol. 2.

anything of interest, that is, other than that which is preserved in the oral tradition of esoteric currents, and the fragmented evidence detected in historical accounts, as noted. Or perhaps key evidence is provided in the Arabian case in Islam itself!

Regarding this last point, we must face up to the egalitarian spirit as a social-religious character clearly held in common in both Mazdakism and early Islam, and one needs to gauge this spirit as a crucial lineament in the history of ideas from Mazdak to Mohammed. The basic equitable character of the early Islamic community corresponds to a uniquely Mazdakite feature that granted rights to women and promoted a commanding egalitarian ideology, which was initiated by Mazdak's *batini* or "closer" reading of the *Avesta*.[75] Both Islam and Mazdakism were fundamentally concerned with the less fortunate members of society, and the two movements arose out of a blend of socio-religious reaction to a caste system and a heavily ethnic religious establishment.[76] In addition, it can hardly be denied that key features of military success for the Moslem campaign against the Sasanians were based on the significant portion of Persian supporters. Now these supporters included Persian exiles, intellectuals and craftspeople, partially assimilated Persians in Arabian lands, as well as former members of the official Persian military forces.[77] Tabari mentions that Arab subjects of the Persian army were among the first converts to Islam, which also affected Persian officers and soldiers who hoped to keep their position.[78] In dealing with subtlety of ideas, the Mazdakite element should not be left out. This could be imagined, in light of Ibn Saad's comments,[79] as consisting of "former" Mazdakites, Mazdakite sympathizers, or even groups providing signs of the earliest neo-Mazdakite resurgence in Arabia. The strength of such a notion is supported by our prior account of existing cultural and religious resilience, seen in the persistence of suppressed (or rather oppressed) nuances in the indigenous imaginings of Persian consciousness.

The Arabs, as previous subjects of the Persians, once formed the front ranks of the Persian army, but the reverse was to occur with the conquest of Iran.[80] It is a common misperception that Islam suddenly burst out of the Arabian Peninsula to conquer the great powers of the time; at least it seemed that way to the conquered. The actual detail of Islam's military successes was really

---

75. Of particular note is: Vendidad 4:44: "If fellow-believers (*ham-daena*), brothers or friends, come to ask for money, wife, or wisdom (*xrato*), he who asks for money should be given money; he who asks for a wife should be given a wife to marry; he who asks for wisdom should be taught the holy word." Cf. Yarshater, "Mazdakism", 997.

76. This is referring of course to the monopoly of the Quraysh in Mecca and the Sasanian elite (*bozorgan*), and to the cult of Kaaba and Zoroastrianism of the priests.

77. Cf. Bosworth "Iran and the Arabs", 607.

78. Tabari, *Ta'rikh*, vol. 1, 2278, in B. Spüler, *Iran in früh-islamischer Zeit* (Wiesbaden, 1952), 134, cited by Duchesne-Guillamin, "Religion of Ancient Iran", 237.

79. Cf. Kister, *Studies*, 144–5.

80. *Ibid.*, 237.

based on utilizing dissident internal forces and resistant cultures. As with Persia, so with the undoing of Byzantium, for Mohammed was well placed from both a religious and political vantage point to gain significant support from "internal components".[81] In fact the same method was employed when Mohammed gained control of Arabia, in building the security of *pax Islamica* at his power base in Medina.[82] This certainly connects back to the questions raised at the beginning of the twentieth century by Islamicists regarding the exact nature, and indeed the exotic question, of a *Persian* origin for Islam, and thus by implication a Persianate impetus to Islamise Persia.

There is a demonstrable connection between Mazdakism and the Islamic conquest of Persia. We find that the advent of Mazdakism represents one popularized version of an ingrained Persian resistant trend, which surfaces for a short time before it is dispersed again; but then, with regard to the Moslem military conquest, the fall of Persia was closely linked with political, social and religious intrigue propelled by the indigenous and resistant culture presented in Mazdakism.[83] It is, therefore, controversially important to note Mazdak's effect on Arabia and its presence in Mecca both before and during Mohammed's time. Subtle religious currents, as represented by Mazdakism, have had a significant effect in conditioning Arabian socio-religious consciousness towards the formation of Islam, and these previously unexplored Persian ideas persisted beyond the Moslem conquest of Persia and inform the special character of "Iranian Islam".

The advent of Mazdakism, indeed, provides an intriguing background to the case for Salman the Persian, besides the fact that the "Persian continuity" we pursue is further demonstrated in this mysterious figure. As will be explained, Salman can be inferred as a disciple of Mazdak's teachings who transmits its principles to Mohammed directly. Throughout our macrohistorical exercise, therefore, Mazdakism takes a special place in illustrating a "retributive effect" of Iranian components that bounce on and give confidence to collective Arabian consciousness. Was the Arabian Islam a revived Mazdakite project? It is unlikely that an "official" Mazdakism was literally conspiring a negative payback against an "official" Persia, rejecting its truths. Rather, the events are to be perceived as far more natural, in that they unfolded through subtle relations and interactions (of ideas, beliefs and practices) between Persia and Arabia, conditioned by the particular personalities and the work of Mazdak and Salman. Admittedly, in the absence of clinching textual materials, the link between Mazdak and Salman can only present itself as a good inference. The

81. Cf. A. M. H. Shboul, "Arab Islamic Perceptions of Byzantine Religion and Culture", in *Muslim Perceptions of Other Religions: A Historical Survey* (ed. J. Waardenburg) (Oxford, 1999), 122–35.
82. Watt, *Muhammad at Medina*, 122.
83. Zarrinkub, "The Arab Conquest of Iran and its Aftermath", 17.

fact that Salman is seen as a reactionary figure (against the Zoroastrian establishment), however, gives credibility to his likely ideological connection to the "communistic" flavour of Mazdakite teachings, especially given the shared spirit of egalitarianism in Mazdak's and Mohammed's reforms, and their common attempts to break the monopoly of elite classes. To Salman we now turn.

CHAPTER 8

BETWEEN LATE ANTIQUITY AND ISLAM: THE CASE OF SALMAN THE PERSIAN AND WARAQA (THE CHRISTIAN SCRIBE)

For the Sufi acolyte, the presence of a master, often referred to as "the Friend" (also a reference for God), is a necessity. Thus far, what this book has tried to demonstrate regarding this theme is the importance of such relationships throughout the history of Iranian religion. That is to say, that the transference of religious knowledge, especially of a mystical or gnostic nature, depends upon a close bond between two or more initiated individuals. This can also occur when personalities of the past are looked upon by adherents as teachers of sacred knowledge. I do not mean to propose a perennial theory here, but rather observe the landscape of Iranian religion and the major thematic monuments along its route from pre-Islamic to Islamic Iran. Thus Pagan Mithra worship (Anahita), Zarathushtra (Mazda), Mazdak (Zoroastrian *gnosis*), the *ghulat* (neo-Mazdakites) and now moving into the Islamic era are highlighted as important platforms in the landscape of Iranian identity.

Enter Salman the Persian, at times made synonymous with Gabriel, and thus emerging as the legendary figure responsible for the direct pollination of ideas and practices from Iran to Arabia. Like Mazdak, Salman is another generally overlooked figure who bridges the historical gap between two periods (that of the Persian and Arab). Importantly, he is not only a missing puzzle of Persia's hidden past, crucial for our work on the macrohisotry of Iranian religion, but also fills in links between Mazdak and Mohammed.

SALMAN THE PERSIAN

Salman, the hidden "gate" between Pre-Islamic and Islamic Iran?

Born Ruzbeh Khoshnudan, the man who later acquired the name "Salman the Persian" or "Salman-e Farsi" was also known as "the Barber" (an epithet of his name in Pers. *Salmani*), because it is said he served the Prophet in that capaci-ty.[1] The relationship of Salman and Mohammed is a classic image of Islam that was entertained by the poetic imagination, up to Iqbal, painting the com-plementary theme of "the poor Persian and the mighty prophet-king".[2] But, as Dwight Donaldson had contested, Salman "appears to have done more, however, than to shave the head and trim the beard of the Prophet", for he was able "to establish himself in his intimate friendship and confidence".[3] Indeed, there is more to the figure of Salman than is readily admitted by the Islamic establishment. In fact, much more is revealed about the figure of Salman from resistant cultures and esoteric currents of spirituality within the milieu of Persian religious consciousness. As will be demonstrated from eso-teric (Persian Sufi and Shi'a Imami) materials, Salman was so much more to Mohammed than mainstream, and especially Sunni, traditions suggest. These are remains of references to Salman in major works of philosophy and theol-ogy of Islamic Persia. An early allusion to the legacy of Salman the Persian and his relationship with Mohammed is found in Ibn Sina's philosophical-mystical narrative work *Fi Maqamat al-'ârifîn* ("On the Station of the Knowers"), where he cites the famed Persian fable of *Salaman and Basal* believed to have been first referred to in the eleventh century, and apparently invented by Ibn Sina himself, who first presented the allusion as an enigma or riddle to his audi-ence.[4] The fable was later popularized by other great poets, such as Fakhr al-Din Razi (d. 1209), Nasir al-Din Tusi (d. 1274) and Nur al-Din 'Abd al-Rahman Jami (1414–92).[5] Razi confirmed Ibn Sina's reference as an "insoluble enigma",

---

1. In Persian Ruzbeh means "a good day". See Abu Nuaim al-Isbahani, *Dala'il an-nubuwwa* (Hyderabad/Deccan, 1950), 213–19; R. Paret, *Die legendäre Maghâzî-Literatur. Arabische Dichtungen über die muslimischen Kriegszüge zu Mohammads Zeit* (Tübingen, 1930), 189–30; D. M. Donaldson, "Salman the Persian", *The Muslim World* 19(4) (1929), 338–52; J. Horovitz, "Salman al-Farisi", *Der Islam*, 12 (1922), 178–83; C. Huart, "Selman de Fars", in *Mélanges Hartwig Derenbourg* (Paris, 1909), 297–310; L. Massignon, "Les origines de la méditation Shiite sur Salmân et Fâtima", in *Mélanges H. Massé* (Tehran, 1963), 264–6; and "Salmân-i Pak et les prémices spirituelles de l'Islam iranien", in *idem* & V. Monteil, *Parole Donnée* (Paris, 1962), 91–128.

   A. Schimmel, *And Muhammad is His Messenger* (London, 1985), 267, notes that "in Turkish barber shops, one might find, in former days, a plate with the verse:

   > Every morning our shop opens with the *basmala*;
   > Hazret-i Salman-i Pak is our *pir* and our master.

   She also noted that in some Turkish dervish orders, the expression *selman etmek*, "to make someone Salman", meant to send him out to beg and learn humility. See A. Gölpînarlî, *Tasavvuftan dilimize geçen deyimler ve atasözleri* (Istanbul, 1977), 288–9.
2. Cf. Schimmel, *And Muhammad is His Messenger*, 267.
3. Cf. Donaldson, "Salman the Persian", 341.
4. See S. Inati, "Fi Maqamat al-'ârifîn ['On the Station of the Knowers']", in *Anthology of Philosophy in Persia* (eds. S. H. Nasr & M. Amirnazavi) (Oxford, 2001), vol. 1, 251.
5. On Jami's version and summary of others, see I. Dehghan, "Jami's Salaman and Absal", *Journal of Near Eastern Studies* 30(2) (1971), 118–26.

supporting the view that the two words "Salaman" and "Absal" were invented by him for purposes known only to himself. But Tusi, who was equally puzzled by the allusion, maintained that the two words could not have been the invention of Ibn Sina, even while failing to establish their original source. Then there is the highly revered work known as *Umm al-Kitab*, a Shi'a Imami/Isma'ili text whose production is approximated between eighth and tenth centuries, which contains "nuances attributing a major role in the rise of Islam to Salman al-Farisi, whose gnostic name is al-Salsal".[6] In this work, he is not only referred to with the traditional titles as being the gate to Mohammed, but also counted (along with Mohammed and Ali and his progeny) "truly worthy of praise by God [and] are the chosen ones".[7] Also of interest is to note that the central figure and chief Isma'ili *da'i*, Al-Mu'ayyad Fi'l-Din Shirazi (999–1077), whose real name is Hibat Allah ibn Musa ibn Dawud Salmani, was believed to have been a direct descendent of Salman al-Farisi.[8] In these Persian representations Salman was forced to deliberately disguise his command of religious knowledge from other companions – a secret, it seems, which only Mohammed and Ali (and his progeny) were aware of. Even though Salman's true capacity and favour remained hidden from common view, there is a general commemoration to his extraordinary quality – some parts of which are obvious, others requiring elucidation – that can be identified in orthodox Islamic materials. On the other hand, esoteric readings of Salman offer a radical interpretation of his role that places him at the core of the history of Islam: as being directly involved in the production of its sacred text, traditions and military expansions. Intriguingly, the only "person" involved in such a task, as accepted by Moslem orthodoxy, is none other than the angelic figure known as *Jibril* (Gabriel). Therefore, the provocative question erupts out of subversive Iranian visions of the past: is Salman the hidden identity of Gabriel? This may always remain an unanswerable question only, but it is a question that has to be asked, here, because the two are made *one* in esoteric sources crucial for this work.

The figure of Salman the Persian has a very significant place in the history of both Persia and Arabia. The exercise of our macrohistory has attempted to make this connection as part of a progressive trajectory from Deep Antiquity to the Sufis. Salman provides the final link in a chain that connects Mazdakism to Mohammed's "new society" and thus weds the sacred histories of Persia and Arabia. He is not the only "foreign" aspect to Arabia that links into the rise of Islam, though, as we can see from the case of Bilal, who offers a window into a different, but related, trajectory of investigation concerning

---

6. See L. P. Peerwani (intro., M. Amirnazavi), "Umm al-Kitab" ("The Mother of Books"), in Nasr & Amirnazavi, *Anthology of Philosophy*, vol. 2, 17.
7. Cf. Peerwani, "Umm al-Kitab, in *ibid.*, vol. 2, 27.
8. Cf. J. M. Muscati & A. M. Moulvi (intro. M. Amirnazavi), "Al-Mu'ayyad Fi'l-Din Shirazi", in *ibid.*, vol. 2, 281.

the early formation of Islam, that is, that of North Africa. Naturally, for our purposes, Salman pertains primarily to the story of Persia and the Moslem conquest of that land. Whereas in the past Salman was strictly limited to a "Zoroastrian" image, our observations have presented a more complex character. Salman seems to have spent quite some time travelling the Near East and the Fertile Crescent before entering Arabia, spending his time, indeed, in the company and service of specific "unorthodox" Syrian monks. Therefore, it is with caution that we refer to Salman as a "Persian", so as not to confuse him with the Zoroastrian establishment. It is also with due caution that we refer to his Syrian monastic *encounter*, so as not to put an official "Christian" affiliation upon him. From the standard material available to us, Salman becomes a good example of an adherent to the Moslem perspective of the *hanifi* religion. In particular, given that he is neither placed as Zoroastrian, Jew, Christian or pagan by affiliation, he holds all the prerequisites necessary for a *hanif* or otherwise "natural *moslem*". This would be fascinating in itself to "prove" with any finality, yet there are too many problems about it to address here, since both the term *hanif* and its conceptual affiliation warrant much scholarly inquiry.[9] Admittedly, the link between Salman and Mazdakite teachings can be no more than an inference as far as the late antique textual date is concerned, but it is based on a Sufi "[macro-]myth-history" later arising and in turn deriving from crucial oral sources. We have already discussed how Salman is a cue for esoteric themes in the Nusayri theological triad and in Ahl-e Haqq, but through this we can also go on to say that our hunch about Salman's possible initial role in mediating a connection between Mohammed and Persia, in the so-called Persian "alternative tradition", has been further substantiated from pockets of evidence available to us within both traditional and non-traditional Moslem sources. The correspondence of Mazdakism and Islam via Salman is indeed an intriguing, if controversial, one, but one which may also be further explored through a better understanding of the notions of *dorost-din* and (as far as we can go here) the *"hanifi*-religion". Therefore, the Persian aspect of Salman is highly pertinent to our macrohistory, seen as a lineament of anti-establishment activity: he affects the Zoroastrian establishment and the Sasanian state as a component of Islam. His persona is later taken up by resilient currents in Iran (indeed indigenous movements elsewhere) and used to present an alternative (macro)history to curb limitations imposed by the Islamic establishment in mediaeval times.

The present chapter goes on to investigate the esoteric claim that Salman and the archangel Gabriel are synonymous. Therefore, the clearest point of departure is the Qur'an itself, held in Islamic orthodoxy as the record of

---

9. A. Guillaume, *Islam*, 171 and 174–5; cf. F. de Blois, *"Nasrani* and *hanif*: Studies on the Religious Vocabulary of Christianity and of Islam", *Bulletin of the School of Oriental and African Studies* (University of London) 65(1) (2002), 1–30.

those "formal utterances and discourses, which Mohammed and his followers accepted as directly inspired" and as the "literal Word of God mediated through the angel Gabriel".[10]

ALLUSIONS TO SALMAN IN THE QUR'AN IN THE LIGHT OF THE "HADITH OF GABRIEL"

The "bismillah" and the pollination of Persian ideas

The first instance of a possible Salman/qur'anic link that requires noting is the phrase *bismi llahi l-rahman al-rahim*[11] ("In the Name of God, the Merciful, the Compassionate"), an invocation preceding all but one of the qur'anic surahs. Since the divine epithets *al-rahman* and *al-rahim* are derivatives of the noun *rahmah*, signifying "mercy", "compassion", "loving tenderness", we should be immediately struck by the thematic correspondence between this phrase and the ancient Persian formula, *Mehr-Aban* (invoking Mithras and Anahita) or *Mehraban* ("Loving-Kindness").[12] This is not to say that such a connection literally exists, nor is Salman here implied as conveying this. A simple explanation of it may be an account of New Testament influence (notions about the love of Christ etc.) on the Qur'an's architect. The correspondence may, however, be argued to demonstrate pervading Persian motifs which are similarly picked up on. Regardless, there is debate as to whether the so-called *bismillah* is originally a part of the main body of qur'anic text or formally separated from it.[13] Qur'anic scholar Muhammad Asad retains its inclusion, counting it as part of the first verse of the Surah *al-Fatihah* (The Opening), which is also held to be one of the earliest, if not *the* earliest (according to the authority of Ali Ibn Abi Talib).[14] Besides, the words *rahman al-rahim* occurs once again, as if enforcing its value, in the third verse of "The Opening" surah (Q 1:3).[15] The inclusion of the *bismillah* is a consistency throughout the Qur'an with the exception of Surah 9, which gives rise to the suspicion of its integral place in the Holy Book. Over two decades ago, however, Philippe Gignoux and company formulated the hypothesis that the influence of the Zoroastrian formula *pad nam i yazdan*, "By the name of the gods", lies behind the Islamic *bismi*

---

10. H. A. R. Gibb, *Islam: A Historical Survey* (2nd edn) (Oxford, 1953), 24.
11. Cf. M. Asad, *The Message of the Holy Qur'an* (London, 1980), 1 and note 1.
12. For the translation offered on the terms *rahman* and *rahim*, see M. Asad, *Qur'an*, 1 and note 1.
13. For more discussion on this, *ibid.*
14. *Ibid.*
15. And again it is found in Q 2:163. There are also allusions to its theme throughout the Qur'an, as undoubtedly detected in the following surahs, e.g. 9:103, 27:11, 27:29, 27:41, 30:50, 33:51 and 39:54.

llahi l-rahman al-rahim,[16] although, as pointed out by Shaul Shaked, Edgar Blochet had already proposed this idea almost a hundred years before.[17]

Shaked presents the contrary argument to Gignoux – that the influence seems better derived from Jewish and Christian domains, without disproving the suggestion of the Zoroastrian formula.[18] His instincts put us on a better track, since in our view the thematic correspondence is not ("establishment") Zoroastrian, but rather Mithraic (though not "Mithraist", as in the *Mithraism* of the Roman soldiers). The point is that the notion contained by the phrase goes deep into Persian Antiquity to the core of Iranian religious conscious-ness (pre-dating the *Gathas*). It is from here that the themes of "Love" and "Kindness", represented by the ancient divinities of *Mehr* (Mithras) and *Anahid* (Anahita), were assimilated into the poetic verses of Zarathushtra, and later derived in the Persian language. While Shaked's thesis for the Hebrew and Aramaic origins of the verse has structural validity, it lacks substantive support, since the formulae has little sway contextually (or thematically). Shaked's proposal only works for the opening statement, for example "By the [your] name ...", whereas the second half of the formula is much more impor-tant, especially with regard to the subject and theme, where we can see lit-tle in common with either Zoroastrian, Jewish or Christian formulae. Indeed these latter formulae talk about "gods" (e.g. the Zoroastrian "By the name of the gods") and other invocations such as "healing", the "trinity", "life", etc, or about one among pluriform aspects of God, as in the Aramaic *bsmk mry 'swt'*, "By your name, the Lord of healing."[19] The same is true of other instances given for example of the Christian (Trinitarian) formula, "By the name of the Father, Son, and the Holy Ghost";[20] the Mandaic, "By the name of Life";[21] and the lengthy Manichaean amalgamation, "By your name, by your will, by your command and by your power, Lord Jesus Christ. By the name of Mar Mani the Saviour, the apostle of the gods."[22] The closest to the Islamic theme of "mercy" is the Aramaic magic formula, "By the mercy of heaven",[23] but arguably if we are going to look for its origins in any known prior formulaic saying, there is

---

16. Cf. P. Gignoux, R. Curiel, R. Gyselen & C. Herrenschmidt, *Pad nam i yasdan: Études d'épigraphie, de numismatique et d'histoire de l'Iran ancien*, Université de la Sorbonne Nouvelle: Travaux del'Institute d'Études Iraniennes 9 (Paris, 1979), 159–63.

17. E. Blochet, "Études sur l'histoire religieuse de l'Iran, I", *RHR* 38 (1898), 26–63; cf. Shaked, "Some Iranian Themes", 152.

18. Cf. Shaked, "Some Iranian Themes", 152–4.

19. See J. A. Montgomery, *Aramaic Incantation Texts from Nippur* (Philadelphia, PA, 1913), 127 (Bowl No. 3).

20. J. A. Montgomery, "A Syriac Incantation Bowl with Christian Formula", *American Journal of Semitic Languages and Literature(s)* 34 (1917/8), 137–9.

21. Montgomery, *Aramaic*, 252 (No. 40).

22. W. B. Henning, "Two Manichaean Magical Texts, with an Excursus on the Parthian Ending –*endeh*", *Bulletin of the School of Oriental and African Studies* 12 (1947), 50 (repr. in *Acta Iranica* 6 (1977), 273–300.

23. Montgomery, *Aramaic*, 193 (no. 18).

good enough reason to propose that the Islamic formula closely reflects the Gathic appeal and reference to *Vohu Mana* ("Loving-Mind")[24] as a primary and consistent invocation throughout the *Gathas* (and also as the highest attribute of Ahura Mazda) (see Chapter 2). This particular *Gathic* appeal recapitulates the "Mithraic" element of pagan Iran. In the end, Shaked does admit a degree of support in favour of retaining the value and precedence of an overarching Persian ethos.[25]

The mysterious teacher

An intriguing verse from the Qur'an states, "Say: 'The Holy Spirit [Gabriel?][26] brought it [the Qur'an] down from your Lord in truth to reassure the faithful, and to give guidance and good news to those that submit.'" It is then followed by a most peculiar statement, "We know they say: 'A mortal[27] taught him'. But the man to whom they allude speaks a foreign tongue, while this is eloquent Arabic speech."[28] In connection to this, the famous "Hadith of Gabriel" attributed to Omar Ibn al-Khattab reports how "a [strange] man in white clothes and very black hair" came to Mohammed and his companions, sat down with his knees pressed against Mohammed's, and questioned him Mohammed on the meaning of Islam. Mohammed responded by explaining the "pillars". Upon the departure of the stranger, Mohammed was asked by his companions to explain this odd event, and he answered, "He was Gabriel who came to ... *teach you* your religion."[29] With regard to the "foreigner" and the "stranger", in both Moslem sources, there is no certainty as to who is implied, but most

---

24. Cf. Taraporewala, *Divine Songs*, 1039–40.
25. Cf. Shaked, "Some Iranian themes", 154.
26. *Ruh al-Qudus* = Gabriel in Qur'an: cf. Muhammad Taqi-ud-Din al-Hilali & Muhammad Muhsin Khan, *Interpretation of the Meanings of The Noble Qur'an in the English Language: A Summarised Version of At-Tabari, Al-Qurtubi, and Ibn Kathir with Comments from Sahih Al-Bukhari* (Riyadh, 1997), 393, and S. V. Mir Ahmed Ali, *The Holy Qur'an: Text, Translation and Commentary* (New York, 1988), 867.
27. The Arabic term *'Ajami* "properly means" Persian, although is also applicable by implication to other foreigners; cf. W. St Clair Tisdall, *The Original Sources of the Qur'an* (London, 1905), 134.
28. Q 16:102–3. Cf. N. J. Dawood (trans.), *The Koran* (Harmondsworth, 2003), 195. The Bee Surah (*al-Nahl*) was revealed a few months before Mohammed's emigration to Medina, and entitled this way because in vv. 68–9 we have an allegory of God's creativeness as manifest in observing the instincts given the bee. Paralleling God's creativeness with the mysterious activity of the bee could at this particular verse point to a human's creativeness, implying a man passing truths on to Mohammed; cf. M. Asad, *Qur'an*, 393; yet for Asad's contra argument on the possibility of a foreign informant for the Qur'an, page 412, notes 130–32.
29. G. Webb, "Gabriel", *Encyclopaedia of the Qur'an* (hereforth *EQ*) (general ed. J. D. McAuliffe) (Leiden, 2002), vol. 2. For the Tradition, Bokhari, *Sahih*, vol. 1, 41; cf. also al-Tabrizi, *Mishkat al-Masabih*, vol. 1, 5.

likely a *Persian*. Correspondingly, Nessim Joseph Dawood[30] cites Salman as a candidate, followed by two other equally intriguing figures, namely Suhaib ibn Sinan (Suhayb al-Rumi)[31] and 'Adas the Monk,[32] as possibly intended by Q 16:103. It was St Clair Tisdal, however, who in his 1905 publication points out that the above qur'anic defence does not discount the view of a foreign informant, since the question does not concern "the language" but the "matter" or "subject" transmitted (to Mohammed).[33] On the identity of this figure, Tisdal was already looking towards the predominance of Salman the Persian chiefly as the mediator to Mohammed of Zoroastrian scriptures.[34] Not long after, both Fr J. L. Menezes and James Gardner corroborated the presumptions of Tisdal, presenting Salman and "Sergius Boheria" (Bahira?), "a Nestorian monk", as "chief factors in the composition of the Qur'an".[35]

The task then is to pick up the trail on the investigation into the legend of Salman without making a finalized claim that Salman instructed Mohammed or that Salman wrote or co-authored the Qur'an. In our macrohistory a special concern is expressed with significant pieces of information that have been ignored by previous academics regarding the role of Salman and his relation to Mohammed. Our research relies on detection into both traditional and non-traditional Moslem sources, including tantalizing esoteric material (that is, alternate, esoteric or "hidden histories" found in the Persian ambience) that sometimes implicitly, and other times explicitly, disclose the special place of Salman in Islamic history.

CORRELATIONS BETWEEN SALMAN AND GABRIEL

Salman the Persian is without doubt a historical figure, but one whose historicity is kept in the haze of legend now surrounding him. There have been many stories passed on about him, but here we will venture to address those

---

30. Dawood, *The Koran*, 195 note.
31. J. E Brockopp "Captives", *EQ*, vol. 1; M. Lecker, "Al-Namir b. Kasit, Banu", in *EIs*. Cf. al-Dhahabi, *Ta'rikh al-Islam* (Beirut, 1991), 600, cited by Brockopp, "Slaves and Slavery", *EQ*, vol. 4. Also, cf. Ibn Kathir, *Tafsir* (Beirut, 1987), vol. 1, 254, cited in Mawil Y. Izzi Dien, "Shira", in *EIs*, vol. 9.
32. R. Tottoli, "Muslim Attitudes Towards Prostration (*Sujud*), I. Arabs and Prostration at the Beginning of Islam and the *Qur'an*", *Studia Islamica* 88 (1998), 14 and note 33, and *idem*, "Muslim Attitudes Towards Prostration (*Sujud*), II. The Prominence and Meaning of Prostration in Muslim Literature", *Le Muséon* 66–7 (forthcoming). Cf. also, Haythami, *Majma' al-awa'id wa manba' al-fawa'id* (Beirut, 1967), vol. 4, 309–10, and Fakhr al-Din Razi, *Al-Tafsir al-kabir (Mafatih al-ghayb)* (Beirut, 1990), vol. 2, 149.
33. Tisdall, *Original Sources*, 134.
34. Cf. *ibid.*, ch. 5.
35. Cf. Menezes, *The Life & Religion of Mahommed, The Prophet of Arabia* (London, 1912), 163; cf. also J. Gardner, *Faiths of The World* (London, 1920), vol. 2, 279.

that deal with the association of Salman with Gabriel. For this task a consultation of both traditional Moslem accounts and resilient Persian cultural and religious currents of spirituality is first necessary. For the former we have the most complete version of the life of the Prophet Mohammed as preserved by Mohammed Ibn Ishaq in the *Sirat Rasul Allah* (*Sira*)[36] and available hadith. For the latter we possess alternate histories (sometimes macrohistories) within the esoteric currents of spirituality and interpretations of traditional sources, as well as information detected by inference as nuances from materials garnished by our own research. The aim here is to tease out all available correlations and parallels that exist between the historic figure of Salman and the angelic visions of Gabriel in the life of Mohammed. Indeed, the intention here is to consider the claim that they are the one and the same person.

My attention was first brought to the whole matter when observing a correspondence between the traditional relationship of Mohammed and Gabriel, and that of the master/apprentice relation in Sufism, such as the most famous one of Rumi *vis-à-vis* Shams. The subtleties of the accounts explain a "phenomenal" encounter between two parties, in both cases, such that the sudden appearance of Shams and his profound effect on Rumi results in a total transformation of consciousness, to the point of Shams' disappearance and subsequent claims that he was a figment of Rumi's imagination. This led me to observe the profound extent of Gabriel's involvement in Mohammed's mission. Naturally, Gabriel, who is never literally identified with any known person, except in one case,[37] prompted me to search for allusions to already known or previously discussed candidates. Pockets of sentiments found in various Sufi materials relating to Salman the Persian soon presented themselves and these were again confirmed by several (anonymous oral) sources on the "Salmanian myth" that credited Salman with a suspicious involvement in the history of Islam.[38] Salman's identification with Gabriel is more or less made transparent by the Nusayri, the Druze and the Ahl-e Haqq (*Yaresan*) traditions, but we will have to add, as the following pages illustrate, that the synonymity is also there in the long history of Persian cultural resilience. This is because Salman becomes the patron saint of many early Persian converts to Islam. In fact, he presents a very likely source of the majority Persian support for the cause of Islam. He is therefore rightly depicted as an icon of Moslem Persia, especially winning favour among the *Shuubiyya*, the propagators of Persian culture and learning. Conversely, Salman also became the means by which Persian propaganda was later spread by reactive cultural and

---

36. Ibn Ishaq, *The Life of Muhammad*; also Ibn Hisham, *Sira* (ed. F. Wüstenfeld) (Göttingen, 1859–60).
37. Hadith tradition, Cf. *Sahih Muslim*, Book 31, No. 6006, www.usc.edu/dept/MSA/fundamentals/hadithsunnah/muslim/031.smt.html#031.6006. See below.
38. Three in particular that remain anonymous: male, late 30s (henceforth X), male, late 50s (Y), and male, early 50s (Z).

religious elements wanting to undermine Arab dominion over "their" Islam.[39] These resistant elements show up above all from the early ninth century, in the prominent, reactionary movement of Shi'a extremists known under the umbrella term of *ghulat*. They constituted the non-Arab cultures assimilated by the Islamic conquests, with its majority being Persian clients or *mawali*. From these groups that were now reacting against the Islamic establishment, some in particular came to hold special reverence for Salman, regarding him as a prophet or even a divine emanation superior to Mohammed and Ali.[40] Moreover, the weight of Salman's presence in esoteric currents of spirituality throughout this adjustment period adds further substantiation of the connections we have been tracing from pre-Islamic Iran to the neo-Mazdakite (Mazdakiyya/Khorramiyya) activities that formed the backbone of the *ghulat* revolutionary movements. In addition, the claims of these movements lends weight to the theory of Salman's possible Mazdakite association and thus helps pick up the trail of continuity and connection with Iran's gnoseological and sapiential heritage dating at least to Zarathushtra.[41]

SALMAN IN HADITH TRADITIONS

Sources from hadith literature relate the extraordinary presence of Salman, and attribute to him a degree of conspicuous authority. As Abu Juhaifa narrates:

> The Prophet made a bond of brotherhood between Salman and Abu Ad-Darda'. Salman paid a visit to Abu Ad-Darda' and found Um Ad-Darda' dressed in shabby clothes and asked her why she was in that state. She replied, "Your brother Abu Ad-Darda' is not interested in (the luxuries of) this world." In the meantime Abu Ad-Darda' came and prepared a meal for Salman. Salman requested Abu Ad-Darda' to eat (with him), but Abu Ad-Darda' said, "I am fasting." Salman said, "I am not going to eat unless you eat." So, Abu Ad-Darda' ate (with Salman). When it was night and (a part of the night passed), Abu Ad-Darda' got up (to offer the

---

39. Cf. Goldziher, *Muhammedanische Studien*, 117, 136, 153 and 212.
40. Halm offers a useful clue in stating that only two references to a sect exist that originated from Rayy and thereabouts. They were allegedly called the *Salmaniyya* and are mentioned by the Isma'ili author, Abu Hatim al-Razi (d. 933/4) in *Kitab al Zina*, not yet printed. Also, Ali ibn Abbas al-Kharadini al-Razi (a native of the village of Rayy) is said to have written a refutation of the sect in his *Kitab al-Radd 'ala'l Salmaniyya*. For details, Halm, "Salmanniyya", in *EIs*, vol. 8.
41. A source, which is said to have discussed the connection between pre-Islamic Mazdakite teaching and the advent of Salman rather openly, is a book by the Iranian political theorist Ehsan Tabari that we have not been able to obtain; the book is possibly entitled "Barkhi az didgaah-haa bih adyaan".

night prayer), but Salman told him to sleep and Abu Ad-Darda' slept. After some time Abu Ad-Darda' again got up but Salman told him to sleep. When it was the last hours of the night, Salman told him to get up then, and both of them offered the prayer. Salman told Abu Ad-Darda', "Your Lord has a right on you, your soul has a right on you, and your family has a right on you; so you should give the rights of all those who has a right on you." Abu Ad-Darda' came to the Prophet and narrated the whole story. The Prophet said, "Salman has spoken the truth."[42]

It is said that Salman held a vast knowledge of holy texts, such as those of the Persians, Greeks, Christians and Jews. For instance in a hadith associated with Salman, we find him saying: "I read in the Torah that the blessing of food consists in ablution before it. So I mentioned it to the Prophet. He said: 'The blessing of food consists in ablution before it and ablution after it.'"[43] Ali ibn Abi Talib, who reveals Salman as an extraordinary individual among the Moslems and as one possessing profound wisdom, confirms the unique status of Salman: "He was a man of us and for us, the line of prophetic house, and in relation to you as the sage Loqman, having learned the first knowledge and the last, read the first scripture and the last: an exhaustive sea."[44] Yet it is Mohammed who placing his hand upon Salman saying "were faith [wisdom and learning] to be suspended from the highest point in heaven, a man such as this would attain to it."[45]

SALMAN AS GABRIEL

The Moslem Tunisian scholar and historiographer Ibn Khaldun (1332–1406) offers a rather telling depiction of the role of Persia in Islam, and it is worth repeating here as a reflection on the importance of Salman:

---

42. Cf. Bokhari, *Sahih*, vol. 3, 107, h. 189.
43. Sunan Abu Dawud, Book 27, No. 3752. Cf. University of Southern California, USC-MSA Compendium of Muslim Texts: www.usc.edu/dept/MSA/fundamentals/hadithsunnah/abudawud/027.sat.html#027.3752.
44. Ahmad Ibn Naqib al-Misri, *'Umdat al-salik [Reliance of the Traveller: A Classic Manual of Islamic Sacred Law]* (ed. Nuh Ha Mim Keller) (Beltsville, MD, 1994), 1093. Note the allusion to Jesus' statement of "I am the alpha and omega". The reference to the "first and last scripture", of course, is a typically Moslem mode of placing importance upon textual transmission.
45. Cf. Ibn Khaldun in F. Rosenthall (trans.), *The Muqaddimah: An Introduction to History* (London, 1978), vol. 3, ch. 4, 311–15. This is the famous hadith that refers to Mohammed's special praise of the Persians with regard to their piety and learning. Cf. Bokhari, *Sahih*, vol. 6, 390, h. 420. The account in *Sahih Muslim* is slightly varied to indicate a reference to the person of Salman specifically, rather than the commonly perceived allusion to the entire nation of the Persians. Cf. *Sahih Muslim*, vol. 3, Book 31, No. 6178, www.usc.edu/dept/MSA/fundamentals/hadithsunnah/muslim/031.smt.html#031. 6178.

It is a remarkable fact that, with few exceptions, most Moslem scholars both in the religious and in the intellectual sciences have been non-Arabs ... Thus the founders of grammar were Sibawayh[46] and after him, al-Farisi[47], and Az-Zajjaji[48]. All of them were of Persian descent and they invented rules of [Arabic] grammar. Great jurists were Persians. Only the Persians engaged in the task of preserving knowledge and writing systematic scholarly works. Thus the truth of the statement of the Prophet becomes apparent, "If scholarship hung suspended in the highest parts of heaven the Persians would (reach it and) take it."[49]

That the Persians are dubbed as inventors of Arabic grammar is of note here, considering that Salman the Persian is held to be the first patron of religious and intellectual sciences, and crafts.[50] Also of note is the so-called, "Hadith of the Persians", (albeit in varying form) confirming the important role of Salman (and the Persians) within Islam.[51] This particular hadith is set in the context of Mohammed foretelling that the Persians would form the better part of the Moslem community, clearly establishing the close affinity of Mohammed's mission with Persian components.

The fact that Persia was an obvious pillar of wisdom, learning and culture to the Arabs confirms the respect given to Salman – even if typically attributed in an allegorical way. For those who accept the non-literal view of Salman in Islamic history,[52] his figure is nevertheless (and without doubt) the prototype of converted Persians and thus plays a crucial role in the course of Islamic history. If any credit is to be given to the esoteric transmissions that directly link Salman and Gabriel, though, problems of their anachronistic character have to be admitted, in that "orthodox Moslem tradition" only has Salman entering Mohammed's company in Medina and not before. However, this is not to deny the implications that carry the importance of Salman *and* Persia as being involved in the very birth and development of the religion of Islam. In effect, the presence and active involvement of Salman as a prestigious feature of Mohammed's entourage is undisputed historically, even though certain details of his career may be questionable.[53] Yet it is nonetheless

---

46. Died *c.*800. Cf. Ibn Khaldun, *Muqaddimah*, 323.
47. Not to be mistaken with Salman al-Farisi, Ibn Khaldun's figure here is Abu Ali al-Farisi (al-Hassan ibn Ahmad) (901–87); Khaldun, *Muqaddimah*, 323.
48. I.e. Abd al-Rahman ibn Ishaq (d. 949); Khaldun, *Muqaddimah*, 323.
49. Using Khaldun, *Muqaddimah*, 311–15.
50. Cf. S. H. Nasr, "The Religious Sciences – II. The Qur'anic Sciences" (with R. Frye), in *CHI*, vol. 4, 466; also S. H. Nasr, "III. The Science of Hadith", in *CHI*, 472.
51. Cf. G. della Vida, "Salman al-Farisi", in *EIs*, vol. 12 (supplement).
52. Cf. G. della Vida, "Salman al-Farisi or Salman Pak", in *EIs*, vol. 12 (Supplement).
53. Cf. *ibid.*

Salman's recurrent association with Gabriel in esoteric thought that raises the real intrigue.

Certainly the reputed status of Salman (within the Islamic tradition alone), as a character of wisdom, learning and knowledge, placed alongside the role and significance of the archangel Gabriel (in relation to Mohammed) as the bearer of revelation (i.e. the Qur'an), is a far too curious a phenomenon to pass as mere coincidence. The reality of Gabriel is without question implied both within the Qur'an and outside of it in countless hadiths and verbal transmissions, especially in Islamic philosophy and theosophical Sufism.[54] Although the nature in which the archangel is depicted is at times somewhat elusive, his soteriological function is always clear. In the Qur'an Gabriel's presence is synonymous with mention of the Holy Spirit, and as such, Ibn Sina conceived of Gabriel as the "active intellect" or a sort of higher consciousness as part of Mohammed's (ultra-)cognitive status, and a similar treatment was given by both Ibn Arabi and Sohravardi (and also resonating in Rumi) when they placed Gabriel as the agent of mystical illumination and the medium of divine unification. Nevertheless, in the Islamic tradition, Gabriel is grounded as a literal figure: with over one hundred hadith references to him (144 to be exact),[55] the majority of these bearing direct witness to Gabriel's actual presence in delivering revelations to Mohammed, and they also speak of Mohammed's careful imitation of the archangel's words. For example, one transmission relates, "Allah's Apostle used to listen to Gabriel whenever he came and after his departure he used to recite it as Gabriel had recited it."[56] It only remains to ask the question that, if Gabriel was a name tagged onto this mysterious figure of revelation at a later date, could this not have been a person already identified but whose active participation in the life of Mohammed is overlooked due to the state of current research or due to limitations of a cultural and religious nature? Hence, this is why we must look to the subterranean and resilient currents that offer what little clues they do to the mystery of Salman and his possible correlation with Gabriel, because the question posed might as well be an "esoteric Persian" one.

Apropos these possibilities a further degree of insight about the Mohammed/Salman correlation may be gathered from materials in the Iranian heartland, that is, through the sayings of Shi'ite communities and some of their Imams.

---

54. In particular the works of Ibn Sina (d. 1037), Muhi al-Din Ibn al-Arabi (d. 1240) and Shihab al-Din Yahya ibn Habash al-Sohravardi (d. 1191), and of course Rumi. For a specific categorization and use of Gabriel in these schools of thought, cf. G. Web, "Gabriel", in *EQ*.

55. Cf. Compendium of Muslim Texts; *Sahih Bukhari*, *Sahih Muslem* and *Sunan Abu-Dawud* at www.usc.edu/dep/MSA/.

56. Transmitted by Said ibn Jubair; cf. Bokhari, *Sahih*, vol.1, 6, h. 4.

SHI'ITE TRADITIONS CONCERNING THE KNOWLEDGE AND
AUTHORITY OF SALMAN

In relation to the *Sira*, one known Hijazi/Medinese legend mentions that "some palm trees spoke to Muhammad and Ali, proclaiming that he [Mohammed] was the Prophet and Ali his *wasiy*", which refers to the original palm trees allegedly planted by Salman the Persian (upon the instruction of Mohammed).[57] These trees were apparently cut down fairly recently (probably in the 1970s) due to Wahhabi protests against their veneration shown by Iranian and other visitors (including local Shi'ites).[58] Of course the veneration of trees or the existence of a "tree cult" in Iranian Kurdistan, during the Parthian period, is particularly interesting. The point here is that the Medinese legend confirms the esoteric authority of Salman the Persian (as seen throughout the Islamic tradition), especially concerning his declaration of Ali after Mohammed. For, after the death of Mohammed, Salman was counted among those Companions who were in the circle of Ali. In another tradition (transmitted by a Sunni source), which is paraphrased here, it is said that Salman the Persian attested to the *wilaya* of Ali after attesting to the *risala* (prophecy) during the time of Mohammed. Then a certain man went to see Mohammed about this, saying, "O Prophet of God, I have heard a thing which I have not heard before." Mohammed then said, "What is this?" The man said, "After the *shahada* to the *risala*, Salman bore witness in his *adhan* a *shahada* to the *wilaya* of Ali." Mohammed replied, "You have heard a good thing."[59] Also important are several traditions about Ali's unsurpassed courage and devotion to Mohammed. One in particular, recounted on the authority of Salman the Persian, is a lengthy and emotional excerpt that speaks of the overwhelming invasion of the Khathaam tribe and their intention to kill the Prophet and his men, and how Mohammed was brought to tears by this, and how it was Ali alone who comes to Mohammed's aid and leads a victorious expedition against the enemies of Islam:

> Ali wiped the Prophet's tears ... he merely asked for the description of the palaces, which the Prophet would give him; the Prophet

57. W. Ende, "The *Nakhawila*, a Shiite Community in Medina Past and Present", *Die Welt des Islams* (spec. issue on Shiites and Sufis in Saudi Arabi) New Series 37(3) (1997), 236–348; Mohammed Labib al-Batanuni, *Al-rihla al-hijaziya* (Cairo, 1329/1911), 254; Abdallah al-Yusuf, *Al-masajid wa-l-amakin al-athariya fi'l-Madina a-Munawwara* (Beirut, 1416/1996), 72–3; and note the account in the *Sira* (Guillaume), 97.

58. Guillaume, *Sira*, 87–9; Yousif al-Khoei, "The Shi'a of Medina", in *Dialogue* (London, 1996), 5; Omar Abd al-Qadir Maghribi, *Al-muhaddam min athar al-Madina al-Munawwara* (Tehran, 1367/1988), 42. Cf. Ende, "The *Nakhawila*", 297, note 128.

59. Told by the author of *Kitab al-salafa fi amr al-khilafa*, Shaykh Abd Allah al-Maraghi al-Misri; an excerpt taken from Riza Ustadi, "*Kalimat al-a 'lam hawl jawaz al-shahada bi'l-wilaya*", cited in L. A. Takim "From *Bid'a* to Sunna: The *Wilaya* of Ali in the Shi'i Adhan", *Journal of the America Oriental Society*, 120(2) (2000), 176.

then described vividly and in detail the beautiful gardens, rivers, and edifices and the graceful houris.[60]

Regarding esoteric knowledge, Ali is of course of well-known stature for hidden and inner meanings in early Islam, recognized as gnostic *par excellence* among the Shi'a, in whose tradition Salman is depicted as a prominent Shi'ite and counted, along with Ali, as among the eminent gnostics.[61] However, Salman's authority (even after the death of Mohammed) is reiterated in the Shi'ite tradition and developed because of the "palm tree" and "declaration" narratives. One traditional theory about him truly exemplifies his esoteric associations, in a discourse on the subject of *taqiyya* (the concealment of one's true knowledge), a withholding that applies not only to outsiders and enemies, but also as occasionally to relationships between the faithful (in this case, Shi'ites):

> The pro-Alid Companion Salman al-Farisi, for example, was noted for the esoteric knowledge which he possessed. According to Shi'i tradition he concealed this knowledge even from Abu Dharr al-Ghifari, a close friend of Salman and a loyal follower of Ali. The reason given for this behaviour is that if Salman's knowledge had been communicated to Abu Dharr he would have been unable to grasp its true significance and would have felt obliged to denounce Salman or even to kill him as a heretic.[62]

The fourth Imam, Ali ibn al-Husayn, who also cites the case of Salman "saying Abu Dharr would have killed Salman if he had known what was in Salman's heart", makes the same appeal to *taqiyya*.[63] It leaves no question as to the degree of knowledge and authority in Salman's role, which the Shi'ite tradition certainly brings to the fore.

---

60. Taken from Furat ibn Ibrahim al-Kufi, *Tafsir* (al-Najaf, n.d.), 222–6, cited in M. J. Kister, "On the Papyrus of Wahb b. Munabbih", *Bulletin of the School of Oriental and African Studies* 37(3) (1974), 562.
61. One list of these includes Maytham al-Tammar and Hasan al-Basri, given in Allamah Sayyid Mohammed Hussein Tabatabai, *Shi'ite Islam* (trans. and ed. S. H. Nasr) (Albany, NY, 1975); cf. J. Eliash, "Review of *Shi'ite Islam* by Allamah Sayyid Muhammad Husayn Tabatabai", *International Journal of Middle East Studies* 8(2) (1977), 283. Other noted associates of Ali were Zubayr, Talha, Miqdad and Abu Dharr Ghifari; cf. D. Steigerwald, "Ali", in *Encyclopaedia of Islam and the Muslim World* (ed. R. C. Martin) (New York, 2004), vol. 1, 35b.
62. Muhammad ibn al-Hasan al-Saftar al-Qummi, *Basa'ir al-darajat* (Tehran, 1285/1906), 87b; E. Kohlberg, "Some Imami-Shi'i Views on *Taqiyya*", *Journal of the American Oriental Society* 95(3) (1975), 397.
63. Cf. *ibid.*, p. 397, note 15.

OVERLAPPING THEMES: RUMI AND SHAMS/MOHAMMED AND SALMAN (GABRIEL)

It is made quite clear in normative Moslem traditions that the Qur'an was revealed to Mohammed via the agency of an angel. It is worth repeating that in such traditions neither Islam itself nor the Qur'an is an invention of Mohammed, and that the latter was written in Arabic so that Mohammed (who was chosen as prophet of God) would understand it. Strictly speaking, tradition does not enforce the idea that Islam is merely an Arab invention. It is said that during the time of Mohammed, a certain Qays ibn Mutatiyah criticized the fact that Mohammed kept foreign company (referring to Salman, Suhayb and Bilal), arguing the fact that the Arabs of Aws and Khazraj have defended Mohammed's cause (and not them). When Mohammed heard this he replied, it is said, "Your Lord is One. Your ancestor is one. Your religion is one. Take heed. Arabism is not conferred on you through your mother or father. It is through the tongue [i.e. the language of Arabic], so whoever speaks Arabic, he is an Arab."[64] Indeed, Abu Bakr's famous statement disassociates Islam from such a notion, even in the case of Islam being limited to Mohammed.[65] This leaves space for Salman. And it is worth noting that, as with the relationship of Rumi and Shams, there is no reason to undermine the significance of Mohammed or to take from the beauty of the tradition in associating Gabriel with Salman. On the contrary, the mysterious relationship serves to expose the performative potential of the qur'anic text as hierophany (à la Mircea Eliade), at least in understanding the text as a masterpiece within the macrohistorical course of a "sacred wisdom" tradition and of world religions.[66]

There are certain parallels worth considering here. The *Diwan-e Shams* and *Mathnawi-e manawi* are direct results of Rumi's experience of Shams. Indeed, they are the depositories of the sacred knowledge bestowed to Rumi by Shams (*c.*1240s CE). As it is written, Shams embarks upon a life journey in which his travels consist of two phases: the first was to quench his thirst for spiritual knowledge, which involves his meetings with numerous mentors;[67] the second

---

64. Cf. www.geocities.com/mutmainaa/people/al_rumi.html.
65. "Those of you who have worshiped Mohammed know that he is dead. Those of you who have worshiped God, know that He is alive and never dies. The first act of Abu Bakr, however, after returning on horseback from expeditions in Sunh, was to go straight to his daughter's house, draw back the cloak that covered Mohammed's face; he gazed at him and then kissed him, and said 'Dearer than my father and my mother ... thou hast tasted the death which God decreed for thee. No death after that shall ever befall thee.' Then, reverently he drew the cloak over his face again and went to address the people." See M. Lings, *Muhammad* (New York, 1983), 342.
66. Cf. M. Eliade, *The Sacred and the Profane* (trans. W.R. Trask) (New York, 1959), esp. ch. 4.
67. Cf. F. D. Lewis, *Rumi: Past and Present, East and West* (Oxford, 2000), 145–6. Cf. also T. Graham, "Shams of Tabriz and His Masters", *Sufi* 48 (Winter 2000/1), 30.

was to find (not a mere pupil or apprentice, but) a successor, an inheritor, an heir to the *gnosis* he then contained.[68] About this latter matter, the *Maqalat* reveals Shams' intimate confession, when he says:

> I came to Mawlana. The first condition of this was that I did not come as a master. God has not brought onto the earth one who could be Mawlana's master, and he could be no human being. Neither am I one who could be a disciple. I have passed that stage[69] … I am Mawlana's friend, and I know certainly that Mawlana is a *wali* ("friend") of God. I could not acquire a tenth of his knowledge and facility[70] … he thinks that in listening to me, he − I'm embarrassed to say it − is but a two-year-old with his father, or like a new Moslem who knows nothing of Islam![71]

Despite Shams' radical humility, he was nevertheless known as an incredibly robust and highly charismatic individual.[72] It is said that Shams searched the entire world to find a worthy receiver of his truth, going through a host of great men, such as Ibn Arabi and Sohravardi Maqtol, but was not satisfied.[73] For Shams was a wild man dressed in black woollen robe appearing no better than a beggar; and that he was best described as an intolerable character, "a wild darvish"[74] unrestrained by the norm.[75] It is said that, in the end, he makes a bargain with God to reveal to him just one man who could tolerate him in exchange for his life.[76] Hence, Rumi was revealed to him. There is much to be said for these fables that surround the meeting of Rumi and Shams, and their significance for the student of Sufism. However, here it will only serve as a corresponding theme to give new light to the discourse of Salman as Gabriel and his presence in the life of Mohammed.

There are some very obvious parallels to be spotted here, in fact, that may account for the story of Rumi and Shams as being a possible relay or indirect transmission of omitted details in Mohammed's encounter with the angel of God. This is not a wholly strange idea, since poetic works are typically engineered to convey double meanings that allude to the author's primary intentions. By way of example we can observe Rumi's own confession in this regard: "The lover's secret that's been kept concealed, is best through tales

---

68. A. Harvey, *The Way of Passion: A Celebration of Rumi* (Berkeley, CA, 1994), esp. 21–7.
69. T. Graham, "Shams of Tabriz and His Masters", 30.
70. S. Tabrizi, *Maqalat-i Shams-i Tabrizi* (ed. M. A. Mowahhed) (Tehran, 1990), vol. 2, 179–80.
71. *Ibid.*, vol. 1, 132.
72. T. Graham, "Shams of Tabriz", 35.
73. For those Shams encountered cf. Lewis, *Rumi*, 147–56; and for a detailed examination of Shams' masters, T. Graham, "Shams of Tabriz".
74. Cf. Harvey, *The Way of Passion*, 21.
75. Cf. Lewis, *Rumi*, 135.
76. Aflaki; cited by Harvey, *The Way of Passion*, 22.

of other loves revealed."[77] An obvious crossover theme is the fact that Rumi's *Mathnawi* is indeed called "The Qur'an in Persian" (along with the *Diwan* of Hafez revered as equal to, if not second only to, the Holy Book), for the *Mathnawi*, like the Qur'an, is taken as an inspired text by the Sufis (especially those that inhabited exotic cultural terrains of Persia and India). For it was Jami in the fourteenth or fifteenth century who openly revered the *Mathnawi* in a verse saying:

> The mystic *Masnavi* of our Rumi:
> > *Qoran* incarnate in the Persian tongue!
> How can I describe him and his majesty?
> > Not prophet, but revealer of a Book.[78]

Now, the *Mathnawi* was not written by Shams, although it specifically relates his wisdom. Ironically, it is Rumi and not Shams who is revered as "Mawlana" (Our Master) and who is the recognized founder of the Mevlevi Order[79] – a point considered, since it is Mohammed who is revered as the founder of Islam and not Gabriel (or Salman). Now, Shams and Salman appear in common with regard to their rugged and wild dress.[80] Also shared in both the legends of Salman and Shams is the element of a break with a dominant father figure.[81] Both Salman and Shams travel extensively, learning from other masters and finally seeking out a singular individual of importance.[82] In connection with the degree of their *spiritual* gnosis, they are also admittedly unsurpassed. Also, like Shams, who is the object of envy among Rumi's disciples, Salman walks a fine line in keeping the full extent of his knowledge hidden from other Companions.[83] It can be surmised that Salman may have resorted to an anonymous alias (even appearance) when unveiling his true capacity, a guise suitably

---

77. See Mojaddedi's translation of the Mathnawi text of Rumi, I:137, 12.
78. Cited in Lewis, *Rumi*, 467: "[E]very Sufi after [Rumi] capable of reading Persian has acknowledged his unchallenged leadership". Schimmel's attestation to the "omnipresence" of the *Mathnawi* may be excessive, but the sheer influence of its literary narrative upon later Sufi poets is unquestionable. Cf. A. Schimmel's "Mawlana Rumi: Yesterday, Today, and Tomorrow", in *Poetry and Mysticism in Islam: The Heritage of Rumi* (eds A. Banani, R. Hovannisian & G. Sabagh) (New York, 1994), cited in Lewis, *Rumi*, 467 and 661–2, note 1.
79. See Lewis, *Rumi*, ch. 11; esp. 431–2.
80. Donaldson, "Salman the Persian", 348; Al-Mas'udi, *Muruj al-dhahab* (eds C. Barbier de Meynard & P. de Courteille and trans. C. Pellat) (Paris, 1861–77), vol. 4, 195–6, cited in W. G. Millward (trans. and annot.), "The Adaptation of Men to Their Time: An Historical Essay by Al-Yaqubi", *Journal of the American Oriental Society* 84(4) (1964), 344.
81. For Shams' relationship with his father, cf. S. Tabrizi, *Maqalat*, vol. 1, 77; cf. T. Graham, "Shams of Tabriz", 31.
82. Aflaki and Dawlatshahi. Cited in Harvey, *The Way of Passion*, 22.
83. Cf. Kohlberg, "Some Imami-Shi'i Views on Taqiyya", *Journal of the American Oriental Society* 95(3) (1975), 397 and note 15.

"reciprocated" by Mohammed in addressing his visitor as Gabriel. In drawing this correspondence, it is also interesting to point out the specific overlap of the functional and performative roles of the characters involved in these traditions. In particular, Shams and Salman fulfil the role of divine harbinger, performing the task of delivering revelation to *one* individual specifically, whereas Rumi and Mohammed serve the figurative function of *disseminating* revelation.

Apart from Ali, whose relationship with Mohammed is well accounted for (depicting Mohammed's special affection and fondness for him), it is Salman the Persian whose intimacy with the Prophet is paradoxically less enunciated. Yet arguably his friendship with Mohammed was unequalled by any other Companion. One particular tradition demonstrating the degree of Mohammed's fondness for Salman is found in the story of Mohammed's first encounter with him in Medina. We will here limit the focus to two versions of this story, dealing with only one specific theme therein. In the traditional account in the *Sira*, the story illustrates a touching scene whereby Mohammed frees Salman from bondage, which on the surface mainly emphasizes the generosity of the Prophet toward a slave.[84] In another version of the story (with a fuller account than given in the *Sira*), Musa ibn Jafar (the seventh Imam) says that his father related Salman's story as told by Ali who requested that Salman explain his meeting with Mohammed, to which Salaman replied, "I swear before God, O Prince of Believers, if any one else had requested this of me I would not have complied."[85] In this version, Salman's Jewish master sells him for fear of his being a sorcerer to a woman of the Beni Salmiyah. She was very fond of Salman, and had a garden that she entrusted to him. Upon Mohammed's request to purchase Salman, she is so reluctant to release him that she demands (in this version) 400 (as opposed to 300 in *Sira*) date palms (half yellow dates and the other red) in exchange for him. And when these are miraculously delivered – for the date palms in both accounts are grown on that day – Mohammed says "come get what you wanted and give me what I wanted".[86]

The key in both narratives is the fact that Salman is in effect equalled to date palms. The significance of dates, especially in the vicinity of the holy city (*medinat al-nabi*), is unquestionably unsurpassed. It is noted that several of the early Imams reportedly owned large palm groves there, whose sayings with regard to the special qualities of their dates are noted in several sources.[87] Both the palm tree and its fruit have special significance for the Shi'ite tradition, as there are numerous sayings of Mohammed and of his Companions

---

84. Cf. Ibn Ishaq, *Sira*, 97–8.
85. Recorded in the *Kamal al-Din* of Babuwaihi al-Saduk cited by Donaldson, "Salman the Persian", 341.
86. Cf. *ibid.*: 344.
87. Ende, "The *Nakhawila*", 297.

to this effect.[88] An anecdote concerning the Eighth Imam, Ali al-Riza (d. 818) should here suffice:

> I really love (eating) dates … because the Messenger of God was a *tamari* [*kana tamariyan*, meaning he was very fond of dates, *tamari*, i.e. especially dried ones]. Likewise, Amir al-Mu'minin (Ali) was a *tamari*, and also (the Imams) al-Hasan, Abu 'Abdallah al-Husayn, Sayyid (Ali Zayn) al-'Abidin, Abu Ja'far (Muhammad al-Baqir) as well as Abu 'Abdallah (Ja'far al-Sadiq) and my father (Musa al-Kazim). So I myself am also a *tamari*. [In general the followers of] our *shi'a* love the fruit of the palm tree because they are created from our stuff (clay, *min tinatina*), while our enemies love intoxicating beverages (*muskir*) because they are created from (smokeless?) fire (or: from a flame of fire, see Q 55:14–15).[89]

The rather cosmological (theological) ending of the quotation relates to a tradition transmitted on the authority of Salman, giving us the cue to further investigate nuances of notable Persian Mazdakite elements. Take one tradition preserved by al-Tabari:

> God caused Adam's clay to ferment for forty days and then put him together with His own hands. His pleasant part came out in God's right hand, and his unpleasant part in God's left. God then wiped His hands one with the other and so mixed both (pleasant and unpleasant). That is why pleasant comes forth from unpleasant, and unpleasant from pleasant (in man's constitution).[90]

Given our previous discussion on the currency of Mazdakite doctrine in Islam via the neo-Mazdakites, there is little need to further investigate all the ins and outs of these correlating themes.

---

88. *Ibid.* Cf. Adib Omar al-Husari, *Al-nakhil fi 'ahd al-nabi* (Damascus and Beirut, 1414/1994), 241–5; Daoud S. Casewit, "Fada'il al-Madinah. The Unique Distinctions of the Prophet's City", *Islamic Quarterly* 35 (1991), 13–14.
89. Ende, "The *Nakhawila*". Cf. Muhammad Baqir al-Majlisi, *Bihar al-anwar* (Beirut, 1403/1983), vol. 49, 102–3.
90. F. Rosenthal (trans. and annot.), *The History of al-Tabari* (*Ta'rikh al-rusul wa'l-muluk*) (Albany, NY, 1989), vol. 1, 262–3.

SALMAN IN THE *SIRA* AND EXAMPLES OF PERSIAN CULTURAL AND RELIGIOUS RESILIENCE

Peculiar sources on the role of Salman

Below we offer a comparative account of Salman's life in the key sources. For convenience, we shall start with three versions or alternate transmissions of his story in Persianate thought, then making comparisons with orthodox accounts, especially in Ibn Ishaq's *Sira*. Lastly, we will take into account the mysterious Hadith of Gabriel to complete the picture, this text being one of the most renowned of all hadith about the Prophet in Islam. The first of the three Persian stories runs as follows:

> In growing up, S[alman] was attracted to the movement of Mazdak, Ruuzbih [i.e. Salman] … grew up in the wake of the Mazdakian era, filled with the spirit of humanity and universal justice. Because he was politically active, he was eventually betrayed by his own father. Through his father [who was the marzban or general of Esphahan] …[91] he was thrown in prison. His comrades contrived to liberate him, and he escaped across the western desert to Syria. His last master was Bahiiraa, the Nestorian monk, who had been the guide of Muhammad, when the latter was leading the caravans from Mecca to Damascus for his wife Khadija. B[ahira] discouraged Salman from becoming a Christian, telling him his destiny was with Muhammad, not mentioning the latter by name but giving him indications of how to find him.[92]

The above is an obvious synthesis of multiple sources that basically relays the traditional story of Salman with a twist. Moving on the second:

> The greatest Persian Traitor, Salman-e Farsi who was an ex-Mazdaki … and after Persian Shahanshah arrested and executed Mazdakis, he fled to Arabia and became the Arab Prophet Muhammad's left hand. Salman practically adapted all the brotherly love theories of Mazdakism to Islam, Salman was a major theoretician of Islam. Salman established the political ideology of Islam. Muhammad with the help of Salman, Ali (fourth Khalifat of Rashedin) and Abu Bekr (first Khalifat of Rashedin) wrote the Koran and practically stole most verses from book of Mazdak, Mitraism, … Bible, Tora and even parts of Avesta, the holy book of Zaratushtra Spitmata.

---

91. A case similar to that of many children of establishment parents in the latter-day Pahlavi era, who turned to various Marxist movements or the People's Mojahedeen.
92. Anonymous account.

... The rest of Koran is basically creations of his delusional epileptic schizophrenic mind or his opportunist charlatanism and con artist behavior depending on daily opportunism in Arabia. What Salman did to Iran, no other Persian ever done to Iran! Salman is the number one Persian traitor, an opportunist who sold Iran to Arabs for personal and political reasons.[93]

The second transmission appears to be an "anti-Salmanian" spill by disgruntled pristine Persian nationalists blaming Salman for the fall of Persia. The piece carries certain overtones of early-nineteenth-century Judaeo-Christian anti-Moslem propaganda. The document is primarily anti-Moslem but specifically focuses on Salman in claiming his direct involvement in the early development and rise of Islam and thus the demise of Persia. Further alleging the co-authorship of the Qur'an as partly being Salman's adaptation of key Persian works, the piece also rejects the remainder of the Qur'an as the product of Mohammed's misguided efforts. This source helps confirm our suspicions surrounding the role of Salman in relation to Mazdakism, Mohammed and Islam. The above can sources represent a residue of the subterranean trajectory hitherto traced in this book. What is particularly novel about the second source however is the vicious attack on Salman, a twist possibly effected by certain Assyrian Christian elements, some of which also take the Biblical Daniel as a Jewish spy in Persia who caused long term trouble.[94]

As with the *Sira*, this anti-Salmanian story putatively places the formal meeting of Salman and Mohammed in Medina. This is most intriguing, in that the strategic importance of Yathrib was a pivotal manoeuvre for Mohammed in securing his success. Could it have been possible that they were first acquainted (in secret) in (the mountains of) Mecca (i.e. Mt. Hira), to make an obvious reference to Surah 96? Such a version of the story would place Salman in league with Waraqah (Khadija's cousin), and together they help Mohammed lead the people through a socio-religious revolution that was to affect first Arabia and later Persia. This version of events would also confirm Salman's role in the fall of Sasanid Persia. To draw out the idea, it would then seem that Salman was to play the role of *Jibril*, and Waraqa was to be Mohammed's confidant. And we are left contemplating the role of Salman as a principal architect of the Qur'an and founder of Islam, however aided by the aging Waraqa, already a well known scribe and translator of the Gospel

---

93. Cf. www.geocities.com/hammihanirani/islam.html; cf. a designation in plural, "Salman Farsis", as referring to what this site calls "Muslim-Iranian Traitor". Cf. http://iranpoliticsclub. net/history/aryamanesh/, a forum discussion on a depiction of Salman as a revolutionary prince aspiring to overthrow the Sasanian Empire with the help of Arabs and a proposed prophet; cf. http://majorityrights.com/index. php/forums/viewthread/58/. The site also contains an allusion to a Moslem training camp in Iraq named after him.

94. Oral testimony, Milton Tariveran to Trompf, 1999.

into Arabic (discussed below). This would also fit in nicely with the Sufi myth-history that the ancient Persian teachings of brotherly love and unity are at the centre of Islamic teachings, which have since been overshadowed by dogmatism. Accordingly, could Salman have been sent by desert monks (and not Mohammed, as in the *Sira*) to find Waraqa, who then turns Salman's attention toward Mohammed?

The Sira

What now of the *Sira*? We can deal with Ibn Ishaq's biography as best embodying the traditional orthodox Moslem account of Salman, comparing it with these Persian strands of interpretation (which do have common elements). First, we find that the *general gist* of the *Sira* does not necessarily clash with these versions of Salman's life, even though the obvious differences need to be taken into consideration throughout the chapter. Of course one clear difference lies in the *Sira*'s presentation of Salman as a humble slave in search of the "the true religion" (Islam by implication), while the alternate currents hint at Salman's authority. Nevertheless, it is through an exegesis of Sufi motifs that a subtle complementarity, a shifting of notes, can be detected. The case of Rumi *vis-à-vis* Shams, to reiterate, has already helped solve the dilemma as to whether Salman instructed Mohammed or vice versa. Thus the time came when (the great) Shams solemnly reduced himself to confess Rumi's superiority in awe,[95] providing the clue as to how Salman plays a somewhat similar hidden role in relation to Mohammed, or at least read to the most profound esoteric rendition of Sufistic thought. The aim here, after all, is to draw attention to the many subtle nuances within the legend of Salman that should not be missed, especially with regard to his role in Mohammed's mission. For the most part Salman's spiritual quest from Persia to Syria to Arabia (through a series of masters) is commonly portrayed in all accounts of his life, in normative Moslem traditions or otherwise, yet with Persianate esoteric versions comes the special twist that Salman was in fact Gabriel who brought the Qur'an and Islam.

Who is Salman?

Having introduced the three major sources, we are still left asking: who is Salman? Now, as far as any source reveals (given minor variations), Salman was of noble lineage and born Ruzbeh or Mahbeh (Mayeh) in Jey (or classical Jayy), a district of Esfahan (Espahan, Mid. Pers. Spâhân). Esfahan, meaning

---

95. Cf. Kohlberg, "Some Imami-Shi'i Views on Taqiyya", 397; *Maqalat*, vol. 2, 175; cf. also T. Graham, "Shams of Tabriz", 30.

"the armies", took its name from the fact that it was the greatest army camp built in central Iran by the Sasanian *shahs*, as it was home to important Iranian noble families and also a large Jewish and Christian population. In one particular hadith, Salman mentions he is from Ramhormoz,[96] though this is a reference to his ancestry as his father was transferred from Ramhormoz to Esfahan, residing in Jey (just outside the military camp), which was designed to accommodate the domestic requirements of military personnel.[97] As a boy, Salman led a relatively sheltered life under the shadow of his father, and sources implicate his father's national and religious dogmatism. The *Sira* indicates Salman's early attraction toward another religion belonging to a group of Syrian Christians near his hometown:

> I told him [his father] that I had passed by some men who were praying in their church and was so pleased with what I saw of their religion that I stayed with them until sunset. He said, "My son, there is no good in that religion; the religion of your fathers is better than that." "No," I said, "It is better than our religion." My father was afraid of what I would do, so he bound me in fetters and imprisoned me in his house.[98]

In the *Sira* Salman confesses, "I was such a zealous Magian that I became keeper of the sacred fire, replenishing it and not letting it go out for a moment."[99] Both literally and figuratively, the "keeper of the sacred fire" (i.e. the divine flame within the heart) is a powerful investiture. The fifth-century tension between the Zoroastrian and Christian church is also a reflection of note in the dialogue with his father, just mentioned. A more relevant factor to consider here, though, is the likelihood that Salman grew up in the wake of the persecutions against Mazdakism, in which case the above signifies a particularly paranoid Zoroastrianism, with the desire to secure its future.

Whether Salman was directly involved as a Mazdakian activist or associated with them in any way remains unknown for certain, but his *imprisonment* and confinement under his father points to this hidden factor. It is clear enough from the evidence at hand that Salman was intrigued by the search for liberation and truth and that he pursued learning and understanding beyond conventional bounds. There is a curious hadith that narrates, "That he [Salman] was sold (as a slave) by one master to another for more than ten times (i.e.

---

96. Cf. Bokhari, *Sahih*, vol. 5, 194, h. 283.
97. Concerning the village of Jey, cf. F. Hooshangi, "Isfahan, City of Paradise: A Study of Safavid Urban Pattern and a Symbolic Interpretation of The Chahar-Bagh Gardens" (Master's dissertation, Carleton University) (Ottawa, 2000), 17–20. Regarding Salman's father, Ibn Ishaq states that he was a *dihqan* of Jey; cf. della Vida, "Salman al-Farsi or Salman Pak".
98. Ibn Ishaq, *Sira*, 95.
99. *Ibid.*

between thirteen and nineteen masters in total),"[100] which, in our opinion, is merely an encoding of the number of "spiritual masters" he served. The stories reveal that he changed teachers several times, each revealing the next on their deathbed until the alleged climax with his meeting Mohammed.[101] It is probably also true that he was sold into slavery, but the tales related to his rescue by Mohammed carry a natural bias.[102] Salman's teachers are never specifically identified, though all sources recognize that most were Syrian-Christian, possibly Nestorian, monks – though, we believe this contact to be of little value in the face of the overwhelming Persian ethos that accompanies Salman's legend. However, Salman's contact with these monks does help explain the Christian presence in the sources on Mohammed's life. In brief, Persia and Arabia were basically separated by scattered and independent "monastic" activity (in the Syrian desert) typical of the Eastern Syriac orthodox varieties.

According to traditional sources, Salman travelled as far into the Arabian Peninsula as the Wadil-Qora[103] (western Arabia), seeking "the prophet of Arabia", as instructed by his last mentor on his deathbed (possibly Bahira).[104] Of course, in all stories "Mohammed" is never named, but Salman is to follow rumours of the Arabian prophet who is specified by distinct signs.[105] The twist in the story, however, is read between the lines, whereby Salman's flight from Sasanian oppression is a major component. There is enough indication toward Mazdakism that can lend support to the thesis of Salman's involvement with Mazdaki revolutionaries (possibly still active in north Arabia after the great persecution of Anushirvan (Khosrow I)). In Moslem tradition, Salman sends for his Christian friends to smuggle him across to Syria,[106] while in the alternate version (mentioned above) it is his Mazdakite comrades. Another pertinent factor to consider is the point of his service to several monks before being directed to Mohammed, which can just as easily be read as Salman being instructed in selecting a pupil, as he had by then fulfilled his period of discipleship (a likely omission on behalf of traditional bias perhaps?). It is important to note in this regard that all of Salman's teachers were older (hence the reason for the change), and that Mohammed was either younger or at the very least a contemporary.[107]

---

100. Cf. Bokhari, *Sahih*, vol. 5, 194, h. 282.
101. Cf. Ibn Ishaq, *Sira*, 96; cf. also della Vida, "Salman al-Farsi or Salman Pak".
102. *Kamal al-Din* of Babuwaihi al-Saduk; cited by Donaldson, "Salman the Persian", 343–4; cf. also Ende, "The *Nakhawila*", 297.
103. "The valley of villages", a once prosperous region including several valleys in northern Hijaz, four or five days' journey from Medina. Cf. M. Lecker, "Wadi'l-Kura", in *EIs*, vol. 11.
104. Cf. Ibn Ishaq, *Sira*, 96.
105. *Ibid.*
106. *Ibid.*, 95.
107. This is based on the assumption that Salman's death is during the period of Othman's caliphate (644–56), as the sources are silent regarding Salman after this period. Nevertheless his respected position and status among the Moslems does imply a sense of seniority.

Traditional Moslem sources tell us that Salman is discouraged from becoming a Christian, despite the fact that all of Salman's teachers were indeed technically Christian. It is possible that Christianity plays an important role in the life of Salman and Mohammed as an informal and non-establishment interaction. Salman received his teachings from individuals who directed him to others alike to themselves, at best demonstrating a chain of esoteric teaching or understanding of Scripture specific to these particular monks. Ibn Ishaq styles these men as "natural Moslems", who always refer to a "true religion", indeed implying (and even stating)[108] the religion of Abraham.[109] This, however, can be taken as a better description of the "religion of the *hanif*" (*hanifi* religion), those righteous individuals who were neither polytheists, nor Jew, nor Christian but naturally "inclined to a religion of their own", in other words "one who has reached monotheism by means of individual insight".[110] This is a salient point pertaining to the legacy of Salman and Mohammed and, indeed, at the very core of Islamic teaching. I argue that the *hanifi* notion of the "true religion" is curiously reminiscent of the Mazdakite notion of *dorost-din*, that is, "of the right faith" (as Yarshater offers) or "the true religion" (as we render it here). In particular as it stands in opposition to the Zoroastrian, *veh-din* "good [or "better"] religion". Indeed, to make our point explicit: could this very *hanifi* religion, depicted to be an *essential* Christianity by Moslem sources, be taken to mean Mazdakism (or a Mazdakite ethos of resistance) alternatively? To investigate the possibility of this continuity a closer look at the "Hadith of Gabriel" is necessary. This particular hadith serves as a vital key to the literal presence of the figure of Gabriel, whose identity was concealed from all except for Mohammed. This particular hadith offers further clues to the doctrinal relation between *hanifi* "true religion" and Mazdakite teachings, and to Sufi interpretations of this "true religion" as central Islamic doctrine.

THE "HADITH OF GABRIEL" IN THE LIGHT OF PRINCIPAL ISLAMIC DOCTRINES AND MAZDAKITE TEACHINGS

In the previous chapter we surmised that Mazdakism was probably an active movement well before its apparent founder, Mazdak, came on the scene. It would seem then that Mazdakism could have been a re-expression of the doctrines that allegedly descended from the teachings of Zarathushtra, perhaps

---

108. The last teacher of Salman who directs him toward Arabia and Mohammed by signs, mentions as one of these that this prophet will bring the "religion of Abraham"; *Sira*, 96.

109. The gist of this is noted in a conversation recorded by Ibn Ishaq between Salman and his master, who says to him on his deathbed, "My dear son, I do not know anyone who is as I am. Men have died and have either altered or abandoned most of their true religion": *Sira*, 96.

110. Q 6:75–9; cf. U. Rubin, "Hanif", in *EIs*, vol. 3.

even earlier. And these teachings persisted beyond Islam's beginnings, going on to inform neo-Mazdakite currents imbibed by the *ghulat* (anti-"Moslem establishment") insurgencies from the ninth century onward. It is important to appreciate, therefore, that Mazdak made explicit the claim to an authentic Zarathushtrian doctrine in what can be described as a gnostic appreciation of Zoroastrian sources. Combined with socialist or "communist" approach to social structures and powers, this he offered as a remedy for the degenerating socio-religious climate of (fifth-century) Sasanian Persia.[111] In addition to this, the inference made or rather the idea entertained here in our macrohistorical perspective is that Salman may have also been a possible disciple of Mazdakite teachings or a man of strong Mazdakite sympathies (with regard socio-political elements at the very least). The transfer of ideas from Persia to Arabia, then, could have easily occurred with Salman's adaptation of the Mazdakite egalitarian principles for the environs of Arabia. The task is to connect the dots scattered along the plane of the history of ideas in both Persia and Arabia. An understanding of the Sufi appreciation of core Islamic principles will act as the means by which such past connections to be made transparent, and whether these connections can all be corroborated or not, the pattern of them remains the schema of the Sufi alternative and "secret history" of Persia.

The Hadith of Gabriel: a record of exchange between master and disciple

The "Hadith of Gabriel" (henceforth HG), as found in the renowned collection of hadith called *Mishkat al-Masabih*, is basically Omar's eyewitness account of the meeting of Mohammed with Gabriel (quoted *in extenso* above).[112] It is obvious from the text that this is not the first meeting of the pair; but what is unique about the content is that it reveals a sort of "final trial" or a "testing" of Mohammed's knowledge. The HG further stands out for making it plain that none of the Companions present (including Omar) are aware that the figure with Mohammed is actually the archangel Gabriel; so immediately, the impression is that this is a man of flesh and blood clearly described by an eyewitness account.[113] The most outstanding feature of the text, however, in this context,

---

111. The Sasanians had suffered a heavy defeat from the Hephthalite empire (of the largely Buddhist Huns) and the social fabric had plummeted to a chaotic state with major divisions between the poor and the elite. For background, see P. Brown, *The World of Late Antiquity* (London, 1971), 160–69.

112. This is a central hadith in the Moslem tradition containing the essential doctrine and practice of Islam and the highest achievement of its faith (*iman*) as being *ihsan* (explained above). Cf. al-Tabrizi, *Mishkat*, vol. 1, 5; Bokhari, *Sahih*, vol.1, 41.

113. It may be thought that since Omar Ibn al-Khattab was the eyewitness that he may have recognized Salman the Persian if it were he conversing with Mohammed. Several problems deter such an examination: the date of the manuscript is not evident as to it being Meccan or Medinan; Mohammed never identifies Gabriel other than by that name; and thirdly, the

is the condescending tone of this stranger questioning Mohammed and then proclaiming, "You have spoken the truth;" at which all the Companions were surprised.[114] In what follows, we take a closer look at some of the principles of Islamic doctrine contained within HG and touch upon key relevant notions within it that have notable correlations with Mazdaki and Sufi themes.

As related in the *Mishkat*, Mohammed's inquisitor presents five questions, three of which will be elaborated on in detail (these being *islam*, *iman* and *ihsan*). The five questions are posed by the inquisitor in the following order: Islam, faith (*iman*), good conduct (*ihsan*), the Hour, with the fifth question relating to the "signs" of the Hour, which can be counted as part of the fourth theme.[115] Immediately, the number "four" (since there are four main questions) could be taken as a recognizable Mazdakite doctrinal theme,[116] but the number five is central to Islam (representing the five pillars). Also, because the practical side of Islam's overall doctrine is usually perceived in the form of a doctrinal trinity, that is, as "works" (*islam*), "faith" (*iman*) and "perfections" (*ihsan*),[117] it seems that numbers appear to lose any specific importance here, and value should be placed on content as a means to evaluate any connection. In the Sufi tradition too there are *three* stages in the advancement of the Path (*tariqat*) from beginning to end, portrayed as *shariat, tariqat, haqiqat*. This correlates with the Islamic formula for the individual transition "within" the faith, in the form of *islam* (submission), *iman* (faith) and *ihsan* (virtue/good works).[118] The correspondence with Mazdaki (and neo-Mazdakite) doctrine is elucidated by way of Sufistic interpretation of HG. The HG presents *islam* (the first stage of Moslem praxis) as containing the "five pillars", while *iman* and *ihsan* reveal yet deeper truths about the experience of the Moslem fait- Looking at the HG, the first stage (*islam*) contains the five pillars. Apart from the *hajj* (taken in a literal sense) and fasting during the month of Ramadan, which does not appear in Mazdaki doctrine *per se*, the *shahada* (witnessing), *salat* (prayer), and *zakat* (alms) display obvious relation to Mazdaki religious

---

identity of Salman may have been unknown to Mohammed's followers until the Medinan period, as the Moslem accounts suggest.

114. Cf. Al-Tabrizi, *Mishkat*, 5.

115. Cf. *ibid*. When Mohammed modestly declines the task of explaining the Hour, he is then asked to relate the "sign" of the Hour. Hence, this may be taken as technically "four" major themes (rather than five). William Chittick offers a useful explanation of the content of the HG, in particular highlighting the tripartite formula of "Islam", "Iman" and "Ihsan", cf. his *Faith and Practice of Islam* (ed. S. H. Nasr) (Albany, NY, 1992), 3–5.

116. Note the occurrence of the quaternary theme in the segment "The Doctrine of Mazdak and its Currency" in Chapter 5. For reference to the number four as a distinct Iranian mode influencing Sasanian architecture and geography as well as religion, particularly in Manichaean and Mazdakite theology, see Müller, "Mazdak and the Alphabet Mysticism of the East".

117. Cf. Chittick, *Faith and Practice of Islam*, 2–5. Brackets are mine.

118. M. F. Güllen, *Key Concepts in the Practice of Sufism* (Rutherford, 2004), 133–6.

practice. Since ritual prayer (*salat*) and charity or charitable acts and communal sharing (*zakat*) have a fundamental connection with Mazdakite worldview as seen via neo-Mazdakite developments during post-Sasanid (Moslem) Iran, we need not touch on these practices again. Instead I will highlight the relevance of the *shahada* in particular. The *shahada* or "testament of faith", literally "witnessing", becomes the point of bypass from a state of *jahila* ("ignorance") to a state of *islam* ("submission"). At this point a brief reflection on William Chittick's categorization of the term "Islam", that is, the revealed religion, is necessary for clarification. It has to be appreciated that "Islam" covers four distinct senses within the Islamic tradition. The first sense covers the broadest aspect of the term whereby all of creation is in an ultimate state of "submission" to God, as notified in the Qur'an (3:83).[119] Therefore, in principle, all is His will. In a second and third sense, *islam* is further narrowed and taken to mean both one's voluntary submission to God's will, as noted in the case of Abraham and other pre-Islamic figures,[120] and as designating the religion revealed to Mohammed through the Qur'an.[121] The last and narrowest sense refers to the exoteric aspect of the religion.[122] With these points in mind and in returning to the *shahada*, we point out the direct correspondence of these distinctions with the (neo-)Mazdaki doctrine of the Supreme Name (*al-ismu'l-a'zam*) and Highest Mystery (*al-sirru'l-akbar*). We can demonstrate this by way of just one excerpt from a Persian Sufi text (from the thirteenth century).[123] Getting back to the point on Mazdakite correlation with the *shahada*, in the works of the Sufi Sadr al-Din Qonawi (d. 1274),[124] an esoteric account of the *shahada* is given whereby the phrase "There is no god but

---

119. Thus "To Him 'submits' everything in the heavens and the earth"; cf. Chittick, *Faith and Practice of Islam*, 2.
120. Abraham, Q 2:131 and 3:67, and other noted figures: Joseph (Q 12:101), Noah (Q 10:72), Lot and his family (Q 51:36), the Apostles of Jesus (Q 5:111), etc.; cf. Chittick, *Faith and Practice of Islam*, 2.
121. Note Q 5:3: "Today I have perfected your religion for you, and I have completed My blessing upon you, and I have approved Islam for you as a religion." Cf. Chittick, *Faith and Practice of Islam*, 2.
122. E.g., as exemplified by the qur'anic verse (49:14), "The Bedouins say, 'We have faith.' Say [O Muhammad!]: 'You do not have faith'; rather, say, 'We have submitted'; for faith has not yet entered your hearts."
123. The evidence for the Mazdakite doctrine is drawn from a prominent primary source, Shahrestani; cf. Shaki, "The Cosmogonical and Cosmological Teachings of Mazdak", 527–8 (including the translation of the British Library MS).
124. Who is the stepson of Ibn Arabi (d. 1240), and a good friend of Rumi, although it is unclear whether it was Sadr al-Din or a certain Nasir al-Din who wrote the proposed introductory works on Sufism: *The Rising Places of Faith, Clarifications for Beginners and Reminders for the Advanced* and *The Easy Roads of Sayf al-Din* (which are translated and presented in Chittick's *Faith and Practice of Islam*). Chittick does not offer any solid remarks concerning the author, but see xi.

God" is held synonymous to the practice of *dhikr* (remembrance).[125] This is crucial for our work in "making connections", because the act of "witnessing" (*shahada*) is underlined as a sacred act of ritual transformation. Moreover, the *shahada* becomes the "key" or sacred utterance for the adherent of faith.[126] It is not only a testimonial, but an entry into the space of religious consciousness, so to speak. This in turn sheds light on a Shi'a tradition, offered by Qonawi, that has Ali inquiring after the "most excellent" path to God, concerning which Mohammed replies:

> "Ali, you must cling to that which I have reached through the blessing of prophecy."
> Ali said, "What is that, O Messenger of God?"
> Mustafa said, "Constant remembrance of God in seclusion."
> Ali said, "Does remembrance have such excellence, when all people are rememberers?"
> Mustafa said, "But Ali, the Hour will not come as long as someone on the face of the earth is saying 'Allah, Allah'."
> Then Ali asked, "O Messenger of God, how should I remember?"
> Mustafa said, "Close your eyes and hear [this sentence] from me three times. Then repeat it, so that I may hear it from you three times."[127]

Interestingly, in the HG, the first pillar is presented in the form of the "double" *shahada*: "There is no god but God [and] Mohammed is the messenger of God." This is peculiar, because it draws our attention to a subtle point about the significance of Mohammad's name. Of course, Mohammed is not an object of orthodox Moslem worship. Yet, there are traditions that glorify his person, and more specifically his name, "the praiseworthy". Rumi does allude to this in verse:

> His [Mohammed's] name contains the whole prophetic line,
> The way that ten includes one through to nine.[128]

God and the deeper meaning of "Mohammed" is the key, and not Mohammad the human teacher; and Rumi, being a good Sunni, tactfully draws attention away from (worshipping) Mohammed in elucidating the spiritual quality of his name. Once again, the nuances in Rumi touch on theological intricacies; in

---

125. Cf. *ibid.*, 146.
126. Qonawi records Mohammed as saying, "The best that I and the prophets before me have said is 'There is no god but God', and that he related that God says, 'There is no god but God' is My fortress – he who enters it is secure from My chastisement." Cf. *ibid.*
127. Cf. *ibid.*, 147.
128. (Mojaddedi) *M* 1:114, 71.

this verse picking up on Christological issues (on the Divine Nature of Christ) and the idea of Mohammed as the Seal of the prophets. By further implication, mind you, the esoteric value of this last verse does not shy away from heterodox Nusayri or Ahl-i Haqq doctrines, especially that of the Salmaniyya and or the *ashab al-Mim* (Adherents of the Letter M),[129] and nods towards the connection between HG's version of the *shahada* and the Mazdakite Supreme Name and the Highest Mystery (see Chapter 6; also further discussed below).

Iman, the second stage of Islam in the HG, is the article of faith[130] in which is contained six attestations of principal Islamic doctrine: the belief in God, His angels, His scriptures, His messengers, the last day (the Hour), and good and evil.[131] In brief, apart from the notions of "scripture" and "messenger" being in the plural,[132] the others are standard Persian themes corresponding and parallel to Islam that can be readily attested to without explanation. That is, the readiness of the notions of monotheism, angelology, eschatology, and philosophical or ethical dualism are transparent in Persia – including Mazdakism – and for this reason in Islamic doctrine. It is these objects of "faith" that become "systematized into" the three overarching principles of Islamic religion: *tawhid* (unity), *nubuwwa* (prophecy) and *ma'ad* (return to God).[133] Our previous discussion on neo-Mazdakite doctrine (and its pursued connection to Mazdak's teachings), therefore, offer a clear enough demonstration of likely continuity from Mazdak to Mohammed, a linkage particularly elucidated in the Persian Sufi accounts we have presented above.

The third and final stage is *ihsan*, "perfection", "virtue" or otherwise simply "doing good".[134] This idea seems to communicate the deepest understanding in terms of Moslem praxis. For Mohammed's reply, "It [*ihsan*] means that you should worship God as though you saw Him, for He sees you though you do not see Him,"[135] brings into play a deeper dimension of "inner attitudes that accompany activity and thought"[136] that relate to perceptions about the world and the hereafter. A similar idea is teased out in an anecdote about Bayazid,

---

129. The assertions of P. Crone and M. Cook in *Hagarism* are also pertinent here in that Mohammed never referred to himself in the *shahada* and that it was a later insertion by Moslem scribes in reverence for the popularization of the Prophet's character.
130. Chittick, *Faith and Practice of Islam*, 3–4, is correct in stating that although *iman* is often rendered as "faith" or "belief", translators often leave out a most prevalent connotation of its root that means "secure", "safe", "calm" and "tranquil", i.e. that by implication, through faith in God one becomes free from fear, secure from error, and rooted in truth – and by extension, heading toward a direction of certainty.
131. Cf. Al-Tabrizi, *Mishkat*, 5.
132. Cf. Persian term *Saosyant*; e.g. Yas. 34.13. Taraporewala, *Divine Songs*, 392 and notes, 1131.
133. For its systematization into the "three principles", Chittick, *Faith and Practice of Islam*, 4.
134. For the first two, Chittick, *Faith and Practice of Islam*, 5; for "doing good", cf. Al-Tabrizi, *Mishkat*, 5.
135. Cf. *ibid*.
136. Chittick, *Faith and Practice of Islam*, 5.

who while on a journey happened upon a severed head on which was written the qur'anic verse "He loseth both the world and the hereafter" (Q 22:11),
whereupon Bayazid picks up the head and kisses it, explaining that "this is the
head of a *darvish* who gave up both worlds for God".[137] So it is that in the HG,
where the *shahada* is the sacred formula entrusted to the adherent, its functional quality and pragmatic end is defined by the achievement of *ihsan*. In this
third stage of transition, there is thus an unspoken or "hidden" quality through
which the adherent is invited to consider. Could it be that there is message
that *ihsan* is to be the "end" of or "release" from religious duty and obligation?
It certainly makes no sense for the orthodox Moslem. Perhaps the Shi'a gnoseological sensitivities give clues as to its extant secret meanings, especially
if one applies an esoteric reading to the innate process of Islamic theology
whereby the individual is meant to traverse from *tawhid* (unity) to *nubuwwa*
(prophecy) to *ma'ad* (return to God). And perhaps important indicators can
be detected in the dialogue of Mohammed's council to Ali (just noted above).
This third stage (*ihsan*) is not a mere "conformity with works and faith" as
read by conservative approaches to it, but, in an esoteric light, an extension
and expansion *beyond* the normative confines of religious consciousness. This
condition is prescient in our imagining of Persian history, and one which persisted (and came to be most profoundly retained in the Sufi understanding of
its past) in spite of the late antique and early mediaeval Islamic trends to fixate
on legalism and authentication of established religious traditions.

A fascinating comparison between the HG and Mazdaki doctrine lies possibly in connections between the notion of *hanifi*, "true religion", and that
of Mazdakite "*dorost-din*". To begin with an obvious parallel, according to
Shahrestani, who documented Mazdak's doctrine, the above point about *ihsan*
being about "going beyond religious formalism" is an idea readily made clear in
Mazdakism: "Every person in whom these powers ... unite, he becomes (part
of) God in the world below and will be relieved from religious obligation."[138]
Moreover, to this person is revealed the Highest Mystery (Truth), whereby
he is permitted to conceive anything of the Supreme Name.[139] We should not
forget the common factor of Mazdakite and Islamic doctrine being grounded
in their shared egalitarian philosophy. To take this further, perhaps even conveyed in what seems to have been originally a "democratic theology" that "He
sees you though you do not see Him" and in that whoever comprehends "anything" (and not all) of these letters will be "divulged" the Truth.[140] For the Sufis,
it is put plainly into verse: "The Sufi comes to know a hidden mystery through
a drop of wine; you can come to know everyone's essence through this ruby

---

137. Cf. J. Nurbakhsh, *The Path*, 40.
138. Cf. Shaki, "The Cosmogonical and Cosmological Teachings of Mazdak", 529.
139. *Ibid.*
140. *Ibid.*

wine."[141] To explain, the Mazdaki doctrine makes explicit a progressive out-look from a formalist to a non-formalist state by which the normative mode of religious function is then made obsolete for any of those who achieve the requisite level, a type of "process theology". The same potential is seen in Islamic doctrine, the original purport of which is brought out in the Sufi stream. This is similarly witnessed in the Sufi categorization of religious consciousness in which *shariat*, *tariqat* and *haqqiqat* (as noted above) form a progressive (spiritual, rather than theological) development. Also of note is the sacred quaternary distinction in rendering the meaning of the Qur'an in that the Holy Book has four layers that sequentially lead into a deeper understanding of the written text.[142]

Although usually left out in principle, the fourth question by the inquisitor in HG is of most importance and relevance here. Mohammed is asked to speak about the Hour, but wittingly avoids the question in a display of genuine humility and sincerity as an ultimate sign of *true* wisdom and gnosis, saying, "The one who is asked about it is no better informed than the one who is asking."[143] As a final note on the HG, we may consider the possibility of looking at the text to be about an initiatory rite, given not only the significance of the *shahada* in Sufi Sadr al-Din Qonawi (above), but more intriguingly the overall manner of Gabriel and Mohammed's discourse in the text, and especially the formal (or intimate?) seating position of Gabriel, who "sat down with his knees pressed against Muhammad's".[144]

THE PRE-EMINENCE OF THE GABRIELIC THEME IN THE EXPECTATION OF KHADIJA AND WARAQA

This brings us to the point of the meeting of Salman and Mohammed. In order to understand this relationship, though, it is necessary to define or at least clarify the position and significance of Gabriel in Islamic doctrine. The role of the archangel Gabriel, Heb. *Gabri'el*, Ar. *Jabra'il* or *Jibril*, meaning "man of God", features in Islamic literature (in continuity from Judaeo-Christian tradition) as the Messenger of God to Man. Gabriel is depicted as one who appears in the shape of a man in order to explain mysterious phenomena to God's chosen. Gabriel is not always actually named in the 96th surah (*Al-'Alaq*), neither is he always explicitly referred to in the corresponding hadith account of Bukhari, or even in the *Sira* of Ibn Ishaq; yet he is implied in every aspect. The first of

---

141. Hafez quoted in J. Nurbakhsh, "Darvish or Sufi", *Sufi*, 68 (Winter 2005/6), 30.
142. Cf. Abol Fazl Rashid al-Din Meybodi, *Kashf al-Asrar* (The Unveiling of the Mysteries and Provisions for the Righteous).
143. Cf. Al-Tabrizi, *Mishkat*, 5.
144. Cf. Web, "Gabriel", *EQ*. Robson's translation has: "Sitting down beside the Prophet, leaning his knees against his, and placing his hands on his thighs." Cf. Al-Tabrizi, *Mishkat*, 5.

these does not identify who is giving command, while the latter two invoke an "angel" (*al-malaka*) or "Namus"[145] to infer Gabriel.[146] Therefore, Gabriel's identification with the bringer of Revelation to Mohammed is very quickly (almost too readily?) taken to be a fact by those who hear of the Prophet's experience, and Mohammed appears to have adopted this trend without delay. This is particularly evident from the number of collected hadith that mention Gabriel's association with Mohammed,[147] and Gabriel is a keyword in describing the mediation of the divine to the Prophet. Moslem understanding of Gabriel follows from earlier references to the archangel in the Old Testament, this figure appearing for the first time in Daniel 8:15-16 and 9:21 and later in the New Testament (Lk. 1:19 and 26). It is very clear from angelology that Gabriel must appear in the form of a man visible to others physically but either possessing a "terrifying" or "hidden" presence (bearable or visible only to whom God wills). A vivid description of Gabriel is given in Daniel 10:4-6, which undoubtedly carries through to current depictions in orthodox Moslem and Sufi thought:

> I was by the side of a great river ... I lifted my eyes, and ... behold a certain man clothed in linen, whose loins were girded with fine gold of Uphaz: his body was like the beryl, and his face as the appearance of lightning, and his eyes as lamps of fire, and his arms and his feet like in colour of polished brass, and the voice of his words like the voice of a multitude.[148]

Even though Mohammed is technically the first person in the *Sira* to whom Gabriel identifies himself by that name,[149] he does not seem to recognize his visitor (neither by appearance nor by name).[150] The first person apparently to acknowledge this fact and make the link between Mohammed's experience (and vision) and the archangel Gabriel was Waraqa ibn Nawfal, the cousin of Khadija, a *hanif* scholar who was familiar with the *Torah* and *Injil* (Gospel).[151] However, it is technically Khadija who first realizes the divine favour bestowed upon Mohammed and reassures him from fears of being possessed by *jinn*, and who then relays news of the event to Waraqa.[152] Mohammed's

---

145. From the Greek *nomos*, portraying a sense of Divine Law or Scripture, here identified with the Angel of Revelation; cf. Lings, *Muhammad*, 44, note 5.

146. Q 96:1-5, cf. M. Asad, *Qur'an*, 963; Bokhari's account concerns a narration by Aisha; cf. Bokhari, *Sahih*, vol. 1, 3, h.3(a).

147. As in the the Compendia of Muslim Texts: *Sahih Bukhari*, *Sahih Muslem* and *Sunan Abu-Dawud*.

148. Cf. also Apoc. Mos. 40:1, 1 Enoch 9–10, and on Gabriel in later Jewish angelology, J. Daniélou, *The Theology of Jewish Christianity* (trans. J. Baker) (The Development of Christian Doctrine before the Council of Nicea, 1) (London, 1964), ch. 4.

149. Ibn Ishaq, *Sira*, 106.

150. *Ibid.*, 106–7.

151. *Ibid.*, 107.

152. *Ibid.*, 106–7.

own account, recorded in the *Sira*, states that "He came to me … while I was asleep [i.e. in a meditative state possibly?]", holding an item with writing on it. Then, the instruction to "Read!" occurs three times, whereupon, from fear for his life, Mohammed makes the plea: "What then shall I read?" After repeating the recitation told to him, he awakens from that state and recalls that it was as though the words were written on his heart.[153] There is immediately an internal conflict when Mohammed reproaches himself as a poet and a man possessed by *jinn*; but a voice intervenes twice to identify Mohammed as the "apostle of God" and itself as "Gabriel". Yet Mohammed still appears unsure of what is happening and again reproaches himself, until he tells Khadija of the event.

There is a strong sense that comes through from the *Sira* of an unspoken narrative. First, it is evident that Khadija is expecting something. Second, the casual invocations made by her such as "I take refuge in God [from *jinn*]" and "Verily by Him in whose hand is Khadija's soul" are neatly underlaid with a subtle but firm monotheistic undertone. Indeed this natural piety is seen in essence to go right back to the time of Khadija's father, Abd Allah, and grandfather, Abd al-Mottalib, who were exemplary men of Quraish (and the latter of whom is said to have known Waraqa).[154] Another interesting point is that tradition speaks of Waraqa's sister, Qotayla, offering herself for marriage to Abd Allah, because she expected that either he or his son would be the foretold prophet of the Arabs (but Abd Allah would not defy his father's wishes of a previous arrangement to marry Amina).[155] The importance of Waraqah and his family (i.e. his cousin and sister) in the traditional account of Mohammed's life and prophetic mission is clearly evident. These connections are hardly coincidental. They indeed illustrate an unspoken and significant narrative that bespeaks of an expectation placed upon Mohammed from very early on, indeed before his birth. Let us consider Waraqa's role.

THE ROLE OF WARAQA IBN NAWFAL IN THE LIFE OF MOHAMMED

Waraqa, the director of a hidden narrative

With regard to Waraqa, two traditions are of particular importance: Qotayla's attraction to Abd Allah and the pregnancy of Amina, Mohammed's mother. In observing Abd Allah, Qotayla is struck by "the radiance which lit his face and which seemed to her to shine from beyond this world".[156] During Amina's pregnancy, a voice spoke to her saying: "You are pregnant with the lord of this

---

153. *Ibid.*, 106.
154. "Abd al-Mottalib knew four of the Hunafa". Cf. Lings, *Muhammad*, 16.
155. Ibn Ishaq, *Sira*, 68; Lings, *Muhammad*, 18.
156. This radiance she had always observed with Abd Allah, which was particularly remarkable on this occasion. Cf. Lings, *Muhammad*, 18.

people and when he is born say, "I put him in the care of the One from the evil of every envier, then call him Muhammad." And she saw a light come forth from her."[157] In these two accounts it is worth noting the allusion to "light" and the importance of "the naming" of the prophet, which relate to the hierophanic discourse within pre-Islamic traditional (including Persian) texts. These two narratives have some parallel to the announcements of the birth of John the Baptist and Jesus in the qur'anic Surah 19 ("Mary"), but here in the *Sira* there is also this fascinating additional element of light – a gnostic touch. If a major theme of Islam, derived from the Qur'an, stresses the passing down of the true way by spiritual descent (as in the case of Abraham Q 2:123–32), there are of course elements of light in this great and holy text as well (Q 24:34–5), but we would still have to say that light, as we find it in the above passages related to Waraqa, is a much more distinctively Persian, and of course also gnostic, feature.[158] The verse Q 42:52 may be brought to mind: "And thus we sent to you a spirit by our command. You did not know what the book was nor faith, but we made it a light with which we guide whom we wish of our servants."[159] This is a verse not only relevant to such Gnosis, but to its imparting by a mysterious guide.

Against this background, if we can now return to Amina, the fact that her pregnancy also directly reflects the story of the qur'anic Mary has significant overtones when considering the element of light/spirit in relation to Gabriel (especially with regard to Persian Sufi imagery).[160] Given that Amina is told to name the child "Mohammed", moreover, this has special significance in that it is the qur'anic Jesus who predicts the coming of "Ahmad" after him (Q 61:6).[161] With regard to the role of Waraqa in Mohammed's life, Qotayla is an obvious connection, but it is "the naming" in Amina's narrative that proves a most thought-provoking point, especially if it was to be

---

157. Ibn Ishaq, *Sira*, 69.

158. Cf. H. Corbin, *Man of Light in Iranian Sufism* (London, 1978). Also, cf. Snouk Hurgronje, *Het Mekkaansche Feest* (Leipzig, 1923), 1–124; R. Paret, "Ibrahim", in *EIs*, vol. 3; D. P. Walker, *The Ancient Theology: Studies in Christian Platonism from the Fifteenth to the Nineteenth Century* (London, 1972).

159. Note also other verses that relate the light theme with revelation of Mohammed in Q 64:8; 4:174; 5:15.

160. Cf. the qur'anic account of Mary, Q 33:42–52 and 19:16–23; for a cross-reference to "light", see Rumi's account of the Virgin Birth in *MJR* 3, 3700–88 and 207–212.

161. Note, the Greek *Periklytos* ("the Much-Praised") as an alleged proper reading of John's *Parakletos* ("Comforter") gathers support from the Bible in that the former is taken to be a Greek translation of the Aramaic *Mawhamana*. It may be possible to connect the Aramaic *Mawhamana* and the Greek *Periklytos*, which have the same meaning as *Mohammed* and *Ahmed* from the verb *hamida* ("be praised") and the noun *hamd* ("praise"). Cf. M. Asad, *Qur'an*, 861 and note 6. For contrasting views on the subject of *The Gospel of Barnabas* as text, cf. J. Joosten, "The Gospel of Barnabas and the Diatessaron", *Harvard Theological Review* 95(1) (2002), 73–96.

Waraqa's contribution (given his recognition as a [Christian] biblical scholar and scribe?). The prediction of Mohammed as prophet is another connecting point between the key figures in the *Sira* – Salman, Waraqa and Khadija – we are discussing here.

In the *Sira*, it was Bahira the Syrian monk who first identified Mohammed as the prophet of the Arabs. It is also he who informs Abu Talib (Mohammed's uncle) to conceal the destiny of the young boy until the appropriate time.[162] A second event, and a point of continuity, comes from another Syrian Christian monk (named in Lings's account), Nestor,[163] who rather strangely distinguishes the adult Mohammed as "none other than" a prophet from among the Arab entourage (accompanying the *caravanserai*).[164] Such identification may imply more than just the repeating of Moslem tradition about Mohammed's legitimacy. There are obvious connections that need to be brought to the fore to explain the subtle links between the Gabrielic theme and Salman, and the expectation of Khadija and Waraqa. The most obvious clue to the connection between these figures is the repeated phrase placed on the lips of all three characters (i.e. Salman, Khadija and Waraqa): "Verily by Him in whose hand is … soul."[165] Then, of course, there is the fact that Khadija goes straight to Waraqa.[166] One is curious to know whether Waraqa and Salman ever actually met (or Bahira and Salman or, indeed, Bahira and Waraqa). For Waraqa is also recorded to have visited Syria (and elsewhere), where he learned from "those that follow the Torah and the Gospel" and from whom he learned written Arabic and Hebrew.[167] Nevertheless, had Salman and Waraqa met, the former is arguably likely to have fulfilled the role of "Gabriel" for Mohammed. Should we entertain this viewpoint then, indeed, a sought-for network of relations between Bahira, Salman and Waraqa is revealed. Accordingly, Bahira may be seen as Salman's mentor, and the one who directs him to Mohammed, via Waraqa. However, Waraqa's connection to Bahira is slightly more complex and requires further elucidation.

---

162. Guilaume, *Sira*, 80–1.

163. Lings, *Muhammad*, 34.

164. *Ibid.*

165. See *Sira*, 107; Salman's statement, "By Him in whose hand lies Salman's soul", is cited in Donaldson, "Salman the Persian", 346. This tradition is also given at www.naqshbandi.org/chain/3.htm.

166. The exact details are difficult to pin down: sometimes Khadija sends Mohammed to Waraqa, while at other times she goes alone to report his words; sometimes she is accompanied by Abu Bakr (which indicates a clear discourse on the first male convert). Cf. C. F. Robinson, "Waraka B. Nawfal", in *EIs*, vol. 11.

167. *Sira* (Guillaume), 107; cf. Robinson, "Waraka B. Nawfal". But this account is deemed anachronistic; cf. S. H. Griffith, "The Gospel in Arabic. An Inquiry into its Appearance in the First Abbasid Century", *Oriens Christianus* 69 (1985), 144–9.

Waraqa and Bahira

There are a number of reasons why Waraqa's role in Mohammed's revelation and mission is unavoidable and in fact paramount. However, this is not to be perceived as Waraqa acting alone, but rather in view of his alleged bond with Salman and in particular, if not additionally, with Bahira prior to this. In this regard, Waraqa's kerygmatic role in the narrative of Mohammed's earliest revelation requires attention, and the fact that Waraqa is without question the authenticator of Mohammed's revelation can hardly be downplayed. Apart from these matters, there is also a tradition worth citing, yet one that cannot be pursued fully in this work due to its limitations. It relates how Waraqa (and an unidentified second figure [a Qorayshi?]) returned a lost young Mohammed "who had strayed from his suckling mother" to Abd al-Mottalib.[168] This legend has a particular importance, in our opinion, for the story of the opening of Mohammed's chest in the desert,[169] the implication being that young Mohammed could have been under Waraqa's tutelage. The kerygmatic quality of Waraqa has raised some important questions that may help delineate an important aspect of Mohammed's career.

Robinson rightly points out that consensus on Waraqa retaining his Christian faith (after confirming Mohammed's prophecy) has no satisfactory answer.[170] His Christian affiliation could very well be a misconception in reading the texts, since some authorities count him among the *sahaba* and others as the first male convert.[171] The uncertainty, we think, stems from the way Waraqa's allegiance is defined in the *Sira*, for there, among the original "four hanifs", only Waraqa and a certain Zayd ibn Amr retain an arguably nondenominational identity. Of Zayd, it is clearly said that he "stayed as he was: he accepted neither Judaism nor Christianity".[172] With regard to Waraqa, as already mentioned, the *Sira* specifically states that he "*had become* Christian and *read* the scriptures and *learned* from those that follow the Torah and the Gospel";[173] this is elucidated by another passage in the *Sira* asserting that "Waraqa *attached* himself to Christianity and *studied* its scriptures *until he had thoroughly mastered them*".[174] And there is a subtle difference in the way the other two hanifs, Obaydullah ibn Jahsh and Othman ibn al-Howayrith, are stated to be Christian: note, "Obaydullah … *adopted* Christianity … and died *a*

---

168. Cf. Robinson, "Waraka B. Nawfal".
169. Cf. Lings, *Muhammad*, 25f.
170. Cf. Robinson, "Waraka B. Nawfal".
171. Al-Zurqani, *Sharh'ala'l-mawahib al-laduniyya* (Bulaq, 1278/1899), vol. 1, 257; al-Diyarbakri, *Ta'rikh al-khamis* (Cairo, 1302/1923), vol. 1, 323; cf. Robinson, "Waraka B. Nawfal".
172. Ibn Ishaq, *Sira*, 99.
173. *Ibid.*, 107.
174. *Ibid.*, 99.

Christian in Abyssinia",[175] and "Othman ... went to the Byzantine emperor and *became* a Christian".[176] Overall a key difference between the four *hanif*s lies in the fact that Waraqa is obviously classified as a *scholar* of Christianity. But the question still remains, of which "denomination"? If he travelled to Syria, then a likely Nestorian influence may be deduced. This may also help explain the pre-rogative in placing a bond between Salman and Waraqa – no doubt a common ground in Nestorianism. However, both Salman and Waraqa remain an anomaly regarding Christianity (as proposed previously), for they are both involved in prophetic expectations outside of the normative stream of Christian establishment. More explicitly (according to both traditional and non-traditional materials), they are both presented as advocates of Mohammed, the prophet of Islam. As an aside, we should note the interesting thesis of Kamal Salibi, a Protestant whose provocative Arab macrohistory places the events of the Old Testament and Jesus's ministry in Arabia (not Palestine), which relates to our story because he devotes a chapter to the "Lost Gospel of Waraqah", which is alleged to influence the qur'anic narrative.[177]

Conceiving whether Waraqa did retain his faith in the face of Mohammed's revelation, one can *almost* interpret his last council to Mohammed as an acceptance of Islam: "thou art the prophet of this people ... if I live ... I will help God in such wise as he knoweth".[178] However, the traditional image that portrays Waraqa as a blind old man is placed under scrutiny. There is a suggestion that Waraqa died in Mecca before Mohammed's public "call to the people that they convert".[179] A more controversial position suggests that he died in Syria, which forms part of an alternative chronology, occurring after the *hijra*.[180] Nevertheless, the sources certainly point to a lively controversy about Waraqa's status in the early Islamic period. We know, for instance, that Mohammed is said to have held the memory of Waraqa as sacred (forbidding insults to him), and even had a dream about him in heaven.[181] Thus, to return to the question of Waraqa and Bahira's meeting, it is agreed that the Syrian connection is of particular importance "among many features" that Waraqa's story "shares with the legend(s) of the monk Bahira". This link was accentuated in the research of Theodore Nöldeke who also argued "the origins of these

---

175. *Ibid.*
176. *Ibid.*
177. Cf. K. Salibi, *Who was Jesus? Conspiracy in Jerusalem* (London, 2007), and his *The Bible Came from Arabia* (London, 1985), discussed in G. Trompf, "When was the First Millenarian Movement? Qumran and the Implications of Historical Sociology", in *The Sum of Our Choices: Essays in Honour of Eric J. Sharpe*, McGill Studies in Religion 4 (Atlanta, GA, 1996), 252 and 263, where it is suggested, to explain the evidence Salibi presents, that exiled Jews tried to reduplicate their holy land in the Arabian wilderness.
178. *Sira*, 107.
179. Ibn Hajar, *Isaba* (Cairo, 1977), vol. 10, 304. Cf. Robinson, "Waraka B. Nawfal".
180. Cf. *ibid.*
181. Cf. *ibid.*

legends" in Waraqa.[182] Perhaps, as Chase Robinson admits, "all this makes evaluating Waraka's significance for the birth of Islam vexing indeed", for it still remains a "difficult" task to "judge what kind of influence (if any) he [Waraqa] exerted on Muhammad's thought".[183] But it is clear that both European and Middle Eastern scholarship have argued for his key role in the affirmative.[184]

GABRIEL IN ISLAM AND FURTHER SUGGESTIONS OF CORRESPONDENCE TO THE FIGURE OF SALMAN

The name "Gabriel" is only mentioned three times in the Qur'an, at 2:97-98 and 66:4. The first passage states that "Gabriel ... brought down upon thy heart this [divine writ]".[185] In other verses a more mysterious tone is suggested, where Gabriel is not named but implied, and made synonymous with *al-ruh* (the spirit), whose main function is in maintaining the correspondence between God and Man.[186] The importance of this is the qur'anic statement that God fortifies the faithful "by spirit from Him" (58:22), and has done so before as he does so again with Mohammed. Not only does Gabriel appear to Mary and not only does the spirit of God impregnate her (in both the NT and Qur'an), but Jesus is also fortified through this same Holy Spirit (Q 2:878 and 253; 5:110). Hence in almost an astounding paradox (contrary to orthodox Islamic rejection of Jesus' divinity) Jesus is named "a spirit from God" (Q 4:171). All this, of course, comes out within the subtleties and grey lines of ongoing theological debate, indicated previously as reflective of the Monophysite/Nestorian dispute. The loose point of relevance is here to show that the general Christian/Moslem narrative on Jesus is more in harmony than often admitted by either party, which is to say that some kind of "Syrian split" that helped allow Islam to appear should constitute the heart of Christian/Moslem dialogue. The Christological dispute seems still an ongoing internal debate within the Islamic body. It is obviously more relevant to our thesis that this dispute is also teased out in the attempt to categorize the figure of Gabriel, since he is both *al-ruh* and a man endowed with "perfect"[187] physical form – a point brought to the fore through the disparity between the Islamic establishment and Persian Sufistic thought, with the latter ready to permit Gabriel to be Salman.

---

182. Cf. Robinson, "Waraka B. Nawfal". For Nöldeke cf. "Hatte Muhammad christiliche Lehrer?", *Zeitschrift der Deutschen Morgenlandischen Gesellschaft*, 12 (1858): 699ff.
183. Cf. Robinson, "Waraka B. Nawfal".
184. For Middle Eastern sources cf. Abu Musa al-Hariri, *Qass wa-nabi* [Priest and Prophet: Research On the Rise of Islam] (Diyar Aql, 1991). Cf. Robinson, "Waraka B. Nawfal".
185. Q 2:97; M. Asad, *Qur'an*, 20.
186. Cf. Q 16:2; 70:4 and 97:4.
187. Cf. Q 19:17, "well-made human being".

The interplay between a "spiritual force" and a "physical man" carries on throughout the Islamic tradition. It also flows into similar theological clashes within the Jewish tradition. An interesting note is that the Jews who query Mohammed about who brought him the revelations reject Mohammed because he identifies Gabriel.[188] Instead they announce Michael as their patron and Gabriel as the betrayer of their secrets, whereby Mohammed answered that both were God's servants and thus neither could be denied, as Mohammed subsequently revealed in sura 2:97–8.[189] Several traditions concerning Salman and the Jews correspond in that they contain nuances of this nature. For instance, as noted, Salman is sold into slavery to Medinan Jews, and in one variant story is re-sold to another from fear of him being a sorcerer.[190] Mohammed indeed speaks of the importance of both Michael and Gabriel in identifying them as the two men in white who perform the "opening of [his] chest" and the "purification of [his] heart" as a young man in the desert.[151] The traditions thus make it clear that Gabriel was more than the harbinger of revelation. Moreover, the idea that he played a direct and active role alongside Mohammed's mission as counsellor and helper was enforced. As alluded to earlier, the alias of Gabriel meant an imminent appraisal and unification of the previous prophetic agencies and their teachings, and also confirmed Mohammed's mission as a continuation (or later conclusion) to these.

There are a series of important events relating the involvement of Gabriel in Mohammed's mission that need to be especially noted. Due to the restriction of space, we will stick to Johannes Pederson's useful collation of Gabriel's involvements, adding our own commentary and additional sources where necessary. It was Gabriel who taught Mohammed *wuzu* (ritual wash) and *salat* (custom of prayer), and guided him on his ascension (*meraj*).[192] At other times Gabriel appears as a terrifying force threatening Mohammed with God's wrath if he failed to comply with his commandments.[193] It was also Gabriel who reproached Mohammed's public acknowledgement of the three goddesses (al-Lat, al-Uzza and Manat), insisting he reveal they were not received from him (i.e. Gabriel).[194] He warns Mohammed of the Meccan betrayal before the *hijra*,[195] and interestingly appears at Badr with thousands of angels in

---

188. Cf. J. Pederson, "Djabra'il, or Djibril, Hebrew Gabri'el", in *EIs*, vol. 2.
189. *Ibid.* On Michael as the patron archangel of Israel in later Judaism, Daniélou, *The Theology of Jewish Christianity*, esp. 117–26.
190. Al-Saduk; cf. Donaldson, "Salman the Persian", 343.
191. Tabari, *Ta'rikh*, vol. 1, 1157; A. J. Wensinck, *A Handbook of Early Muhammadan Tradition* (Leiden, 1927), 166. Cf. Pederson, "Djabra'il, or Djibril, Hebrew Gabri'el". Here we can add how interesting it is that both Waraqa and Salman can be by inference brought into the sphere of Mohammed's boyhood years.
192. Tabari, *Ta'rikh*, vol. 1, 1157–9; *Sira* (Wüstenfeld), 263; Wensinck, *A Handbook*, 25; cf. Pederson, "Djabra'il, or Djibril, Hebrew Gabri'el".
193. Tabari, *Ta'rikh*, vol. 1, 1171.
194. *Ibid.*, 1192f.
195. *Ibid.*, 1231; *Sira* (Wüstenfeld), 325–30.

Figure 8.1 Faravahar (stone carving in Persepolis). Photo by Napishtim, Wikimedia Commons (CC BY-SA-3.0-2.5-2.0-1.0).

support.[196] (Could this last action be taken to imply a possible military intercession in favour of Moslem forces, entailing a Mazdakite related force?). An almost anti-hero façade can be picked up when Gabriel is also said to have ordered the attack on the Jewish tribes of Banu Qaynoka and later Banu Qorayza (which may be read as payback, considering the story of Salman being flogged by Jews for not publicly denouncing his connection from Mohammed).[197] There are also several indications that allow for a Persian connection with the figure of Salman: the first of which is taken from a hadith related by Aisha, who had seen Gabriel twice in his transcendent form (as he was seen by Mohammed in the horizon and at the *sidra*-tree). He is described as having 600 wings with every pair filling the space from East to West,[198]

196. *Sira* (Wüstenfeld), 449f; Ibn Saad, *al-Tabaqat al-kubra* (ed. H. Sachau *et al.*) (Leiden, 1905–40), vol. 2, 1, 2 and 18.

197. See Kohlberg, "Some Imami Shi'i Views", 399; cf. Tabari, *Ta'rikh*, vol. 1, 1360 and 1486. Cf. also Q 8:58 and 59:2; *Sira* (Wüstenfeld), 684.

198. Cf. Tabari, *al-Musamma Jami al-bayan fi tafsir al-Qur'an* (al-Qahirah, 1323–29/1944–50), vol. 27, 26f. Also, Q 53:6. Cf. Pederson, "Djabra'il".

Figure 8.2 A guardian spirit: Cyrus the Great (monument at Sydney Olympic Park). Photo by Siamax, Wikimedia Commons (CC BY-SA-3.0 or CC BY-SA-2.5-2.0-1.0).

an obvious Persian iconographic reference to the *faravahar*[199] (located in Persepolis), and the *fravashi*[200] (guardian spirit or sometimes "intuition" or "intuitive mind") of Cyrus the Great depicted at Pasargardae (the ancient capital of the Achaemenians).

Descriptions of the physical form of Gabriel (echoing those of Daniel) in the Qur'an have him as a "well-made human being".[201] This provides us with another "connection of interest", where he generally appears in Islamic tradition as a strong man[202] clad in green garments and a silk turban, seated upon

199. A prominent motif at Persepolis thought to be the symbol of the Persian Empire and the icon of the Zoroastrian religion.
200. Note on this term the specific conceptual link whereby NPers. *fereshtegan* (*firishtagan*) corresponds to the NPers. *ferestadegan* "those who are sent", i.e. "angels". It was a common neo-Mazdakite Khurrami belief that such *fereshtegan* were messengers who dwelt among them, an idea noted but not elaborated on by Madelung, "Khurramiyya".
201. E.g. Q 19:17.
202. Tabari, *Tafsir*, vol. 27, cited in Pederson, "Djabra'il".

a horse[203] (or mule[204]), trademarks of refinement and sophistication rather fitting to a Persian such as the stature of Salman.[205] Conversely, in other instances Salman is specifically made to be a stout ascetic with few possessions,[206] presented in common or sometimes appalling dress.[207] As a source of divine inspiration, Gabriel's intercession is never limited to any specific time or place in any of the monotheistic traditions that mention him, and it is not the intention of this work to limit his identification to the figure of Salman or the prophecy of Mohammed. Gabriel is seen as an essential component of divine revelation generally, and especially in normative Islamic theology and history, which takes Gabriel as divine aid to God's leading figures, from Adam to Mohammed.[208] Of course, this fits in with a difficult-to-question mystical reading whereby any prophet in question would see an angel while others an ordinary man:[209] a view supported by Islamic sources about Mohammed (although partly contradicted by the orthodox claim that many "pseudo-prophets" would lay claim to inspiration from Gabriel,[210] thus raising the all-round question of "legitimate prophecy".

A curious hadith states that Gabriel came to Mohammed while in the presence of Aisha and conversed with him, after which Mohammed asked Aisha if she knew who that was and what he said, whereupon she answered that it was Dihya Ibn Khalifa al-Kalbi. Interestingly enough, it was Salman who narrated the hadith. In which case, he almost bluntly (and for the first time in any traditional Islamic source) reveals the identity of Gabriel as associated with a known figure.[211] One suspects that the hadith is ironically supportive of Salman's role as Gabriel (even if resorting to a theory of misdirection). Concerning Salman in this role, there are several other noteworthy points to consider in brief. According to tradition, Salman was considered an accepted

---

203. Ibn Saad, *al-Tabaqat*, vol. 2, 1, 9 and 24; Pederson, "Djabra'il".
204. Cf. Tabari, *Ta'rikh*, vol. 1, 1485; *Sira* (Wüstenfeld), 684; cf. Pederson, "Djabra'il".
205. Salman was of notable family whose father was the *marzban* (general, gatekeeper) of Esfahan. Other Persian stories take Salman as a Persian prince. Cf. http://majorityrights. com/index.php/forums/viewthread/58/. And for Salman depicted as being "a man of unusual physical strength", see Donaldson, "Salman the Persian", 348.
206. Al-Masudi *Muruj al-dhahab*, vol. 4, 195–6, cited in Millward, "The Adaptation of Men to Their Time", 344.
207. Donaldson, "Salman the Persian", 348; Cf. Millward, "The Adaptation of Men to Their Time", 334, citing Al-Mas'udi, *Muruj*, vol. 4, 195–6.
208. Cf. al-Kisa'i, *Qisas al-anbiya* (Leiden, 1922). Cf. Pederson, "Djabra'il". For references to Moses, Samuel ibn Bali and David, for example, see W. M. Brinner (trans.) (ed. and annot. E. Yarshater), *The History of Tabari (Ta'rikh al-rusul wa'l muluk)* (New York, 1991), vol. 3, 71, 75, 130 and 149.
209. See Ibn al-Farid, *al-Ta'iyya al-kubra* (Cairo, 1319/1940), vol. 5, 279–84; cf. Pederson, "Djabra'il".
210. Tabari, *Ta'rikh*, vol. 3, 1394; cf. Pederson, "Djabra'il".
211. Cf. *Sahih Muslem*, Book 31, no., 6006. www.usc.edu/dept/MSA/fundamentals/hadithsunnah/ muslim/031.smt.html#031.6006.

member of Mohammed's family, being the first case of a Persian *mowali*. This is a strong indication of Mohammed's fondness of Salman, but, according to a certain unsourced tradition, Aisha would report that Mohammed and Salman would spend hours alone, talking (about issues of religion etc), to the extent that she thought that Salman would spend the night with Mohammed![212] It is without doubt that Salman was a revered Companion with a special place next to Mohammed, doubtless affecting the latter's revelation that "the Persians will form the better part of the Moslem community".[213] Similarly, the Islamic and Sufic traditions continue to honour Salman by variously attributing to him titles such as "imam", "the inheritor of Islam", "the wise judge" and "the knowledgeable scholar".[214] The image that is gathered from the sources portrays Salman as a man of great value for development of the new religion of Islam. And the fact that he was Persian had immense implications, then picked up on and developed to extraordinary lengths. Some relevant claims about his alleged role in the Battle of the Ditch, in the conquest of Iraq and Fars (in which the story of his crossing of the Tigris bears an uncanny likeness to the Mosaic parting of the Red Sea),[215] and his governorship of Madain are admittedly questioned for their historical value due to the controversial authority of their transmitter, Sayf ibn Omar.[216] The historicity of these events is by no means to be discounted outright, however, and in any case it is important that they still retain traditional and esoteric credibility to this day.[217]

Salman is further attributed "as one of the chief pillars and earliest exponents of Sufism", and as the "Grandmaster of Guilds (*asnaf*)"[218] for being a critical figure in the development of the *futuwwa* and "workmen's corporations".[219] His alleged tomb in ancient Madain attracted the growth of a village named after him – Salman-Pak ("Salman the Pure", near the former suburb of Asbandur) – and this was from very early on a centre of worship.[220] Within the

---

212. www.mukto-mona.com/Articles/kasem/quran_origin3.htm.

213. Repeating the "Hadith of the Persians", cited in della Vida, "Salman al-Farisi".

214. Cf. Naqshbandi Sufi transmission "Golden Chain": www.naqshbandi.org/chain/3.htm.

215. Donaldson, "Salman the Persian", 346. The name of Salman "appears also in the list of those saints, other than prophets, who are regarded as having exercised miraculous powers (*karamat*), and both he and Abdol-Darda are said to have walked on the sea." Abu Nasr al-Sarraj, *Kitab al-Luma' fi'l-Tasawwuf* (ed. Nicholson), Gibb Memorial Series 22 (London and Leiden, 1914), 64, 134 and 321, and "Introduction", 52–7, cited in Donaldson, "Salman the Persian", 351.

216. Cf. della Vida, "Salman al-Farisi". For Sayf ibn Omar, see F. M. Donner, "Sayf B. Umar", in *EIs*, vol. 9.

217. For the converse opinion cf. della Vida, "Salman al-Farsi or Salman Pak".

218. Cf. Zarrinkub, "The Arab Conquest of Iran and its Aftermath", 13.

219. della Vida, "Salman al-Farsi or Salman Pak".

220. Al-Yaqubi, *Kitab al-Buldan* (ed. de Goeje) (Leiden, 1892), 321; cf. della Vida, "Salman al-Farisi". Also, M. Streck [M. Morony], "Al-Mada", in *EIs*, vol. 5. His sepulchral mosque was renovated by the Ottoman Sultan Murad IV (1623–40) and further restored in 1904–5. On this, E. Herzfeld & F. Sarre, *Archäol. Reise im Euphrates- und Tigrisgebiet* (Berlin, 1911),

Shi'a tradition Salman commonly features in divine emanations that "immediately" follow Ali,[221] and these are specifically espoused by the Nusayris who claim the trinity of the mystical letters (as noted previously): *Ayn* (Ali), *Mim* (Mohammed) and *Sin* (Salman).[222] A most significant aspect in the career of Salman is that he is credited to be the first non-Arab qur'anic scholar and the first to translate the sacred text (with commentary) into Persian, the first language into which the Qur'an was translated.[223] Similarly, he was the first Persian who recorded and commented upon hadith,[224] a crucial point that may help clarify our earlier discussion on the special place of Salman within Islam, and especially in relation to Persia. If we recall, after the death of Mohammed, Salman became a close companion of Ali. It was Ali who openly favoured the recording of hadith and was opposed by a group of Companions on this.[225] Salman also taught a vast number of Persians in their own language,[226] instructing them in the sciences of Qur'an and hadith. There is no denying that Persians were a volatile component of Islamic history, as demonstrated by the traditions and outstanding legends that surround the figure of Salman. Following on from his *exemplum*, it was indeed the Persians who excelled in the qur'anic sciences and the construction of the hadith traditions, as they did in the learning of Arabic. Many notable authorities in the science of "recitation of the Book" (*qira'a*) are Persian in origin; the transmission of *hadith* literature (in both the Sunni and Shi'a world) is also largely indebted to the Persian contribution.[227] Even purely relying on our traditional sources, Salman is still placed as the primordial link between Persia and Islam and (later on) Sufism. Moreover, he is held by both Sunni and Shi'a as a foremost authority on the esoteric meaning of the Qur'an and spiritual matters pertaining to the secret teachings of the Prophet as passed to the most intimate circle of his Companions – and transmitted by the Shi'ite Imams. For certain, the honour bestowed to Salman in tradition lends support to the alternate (resilient) view of Salman as the author (or co-author) of the Qur'an.

---

vol. 2, 262, note 1, cited in della Vida, "Salman al-Farisi". It remained the object of regular veneration and pilgrimage, paid homage to by Sunni barbers of Baghdad and especially by the Shi'ites who stop over *en route* from Karbala. Other locations are given for his tomb: Esfahan (and elsewhere, e.g. Lydia), where there is evidence of his cult in the thirteenth century. On this, Yaqut al-Hamawi, *M 'jam al-buldan* (ed. F. Wüstenfeld) (Leipzig, 1866–73), vol 2, 170, cited in della Vida, "Salman al-Farisi".
221. Cf. della Vida, "Salman al-Farisi".
222. R. Dussaud, *Histoire et Religion des Nosaïris* (Paris, 1900), 62, cited in della Vida, "Salman al-Farsi".
223. Cf. Nasr, "The Religious Sciences: II. The Qur'anic Sciences", 466.
224. Cf. *ibid.*, 472.
225. Nasr, "Sufism: II. The Spread of Sufism Among the Arabs", *ibid.*, vol. 4, 446; Nasr, "The Religious Sciences: III. The Science of Hadith", 470.
226. Dianner, "Arabic Literature in Iran: I. The Umayyad Age in Iran", *ibid.*, vol. 4, 570.
227. Nasr, "The Religious Sciences II", 467; Nasr, "The Religious Sciences III", 472.

It is worth noting Hossein Nasr in response: he endorses the Persian contribution but holds that the relevant protagonists were "Moslem Persians" working within the frame of Islamic domain and not vice versa. He insists that the philosophical or spiritual activity of these figures strictly adhered to Qur'an and hadith (and the sayings of Ali).[228] Hence in this view, Salman is the "Moslem Persian" *par excellence*, who embodied the true epitome of a foreign convert to the religion of Mohammed. But there are versions of this general approach that actually count in favour of our arguments, for such an Islamic traditionalist view is also supported to some extent by the "anti-Salmanian" Persians who, as noted above, would slander Salman "the greatest Persian traitor", as the cause of the Persian (Sasanid) empire's downfall. They actually reveal a great deal more about Salman in the course of their slander that would truly disturb the core of Islamic establishment. They say, for instance, to take us back to the beginning of this chapter, that Salman "was an ex-Mazdaki", and that he was the "Prophet's left hand", who adapted all the "brotherly love theories to Islam", playing a major role in the formation of Islamic doctrine and political ideology. And they say that Mohammed, "with the help of Salman" and others, "wrote the Qur'an and practically stole most [of the] verses from [the] book of Mazdak, Mitraism" – as well as other Holy texts of the Jews, Christians and Zoroastrians. The rest of the Qur'an, moreover, according to them, came *ad lib* from Mohammed himself. Finally they declare that Salman was "an opportunist who sold Iran to Arabs for personal and political reasons".[229] If according to such groups Salman is used as a foil for the undermining of primary Islamic sources, then it is interesting to re-evaluate Nasr's point about everything being rooted in Qur'an, hadith and the sayings of Ali. The same orthodox material is used by non-establishment currents (such as the Nusayri, Alawite and Sufi components) against the establishment, all offering special theologies and sacred macrohistories of their own. A collation of the material from all available relevant sources, in any case, certainly helps to explain the importance of Salman the Persian, whether as hero or villain. In particular, with regard to our own tracing of an alternate macrohistory of Persian religious consciousness, the case of Salman lends solid support for tracing "counter-establishment" lineaments of Persian thought from Persia to Arabia, from Mazdak to Mohammed, and, as we shall now more clearly see, to Persianate Sufism.

---

228. Nasr (ed.), *Anthology*, vol. 1, xxvi–xxx.
229. Quoted in full above. For the source, see www.geocities.com/hammihanirani/islam.html.

CHAPTER 9

THE END OF THE JOURNEY: PERSIAN SUFISM

Sal-ha del talabeh jaameh jam az maa mikard
Va-an cheh khod dasht ze bigaaneh tamanah mikard

For years the heart had sought after the grail from us
And a needless quest for what the heart had always possessed[1]

Hafez

WHAT IS "PERSIAN" SUFISM?

I use the above quote to open this chapter because it sums up the experience of Sufism as a quest within the self, but the quote is also reflective of the over- all journey of this book and its aim to excavate the Iranian religious conscious- ness. In many ways, this book has been about an exploration of Persianate identity, which covers themes from the wider spectrum of events that have unfolded throughout the history of greater Iran, and which are brought together in the amalgamation of what appears to constitute a typical Persian identity. The extent of the influence of Persian culture upon those nations under the sway of this once mighty empire is plain and obvious. And it is the extent of the cultural products of Persian elements like language, literature and art that presents itself in even the most basic study of Middle Eastern tra- ditions. Weaved within this grand project of writing a macrohistory of Iran is found the distinct brand of Sufism, commonly referred to as "Persian Sufism". "Persian Sufism" is not only a predominant brand of Sufism, one which is local- ized within Iran, but is one whose cultural products have far-reaching effects on other Sufi cultures throughout the East and North Africa, and even other

---

1. My translation. Hafez, *Diwan* (ed. K. Khatib-Rawhbar), 193, ghazal 143, line 1.

places. Still, Sufism, as already mentioned, does not originate in Iran; it is not Persian. Rather, Sufism, which is an Islamic phenomenon, is distinctly permeated by dominant Persianate themes and cultural products, such as its poetry and music and language, for instance, that give the unmistakable impression of it being Persian. It is with this understanding that I refer to "Persian Sufism" in this chapter.

Islamic Mysticism and Sufism

Should Sufism be thought of as its own tradition, that is, as independent from Islam? It appears so. This is certainly possible if we draw on Troeltsch's definition of two ideal types of mysticism: "mysticism" and "technical mysticism".[2] In brief, these represent the types of mysticism with regard to their relationship to "regular forms of worship and devotion". To explain, "Mysticism" appropriates the organization to which it belongs and does not detract from it, but rather embodies the highest form of the religious expression. "Technical mysticism", however, makes a break with traditional religion, and its adherents see themselves as independent from religious principle and institutions and even reject religious morality.[3] In citing this, we can make an important observation from a close reading of Sufi history and analysis of its texts so as to distinguish the two types of mysticism at play within the history of Sufism, while detecting anomalies within Sufi teachings along the way.

If we take the beginnings of Sufism to have been in the ninth century, the period that separates us from its antiquity is about 1200 years. Yet throughout the uneasy relation of Sufism to Islam is revealed. Sufism is received with mixed emotions by the orthodoxy, even today. The variety of Moslem approaches towards Sufism is worth noting. At one extreme we find Salafi/Wahabi attitudes that utterly reject mysticism and heterodoxy, while on the opposite side of the spectrum the Shi'a retain a thinly veiled tolerance for the type of Sufism that feeds into, and venerates, the imamate (especially Ali and Ja'far as-Sadiq). The larger body of Sunni Moslems generally tolerate a conservative Sufism, in the sense of Sufism being the "spiritual" or "inner" (*batin*) aspect of their Islam, which is seen as complementing *fiq* (jurisprudence). The tension between Sufis and the representatives of orthodoxy came to its climax in the tenth century, with the advent of the martyring of Hallaj. Ever since the public crucifixion of Mansour-e Hallaj (d. 922), which marks the first major eruption between Sufis and *ulema*, even a mild and conservative type of Sufism has been suspect in the eyes of mainstream Islamic orthodoxy. The Sufism of the Traditionalists (or the Perennialists) – Frithjof Schuon and Martin Lings, in particular, but also Hossein Nasr (the head of Maryamiyya)

---

2. E. Troeltsch, *The Social Teaching of the Christian Churches* (London, 1950), 231.
3. *Ibid.*

– is a case in point of a tolerated, but suspicious form of Islamic practice. Of note is also the Sufism of René Guénon (although he is not formally counted among the Traditionalist School). These adaptations of the North African schools of Sufism are interesting but will not be pursued here at length, since they highlight aspects of Neo-Sufi tendencies that have been explored elsewhere.[4] Sifting through Sufi materials and the history of its schools, it becomes clear that "Islamic Mysticism", and not "Sufism", is the appropriate place of Moslem spirituals – those firmly grounded in the Qur'an and obedient to the Sunna and the Sharia to the letter. In this strict Islamic context, the term "Sufism" is nuanced as something foreign to Islam and even representing a relaxed approach concerning Islamic Law. Sure enough, one can find in Sufism practices and customs that do not fit, in any shape or form, into daily Moslem worship. Consider the centrality of *samâ'* (sacred [musical] audition) and poetry in the Sufism(s) of North Africa, Iran and India, not to mention the indigenous components of South East Asian (Indonesian) Sufism. What this indicates to me is that the question regarding the analogous relationship of Islam and Sufism is long overdue. In short, given the evidence at hand, can we talk about "Islamic Mysticism" and "Sufism" as being the same? There is no doubt that the Sufis are the "mystics" of Islam, but "Islamic Mysticism" implicates Sufism as distinctly and fundamentally Islamic, which in my opinion is both questionable and problematic. It is time for a recognizable distinction to be made between the mystic Sufi tradition and Islamic piety. Certainly Sufism developed out of the spiritual core of Islamic doctrine and faith, looking to the austerities and spiritual experiences of Mohammed, but it has long since matured as a mystic tradition in its own right. Sufism has not left Islam nor is it to be seen as apart from Islam, but rather the argument is that Sufism has evolved from the puritanical Islamic spiritual piety into a true mysticism. Indeed, the Sufis have long ago gone beyond the basic principles of piety that are found at the core of Islam. It may be odd to talk about Sufism in this way, but supposing we were to talk about Islam and Sufism in terms of *exoteric* and *esoteric* modes of practice within the body of Islam, it would be naïve to ignore the growing independence of the Sufi tradition and the core tension between the mysticism of the Sufis and the piety of Moslems. In short, Sufis like Abu Sa'id Abol Khayr, Hallaj, Ibn Arabi, and many more, are not Islamic spirituals, they are *Sufis*, and their mysticism has a quality very dissimilar to the normative spirituality of the Moslem faithful. Such a disparity may indeed be found in the subtleties of their interpretation of Islam, but it is significant enough to validate a recognizable difference. Sufism, though not necessarily anti-Islamic,[5] disregards the superficial dogma of religion. Its aim,

---

4. Mark Sedgwick, "Neo-Sufism", in *Dictionary of Western Esotericism and Gnosis* (ed. W. J. Hanegraaff) (Leiden: 2006), vol. 2, 846–9.
5. S. A. Chaudhary makes an interesting case for Sufism's anti-Islamism in *Sufism is not Islam: A Comparative Study* (New Delhi, 1998).

as notable Sufis have numerously stated, is to go beyond both faith and infi-delity. And nowhere is this better illustrated than in Attar's verse: *har kera dar eshq mohkam shod qadam, dar-gozasht az kofr va az islam ham* ("whoever sets foot firmly forward in love, will go beyond both Islam and unbelief").[6]

Hamzehee places Sufism within the socio-political history of Islam as a trend advocating a "passive resistance" to the mainstream (see above). Even if we were to argue for a "true" Sufism that is based on the mystical expe-riences of Mohammed, refusing any place for the likes of Hallaj, we are still left addressing fundamental anomalies, such as the centrality of the *pir* or *qutb* ("the master [of the path]" and "[spiritual] pole") and his unquestioned authority over Sufi adherents. When Hojviri wrote the first treatise on Sufism in the Persian language in the eleventh century (which is a thorough attempt to formalize a coherent image of "orthodox" Sufism), naming all heretics and their groups, he did not remove Hallaj from among the paragons of the mystic-Sufi cause. Quite the contrary, he actually attempted to redeem Hallaj as a misunderstood mystic.[7] The life and work of Abu Hamid al-Ghazali (d. 1111) was crucial in the process of aligning the mystical tradition with ortho-dox Islam. The problem was that his efforts produced a compliant form of Sufism, while he spent the better part of his career rejecting great Moslem thinkers like Ibn Rushd (Averoes) and remaining suspicious of esoteric fac-tions like the Isma'ilis. Al-Ghazali is therefore pivotal for making Sufism an acceptable part of orthodox Islam. What emerges is the view that Sufism is not un-Islamic, but rather Sufism has always represented an alternative expression to the mainstream. As such, Hallaj and others were in fact devoted Moslems who intensely followed the qur'anic decree and Sharia Law. "Sufism" then, as opposed to Islamic Mysticism (remembering Troeltsch's definitions) is under-lined as an "unrestrained" mysticism, to use the words of the Dutch theologian Gerardus van der Leeuw; and Islamic Mysticism as likened to a "mysticism of the church".[8] In that light, we must confidently distinguish "Sufism" from "Islamic Mysticism".

Shades of Islamic Mysticism

An example of what both Troeltsch and Van der Leeuw would describe comes up again in thirteenth-century Anatolia. This concerns a famous passage from Rumi's work which directly contrasts the first qur'anic verse of revelation. At the heart of Islam, Surah 96 of the Qur'an, we find:

---

6. Cf. L. Lewisohn & C. Shackle. *Attar and the Persian Sufi Tradition: The Art of Spiritual Flight* (London, 2006), 155.
7. Al-Hojviri, The "Kashf al-Mahjub". On the controversy of Hallaj, see esp. 152 and 260.
8. On the two types of mysticism, van der Leeuw, *Religion in Essence and Manifestation* (New York, 1963), vol. 2, 494.

Read in the name of thy Sustainer ...
Who has taught [man] the use of the pen ...
(Q 96:1-4)[9]

And in the *Mathnawi* of Rumi, a central Sufi work, nay "the Qur'an in Persian",[10] we encounter:

While the pen made haste in writing,
  It split upon itself as soon as it came to Love.
(*M* 1:114)[11]

Rumi was without doubt first and foremost a Moslem, and the essential message of his works serve to extol the superiority and perfection of Islamic religion and doctrine.[12] The comparison made above is not, however, to demonstrate the difficulty in reconciling the two quotations, but in underlining the experience of Sufism within the context of Islamic culture, be it Persian or otherwise. Sufism does not seem to be as much about reconciliation, as al-Ghazali thought, as it is about "going beyond", as Rumi showed. The "pen" of knowledge is contrasted with the "shattering" effect of love, and through it the Islamic institution compared with the spiritual (aspect). But this is not a rejection of the legalistic establishment. What it does is to allude to a repression of the spiritual, where in total abandonment the following verses go on to express the apocalypse of "logic" and "intellect", of rationalization and formalism, and how with the approach of the "sun" (Shams), as Rumi declares, "All things would burn and leave no traces here [in him]."[13] The power of Rumi's verse is found in knowing that an *ummi* or "illiterate" (Q 7:157–8) Mohammed would have the words (of the Qur'an) inscribed upon his heart.[14] It has to be made clear that, for the Sufis, the Islamic form was the means through which to engage the divine, in effect by going *through* and then *beyond* the established practices. Rumi follows this through to conclusion in his works. It is tempting simply to leave the definition of Sufism to its spiritual aim, but we must not ignore the cultural–religious subtleties of its "after-effect". The example of Rumi helps to demonstrate the desire of the Sufi to imitate (and recreate) the experience of the Prophet: that Sufism is the extension and continuation of the mystical relationship between God and Man. For Ibn Ishaq reports Mohammed as saying after the Angel of revelation departed from

---

9. Q 96:1–4. Cf. M. Asad, *Qur'an*, 963.
10. Lewis, *Rumi*, 467.
11. *MJR* 1, 114, vol 1, 10.
12. Lloyd Ridgeon, "Christianity as Portrayed by Jalāl al-Dīn Rūmī", in *Islamic Interpretations of Christianity* (London, 2001).
13. Cf. Rumi, *The Masnavi*, 11–12, lines 112–43.
14. Ibn Ishaq, *Sira*, 106.

him "it was as though these words were written on my heart". Mohammed's revelation was incorporated by the Sufis into a "central ... understanding of Islamic religiosity". For the mystic, just as the "virginity" of Mary is required for an immaculate vessel for the divine word in Christianity, "so in Islam ... God reveals Himself through the word of the Koran", and thereby the Prophet "had to be a vessel that was unpolluted by 'intellectual' knowledge of word and script so that he could carry the trust in perfect unity." This was a view far from being embraced by orthodox Islam, but it represented the experience of the Moslem mystic nonetheless.[15]

The unique Sufi formulation of fana and baqa

The Sufis shed significant light on certain aspects of history that cannot normally be detected in standard historical exercises. Yet ideas about the almost parallel development of Sufism alongside the Islamic "institution", such as proposed by the Nematollahi Sufi order, require careful analysis. The hypothesis for a polarity conveys the Nematollahi concern for distinction and separation, between Sufism and Islam, which has little to do with the actual history of Sufism and Sufi figures. The glorification of the remote northeast Iranian province of Khorasan, away from the caliphates, has more socio-political relevance than it does spiritual. But the way that the Nematollahis envision this imagined past is intriguing and worth a closer look. Till now we have been lacking a sufficient definition of Sufism. Any definition will be limited and practical because as demonstrated experiential Sufism is about "going beyond", which makes the Sufi neither a part of the Islamic body nor separate from it. *In extenso*, the dervish (*faqir*), having realized his "non-existence" or "ego-lessness", no longer partakes in the domain of normative religion at the same level as the lay person. Rumi defined the goal of the mystic in the *Mathnawi* as *fana* "annihilation in God", which he equated with *faqr* ("spiritual poverty", i.e. dervish-hood).[16] And Annemarie Schimmel makes a perceptive connection with Attar before him who placed poverty and annihilation as the final, and seventh, Valley in his *Mantiq al-tayr*, placed after the valleys of search, love, gnosis, independence, unity and bewilderment on the journey towards God.[17]

The notion of "going beyond", however, is not to denote "transcendence" or a "post-theologic" impression in Sufi literature, nor is it technically a "transfiguration" in the way of referring to Jesus' experience as recounted in the

---

15. Schimmel, *Mystical Dimensions of Islam*, 26–7.
16. Cf. *MJR* 5, 672, vol. 6, 43. Also cited by Schimmel, "Mystical Dimension", 123.
17. Cf. Fariduddin Attar, *Mantiq at-tayr* (ed. M. J. Shakur) (Tehran, 1962), cited in Schimmel, "Mystical Dimension", 123. For English rhyme translation of Attar's *Mantiq at-tayr*, see *Conference of the Birds* (trans. A. Darbandi & D. Davis) (London, 1984).

Synoptic Gospels.[18] "Going beyond" relates directly to the Sufi doctrine of *"fana* and *baqa".* This doctrine is a uniquely Sufi formulation that was officially intellectualized in the post-Hallajian period in order to vindicate the place of the mystic in Islam. The Sufis, however, went further to demonstrate that Sufism was, indeed, both "truly Islamic" and "the true Islam".[19] The Sufis were careful not to imply associationism, "the incarnation of God in man" and "the total mergence of the individual and the finite human ego in God".[20] Thus, a strict doctrinal definition was set in the two linked classifications of *fana* and *baqa. Fana,* in the first definition, is the "passing away from the consciousness of the mystic of all things, including himself, and even the absence of the consciousness of this passing-away and its replacement by a pure consciousness of God"; *fana* also included "the annihilation of the imperfect attributes, as distinguished from the substance, of the creature and their replacement by the perfect attributes bestowed by God".[21] In *baqa,* the mystic would experience "persistence in the new divinely bestowed attributes (*baqa bi'llah*)", accompanied by a "return to the mystic's consciousness of the plurality of the creaturely world".[22] This accompaniment to *baqa* is necessitated by the view that "being with God means also being with the world", since it is His creation and "in which He is manifested, however imperfectly",[23] hence, subsequently denoting the sequence of the mystical experience of *fana* (effacement [of self]) leading into *baqa* (subsistence [in God]). In turn, the Sufis aligned their newly formed doctrine with the example of the Prophet, celebrating him as the mystic *par excellence,* and were careful to guard against further public outbursts of euphoria so as not to provoke unwanted judicial onslaught, as happened to Hallaj. But these were the beginnings of a moderate Sufism, sensitized to normative religious concerns, far-flung from the original antinomian spirit of the early fathers of Sufism, or so it would seem outwardly. The Sufis further secured themselves in grounding their mystical experience in an esoteric reading of Mohammed, where the highest station of the mystic was idealized in Mohammed's "servant-hood", and defined by the example of his simultaneous presence with God and with the world. A further doctrinal subtlety is found in the allusion to the "ongoing-ness" of the mystical experience, where *fana* (annihilation) is not seen as the end of the spiritual journey, but rather a "true" beginning, whereby the initiate (now matured) is invited to patiently travel the seemingly endless road of *baqa* (subsistence).[24] The entire mystical

---

18. Matt. 17:1-9, Mk. 9:1-8, and Lk. 9:28–36.
19. Cf. F. Rahman, "Baka wa-Fana", in *EIs,* vol. 1, s.v.
20. There are countless examples of the doctrine, in various Sufi texts, but for the sake of clarity and succinctness, Rahman gives an adequate definition (*ibid.*).
21. *Ibid.*
22. *Ibid.*
23. *Ibid.*
24. Cf. J. Nurbakhsh, *Divani Nurbakhsh* (Tehran, 1379/2000), 113.

meaning of what is being said here, of course, is best explained in the tripartite configuration of "Islam" (i.e. *islam, iman, ihsan*), as already discussed in relation to the "Hadith of Gabriel", and also in its Sufistic expression of *shariah, tariqah, haqqiqah* ("the law", "the path" and "the truth"). Accordingly, it is not strange to find Rumi reverberating this profound notion in a cheeky verse:

> Don't give me duties now I've passed away
> My senses dulled, I've no clue how to pray,
> For anything a drunk might sing is wrong
> Whether he's meek or boastful in his song ...[25]

The mystical tradition of "Sufism" and its genesis

The Nimatollahi "myth-history" advocates an exclusive "Persian" heritage for Sufism (*farhang-e tasawwuf-e irani*). Admittedly, there is some truth to this claim. By this, I mean that "Sufism", the tradition of Troeltsch's "technical mysticism", has its genesis in the Iranian heartland. Yet this is not to denote Sufism as pre-dating Islam in the form of a covert "mystical tradition" that only puts on the garb of Islam after the conquests. In fact, closer examination of Nurbakhsh's own writings doesn't even make such a claim. His position, as I understand it from his own writings, is that Sufism was a Persian phenomenon born out of the mixture of pre-Islamic Iranian strongman cultures and Islam. This view is, to some extent, a tenable position and will be discussed below. The tradition of Sufism, as I see it, began to blossom in (greater) Iran, expanded on the ascetic and spiritual tendencies of early Moslem pietists that occupied Baghdad and Basra. With this, influences from the Khorasan province, and perhaps even further east contributed to the distinct culture of Persianate Sufism. Nurbakhsh has certainly picked up on this detail, and has made it a dominant theme of discourse within the order's myth-history. However, the point is that the Khorasan school, founded by the legendary Ibrahim Adham (d. 777?) and led by Sufis like Bayazid-e Bistami (d. 874) and Attar Neyshaburi (d. 1221), was not the birthplace of Sufism, but that its style was influential, especially on other forms of Sufism closer to the caliphate. This again differs to Nurbakhsh's postulation that Sufism is first born in Khorasan. The difference is that those Sufis belonging to the school of Khorasan favoured the method of "intoxication", in contrast to their brethren in the Baghdad school who upheld the importance of "sobriety". It is not useful or appropriate to promote a narrowly "nationalistic" Sufism, as Nurbakhsh does in stressing the importance of the Khorasan masters, for the difference between the two schools of thought

---

25. (Mojaddedi) M 1, 128–9, 12.

is merely one of methodology. The mysticism of Sufis is much more coherent than previously given credit, since an equally robust and liberal environment as that of Moslem Spain allowed the likes of Ibn Arabi (d. 1248) to explore the full depths of mystical experience. We can even cite the early ecstatics such as Abol Husayn Nuri (d. 907) and Hallaj (d. 922) of Baghdad and Ibn Farid (d. 1235) of Cairo as cases of antinomian Sufism outside of Khorasan. Even so, such Sufis were extremely rare cases in a formalist environment and two of them we know to have been severely rejected by the authorities, Hallaj being dismembered and burnt and Nuri banished to Syria. Certainly, the Sufism of Persia and Moslem Spain is an example of an atmosphere of cultural and intellectual liberalism, but specifically as a result of the meeting of Islam with the Persian and Iberian cultures where music, dance, diversity and literature flourished. This helps us understand, for instance, the full implication of Rumi's verse given above and the powerful mystical imagination of Ibn Arabi in two quite separate regions, while also acknowledging that both kept carefully to the parameters of Islamic tradition. On the one hand, the general influence of Persian heritage is discernible in the Sufism of the Near and Middle East; while on the other hand, the Iberian influence on Spanish Sufism of Al-Andalus, and that of the Berber culture on North African Sufism are notable cases of geo-social forces at work. In light of this, we can talk about Berber culture, which was repressed by Arab Moslems and which still persists in the Sufism of these regions, especially in Tunisia (Nafta). In the same way, we can talk about "Persian" Sufism as being defined and shaped by its own unique heritage and indigenous spirituality; and this is different to Nurbakhsh's argument for an unbroken tradition of "Iranian mysticism" rooted in pre-Islamic Iran. Now in this work it has not been our concern to investigate the "broad effect" of Sufism, and the many places that it has since affected, such as Southeast Asia, or more recently the West, but we have decidedly come to the heart of Sufi history and tradition by exploring its "Persianate" sensibilities.

What is Sufism?

There is no need to offer a tedious and a technical analysis on the terminology of "Sufi" and "Sufism", especially given the substantial reckonings one finds in extant works,[26] but suffice it to say Sufism is the mystical belief and practice in which Moslems seek to find the truth of divine love and knowledge through direct personal experience of God. As such, Sufism would properly be defined not as the worship of God, to distinguish it from Moslem piety, but the annihilation in God. That is, Sufism is not monotheism, but an absolute monism.

---

26. In particular cf. Schimmel, "Mystical Dimension"; Nasr, "Sufism" (ed. Frye), *CHI*, vol. 4, 442–63.

Besides, whenever Sufis are asked to define Sufism or explain it they do so in riddles. So any definition must in fact come from observation of what they do, not necessarily what they say. Shebli (d. 846), the great *majzub* (attracted lover) was once asked why Sufis are called "Sufi". Expecting an elaborate answer such as it being due to their woollen attire (*suf*) or to do with their purity (*saaf*), he only answered:[27]

Because there is something still left of their identity.[28]

When asked what is Sufism, Abol Hassan al-Bushanji said:

Today it is a name that has no reality; but it used to be a Reality without a name.[29]

Consequently, Hassan al-Basri (most likely in honour of Rabea) was known to have said:

Sufism is only found in books, and [all real] Sufis are dead.[30]

We are then directed to the Prophetic saying, "Die before you die", about which Rumi avers:

O you who possess sincerity, [if] you want that [Reality] unveiled, choose death and tear off the veil –
Not such a death that you will go into a grave, [but] a death ... so that you will go into a Light.[31]

THE INDIGENOUS FEATURES OF PERSIAN SUFISM

The notion of an "indigenous" origin for "Persian Sufism" is not to challenge the traditional idea of Sufism as an Islamic phenomenon, but rather an attempt to address directly problematic concerns held about Sufism in the Islamic worldview. In one sense this concerns Sufism's notably independent missionary activities in the outer regions of the Islamic empire, which continue today in the West away from the central heartlands of the Islamic establishment. In which case, where Sufism operates under the banner of

---

27. For a brief definition and discussion of these terms, see esp. L. Lewisohn *et al.*, "Tasawwuf", in *EIs*, vol. 10; Nasr, "Sufism", 443f.
28. J. Nurbakhsh, *Shibli: Mast-i Haqq va majdhub-i haqiqat* (London, 1997), 3.
29. Fariduddin Attar, *Tadhkeratol-Auliya'* (ed. J. Salmasi-zadeh) (Tehran, 1381/2003), 546.
30. *Ibid.*
31. *MJR* 5, 723, vol. 6, 298.

Islam, it must be viewed as derived from Islam. From its inception, Sufism has always drawn on the "inward" meaning of religious practice, even at times looking past the boundaries of the Islamic norm, and finding ways to bridge gaps within religious diversification. This attitude, not foreign to the initial Islamic ideal, became increasingly the Sufi "norm" and fed its "spiritual quest". Therefore, as a result of increasing materialism in the Umayyad period, the Sufis would not only idealize the "inner" and sacred qualities of the experiences of Mohammed, but they made increasing appeal to the "Meccan period" as their preferred or ideal Islam. Indeed, in a highly provocative sense, were we to give any value to the archangel Gabriel as the source of revelation, the mystical roots of Sufism could very well be said to "go beyond" Mohammed, perhaps opening the debate for "indigenous" origins of Sufism and, moreover, laying bare the "the problem of Sufism" in general. In this chapter we allow ourselves a brief immersion into the esoteric or vertical axis of Sufi thought if only to get a better "feel" for the deeper understanding of Persia's repressed past. The difficulty in simplifying a "standard" for Sufism arises because of its unique adaptations − as expressions of Islam into the many foreign regions of the Moslem empire(s). Hence, although the qur'anic language and content is paramount to the foundation and understanding of Sufi texts and principles, at the same time one must also appreciate that historically Sufism is not homogeneous in its development throughout the regions where it is practised. Sufi identity is as multitudinous and multifaceted as its *tariqahs* ("schools" or "communities"), which makes it risky to attempt any superficial classification.

This enterprise began with a look at the ancient religious complex of the Iranians, and traced the history of the "Persians", that is, the Pars tribe of southwestern Iran which arrived from the northeast and how it was connected with the Kayyanid line that gradually dominated the entire Iranian plateau and established Achaemenid Persia. With them survived the major religious themes of Iran's past as collated in the *Avesta*, and from then on the sapiential doctrines coming from the Achaemenid impact permeated the entire fabric of Iran's religious life, even under the ascending moon of Islam. We have to be careful here not to assume an unbroken chain of Persian religion, but rather the influence of the cultural products of a nation that has presided over the terrain for long periods of time. Persian and broader non-Arab cultural influences, we have been arguing, were there at the very outset of Islam itself, and continued to flourish in its so-called Golden Age; and even when this period came to a halt, it was Sufism, more specifically Persian Sufism, that mainly contributed in the Persian cultural revival, through its literary effort. It fell upon key Sufi figures, such as Sohravardi Maqtol and, although not Sufi, to a great extent Ferdowsi, to carry the ongoing torch of Iranian esoterica until Persianate Sufism and Sufi brotherhoods were eventually formed and chains were established, capable and independently transmitting lines of arcane wisdom tradition.

215

Islam did indeed facilitate the Iranian imagination. According to Nasr, "Islam possesses a unique power of assimilation and synthesis."[32] This is a character that enabled Islam to retain its identity while allowing the Persians to "participate in its life and to contribute fully to its elaboration". Islam, according to Nasr, actually allowed them "to contemplate ... the most profound elements of their religious and spiritual past", which, "far from dying out, gained a new interpretation and became in a sense resurrected in the new spiritual universe brought into being by the Islamic revelation."[33] *Pace* Nasr's view, however, there remain points of a subtle nature from the history and development of Islam and Sufism that need to be unravelled – and to some extent have been – and correlated to the ancient world of Iran and that sit rather outside traditionalist Moslem expectations. For Nasr, Sufism became what it became precisely because of the strong Islamic influence on Iranian thought, but we propose a sprouting at least from a mutual and concurrent exchange, and at the most a sprouting from the inside out. Quite apart from the unique phenomenon of "Iranian Islam", its independent formulation of the Twelver tradition, it seems more likely that "formal Islam" is a sheet that covers the contours of the Iranian psycho-spiritual plateau.[34] In fact, what Nasr is (directly or indirectly) promoting in his work is no doubt primarily concerned with this "Iranian [formulation of] Islam", a stress noticeable from a wide range of his works where his acute awareness of Persia's past forms a truly "Persian" idealization of Shi'ite Islam in his many books.[35] This reflects Nasr's collaboration with Henri Corbin, Allame Tabatabai and their Tehran circle before the 1979 Islamic Revolution, and their grand attempt that "re-wrote Shi'ism into otherworldly gnosis".[36] Gathered from a memorable dialogue between Corbin and Tabatabai, which was recorded by Nasr, we can see that their conceptualization of Islam was not far removed from the deeply esoteric:

> Corbin ... once said to Tabatabai ... "Western scholars claim that Ali is not the author of *Nahj al-balaghah*. What is your view and whom do you consider to be the author of this work?" Allamah Tabatabai raised his head and answered in his usual gentle and

---

32. S. H. Nasr, "Elements of Continuity in Iran", in *Acta Iranica: Commemoration to Cyrus* (Leiden, 1974), vol. 1, 266.

33. *Ibid.*

34. For Nasr's view of Persian Sufism, cf. "The Rise and Development of Persian Sufism", in *The Heritage of Persian Sufism* (ed. L. Lewisohn) (Oxford, 1999), vol. 1, 1–18.

35. E.g. cf. S. H. Nasr, *Ideals and Realities of Islam* (Cairo, 1989). On Persia's past and Shiite Islam, in particular, see also his introduction to Nasr & Amirnazavi (eds), *Anthology of Philosophy in Persia*.

36. Cf. M. van den Bos, *Mystic Regimes: Sufism and the State in Iran, from the late Qajar Era to the Islamic Republic* (Leiden, 2002), 37. For more discussion on the positions of Corbin and Tabatabai on Shi'ism and their relation with Iran, see *ibid.*, 36–7.

calm manner, "For us whoever wrote the *Nahj al-balaghah* is Ali, even if he lived [only] a century ago."[37]

This is a view rightly suggested as being in conflict with the Ayatollah Borujerdi, who kept his distance from Corbin's circle and felt Tabatabai to be too philosophical and distant from jurisprudence (*fiqh*), and was far from accepting "Corbin's ecumenicalism".[38]

Beyond this circle of academic intellectuals, we now approach that of the Sufis, more particularly the Nematollahi Order, which offers a far more radical interpretation than that of the Tehran circle. Nasr was initially involved in the Nematollahi publications (early on) but soon drifted away, no doubt due to the order's steady shift away from traditionalism and its increasing emphasis on a non-Islamic origin of Persian Sufism.

NEMATOLLAHI MYTH-HISTORY AND PUBLICATIONS

Leonard Lewisohn's contribution to Jamal Malik and John R. Hinnell's *Sufism in the West* details the basic overview of Nematollahi history and doctrine from its genesis to the present day.[39] Lewisohn has also edited the three volumes of *The Heritage of Sufism* in which the imporant articles deal with the history and doctrine of the Nematollahi Sufi order.[40] The Order is one of the largest Sufi orders in Iran, but it is divided into three primary branches: Monawwar Ali Shahi, Safi Ali Shahi and the Sultan Ali Shahi (or Gonabadi). In this book I've dealt chiefly with the views of the first sub-group, since they have a more significant presence outside of Iran. In contrast, the Gonabadi branch is by far the largest and best known of the three within Iran. Lewisohn outlines the Nematollahi "myth-history" by analysing the content of the later publications by Javad Nurbakhsh, from the 1990s onward, and the articles featuring in the Order's quarterly journal *Sufi* for the past ten years.

---

37. Cf. *ibid.*, 37–8.
38. *Ibid.*, 38.
39. See L. Lewisohn, "Persian Sufism in the Contemporary West: Reflections on the Ni'matullahi Diaspora", in Malik & Hinnells, *Sufism in the West*, 65, note 3; also his "An Introduction into the History of Modern Persian Sufism", *Bulletin of the School of Oriental and African Studies* 61(3) (1998), 437–64, and 62(1) (1999), 36–59.
40. L. Lewisohn, "Persian Sufism". This article stands as the most comprehensive critical survey of the Nematollahi history to date; cf. also T. Graham, "The Ni'matu'llahi Order under Safavid Suppression and in Indian Exile", in *The Heritage of Sufism* (ed. Lewisohn) (Oxford, 1999), vol. 3, 165–200, and S. A. Quinn, "Rewriting Ni'matullahi History in Safavid Chronicles", *ibid.*, 201–2.

Khaneqahi Nematollahi Sufism

All of the Nematollahi branches trace their foundation to fourteenth-century Iran, under the saintly figure of Shah Nematollah Wali (1330–1431).[41] The Order was moved to the Deccan (India) in the fifteenth century, until it returned to Iran and inaugurated a full revival by the end of the eighteenth century.[42] The Order continued along relatively traditional lines until quite recently, when a marginal shift in the attitude of the first group (Monawwar Ali Shahis) took place under the influence of Javad Nurbakhsh. This shift came fully into effect following the Revolution of 1979, after which Nurbakhsh left Iran and moved the headquarters of his group to England.[43] In the West, Nurbakhsh's group was formally established as the Khaneqahi Nematollahi Sufi Order (KNS). This group is distinguished by an air of "progressive spirituality", hence its marginalized status in Iran, that was gradually vocalized through Nurbakhsh's later discourses and writings. His progressive attitude has greatly affected the direction of the KNS and the group's projection of what Sufism entails. Nurbakhsh's inauguration as *pir* or *qutb* ("master" or [spiritual] "pole") of all Nematollahis, a view challenged by the other two branches, in a sense marked the break with traditional Islamic forms of Sufi practice. Indeed, Nurbakhsh, who died in 2008, is deemed the most "intellectually formidable Persian Sufi master" of the age. He was a prolific author who produced many publications in Persian, the majority of which are available in English.[44] Now, the central thesis of these works and other publications under its quarterly journal *Sufi*[45] – two independent versions are produced in Persian and English – is the affirmation of the "innate Iranian nature and native Persian origin of Sufism" and the idea that the universally humanitarian doctrines of Sufism are a "quintessentially Iranian cultural phenomenon".[46]

Nurbakhsh openly espouses the prominence of Khorasanian Sufism, from which Sufism spreads to Baghdad, forming "the moderate" Baghdadian Sufism. This is juxtaposed with Hossein Nasr's view, a leading Shaykh of the Maryamiyya Sufi Order and once collaborator with Nurbakhsh in the promotion of Sufi studies in the West. The contrast here is effective in demonstrating

---

41. On the life and teachings of Shah Nematullah, see T. Graham, "Shah Ni'matullah Wali: Founder of the Ni'matullahi Sufi Order", in *The Heritage of Sufism*, 173–90. Also, *Classical Islam: A Sourcebook of Religious Literature* (eds and trans. N. Calder, J. Mojaddedi & A. Rippin) (London, 2003), 262–8; also T. Graham, "Yafei: The Master of Shah Nematollah", *Sufi* 46 (Summer 2000), 35–41.
42. Cf. T. Graham, "The Ni'matu'llahi Order", 167–8.
43. Cf. L. Lewisohn, "Persian Sufism", 66, note 19. The present master of the Order is Alireza Nurbakhsh, the son and successor of Javad Nurbakhsh.
44. For a listing cf. *ibid.*, 56–60.
45. The quarterly journal began to be published in 1988 by the Khaniqah-i Ni 'matu'llahi Press in London in both Persian and English.
46. Cf. L. Lewisohn, "Persian Sufism", 56.

the competing notions of the historical imagination of particular Sufi figures or groups explored throughout this book. The distinction clearly underlines the concern of this book with Iranian and by extension Sufi identity as a result of the introduction of Islam to indigenous cultures. Nurbakhsh and Nasr represent the two classic attitudes toward the conundrum of Iranian (Sufi) identity in an Islamic age. The parallel also helps outline the general worldview of the KNS. As such, Nasr has the cradle of Sufism in Basra and Kufa and then extending out towards Khorasan, while Nurbakhsh focuses on Bayazid and presents the notion of the *khorasani* "Bayazidian Sufism".[47] Nasr places Bayazid, along with other notable Persian Sufis of Khorasan, as later members who are influenced by the Baghdad School.[48] For Nasr, the history of Sufism is a result of Islamic expansion from Arabia to the garrison towns of Basra and Kufa and follows it into Iran, whereas Nurbakhsh offers a "hidden" or alternate history of Sufism that has its roots in Iran before the coming of Islam that only adopts the name "Sufism" as a result of the Islamic experience. There are problems with Nurbakhsh's thesis, however, which is poorly presented in terms of cultural history by Nematollahi publications, but which remain valuable to our macrohistory.

The exposition of the Nematollahi myth-history

The core of the Nematollahi myth-history is derived from a two-part article written by Parviz Nawruziyan.[49] The first part sets the backdrop with the dawn of Persia's mystical tradition – beginning with the enigmatic mythical king Kay-Khosrow of Ferdowsi's *Shahnameh*. This is then linked with Sohravardi Maqtol (or *shaykh ol-eshraq*) through his doctrine of light, emphasizing the "over-riding" influence of the Khorasanian Sufi tradition on Sohravardi. Kay Khosrow is portrayed as an "Iranian prophet", and he sits along with other notables of Sufism who are sacrally initiated members of a tradition of Sufi chivalry (*javânmardî*), which is really "a Zoroastrian mystical chivalric order" of the ("mythical") Khosravani tradition or *ayin-e khosravani*. The second part

---

47. A. Nurbakhsh, "Bayazidian Sufism: Annihilation without Ritual", 8–13, and also J. Nurbakhsh, "Bayazid Bistami" (n.p., 1995). Nurbakhsh explains, "Bayazid undertook to establish a humanist school of thought (maktab-i insaniyyat) under the banner of mysticism (irfan) during a time when Iranians were engaged and preoccupied in the struggle against the alien culture [of the Arabs] (mubariza-yi farhang-i bigana). With his creatively original words he managed to preserve and protect Iranian culture from the influence of foreigners [i.e. Arabs]", J. Nurbakhsh, "Bayazid Bistami", 4, trans. offered by L. Lewisohn, "Persian Sufism", 67.

48. According to Nasr, Bayazid and others came to prominence after the School of Baghdad influenced the School of Khorosan. Cf. Nasr, "Sufism", 451.

49. Cf. P. Nawruziyan, "Taj-i Kay Khusraw bar sar-i Shaykh Ishraq I", *Sufi* 34 (1997), 26–31; P. Nawruziyan, "Taj-i Kay Khusraw bar sar-i Shaykh Ishraq II", *Sufi* 35 (1997), 26–34.

of the article then moves to explain the non-Iranian elements of Sufism, such as the doctrine of "trust in God" or *tavakkol*, as inherited by Egyptian and Syrian Christianity. Moreover, the "doctrine of activity" and "social exertion" (*kasb*, *amal*) is portrayed as purely a pre-Islamic Khorasanian phenomenon of the *javânmardân*, the strongmen or chevaliers. We also learn that the notion of asceticism (*zohd*) is absent from and therefore alien to both Sohravardi and the *Shahnameh*, further reflecting "a pristine pre-Islamic mysticism". All in all, the Nematollahis give a great deal of importance to the *Shahnameh*, in that this great epic contains basic Sufi doctrines and these doctrines find their origin in Zarathushtra's teachings.[50] In short, there is a manifest component of chauvinist advocacy of Iranian nationalism.[51] Despite this, the KNS appear more socially and politically savvy compared to "other Sufi groups". In fact, their publications have a New Age edge to them, which may be a result of a conscious choice to tap into that market; indeed, the KNS attract a substantial non-Iranian following.

The crux of Nawruziyan's work is loosely based on the researches of Abdol-Hossein Zarrinkub (1923–1999), who in turn based himself on Richard Hartmann's theories of the Persian origin of Sufism. However, there is a critical difference between Nawruziyan's own work and Zarrinkub's. Zarrinkub highlights Persia's rich heritage and carefully suggests the valuable effects of Persia's cultural and religious history behind the unique expressions of the great Persian Sufis. Yet he never denies the centrality of the Qur'an and the Sunna, even if asserting the influence of Mazdaeism throughout the first few Islamic centuries, and the particular role that this played in establishing "Sufism" in Iran.[52] Nawruziyan is more forthcoming in his position, perhaps being influenced by "Nurbakhshian Sufism", in proffering the legacy of Zarathushtra as an essential marker for the eventual success of Sufism among Iranians.[53]

The Persian objection

The Persian generally objects to a solely Arab-Islamic image of Sufism. This inherited "psychosis" is based on the theme of repression noted in the opening of this book and it leads back to the Arab-Islamic, specifically Umayyad, occupation of Iran. The Nematollahi dogma can be linked with a *shu'ubiyya*-type attitude that sees Islam, in general, as oppressive. This "Iranian reactionism" seems to go back to the alleged "anti-Persian policies" of the Umayyads,

---

50. Cf. Nawruziyan, "Zartusht u hukamayi bastani-yi Iran", 12–18.
51. L. Lewisohn, "Persian Sufism", 59. On Boroujerdi, cf. M. Boroujerdi, *Iranian Intellectuals and the West: The Tormented Triumph of Nativism* (Syracuse, 1996).
52. Esp. A. H. Zarrinkub, *Justuju dar tasawwuf-i Iran* (Tehran, 1978), 22.
53. Cf. Nawruziyan, "Zartusht u hukamayi bastani-yi Iran", 18.

but the outcomes of the 1979 Revolution were not regarded as conducive to the liberation of Iranian people by those who were less sympathetic to the Mullahs.[54] The fact of the matter is not entirely embraced by the KNS, at least not openly; that is, both Iranian and Arab Moslems, prior to Umayyad rule, shared a close relationship that was marked by their efforts to uphold the pristine notions of Islam, as idealized in the Imams – the progeny of Ali. Indeed, the importance of Salman in this regard needs to be highlighted, for it was he who after the death of the Prophet favoured the company of Ali. Salman the Persian is a model for all Iranians to follow. Therefore, Salman can be seen as an important contributor to the Iranian Islamic identity. This is a point completely overlooked or ignored by the KNS. The KNS have sought a completely different trajectory, over the past two decades, to promote a *revival of earlier theories* that favoured the Persian origin of Sufism, a Sufism underpinned by the development of the "Primeval Religion of the Aryan race".[55] For example, the German Protestant Church leader August Tholuck (1799–1877) proposed, and later rejected, the theory that Sufism has a "Persian Magian" rather than an "Arab Islamic" origin.[56] The English Orientalist Edward Palmer (1840–1882) explored these ideas further, though they were best purveyed throughout the second half of the nineteenth century by the Franco-Dutch Arabic scholar Reinhart Dozy (1820–83), who was assured that "mysticism came from Persia",[57] before the culminating statement made in the next century by Hartmann (1881–1965). Hartmann's attempts were theories resonating most clearly with the recent aspirants of "Nurbakhshian" publications, as he stressed: "It becomes clear beyond all dispute that Sufism flourished first and foremost in Khorasan; indeed it seems that we must regard as its cradle the eastern legacy of Khorasan."[58] In the wake of this scholarship, Reynold Nicholson and Louis Massignon attempted a rebuttal of the general case for a Persian origin of Sufism, in principle, and disputed the centrality of Persia for the study of mysticism. Nicholson, who was a noted scholar of Sufism and a faithful translator of Sufi works, pointed out the Greek origin of much of Islamic intellectualism. Yet he firmly placed Sufism in the Islamic frame as forming out of the inherent tendencies of asceticism found there.[59] Concurrently, Massignon

---

54. Cf. Zarrinkub, *Du qarn-i sukut.*
55. E. H. Palmer, *Oriental Mysticism* (1867) (ed. and intro. A. J. Arberry) (London, 1938), 11, cited in L. Lewisohn, "Persian Sufism", 60.
56. F. A. D. Tholuck, *Sufismus sive Theologica Persica pantheistica* (Berlin, 1821), cited by L. Lewisohn, "Persian Sufism", 59–60.
57. Cf. A. J. Arberry, *An Introduction to the History of Sufism* (the Sir Abdullah Suhrawardy Lectures for 1942) (New Delhi, 1992), 25, cited by L. Lewisohn, "Persian Sufism", 60.
58. Cf. R. Hartmann, "Zur Frage nach der Herkunft und den Anfängen des Sufitums", in *Der Islam* (Berlin, 1916), vol. 6, 31, cited in L. Lewisohn, "Persian Sufism", 60.
59. Cf. R. A. Nicholson, "A Historical Enquiry Concerning the Origin and Development of Sufism, with a List of Definitions of the Terms 'Sufi' and 'Tasawwuf', Arranged Chronologically I", *Journal of the Royal Asiatic Society* (1906), 309–53.

held that Sufism was no doubt based on qur'anic vocabulary for its expression of technical principles, and that the Iranian influence was simply derived *a priori*, and a claim unsubstantiated, by Iranian hopefuls.[60] Massignon highlights the Semitic heritage, and against the common accentuation of Aryan origins he explains away the Persian origin of Sufism and denies Persia the right to it as any kind of "cultural possession".[61] Yet ironically, both these authors, wanting to preserve the authenticity of Islamic mysticism, are forced to concede the impact of certain external ethnic and cultural factors. Massignon, for instance, while shying away from classifications of Moslem thinkers based on their "Persian" origins, was a Catholic very ready to see close comparisons between Moslem mystics and such Christian thinkers as Augustine in their Roman context.[62] The point of this book, therefore, has been to bring to the fore the important influence of Persian cultural components that have affected the terrain and activities therein for over a millennia, and which have produced the unique expression of an indigenous Iranian brand of Sufism. A point which has little to do with promoting a purely Persian origin of things, but one which to a great extent – through the reproduction of an "alternate [macro-]history" of Persia – seeks to address the repressed agenda for Persian studies and the heritage of Persian wisdom and spirituality. But it is time to set aside others' conclusions and offer our own.

60. Cf. L. Massignon, *Essai sur les Origines du Lexique Technique de la Mystique Musulmane* (Paris, 1954), 63–8.
61. *Ibid.*, 64.
62. *Ibid.*, 65.

CONCLUSION

In the course of this thesis a number of sensitive issues have been raised as we advanced the "esoteric" and "alternate" view of Persia — a past summarily unveiled to us through the mystical poetry of the Sufis. Persian Sufism tells us of a great indigenous wisdom tradition of Khorasan, celebrated as *hekmat-e khosravani*. This is "the flowing wisdom" that for Persia was supposed to be initiated in pre-Zarathushtrian times by the mythic king Kay Khosrow. Such is the basic image of Persianate Sufi myth-history or "mythological macrohistory". Partly in response to it, we have presented our own "hidden" history of Persia, and concurrently with the Sufi paradigm we have critically explored relevant aspects of a number of traditions in Iranian religious history, namely Zoroastrianism, Mithraism, Mazdakism and Islam, up until Sufism itself. Certainly Sufism has also come to be placed among past "fixtures" because of the establishment of fraternities and "chains" of spiritual authority that locate different schools in their own special relation to the Khorasan tradition. Thus, it has been a key intention of this work to present a case for a "re-thinking" of the history of Sufism, partly by understanding the narration of the Sufi "myth-history" in detail, yet above all by taking its lead to reconstruct the "esoteric current" of Persia's spiritual heritage in the manner of a critical historiography, including the history of ideas.

It was always assumed that Islamic Persia was linked to her most ancient past especially as conveyed by the great national epic of Ferdowsi, but many gaps need filling for an adequate re-visioning. Hence, the bigger links have been most telling in our argument. Consider how the legacy of Mazdak gathered up Zarathushtra's original teachings, for example, and notice what happened each time religious establishments, whether Zoroastrian or Islamic, became "too normative". Then we have the provocative enigma of Salman the Persian that helped to bridge the gap further between Islamic Persia to her pre-Islamic heritage, and entailed a deep reading of materials contained within the Islamic tradition itself. Admittedly, one cannot claim all the constituent parts of our argument to be entirely new. But what has been said before has been put in less effective ways and never in a critical macrohistory, with the whole matter enduring "centuries of silence", to adapt Abdolhossein Zarrinkoub's provocative title, as far as modern scholarship is concerned. To resurrect the indigenous idea of Persia's mystical past, then, and to retrace the "typical" historical steps suggested by traditional materials, has beckoned as a worthwhile if not necessary exercise. In the process linkages have been made and probed between ideas and movements previously left unaddressed; and from a methodological standpoint our work has escaped the limitations of a particular cultural and religious time frame, that is, the Islamic, in which Sufism still finds itself. Paradoxically, though, the macrohistory and "perennial" vision of the Qur'an itself uncannily looks beyond the specific historical context of its first expressions.

Sufism as a whole is inextricably and simultaneously linked to a number of pasts, yet a prominent one – for us most crucial – is the Persian, which has been explored here. It should not come as a surprise to the reader that one can talk about plural "Sufisms", that is, the "Sufi tradition" in such various regions as Iran, India, Egypt, North Africa, Spain and South East Asia, sometimes operating with minimal presence – even independently – of an Islamic community, and also overlooking judicial authority, as with the increasing spread of Sufism in the West. The argument put forward in this work has been to state the case, but not a final judgement, for the Iranian origin of the "Sufi" tradition, as opposed to Islamic mysticism. Confessedly, the tracing of a Zarathushtrian connection to Sufism needs much sensitive scholarship to clinch it, yet, however unorthodox this view will be in today's atmosphere, the rise and development of Sufism in Iran cannot be properly explained without such "archaeology". Consequently, we have called for a careful distinction between "Islamic Mysticism", or the mystical component of Islam, and that of the "Sufi tradition", the difference being that the latter has been forever subject to periodical fluctuations in its relationship with the Islamic establishment. In fact, since its suppression in the tenth century, only in its extremely "moderate" forms has Sufism ever been accepted from the post-Hallajian period onward, and its "promiscuous spirituality" barely tolerated by both the Sunni and Shi'a orthodoxies. Indeed, where Shi'ism is seen as the protestant offshoot of a catholic Sunni Islam, Sufism goes a step further – in the Christian analogy towards Quakerism, let us say – and of course how close Sufism is to (or far from) a *true* sense of "Islam" will remain an intriguing matter of debate.

In a somewhat unexpected way we have presented a "stepping-stone" macrohistory uncovering the origins of Sufism. Islam itself is not in question, because Islam is a continuation of the wisdom tradition in a quasi-perennialist form. Contextually, it is our suspicion, as also that of many Orientalists from the start, that Islam is a unique offshoot of the Judaeo-Christian tradition injected with Greek, and even Persian, sensibilities. Our case is that it is moved by a strong spiritual undercurrent fed by the great rivers of ancient Persian, but also Greek and Egyptian, wisdom traditions, as indeed Sohravardi suspected, and to some extent demonstrated. Whether Rumi knew this directly or not, he was a major influence in the revival of the suppressed Persianate Sufi tradition of Bayazid and Hallaj. Yet his work was tempered in a way to unite the religious front rather than divide or provoke it as his forebears had done.

The overarching purpose in this book has been the re-working of the history of Persia in light of its Sufi tradition. As stated in the opening of this work, the history of Persia is one which deals to a large extent with a suppressed past, though occasionally with the "cork popping out of the bottle" so that we can see what has gone on – as an ongoing cultural complex of resilience. This befits the title of Hamzehee's book, *Land of Revolutions*, used to describe the history of Persia: for him Iran is a land linked through the chain of its revolutions.[1] Such socio-political eruptions can only be nourished by highly charged religious components ruffled by religious-political establishments. Thus it may be appreciated that Sufism is the evolutionary outcome of this "eruptive Iranian religious condition", and it is hardly a coincidence that Sufism would arise at such a critical point in the history of Iran, during the eighth and ninth centuries,[2] when a revival of her past – in the "Persian renaissance" – was inaugurated under the Abbasids, when the New Persian language was born. In the cultural renaissance of the Abbasid era, everything Persian is long thereafter celebrated and honoured throughout the Islamic Empire, from Turkey to the Indus, as the official language of the court, the international language of poetry and, of course, Sufism. The survival of Sufism is testament to the quality of Persia's psycho-spiritual tenacity, which was able to survive and adapt to the long and frenzied history of Islam in the Persian lands through Mongol, Seljuk and Torkoman invasions – a true test of Persia's wisdom tradition. Indeed, given the presence of pre-Islamic Persian elements in the Sufism of Iran, we have to face up to the fact that there are now obvious religious reasons why Persia's wisdom tradition endured the Arab (Umayyad) domination, as Iranian culture always did *vis-à-vis* all its assailants throughout its illustrious history.

This explains why we have been looking at Sufism all the way through the book, because the key contention is that the dense Sufi materials are best explained by delving into the Persian past as uncovered in this exercise. And in the end Persianate Sufism's own myth-history actually finishes putting together the jigsaw puzzle that has been collected and identified in this work. Indeed, the Sufis richly illustrate in their spiritual outlook what this book has

---

1. Hamzehee, *Land of Revolutions*, 11.
2. See E. G. Brown, *A Literary History of Persia* (Cambridge, 1902–6), vol. 1, 418. Hamzehee makes this a pivotal point in his placement of Sufism as very much attuned to the social-political climate of Iran in *Land of Revolutions*, 61.

attempted to demonstrate in critical detail, and they, the Sufis, have preserved the macrohistory *in nuce* in oral traditions to provoke the efforts brought forth here. Through their traditions, indeed, bits and pieces that we wanted to know about Mithraism and Mazdakism, for instance, have fallen into place, and in the end this book has done more than just carry the critical task of explaining what the Sufis have been saying: this work has also honoured their acts of "spiritual conservation".

SELECT BIBLIOGRAPHY

PRIMARY SOURCES

Attar, F. 1381/2003. *Tadhkirat al-Awliya*, J. Salmasi-zadeh (ed.). Tehran: Talayeh.

Dawood, N. J. (trans.) 2000. *The Koran*. London: Penguin.

Ferdowsi 1838–78. *Shahnameh*, 7 vols, J. Mohl (ed. & trans.). Paris.

Ghazali, A. 1986. *Sawanih al-Usshaq*, N. Pourjavadi (trans.). London: KPI in association with Iran University Press.

Hafez 1976. *Diwan-e Hafez*, S. M. Reza Jalali Naini & N. Ahmad (eds). Tehran: Amir Kabir.

Hojviri, O. [1911] 1959. *The "Kashf al-Mahjub": The Oldest Persian Treatise on Sufism*, R. A. Nicholson (trans.). London: Luzac.

Ibn Al-Nadim 1970. *Ketab al-Fehrist*, 2 vols, B. Dodge (trans.). New York: Columbia University Press.

Ibn Ishaq, M. [1955] 2004. *The Life of Muhammad*, A. Guillaume (trans.). Oxford: Oxford University Press.

Kashifi, H. V. 2000. *The Royal Book of Spiritual Chivalry (Futuwat nama-yi Sultani)*, J. R. Crook (trans.). Chicago, IL: KAZI Publications.

Monawwar, M. 1899. *Asraru'l-tawhid fi maqamati'l Shaykh Abi Sa'id*, Zhukovski (ed.). Petrograd.

Porphyry 1969. *The Cave of the Nymph in the Odyssey* (*De Antro Nympharum*). Buffalo, NY: Arethusa.

Rumi, J. 1925. *Masnavi-ye manavi*, 6 vols, R.A. Nicholson (ed.). London: Luzac.

Shahrestani 1985. *Kitabo'l-milal wa'l-nihal* ("The Cosmogonical and Cosmological Teachings of Mazdak"), in *Acta Iranica*, M. Shaki (trans.), vol 11, 527–43. Leiden: Brill.

Sohravardi, S. 1954. *Hekmat al-eshraq* in *oeuvres philosophiques et mystiques. Opera metaphysica et mystica*, H. Corbin (ed.), 3 vols. Tehran: Institut franco-iranien.

Taraporawala, I. J. S. [1951] 1993. *The Divine Songs of Zarathushtra*. Bombay: D. B. Taraporevala Sons.

SECONDARY SOURCES

Arberry, A. J. [1942] 1992. *An Introduction to the History of Sufism: The Sir Abdullah Suhrawardy Lectures for 1942*. London: Longman.

Asmussen, J. P. [1947–60] 1962. "Das Christentum in Iran und sein Verhältnis zum Zoroastrismus". *Studia theologica* **16**: 1–24.

Bausani, A. 2000. *Religion in Iran: from Zoroaster to Baha'ullah*, J. M. Marchesi (trans.). New York: Bibliotheca Persica Press.

Bidez, J., & F. Cumont [1938] 1975. *Les Mages héllénisés: Zoroastre, Ostanes et Hystaspe d'après la tradition grecque*. Paris: Belles Lettres.

Blochet, E. 1898. "Études sur l'histoire religieuse de l'Iran I". *Revue de l'histoire des religions* **38**: 26–63.

Blochet, E. 1899. "Études sur l'histoire religieuse de l'Iran, II". *Revue de l'histoire des religions* **40**: 1–25.

Blochet, E. 1902. "Études sur l'ésoterisme musulman". *Journal asiatique* **19**: 489–531.

Blochet, E. 1913. *Études sur le gnosticisme musulman* (Extrait de la *Rivista degli studi orientali*, 2, 3, 4, 6). Rome: Casa editrice italiana.

Boroujerdi, M. 1996. *Iranian Intellectuals and the West: The Tormented Triumph of Nativism*. Syracuse, NY: Syracuse University Press.

Boyce, M. 1975–91. *History of Zoroastrianism*, 3 vols. Leiden: Brill.

Brown, P. 1971. *The World of Late Antiquity*, London: Thames & Hudson.

Caetani, L. [1904–26] 1972. *Annali dell'Islam: Compilati de Leone Caetani*, 10 vols. Hildesheim: Olms.

Chaudhary, S. A. 1998. *Sufism is not Islam: A Comparative Study*. New Delhi: Regency Publications.

Christensen, A. 1925. *Le regne du roi Kawadh I et le communisme mazdakite*. Copenhagen: Host & Son.

Cook, M. & P. Crone. 1977. *Hagarism: The Making of the Islamic World*. Cambridge: Cambridge University Press.

Crone, P. 1987. *Meccan Trade and the Rise of Islam*. Princeton, NJ: Princeton University Press.

Crone, P. 1991. "Kavad's Heresy and Mazdak's Revolt". *Iran* **29**: 21–42.

Crone, P. 1994. "Zoroastrian Communism". *Comparative Studies in Society and History* **36**(3): 447–62.

Cumont, F. 1903. *The Mysteries of Mithra*, T. J. MacCormack (ed. & trans.). Chicago, IL: Open Court Publishers Co.

Daftary, F. 1998. "Sectarian and National Movements in Iran, Khurasan and Transoxania during Omayyad and Early Abbasid Times". In *History of Civilizations of Central Asia*, vol. 4: 41–60, M. S. Asimov and C. E. Bosworth (eds). Paris: Unesco.

Daniel, E. L. 1979. *The Political and Social History of Khorasan under Abbasid Rule 747–820*. Minneapolis, MN: Bibliotheca Islamica.

De Bruijn, J. T. P. 1983. *Of Piety and Poetry: The Interaction of Religion and Literature in the Life and Works of Hakim Sana'i of Ghazna*. Leiden: Brill.

De Epalza, M. 1982. "Le milieu hispano-moresque de l'Évangile islamisant de Barnabé (XVI–XVII)". *Islamochristiana* **8**: 159–83.

De Jong, A. 1997. *Traditions of the Magi: Zoroastrianism in Greek and Latin Literature*. Leiden: Brill.

Donaldson, D. M. 1929. "Salman the Persian". *The Muslim World* **19**(4): 338–52.

Duchesne-Guillemin, J. 1973. *Religion of Ancient Iran*. Bombay: Tata Press.

Dussaud, R. 1900. *Histoire et religion des Nosaïris*. Paris: Et Boullion.

Edmonds, C. J. 1969. "The Beliefs and Practices of the Ahl-i Haqq of Iraq". *IRAN: Journal of the British Institute of Persian Studies* **7**: 89–101.

Ende, W. 1997. "The *Nakhawila*, a Shi'ite Community in Medina Past and Present". *Die Welt des Islams* **37**(3): 236–348.

Frye, R. N. 2005. *Greater Iran: A 20th Century Odyssey*. Costa Mesa: Mazda.

Gershevitch, I. 1964. "Zoroaster's own Contribution". *Journal of Near Eastern Studies* **23**: 12–38.

Gibb, H. A. R. 1975. *Islam: A Historical Survey*. Oxford: Oxford University Press.

Gignoux, P. (ed.) 1992. *Recurrent Patterns in Iranian Religions: From Mazdaism to Sufism*. Paris: Association pour l'avancement des études iraniennes.

Ginsburg, C. D. [1865] 1971. *Kabbalah: Its Doctrines, Development and Literature*. London: Routledge.

Gnoli, G. 1980. *Zoroaster's Time and Homeland*. Naples: Istituto universitario orientale.

Goitein, S. D. 1966. *Studies in the Islamic History and Institutions*. Leiden: Brill.

Goldziher, I. 1971. *Muslim Studies* (*Muhammedanische Studien*), S. M. Stern (ed.). Chicago, IL: Aldine Publishing Company.

Gölpînarlî, A. 1977. *Tasavvuftan dilimize geçen deyimler ve atasözleri*. Istanbul: İnkılâp ve Aka Kitabevleri.

Gropp, G. 1993. *Zarathustra und die Mithras-Mysterien*. Bremen: Edition Temmen.

Guillaume, A. 1956. *Islam*. Harmondsworth: Penguin.

Hamzehee, R. 1991. *Land of Revolutions: A Historical and Typological Study of Iranian Social Movements*. Göttingen: Edition Re.

Hanif, N. 2002. *Biographical Encyclopaedia of Sufis: Africa and Europe*. New Delhi: Sarup.

Hartmann, R. 1916. *Zur Frage nach der Herkunft und den Anfängen des Sufitums*. Strasbpurg: Karl J. Trübner.

Hinnells, J. R. (ed.) 1975. *Mithraic Studies*, 2 vols. Manchester: Manchester University Press.

Hodgson, M. G. S. 1974. *Venture of Islam: Conscience and History In a World Civilization*. Chicago, IL: University of Chicago Press.

Horovitz, J. 1922. "Salman al-Farisi". *Der Islam* **12**: 178–83.

Huart, C. 1909. "Selman de Fars". In *Mélanges Hartwig Derenbourg*, 297–310, H. Derenbourg (ed.). Paris: Leroux.

Ivanov, V. 1953. *The Truthworshippers of Kurdistan*. Leiden: Brill.

Izady, M. R. 1992. *Kurds: A Concise Handbook*. Washington, DC: Crane Russak.

Jeffery, A. 2007. *The Foreign Vocabulary of the Qur'an*. Leiden: Brill.

Johansen, J. 1996. *Sufism and Islamic Reform in Egypt: The Battle for Islamic Tradition*. Oxford: Oxford University Press.

Jones, H. 1963. *The Gnostic Religion: The Message of the Alien God and the Beginnings of Christianity*. Boston, MA: Beacon Press.

Khorram, M. 1984. *The Long Search: Story of Salman the Persian*. Leicester: Islamic Foundation.

Kister, M. J. 1968. "al-Hira. Some Notes on its Relations with Arabia". *Arabica* **15**: 143–69.

Kister, M. J. 1980. *Studies in Jahiliyya and early Islam*. London: Variorum Reprints.

Klima, O. 1957. *Mazdak: Geschichte einer sozialen Bewegung im Sassanidischen Persien*. Prague: Nakladatelství Československé Akademie Věd.

Klima, O. 1977. *Beiträge zur Geschichte des Mazdakismus*. Prague: Academia.

Kolesnikov, A. 1997. "The Early Muslim Geographers on the Ethnic Situation in Khurasan (IX–XII A.D.)". In *Iran and Caucasus 1: Research Papers from the Caucasion Centre for Iranian Studies*, 17–24, G. Asatrian (ed.). Tehran: International Publications of Iranian Studies.

Kruke, R. 2001. "Sharaf Az-Zaman Tahir Marwazi (fl. *ca*. 1100 AD): On Zoroaster, Mani, Mazdak, and other pseudo-Prophets". *Persica* **17**: 51–68.

Laeuchli, S. 1967. *Mithraism in Ostia. Mystery Religion and Christianity in the Ancient Port of Rome*. Evanston, IL: Northwestern University Press.

Laeuchli, S. 1968. "Urban Mithraism". *The Biblical Archaeologist* **31**(3): 73–99.

Lewis, F. D. 2000. *Rumi: Past and Present, East and West*. Oxford: Oneworld.

Lewisohn L. (ed.) 1999. *The Heritage of Persian Sufism*, 3 vols. Oxford: Oneworld.

Lings, M. 1983. *Muhammad: His Life Based on the Earliest Sources*. New York: Inner Traditions International.

Loewen, A. 2003. "Proper Conduct (*Adab*) is Everything: The *Futuwwat-namah-i Sultani* of Husayn Va'izi-i Kashifi". *Iranian Studies* **36**(4): 557–62.

Malik J. & J. Hinnells (eds) 2006. *Sufism in the West*. London: Routledge.

Massignon, L. 1994. *The Passion of al-Hallaj: Mystic and Martyr of Islam*, H. Mason (ed. & trans.). Princeton, NJ: Princeton University Press.

Melikian-Chirvani, A. S. 1990–91. "From the Royal Boat to the Beggar's Bowl". *Islamic Art* **4**: 3–111.

Menzes, Rev. J. L. 1912. *The Life & Religion of Muhammad, The Prophet of Arabia*. London: Sands & Company.

Messina, G. 1951. *Diatessaron Persiano*. Rome: Pontificio Istituto Biblico.

Minorsky, V. 1953. *Studies in Caucasian History*. London: Taylor's Foreign Press.

Mirza, K. 2000. *Ancient and Middle Iranian Studies*. Mumbai: K. Mirza.

Moezzi, M. A. 1994. *The Divine Guide in Early Shi'ism: The Sources of Esotericism in Islam*, D. Streight (trans.). Albany, NY: SUNY Press.

Mojaddedi, J. 2001. *The Biographical Tradition in Sufism: The Tabaqat Genre from al-Sulami to Jami*. Richmond: Curzon.

Moulton, J. H. 1917. *The Treasure of the Magi*. Oxford: Oxford University Press.

Negosian, S. A. 1993. *The Zoroastrian Faith*. Montreal: McGill-Queen's University Press.

Nurbakhsh, J. 1379/2000. *Piran-i Balkh*. Tehran: Khaniqahi Nimatullahi Publication.

Nyberg, H. S. 1938. *Die Religionen des Alten Iran*, H. H. Schaeder (trans.). Leipzig: Hinrichs.

Olinder, G. 1938. "The Kings of Kinda of the Family of Akil al-Murar". *Lunds Universitets Arsskrift 1* **26**(6): 63–4.

Ridgeon, L. 2010. *Morals and Mysticism in Persian Sufism*. New York: Routledge.

Russell, J. R. 1993. "On Mysticism and Esotericism among the Zoroastrians". *Iranian Studies* **26**(½), 73–94, www.scribd.com/doc/62258912/On-Mysticism-and-Esoteric-Ism-Among-the-Zoroastrians-James-R-Russell.

Shaked, S. 1969. "Esoteric Trends in Zoroastrianism". *Proceedings of the Israel Academy of Sciences and Humanities* **3**(7): 175–321.

Shaki, M. 1978. "The Social Doctrine of Mazdak in Light of Middle Persian Evidence". *Archiv Orientali* **46**: 289–306.

Shboul, A. M. H. 1999. "Arab Islamic Perceptions of Byzantine Religion and Culture". In *Muslim Perceptions of Other Religions: A Historical Survey*, 122–35, J. Waardenburg (ed.). Oxford: Oxford University Press.

Stepaniants, M. 2002. "The Encounter of Zoroastrianism with Islam". *Philosophy East & West* **52**(2): 159–72.

Taeschner, F. 1953. "As-Sulami's *Kitab al-Futuwwa*". In *Studia Orientalia Ioanni Pedersen Septuagenario*, 340–51, F. Hvidberg (ed.). Hauniae: Munksgaard.

Taqizadeh, S. H. 1947. "The 'Era of Zoroaster'". *Journal of the Royal Asiatic Society* 1–2: 33–40.

Troeltsch, E. 1950. *The Social Teaching of the Christian Churches*. London: Westminster John Knox Press.

Trompf, G. W. 1979. *The Idea of Historical Recurrence in Western Thought*. Berkeley, CA: University of California Press. (Vol. 2, "From the Later Renaissance to the Dawn of the Third Millennium", forthcoming.)

Van Den Bos, M. 2002. *Mystic Regimes: Sufism and the State in Iran, from the late Qajar Era to the Islamic Republic*. Leiden: Brill.

Watt, W. M. 1953. *Muhammad at Mecca*. Oxford: Clarendon Press.

Watt, W. M. 1956. *Muhammad at Medina*. Oxford: Clarendon Press.

Ward, C. O. [1900] 1970. *The Ancient Lowly: A History of the Ancient Working People from the Earliest Known Period to the Adoption of Christianity by Constantine*, 2 vols. New York: Franklin.

Zaehner, R. C. 1961. *Dawn and Twilight of Zoroastrianism*. New York: Putnam.

Zarrinkub, A. 1336/1957. *Du qarn-i sukut: Sarguzasht-i havadis va awza'-i tarikhi dar du qarn-i avval-i Islam (Two Centuries of Silence)*. Tehran: Amir Kabir.

INDEX